IRAN FROM CROWN TO TURBANS

ALSO BY GAIL ROSE THOMPSON

All the Shah's Men

All the Shah's Horses

Iran from Crown to Turbans

Gail Rose Thompson

Rev. date: 12/06/2018

To order additional copies of this book, contact:
Xlibris
1-888-795-4274
www.Xlibris.com
Orders@Xlibris.com
773023

DEDICATION

"But all this world is like a tale we hear-
Men's evil, and their glory disappear."

Abolghasem Ferdowsi, Shahmaneh: The Persian Book of Kings

In memory of departed Iranian friends

To all those who are living or wanting the "The Good Life" for Iran

Although this work is a nonfiction I have changed the names to protect the identity of some people.

Because a good portion of this book took place almost forty years ago I had to rely on my memory which at times has a habit of changing or twisting the facts. Dialogue is our main means of communication so I have constructed it to the best of my abilities and as close to the truth as possible.

ACKNOWLEDGMENTS

When my friend James Underwood came to visit me in Virginia, shortly after the Iranian revolution, we decided we would write a book about our times in that country in the 1970s in order to explain what we believed were the reasons for the revolution that shocked us, and the whole world. We worked together for many months pounding on our typewriters and finally put together a manuscript that we presented to many agents and publishers, none of whom were interested in what we thought as brilliant piece of work. The copy of "2537", the Persian year of the revolution, went into a box where it resided for almost forty years. When I was cleaning the attic before moving to Florida I discovered the old manuscript and I considered trying again. A lot had changed in the forty years so I decided it would be fun to tell stories of the times during the reign of the Pahlavi Crown and also of how things have become under the Islamic Republic's Turbans. I thank James for his part in helping me write this book.

In the two years it has taken me to complete the book, I have had a great deal of help and support from family and friends. My long suffering partner, Mel Stone, has put up with my inattentiveness to him and late nights as well as being asked to do proof reading. My daughter, Helen Parrott, assisted with her artistic abilities designing the crown and turbans. My grandson, Micah Thompson, with his superb grasp of the English language, helped with some final editing. Barbara Zimmerman proof read the chapters as I spewed them out of my printer. Judy Hendry took time to read and correct chapters I emailed to her in Hamilton, Canada. My friends, Fred and Elian Elghanian, hosted me for several days while we went over old times in Tehran. As well, there are many friends and family members who had to listen to me talk about my book incessantly during this time. I want to thank all for their help and patience; without them I would not have been able to complete this project.

Thanks to the Surfiran Team for all their help with visas and guiding me, especially Mehdi Eshraghi, Sajad Bamdad, Sara Azumar, Hoor Mansuri, Elham Babaee, and Leilah Mohasab.

I also want to thank the people at Xlibris. My author representative, production assistant, design coordinator and editor all did a great job.

CONTENTS

PART II. Turbans

PREFACE

Iran has been consuming the news of the world for the past several years, but the majority of people in the West have little knowledge of the country, its history, or its people.

The Iranian nation is one of the oldest civilizations in the world. The early population occupied the caves of the Zagros and the Alborz Mountains before descending to the foothills, where they developed farming and raising livestock as well as establishing the first urban cultures in the Tigris-Euphrates basin, which is in present-day Iraq.

The first urban peoples in what is now Iran were the Elamites in the southwest corner of Khuzestan. In the first century BC, the Aryans (Medes and Persians) arrived on the Iranian plateau marking the beginning of the Iranian civilization that rose to the heights of the great Achaemenid Empire of Cyrus the Great. Under his successors Darius the Great and Xerxes, it was extended from northern India to Egypt.

It has been said and continues to be said today that the conquerors of Iranian territory were eventually conquered by the Iranian culture. Over the centuries, Persians worked to protect and revive their distinctive language and culture, a process known as Persianization.

The first conqueror, Alexander the Great, swept through the region and conquered the Achaemenid Empire in 330 BC. After his death, his generals and their descendants established their own sub-empires, which culminated in the establishment of the entirely Persian Sasanian Empire at the beginning of the third century AD. The Sasanians consolidated all territories east to China and India and engaged successfully with the Byzantine Empire.

The second conquerors were the Arab Muslims, who came from Saudi Arabia in 640 AD. They gradually melded with the Iranian peoples, and in 750 AD, a revolution emanating from Iranian territory assured the Persianization of the Islamic world through the establishment of the Abbasid Empire in Bagdad.

The next conquerors were successive waves of Turkish peoples starting in the eleventh century. They established courts and founded several cities in northeastern Khorasan. They soon became patrons of Persian literature, art, and architecture.

The many Mongol invasions of the thirteenth century resulted in a period of instability that culminated in a strong reaction in the early sixteenth century on the part of the Safavids. Their rulers started as a religious movement of adherents of the Muslim-Twelver Shi'ism (belief in the twelfth hidden Imam) as the Iranian state religion. This empire, which ranged from the Caucuses to northern India, raised Iranian civilization to its greatest heights. The Safavid capital, Isfahan, was one of the most civilized places in the world, far more advanced than most places in Europe at the time.

Subsequent conquests by the Afghans and the Qajar Turks resulted in their also being Persianized. During the Qajar period, 1785 to 1925, Iran came in contact with Europe for the first time in its history. The Industrial Revolution in the West had seriously damaged Iran's economy, and the lack of modern weapons, transport, and a strong army resulted in serious losses of territory to Great Britain and Russia. The pleasure-loving Qajar rulers began selling concessions for agricultural and economic institutions to their European rivals to raise funds for modernization. Much of this money went straight into the pockets of the Qajars creating a public image of collaboration between the throne and foreign interests.

When Reza Khan and his small band of Cossacks effectively took over the government of Iran in 1925 with the assistance of British funding, training, and arms, he was determined that Iran would again become a strong and independent country. He sought advice from America and continued to take advantage of Britain, Russia, and other European countries that were still aiding Persia in its desire for modernization while keeping their eyes on Iran's lucrative oil fields.

He had himself elected shah by the *Majlis*, the elected parliament, in 1926, so the country continued to be a monarchy after the Qajars were thrown from power by his forces. Ruling the country with an iron hand, he created a modern nation with a strong government, a small but budding industrial sector, and a modern army. He built a railroad from the Caspian Sea to the Persian Gulf, decreed the wearing of Western-style dress, and liberated women. His desire for Persia to remain neutral in World War II led the British and Russians to overthrow him in 1941.

When he was exiled to Transvaal, South Africa, his son, Mohammad Reza Pahlavi, became the shah. His first years were fraught with problems due to oil, the country's main source of revenue. Problems with his prime minister, Mossadegh, and his brief time in exile in 1951, when he was still considered a young playboy, caused him much trouble, but once he was returned to his role as King of Persia, he settled down to develop the country with his plan for a Great Civilization.

The late fifties through the seventies was a golden age for Iran. Oil and industry were flourishing, and life for the people was good. Even in small villages, children were being educated. There was little illiteracy, and there were no starving people. Iran was developing into an important member of the developing nations of the world.

Then in 1979, the monarchy of the Pahlavis was toppled by the supporters of Ayatollah Ruhollah Khomeini, and Iran became an Islamic Republic. Things changed again in this vast country, which is so rich in natural resources. The current Islamic Republic seems to be flourishing, and the people are living worthwhile lives in a country governed by a combination of a democratically elected government and a powerful Ayatollah and his Assembly of Experts. Iran is now a democratic theocracy.

INTRODUCTION

In October 2017, I returned from three weeks visiting Iran. My friends and family had asked me why I had wanted to go to Iran, a dangerous Middle Eastern country that was on Trump's travel ban. They thought I was insane. The country was ruled by a fierce Ayatollah and his Assembly of Experts and was supposedly supporting terrorists and their activities in that part of the world. My answer was that I had been in Iran as the wife of an expatriate American working for a large international company during most of the 1970s. I'd had a fulfilling and exciting life during the five years I lived there, and I loved the country and the people. I wanted to go back and learn how their way of life had changed under the rule of the Ayatollahs and the Islamic Republic. I could not believe that life there was as dangerous and oppressed as the media described it.

When our family arrived in Iran in early 1972, the security officials learned I had expertise in show-jumping horses in my home country, Canada. After I was questioned and later tested about my knowledge of the field, I was asked to help out with the sport, which was in its inception there at that time.

I was soon hired by the *Anjoman-e Sultanat-e Asb*, (Royal Horse Society), the purpose of which was:

> to preserve, propagate, and improve native Iranian breeds, make them known in foreign countries by holding horse shows in Iran and participating in horse shows and sales abroad, create popular interest in the protection and care of horses, promote and develop equestrian sports, and define and register Iranian breeds and issue identifying certificates.

I felt that much of the aim of this society was far beyond my capabilities, but I accepted the position anyway. It was a great opportunity because the organization was a part of Iran's Imperial Court, which was solely the Shah's domain. I was appointed chairman of show jumping for the society; as an employee of the Imperial Court, I became the trainer and manager of the Shah's Imperial Stables at Farahabad as well as the trainer of the Iranian national show-jumping team.

Due to these positions, I was able to meet many members of the royal family in informal moments; it also gave me an entry into high society, where I was able to watch the upper classes at play. I met many officials and members of the court and was able to see, as an insider, how things worked in Iran during the reign of Mohamed Reza Pahlavi. He was always very pleasant when I saw him, and he had great love for his horses; he was a very accomplished rider. He knew every *djelodahr* (imperial servant), by name from the old gatekeeper to the stall cleaners and the imperial riders. He treated them like family, and they loved him very much.

Mohamed Reza Pahlavi had a great vision for his country; he wanted it to be recognized internationally in every field. He followed his father's goals to make Iran the leading power in the Middle East. His was to build a Great Civilization so the country would once again become as powerful as it had been during the great Persian Empire of the past. He believed that by developing industry, education, economics, and the military, his dream would come true.

He was also a sportsman; he realized his people needed leisure time, so he encouraged and supported athletic activities. The Iran of the 1960s and 1970s was a country with the most beautiful snow skiing in the world, it had a world-renowned soccer program, and there were country clubs and civic parks with golf courses, tennis courts, swimming pools, and just about any activity anyone might want.

I had a great respect for what he had done for his country and people over the years. It is unfortunate that the Western world let him down so badly; now, his name is so tarnished. He made mistakes, but he truly loved his people and his country, and he believed he was doing what was right. He was not the cruel monarch the world has made of him today. Unfortunately, many of the people close to him misled him, and he was not able to see what was coming in Iran. He considered himself a benevolent dictator who was trying to do what was best for his country, which was still mainly of the old, feudal mind-set.

The world's leading reporters were so anxious to print their exclusive interviews with the Shah that they forgot to take a close look at the other Iranians or at what was really going on in that vast country. Though they would poke fun at the Shah's dreams and portray him as the megalomaniac he undoubtedly became, they never tried to look further to find out how he managed to wield such complete power for so long over a nation of 30 million.

I saw the boom and the succeeding unrest developing. I saw the breathtaking extravagance and arrogance of the pampered servants and friends of the Shah and his family, their unscrupulous methods of doing business, and their use of their influence to beat down rivals or gain every favor they could for themselves. The competition to gain wealth, build the finest houses, and throw the best parties became so keen among them that they forgot other Iranians existed.

Left to themselves, these other Iranians, a great many of them, mopped up the considerable overflow of money the gigantic oil revenues left over even for them and followed their betters' example. Corruption became relative to status; the smaller you were, the lesser your scale of corruption, but nearly everybody who had the chance was pocketing easy money in the Iran of the mid '70s. It was rumored that many of the Shah's top generals spent much of their time junketing while putting away huge sums they were receiving as their cuts on the treasury of weapons they ordered in the Shah's name. They joined in gambling sprees around the card tables and at the casinos that were mushrooming around the capital, Tehran, and the coastal resorts.

In the midst of all this carousing, however, many serious Iranians did their best to try to improve the lot of their fellow citizens and urged the ruling family and officialdom to adopt a more discreet public image. Foremost among them was Farah Diba, the Shah's third wife. Those who knew her and saw her work at close quarters considered her almost a Florence Nightingale to the general mass of Iranians blinking so confusedly in the light of sudden wealth and the onset of a tide of technology and westernization.

Many good things were going on in Iran along with the bad. But the 150 or so years of Qajar rule the Shah's father had ended had been a period of such isolation and degradation for Iranians that they were in no way prepared for the twentieth century when it arrived almost overnight. Their social attitudes were more suited to the feudal society of the Safavid times when Iran had last competed for a prominent place in the world. Their primitiveness barred them from understanding how to deal with the technology and ideas that were essential for the modern society their rulers were trying to build. They turned to the good life to help forget the hassles of the new Iran on the road to the Shah's much-vaunted Great Civilization.

Foreigners criticized Iranians for their self-indulgence and cowardice in the face of an autocrat who ultimately turned out to be a paper tiger. They failed to understand how the complete absence of contact with the dynamic West over two centuries had left the whole society virtually unable to cope with the demands of even an embryonic Western-style society. This made them easy prey for those who happened to hold the reins of power. So easily, it turned out, that when the grip on the reins was relaxed for a moment, the startled horse galloped away out of control.

When I returned to the United States, in 1977, I was stricken by the ignorance of people I talked to about the real character of the Iran of the last decades. So when people gasped in disbelief as the Shah toppled, I wanted to set down my experience and observations to help people understand why the Shah proved to be such a paper tiger and why the other creatures of the jungle where he was king of the beasts turned tail and fled when they saw there was the faintest possibility of his being mortally wounded.

Much has been made of the failure of American officials to see what was coming in Iran soon enough to begin some corrective action in their policies. I don't see that there was much they could have done to stop the slide that President Carter, in his pressure on the Shah to give his people more Western-style freedoms, had initiated. Carter's mistake was in pressing for changes before he and his men had taken a proper look at the actual state of Iranian society and had learned how flimsy the economic structure was that the boom had created. Neither did he know anything of the character of the opposition in Iran or of how naive and basically apolitical Iranians were.

One section of the opposition that did understand this included those behind Ayatollah Khomeini and his group of zealous priest supporters in Iran. They knew the only way to power in Iran was to offer another charismatic leader as an alternative to the Shah. When the Shah gave away his face in the panic that followed the equivocation of his longtime faithful American friends, Khomeini was there to take his place. It was his men, who were mostly religious leaders or *mullahs*, who took power in Iran, and it will take a long time to wrest it from them. However, many things in Iran today have improved beyond belief, which I will illustrate in this book.

From afar, Khomeini had promised his people that he would bring to Iran a democratic Islamic Republic, a vague utopia designed to maintain the unity of a wide spectrum of leftists, liberal democrats, and Islamist opposition groups.

To the masses, he had become a living symbol of hope through his tapes and broadcasts that targeted ordinary and mostly uneducated Iranians. They wanted a leader who would personify their aspirations, restore their spirituality, and bring freedom, independence, and justice. His goal was chimerical as he wanted to recreate an idealistic past that had never existed. His was not to be an ordinary government but one that was based on Shari'a; any revolt against the government would be a revolt against God and punishable in Islamic jurisprudence.

Iranians who had just emerged from arbitrary imperial rule were about to experience a new autocracy that was divinely inspired. They were about to experience arbitrary arrests, executions, floggings, confiscation of property, and abrogation of women's rights that would bedevil the new regime and begin to erode its legitimacy. The belief of Khomeini's government was that criminals should not be tried—they should be killed. And thus began Khomeini's quarrel with the international world.

In 1980, Iraq declared war on its neighbor, and for the next eight years, the country was in turmoil. Just a year after the UN engineered a truce, Ayatollah Khomeini died. Since his death and the end of the war, Iran has become the most modern country in the Middle East. There are still problems internally and internationally, but with the moderates and reformists becoming more influential by the day, the country is looking to the future.

I hope to show you the Iran of Mohamed Reza Pahlavi and the Iran of the post-revolutionary days up to the present. Little has been written about life in the country as it is now because few people wanted to or were able to get visitors' visas. The press has drawn a picture of Iran that is "fake news."

I want to enlighten readers through this collection of stories about the true nature of the country and its people over the past eighty or so years. I hope you enjoy the stories I have written about how life was in Iran under the Pahlavi Crown and what it has become under the rule of the Islamic Republic, that of the Ayatollahs and their Turbans.

PART I

The Crown

CHAPTER 1

The Shah

It was October 1978. The crowd inside the brand-new Museum of Contemporary Art in Tehran, reputed to have cost $100 million, bubbled with excitement as it followed Shah Mohammad Reza Pahlavi and Empress Farah through the elegant galleries.

For the artsy crowd around the Empress, most of them from the country's elite families, the Shah's presence was tantamount to imperial recognition because His Majesty had little or no interest in the arts or indeed anything cultural unless it was a tome or tableau heralding the monarchy. He reserved his public appearances for inaugurating or visiting industrial or military projects.

For the society crowd sporting a fortune in fur coats and another in jewels, this was the one place in the world anyone would want to be at that moment. A royal occasion in Tehran, even if it boasted only a princeling, was a glittering affair with half the town there. And when it was the Shah himself, the other half came too.

In addition, there was the added attraction of the presence of famous museum directors and figures from the arts scene in the United States, Britain, France, Germany, and other Western countries; they had flown in at the invitation of the Empress for the opening of the new museum, which was designed by her architect cousin, Kamran Diba.

One or two people at the opening even admired the paintings, which were acquired at great cost and ranged from Picassos to French Impressionists and more. Those local artists who were not featured prominently in the Iranian section tried to get their scorn for the display heard above the hubbub. But everyone was concentrating on the royal couple, waiting to applaud them as they approached the entrance to make their departure. The Shah was obviously deeply impressed. As he left, he turned to the officials gathered around, who included most of the ministers of his government, and said, "We must have more of these!"

To Mohammad Reza Pahlavi, that's how it was. You decided you wanted something, and you ordered somebody to do it. It was not for him to worry about the hell the designers had gone through as they tried to equate the essence of traditional Iranian mud architecture with the requirements of a modern cultural facility. Nor did he need to care about the unimaginable hassle of dealing with Iranian builders as they tried to make the building take shape.

Had his wife not told him that the Ministry of Culture and Arts, headed by his brother-in-law Mehrdad Pahlbod, the husband of his elder sister, Princess Shams, had held up the visas for the international experts she had called in to advise on this and other projects? That in spite of Farah's exalted position in the land.

Did he not know that European art dealers had battled for so long to try to make a killing from the Empress's art buyers when they sought pictures for the museum over the previous several years? Some of their representatives were in the crowd gloating over the prospect of making more. Did the Shah not know just how much it had all cost in both effort and money? But then, $100 million was a mere bagatelle for a man who could decide at breakfast to spend another billion on arms purchases for his glorious military forces.

That remark when leaving the museum sums up the apparent weakness of Mohammad Reza Pahlavi. In spite of meeting so many top Western political and business figures, he was startlingly ignorant of the true nature of the modern world. In particular, he could not appreciate the way the changes he was making were inevitably demanding changes in his attitude to his fellow citizens. It was only a couple of years before his regime toppled that he even showed he had become aware that those fellow countrymen were not capable of learning to run sophisticated industries overnight. In his first-ever private interview with an Iranian journalist (he had received hundreds of foreign ones), he conceded his grandiose plans for Iran were going to take a little longer to complete than he had imagined.

Living in Iran for so many years, I had the constant sensation that it would take only a little bit to make ridiculous things sane. It could easily have been so different. So much was ridiculous whether it was the failure to instruct security men on big occasions or just the concession to elitism that turned what could have been a wonderful occasion for the public into a select party for the chosen few. He made speeches in the years after he married the down-to-earth Farah Diba, which made a lot of sense to those of us who heard or read them. For some reason, he didn't realize that his officials were not implementing things the way he said he wanted them.

The Shah enjoyed pontificating, but he showed precious little interest in going out and checking on the day-to-day needs of his flock. So his officials mostly didn't either. On many formal occasions that appeared on television, the Shah's arrogance was so evident. It was usually when he was inspecting or receiving alone. When Empress Farah was with him, he somehow became a different man. She seemed to give him a bit more confidence and humanity. He would smile more and look around him while she occasionally did the talking.

You only have to read his first book, *Mission for My Country*, to sense how his feelings had been blunted by his upbringing and his separation from ordinary Iranians. He talks of his marriages and his wives with the impersonality of a man talking about how he acquired a favorite automobile. Of his first wife, Princess Fawzia of Egypt, the sister of King Farouk, he wrote, "Up to that point I had never laid eyes on the girl. So it was arranged I should go to Cairo to see her. There we had about two weeks to become acquainted with one another." That was all. For Mohammad Reza Pahlavi, no other memories seemed to have remained of those two weeks getting to know a lovely young princess in the fairy-tale city that Cairo was in 1938.

With Soraya, the petulant beauty who seemed to have been a sad combination of the arrogance of the Bakhtiari tribal chiefs and the solidness of middle-class German society, he was a little more humane. People who knew them say he really did love this ravishing beauty who contrived to offend most of Iranian society's worthwhile establishments and the women in particular during her sojourn as empress. She was not averse to acidly telling women with ideas that she was the empress and she would decide on subjects of which she had no knowledge. She was heavy on protocol with other members of the royal family and managed to foster bad feeling among them all—and she had failed to produce an heir to the throne. The Iranian people who mattered were heartily fed up with her by the time the Shah yielded to pressure to divorce her.

If it had been the hand of God that made Soraya barren, the Shah could also thank the Almighty for bringing his third wife, Farah Diba, to his attention. She helped bring some sanity to his court and make development more human. In his book, the Shah wrote about her as if she were the daughter of a friend rather than someone intimately close to him. The details he gave smack of a memo sent to her private office: "Send five hundred words on Empress Farah for inclusion in His Majesty's book."

History will no doubt show how Farah Diba brought out the best of her husband's qualities and shaped so many of his ideas so that they were of practical value to his country. She was a rare bird as young Iranian women went. Like the Shah, she was comparatively uneducated, typical of how modern values are esteemed in the developing world. She had studied architecture in Paris, but she didn't complete her course after meeting the Shah. However, her education first at an Italian school, then by French nuns in Tehran, and followed by two years in Paris gave her solid grounding. Once the Crown Prince was born, Farah was established. When the oil boom came and development plans became a reality rather than just serious hopes of a ruler who felt he should be doing something, she got to work to make the Shah understand that development was meaningless unless it served the people.

All his utterances on previous big occasions had intimated that he thought development was for the glory of Iran and its monarchy. He began to make speeches with a different emphasis; he called on the people to take part in the building of a new Iran. At first, he still made it seem as if they should work for his glory as well as for that of the country, but gradually, he came around to telling the people that it was all for their personal good too.

Not that the Iranians really believed it. The Shah's remoteness from them made him completely unaware of their quite terrifying skepticism, a characteristic of Iranians that always surprised newcomers to their company whether at home or abroad. That underlying characteristic formed by a long history of heartrending cruelty and long periods of hopelessness encouraged even educated and wealthy Iranians who had profited excessively from the Shah's regime to turn to something new when it looked as if it might become stronger than the Pahlavi Dynasty.

Even the multimillionaires in Tehran believed that somebody else, the royal family and their connections especially, were profiting more than they were and that their wealth was due entirely to their cleverness in scraping a bit of treasure from the pile. They were to some extent right of course, but the Shah didn't realize that. He thought they should be kissing his hands and feet for making them prosperous. He must have thought: *Don't those people, who are not yet rich, see that they will soon be prosperous the way things are going?* Surely they could count the new industries and new jobs, compare their salaries with those of workers in neighboring countries, and realize how fortunate they were and what luxuries the future had in store.

When Empress Farah made her famous speech about sycophancy in which she explained how the royal family was unimpressed by streets named after them and the statues that littered the country, the Shah no doubt smiled knowingly to himself when her lecture produced only a new rush to name things for him. If you were important, you expected sycophancy; if you were unimportant, you were expected to give it—it is essential to understand that if you want to begin to understand Iranians. Once a man is on the downward path, you can equally show him no mercy; you help him go down faster. The ability of the opposition outside Iran to understand this better than the Shah did enabled it to turn virtually the whole Iranian nation against him.

Sadly, the competitive, jealous nature of the officials around the Shah led him to grow thoroughly bored with the tales of inefficiency and ill doing that were brought to him. People became afraid to tell him anything of the raw truth. "To Reza Shah, his father, one was afraid to tell a lie; to the present Shah, one is afraid to tell the truth," was a saying one heard frequently.

As an employee of the Imperial Court at the Imperial Stables at Farahabad, which was southeast of Tehran and where the Shah and other members of the family came to ride, I was able to observe him when he was not in the official spotlight. He would usually helicopter in and then be driven the couple of hundred yards to the stable area, where he would mount up and gallop off. He wouldn't ride a horse unless it would jig and prance and look difficult to ride.

He came to ride at irregular intervals until the end of January each year, when this man who was so busy receiving heads of states and dealing with endless problems would suddenly begin to find time to ride frequently. It was a determined effort to get fit to ensure he could be seen to advantage during his Now Ruz, or Persian New Year vacation, when he and the empress received a lot of distinguished guests on the lovely little Persian Gulf island of Kish just off the coast of southern Iran. Every year, the Shah had sixteen horses, a foreign vet, and grooms flown to this paradise, which he planned to turn into the Monte Carlo of the Middle East.

He and his family stayed at a swish little palace he had built there; it was a little away from the villa and hotel development designed to lure millionaires from the play spots of the world for brief winter vacations. Life during the ten days he and his party were there consisted of tennis, diving, swimming, and of course partying as well as riding. He usually rode with his guests in the cool of the morning and the shadows of the late afternoon. A ride meant galloping hell bent for leather along the coral sand beaches; the Shah delighted in outriding his guests. They had had no special preparation for this diversion anyway and so were mostly out of condition. The Shah would gallop until he found his companions wilting. Then he would pull up and laughingly ask why they were panting or perspiring so much. This was the same man who tried to show such a responsible image on the world scene when dealing with political affairs.

It didn't seem to have occurred to him that the people of Iran would resent his plan to turn Kish into a pleasure island project run by a court-owned company. "But it's our island, not his," people often told me. "It's part of our national possessions." The island has links with the story of Dick Whittington of children's story fame according to literary men. The character was based it is said on a badly treated, poor young man from the Persian Gulf port of Siraf, who in the heyday of this coastal region in early Muslim times sailed to India with his cat to seek his fortune. In India, he met a king whose palace was overrun by mice. The young man put his cat to work and cleared them out. The king was so grateful that he generously rewarded his benefactor, who then sailed back to the Persian Gulf and founded the port of Kish to take away the business of his former hardhearted Siraf taskmasters.

Kish had reverted to a small fishermen's village when the court planners came down to assess its potential as a resort. The Shah and his family had spent much of their leisure time and money in the south of France and the casino resorts of Europe, so that was that model that appealed to them. They built their casino and sumptuous villas, imported topless bar girls, let out duty-free shop concessions to their relatives and friends, and took generous cuts out of all the contracts.

Empress Farah, who had originally been interested in the development of the project as a benefit to the islanders, made one of her rare errors of judgment when she consented to fly down to Kish on an Air France Concorde with a team of models for a fashion show and other publicity. She was no doubt under pressure from French contacts who helped her in other domains to give this new moneymaking venture a boost. The ordinary Iranians saw in that the worst excesses of the court people. The prices to fly to the island on special flights and accommodations were astronomical.

I first saw the Shah at close quarters when I was asked to be on the jury for the Aryamehr Cup, the annual show-jumping competition he sponsored; it was held at the Imperial Stables in the early autumn. I had arrived at the venue two hours early as I had been told to. There was much helicopter activity on the helipad for an hour before his arrival. There were SAVAK (secret police) guards sitting in every few seats; I was told they had been there since sunrise.

It was quite a spectacle to see the Shah, the Shahbanou, and the royal children arrive. About ten minutes before the show was to commence, the whirr of the helicopters was heard and what looked like two huge, blue and white dragonflies hovered and landed. Into the ring came the Shah and the Shahbanou riding in an antique landau pulled by four beautiful white horses. Following a few meters behind was another carriage pulled by four black steeds and carrying the royal children and their nanny.

We members of the jury were lined up along the red carpet laid out for the royal party to walk on before entering the royal box. I had not believed it when people told me the Shah had a special aura about him, but I felt it that day as he passed and looked into my eyes. Following the completion of the competition, he again passed the jury members, shaking hands with each of us. I was awestruck.

When I was officially working for the Imperial Court, I would see him often when he came to ride or just see his horses. He had bought a group of horses in Germany for his imperial servants to ride and to pull the carriages. He wanted to become international in every way including in show jumping. He liked to come to see the horses jump, and on those afternoons, I would be on call to put on a little training show for him. The master of his horses for whom I worked always told me, "Don't make a mess of it." It had to look as perfect as possible; that's how the Shah liked it, and that's how his minions had to have it. And that's the way it was.

To his family and his close friends, he was a kind person; he often seemed blind to their faults. He was deeply attached to his mother. When I heard stories of how the Queen Mother influenced the Shah, I recalled how he had written in his first book, "The Persian household has in fact often become a kind of matriarchy. The mother is especially influential with her sons, who almost invariably look to her for advice."

Though she was in her eighties, this diminutive woman still insisted on the Shah's dining regularly with her along with other members of the royal family. She was the second of his father's four wives. People I knew in the court told me that her manner with the Shah was quite extraordinary. She would frequently chide him for not being as capable or as clear thinking as his father had been or for being weak willed. This latter may have been a wry reference to the influence of Empress Farah and other people around him. No doubt his brothers and sisters dropped a few remarks about the more radical ideas of Farah and those often liberal-minded friends she introduced to the Shah.

Others who had had the privilege of being guests when the Shah dined with his mother said they were surprised to hear him boasting too of some achievement like a small child reporting a feat at school. She was a strong element in keeping the Shah loyal to his family. That must have contributed a great deal to his continual indulgence of his relatives when it had already become clear to most people outside their circle that their commercial and other activities were damaging his image. It was hinted that he was afraid to get tough with them when complaints were brought to him because he didn't want to upset his mother. Certainly, his mother was a force in his life when he was seeking a third bride. One girl, who had beauty and a fine university record in Britain to her credit, had even been told to prepare herself for the role when the Queen Mother crossed her name from the list because of her family's links with the Shah's old enemy Mossadeq in the 1953 uprising.

The Shah obviously had a very strong personal attachment to his twin sister, Princess Ashraf, a woman of many different characters who would cruelly destroy somebody with the same ferocity that she would rush to the aid of an acquaintance who was being oppressed. She loved to have handsome young men and good-looking young women around her, and she could never resist the lure of the gambling table. How could he have overlooked her excesses? How could he have sent her to head important delegations for Iran knowing that gossip tied her to excessive gambling and drugs? However, were such accusations true? She served as the Iranian delegate to the UN for sixteen years, she was on and eventually chaired the Human Rights Commission, and she founded and worked diligently for the Iranian Social Services Foundation. Her brother believed in her good, not the gossip.

It was the same with Ardeshir Zahedi, his lifelong friend and for a time his son-in-law. Zahedi had a thoroughly unsavory reputation as a womanizer and having aides who were undisguised pimps. Yet the Shah continued to send Zahedi as ambassador to cities such as London and Washington. And he remained a favored friend even after his marriage to the Shah's daughter, Princess Shahnaz, the only child of the monarch's marriage to Princess Fawzia, had come to an end.

This kind of blind loyalty is a powerful factor in all Iranian families and groups. It was also reflected in the Shah's bland refusal to take sides between two close people such as Zahedi and Princess Shahnaz. It was also demonstrated in the Shah's case where he must have been aware of the bitter feelings of Culture Minister Pahlbod, his brother-in-law, toward Empress Farah, the woman who was doing all the things that Pahlbod had failed to achieve in his field. Did Empress Farah not tell him of the way Pahlbod's people had tried to foul up her work on so many occasions? If she did, it seems his feelings toward his sister Princess Shams, who insisted her husband remained as minister, were too strong to allow him to chide his brother-in-law.

Didn't he mind Shams converting to Roman Catholicism in a country so full of Muslim religious fanatics? She had a chapel built openly at her palace outside Tehran. He could have pressured Shams to convince her husband to let the empress have a clear field in the arts and cultural matters by citing his concession about her religion, but she would probably have gone to her mother, and there would have been hell to pay.

The Shah didn't usually look happy; he always felt he had to look the monarch. When he came to ride, he always looked like something out of *Bazaar* magazine—carefully matched tweed jacket, turtleneck sweater, and breeches. He always sat cross-legged in the royal box during big shows looking imperious, but then he would slowly relax. He showed little animation unless the rider happened to be one of his immediate circle of friends or *djelodards*—his stable riders—riding his horses.

I knew he enjoyed the sport of show jumping; why else would he have put so much money into the stables, horses, and training? He knew every person who worked at the stables by name and always chatted with them asking about their families and if things were going well with them. He was always friendly to me and the Irish resident veterinary, who took care of his horses; we were the only foreigners working at the stables. To all of us at Farahabad, he was the Shah, but he was also just our benevolent boss, and we all loved and respected him.

The Shah really enjoyed playing cards on Friday with his cronies and watching new American films when he had no state functions in the evening. If he didn't like a film, he would merely go to sleep. The films were handed out to his friends as soon as he had seen them; his handsome air force general friend Nader Djahanbani and Armenian Felix Aghayan were always first on the list. They were both arrogant men who took advantage of their relationship with the Shah to make themselves rich as did so many others the Shah liked. Aghayan so wormed his way into the Shah's confidence that he became the representative of Iran's Armenian community in the nation's Senate. He was also appointed head of the Ski Federation with a generous budget; he obtained the cash to build a first-class ski resort with hotel and chalets in the Alborz Mountains near Tehran. At the same time, rumor freely tied Aghayan to illicit trade in antiquities, in which the royal family was involved, and with drug trafficking. It was said his wife was also into drugs. The couple paid the price for this when their two attractive daughters died from the effects of drugs while still in their early twenties.

The Shah and Shahbanou regularly went skiing at Aghayan's ski resort at Dizin. I saw them there quite often enjoying the runs, which ranged between three and seven kilometers. I have skied often in North America and Europe, but the slopes at Dizin were the best I have ever experienced. Snow conditions were perfect throughout most of the winter. The foreign ski instructor hired to train the Iranian national team told me, "The Iranians will never have a successful ski team until they start training in Europe because conditions are too perfect here."

During weekends, Dizin was one big fashion parade; the smart set wore the latest outfits from Europe and the States. Many of them never skied a yard; they were there to be seen. The Shah and Shahbanou went only on weekdays to avoid the crush. After the Swiss government warned the Shah in 1975 that they could no longer guarantee his safety in that country, they went to Dizin more often. I watched them with a friend one afternoon. The Shah was good, but Farah outshone him; she had a far superior speed and style. We had been about to climb into a gondola lift when we were rudely pushed aside and saw the royal party approaching. There were two shahs or so it seemed, but one of them was carrying the skis, so the other was the real one. As he approached, my friend Judi whispered to me, "Take off your sunglasses. Perhaps he'll recognize you and invite us to his chalet for a drink."

"Don't be stupid," I replied, but I did take off my glasses.

Just as the Shah reached us, I heard Judi's rather brash voice chime, "Hiya, Shah Baby!"

I shivered with horror as his majesty turned and looked at me. My heart was in my mouth. He thought I, not Judi, had addressed him.

"Well, hello," he said with a puzzled look. Perhaps he had a feeling he had seen me some place.

I quickly blurted out a humble, "*Gorban-e-shoma, Valazrat*"—roughly, "I'm your slave, your majesty"—and inclined my head respectfully. It seemed to do the trick; he passed on. However, the next day at the stables, my boss, Kambiz Atabai, asked me, "So how was the skiing yesterday? You were seen at Dizin by His Majesty."

Perhaps the Shah thought that was how American women always addressed important people because he wasn't put out either when Lauren Bacall at that now-famous White House ball replied to his compliment that she was a good dancer with, "You bet your ass, Shah!" Lauren came to Iran in 1977 to a film festival; she was not invited to the palace, but she was in stinging form. When asked by a reporter when she would give a press conference, she replied heatedly, "To hell with the press. Where's all that caviar I was promised if I came here?"

As I came to know Iran better toward the end of my stay, I sometimes wondered if the Shah would have replied, "Well, hello" to some enthusiastic Iranian well-wisher in the same circumstances. It was quite clear that this strange man had developed a strong complex about his own people; unless he knew someone very well, he was afraid to trust him or her.

Two of his other friends, physician Yahya Adl and promoter Jamshid Bozorgmehr, developed the Imperial Country Club, a lucrative enterprise that became the social center for much of Iran's upper crust—almost a private preserve. The club had an active riding stable where we held many of our shows in the beautiful sand ring at the bottom of the hill below the clubhouse with a view of the majestic Mount Damavand.

Many international competitions were held on tennis courts there that were often attended by the Shah and Empress, who both enjoyed the sport. The Olympic-sized pool with its high-diving boards hosted swim and diving meets, and the dining rooms served delicious meals prepared by international chefs. My husband, Don, and his friends enjoyed playing golf on the course; they said that the fairways were a little rough and rocky but that the greens were beautifully cared for.

Constant allegations of corruption were leveled at the two developers, but if the shah heard them, he ignored them until Bozorgmehr was kicked out and arrested at the time when the search for scapegoats for the palace was at its height.

One of the Shah's ministers who had been an assistant to the prime minister told me that one of his jobs at that time was to take reports to him from the premier's office. "He never looked at me," the minister told me. "I read the report, and he studiedly gazed up at a portrait of his father or something else on the wall most of the time with his back to me. When it was over, he grunted, and I was dismissed." That was the attitude Mohammad Reza Shah Pahlavi took with his officials. It was the foundation of his troubles and ultimately the cause of his downfall; it led to the unabated rat race among officials to try to show they were doing things to his satisfaction and to the sweeping of every defect under the carpet. Once he had given an order, ministries announced their plans with a flourish of statistics and target dates. They would periodically announce details of what they had accomplished, but the figures were false in most cases.

When Khomeini made himself first known in June 1963 with fiery words about revolution, the Shah was unwilling to issue an order that might have led to civilian casualties. He conceded command to his generals, who declared martial law, and troops began moving through the streets. Gunfire was heard through the night of June 5 and into the next morning. Rumors spread that thousands had been killed, but it turned out that the actual count was fewer than fifty. Even though the *marjas*—the religious leaders—loathed Khomeini for provoking bloodshed and unrest, they petitioned the Shah to spare his life. That the Shah did, but at the same time, he established his personal authoritarian rule. From that time on, the prime minister, cabinet, and parliament could question but never oppose his decisions.

In October 1964, Khomeini delivered a fiery speech denouncing the Shah and the Pahlavi state. That time, the government did not wait for demonstrations to begin; it just put him on an Iranian air force plane and sent him into exile.

Most Iranians were too unworldly to take responsibility for their moral weakness; their traditionally respectful attitude to the monarchy was one of the great strengths of the Shah. I often saw people who were highly critical of him almost moved to tears when he appeared in person. Simply the idea that this was their monarch seized them. Twenty-five hundred years of tradition was too much for them when it came to the crunch.

But it was easy for Mohammad Reza Pahlavi, whose father had taken on the hallowed name of the ancient Persian language, to aggrandize his dynasty and confuse respect for the monarch with reverence for his person. I don't think he ever got as far as trying to disentangle the two. I knew so many young society Iranians who shared his absurd vanity about himself. This characteristic remained unchanged even in the face of disastrous failures in jobs and careers. No man in Iran ever accepted that his failure in any job was due to his own shortcomings; in that jungle of intrigue and corruption, he found it easy to point to scores of reasons why he hadn't made it.

Any hint of privilege would start inflating the balloon of an Iranian's vanity whether he was a servant or a prince. If you performed a favor for him once, you would be expected to do it again. Any concession to him in the way of superior status could cause a crisis if you demanded equality later. How then could you expect Mohammad Reza Pahlavi, who was surrounded by sycophants from an early age and groomed for kingship by people either naively conscious of glory or self-seeking to have kept his feet on the ground?

Those who spent leisure time with him as a young man described him to me as a monster who was unscrupulously arrogant to those around him. I thought of that when I watched Crown Prince Reza at the odd public occasions he attended and on his visits to the Imperial Stables. Only in the year before he left for the States to learn to fly military planes did he begin to show any signs of consideration for others. Before that, he was the typical spoiled puppy that almost all Iranian boys of the better class were. Presumably, the fawning attention he received from courtiers fed his arrogance. In addition, he was given special small automobiles at an age most boys were still playing with toys, was handed his own private palace to live in when he was ten, and by age fourteen, he had earned a pilot's license. No wonder he resented having to attend functions because his parents or somebody else thought he should.

A prominent British journalist whom the Shah regularly received told of a visit he paid to the palace when the Crown Prince was only seven or eight. The audience was in the early evening, and the Shah suggested that he should accompany him to say goodnight to the Crown Prince in his room. The Shah opened the door, and the Crown Prince hurled a toy locomotive at the royal head. The prince was in a bad mood, but the Shah seemed to accept the tantrum as fairly normal. He laughed and made some offhand comment.

I recalled this story when I saw the Crown Prince's younger brother, Ali Reza, riding at the stables. He was not happy on the horse, but my boss, Kambiz Atabai, who was teaching him, insisted he continue his lesson. He said it would do "the little devil" good, a hint that this little prince too was wayward. When the lesson was over, the boy, only five, spat on the ground near Kambiz to show his anger—a not very princely gesture. Where had he learned that? Perhaps that kind of behavior was hereditary in Iranian boys of that class; I saw so many of them forget their manners when crossed in any way.

The Crown Prince demonstrated selfishness in another incident after he returned from the finals of a national youth soccer tournament one year. He had obviously found the whole business such a trial that he told Kambiz, the organizer, that he would make no more public appearances until he was twenty-one, several years hence. But he was mellowing fast in the last year in Iran, a reflection one felt of the influence of his mother and grandmother Madame Diba. When he went to Kerman for the same youth soccer final that year, he showed much more patience, and people were impressed by his developing charm.

Empress Farah's influence on the Shah became steadily more noticeable during their married life. It first appeared in the new, relaxed smile he occasionally flashed and in the photographs of himself with the children. He went along with playing the family man instead of the glorious monarch standing on a globe and waving to the world that had been on posters of him. And his speeches began to reflect a greater understanding of the mental processes than they had before. Finally, he began to take the

Shahbanou to state functions, and she was allowed to sit next to him and comment at his annual meeting with his chief executives on education in the Caspian resort of Ramsar every autumn.

Watching him on television at these meetings, I felt considerable sympathy for him. Here was a man who wanted the best for his people but somehow could not relate those instincts to the problems when talking about them. The Empress often seemed to be there to dot the *I*s and cross the *T*s for the viewers' benefit.

The foreign businessmen and planners who talked to him about his heavy industries and general development program were always extremely impressed by his knowledge and understanding of those subjects. The Shah seemed to have a very clear grasp of such matters, but was he misled by the insistence of a few of his technocrats that these ambitious dreams were possible within the time he was giving himself? The only clue to that was in the way those few visitors who did venture to question the possibility of achieving them were scoffed at by people such as Hushang Ansary, the capable and ambitious financial adviser to the Shah and his minister of economy and finance. "You are too old fashioned," the doubters were told. "You don't appreciate the possibilities with modern technology and proper financing that we can afford."

I have often wondered if things would have been different for the Shah if he had chosen the worldlier Ansary instead of Jamshid Amuzegar to be his premier after Hoveyda. Ansary was a much smarter operator than was Amuzegar, who was more the old-fashioned type of distant intellectual from a Third World country. But many of his advisors felt Ansary was too sharp and clever, so the Shah was advised against him. Amuzegar seemed to make foreigners wary as he climbed the ladder. Always impeccably dressed, he was constantly aware of his image as an educated man and was aloof from much of what was going on in Iranian politics. Ansary on the other hand was too clever to give in to personal animosities when they might hurt him. He came from Isfahan, and he was as hardheaded as the business-minded Isfahanis usually were.

The Shah first noted him after he handled his visit to Tokyo so well while he was a young diplomat there. When he was appointed Minister of Information he proved efficient and contactable unlike most officials. One got the impression that he was a much abler politician than Amuzegar turned out to be. He would have continued in the Hoveyda style, I think, not casting doubts about what had gone before as Amuzegar had.

The blunt truth about Mohammad Reza Pahlavi, however, was that he was dedicated to an Iran of his imagination, not the Iran that existed. He didn't recognize that other Iranians had just as much stake in their country as he had and that they wanted some say in what was happening. He became so convinced that his vision was right that he discounted all dissents and sacked everyone who dared to suggest his vision should not be taken into account. This is what opened the way for corruption and made it endemic in his regime. He made himself a business manager with absolute power over every detail of policy; he was determined that nothing and nobody would stop the country from achieving his targets.

Many Iranians and foreigners felt that his way of forcibly pushing Iranians into the twentieth century was the only one. Others decided that they couldn't fight him so they'd go along with him. Everyone found it easier to sit back and eat the fruits rather than try to point out better ways of doing things. It was those people and their monarch's downfall that they did.

In his last book, 'Iran's Domestic and Foreign Policy', published shortly before the revolution, he wrote,

> Our revolution, which started fifteen years ago, constitutes the greatest change in the history of Iran … Through it, all barriers and positive action have been removed, thus allowing the free flowering of all talents, and potentialities, as well as the Iranian people's equitable enjoyment of the product of their labour … Today our economy founded on realism and foresight, is growing daily more sound, and thanks to that a new Iran is being born, benefitting all its citizens … When it comes to halting inflation, ours is an unbeaten and unprecedented record in the world.

He believed that all who read it were saying nothing but good things about the book, and he felt it was crucially important to the development of the country. In the thirty-seven years of his reign, he never understood the dangers of flattery.

In the end, the oil that gave him and his country so much wealth got him. He controlled oil prices for years as the head of OPEC, but as the world economy was fearing recession, his price hikes to finance the billions he was spending on military toys were not supported by the other Middle

Eastern countries especially Saudi Arabia, which was the biggest producer at the time. Things became agitated in the area, and the United States, which had been his best friend, decided to drop him under the Carter administration.

Washing day in the village

Shah skiing

CHAPTER 2

Iran's Black Panther and Siblings

The panthers, they say, have disappeared from Iran. Until the fall of the Pahlavis, there was certainly one still there. It was Princess Ashraf, twin sister of the Shah and one of four daughters and six sons of Reza Shah. She liked being called the Black Panther, a name given to her by the French press. She felt the name suited her. In her book, she wrote,

> Like the panther, my nature is turbulent, rebellious, and self-confident. Often, it is only through strenuous effort that I maintain my reserve and my composure in public. But in truth, I sometimes wish I were armed with the panther's claws so I might attack the enemies of my country. I know that these enemies-and particularly in light of recent events-have characterized me as ruthless and unforgiving; almost a reincarnation of the devil himself. My detractors have accused me of being a smuggler, a spy, a Mafia associate (once even a drug dealer), and an agent of all intelligence and counterintelligence agencies in the world.

She was remarkably attractive for a woman in her fifties, when I knew her. Somebody with real skill helped her with her face of course, but she looked decidedly less doll-like and more natural in her beauty than did her year-older sister, Princess Shams. The latter looked too good to be true, more like a thirty-year-old and too artificial with her jet-black hair and makeup.

I saw Ashraf once at a dinner party and was astonished by the speed with which she ate. She used a small wooden toothpick with the same energy afterward. Her conversation came bursting out, and she moved as if she had pressing engagements waiting.

She had a constant stream of younger men friends, usually in their early thirties and tall, dark, and handsome. When she made her rather rare public appearances in Tehran, one or two of them were usually in her entourage. Some who had been her close friends and later married still turned up on occasion along with their wives still part of her entourage.

One day when she came to see an exhibition of paintings by a friend, she breezed in and tore around the exhibits so fast that she had seen them all before her entourage had finished greeting and gossiping with other friends of the artist. As she reached them at the end of her lightning tour, she called out, "Are you still here? I've seen them all." She obviously was pleased by her powers of absorption compared to that of her friends.

It was difficult not to be fascinated by her. I saw her on another occasion when she again came to see a showing of one of my friend's paintings. These were special favors she accorded because she didn't bother much with art. She must have thought that the elegant women at this private affair, many of them ambassador's wives, were impressed by her royalty. It wasn't that at all. It was her animal vigor and all the stories they had heard that kept their gaze fixed hungrily on her. Perhaps a little envy was in it for the way she contrived to get away with things they wouldn't dare try. Their eyes were taking in the young men lined up among the other guests to greet her. Two or three of them had been set up as directors of new businesses in which she had the Iranian interest. People said that was a common reward for favorites. They were real husky, he-man types, and I wasn't alone in admiring them.

The princess had been married in 1937 when quite young to a son of the leading family, the Ghavams, in Shiraz, the southern capital. Mirza Ali Muhammed Khan Ghavam became the assistant attaché in Washington for Iran in 1941. She had one son from that marriage, the good-looking and bright Prince Shahram, whose Harvard education didn't stop him from becoming one of the most unscrupulous businessmen in all Iran. There were dozens of stories of his grabbing contracts and using strong-arm methods on competitors. Some of the stories that reached the Shah's ears led him to exile Shahram for six months.

An attempt to kidnap Shahram outside his office in downtown Tehran failed because there were too many people in the street outside when it was tried. During my time in Tehran, I had no doubt many people in Iran wanted to take revenge on him. Handsome, rich, and intelligent Shahram had everything going for him from the start. He had a lovely wife and an equally lovely daughter, but he was too Iranian to be content with that. He obviously felt that his good looks, personal attributes, and connections entitled him to be the biggest guy around after the Shah. His greed seemed to know no bounds. In addition to his ordinary commercial interests, he was also linked closely with the illegal export of antiquities from Iran. In spite of his royal connection, he obviously lacked the patriotism to resist even that degrading means of making money.

Princess Ashraf's second husband, Ahmad Chafik, was a charming Egyptian who was one of the founders of Iran's civil aviation organization. Once again, however, this marriage ended in divorce after one son, Prince Shahriar. Unlike his elder brother, this young man settled on a career in the navy and abjured business. The princess was very proud of him for that; she was obviously surprised that he didn't want to do something less strenuous and more profitable. Shahriar was so happy in his job and got on so well with his colleagues that he was encouraged to believe that when the revolution came, he would be justified in staying at his post. But at the last moment, he was persuaded to take a vessel across the Persian Gulf to safety. It was a sound decision as events turned out. He was unfortunately assassinated in Paris in December 1979.

Later, Princess Ashraf married Mehdi Bushehri, a sophisticated and cultivated Iranian from a leading family whose cultural interests made it very surprising he should tie himself up with this woman. This marriage also went on the rocks, but it was reported that the Shah would not allow any more divorces. The couple remained on good terms, though. Bushehri settled down in Paris and represented the court's interests there; he was involved much more in the Empress's cultural activities than in his wife's affairs the last few years.

The princess's reputation of wild gambling and her involvement with drugs tended to overshadow the good work she did in the field of women's rights and other social areas. She supposedly lost millions in the casinos of Europe and the United States, and people contended that she used her diplomatic immunity to allow her entourage to bring in and carry out with her large quantities of drugs. Stories of drug parties at her palace were commonplace, but that was all rumor and most probably not true.

Ashraf was serious about her work in women's rights. One courtier acquaintance of mine told me of an occasion when she stormed out of a meeting at which Ardeshir Zahedi and other senior officials were making speeches about women's rights. As she left, she said loudly, "If you cared at all about women's rights, you wouldn't be here just talking about them." She was right.

As well, many other women in Iran including Empress Farah were setting a good example of what women could do if given the chance. Iranian men's attitude toward women was always ambivalent. Islam had been exploited by men to ensure a life free from women's interference over the centuries, and they didn't want to give up its protection. But Islam was not such a natural phenomenon for Iranians as it was for Arabs, and their constant looking back at their early Iranian history reminded them that women had never been subjugated in that way before the Arabs came.

The scandal of the parties hosted by the princess and the suspicion that many of the drugs being used by an increasing number of young people were being brought in by her entourage caused a great deal of resentment for her. That led many people to regard her do-gooding activities as merely a game, but they were not. Her chief aide in women's affairs, Mahnaz Afghami, was a serious woman who built up the Iranian Women's Organization into a prestigious body that achieved a great deal in improving women's rights during the last decade of the Shah's reign. The family protection law, giving wives the right to financial security and making divorce much more difficult for men, was one of its main achievements. Its efficacy was confirmed when a suggestion that Khomeini would revoke this law caused such a nationwide outcry after the revolution. Women and liberal-minded men were well aware of its value. The real women's libbers were critical of Afghami, who for a period was Minister of Women's Affairs, because as a politician, she went too slowly with her campaign. But I think she was right.

After the big meeting of women in Mexico in 1976, Princess Ashraf obtained funds to set up an Asian and Pacific regional center in Tehran for planning a program meant to obtain a better deal for women of the East. She didn't have a good grasp of the technical problems she was dealing with when chairing international meetings, but she gave her strongest backing to those who did.

It was the same with the vocational or functional literacy projects that UNESCO launched in a dozen developing countries in the late 1960s. Ashraf had the Shah give all the money and logistical support this project needed, and the result was the best evaluation of all the projects around the Third World. UNESCO learned more about the possibilities for this through Iran than anywhere else it tried it. The princess dealt just as firmly with the older officials, who true to Iranian form, tried to denounce the UN experts on this project in Isfahan and Dezful in southeastern Iran as Communists who were plotting against the Shah.

One of the UN people told me that without her steadfast support, there was no doubt they would have been expelled and the whole project abandoned. Ironically, the foreign officials often told people privately that the success of their project, which taught workers to read and write what they needed for their work rather than abstract sentences, would bring revolution against the Shah closer. People told him that, but his confidence that the majority of Iranians would recognize he was working for their interest made him scoff at that. He was probably lulled a little by a suggestion by Pierre Henquet, the brilliant Frenchman in charge of the experiment in Iran, that it might be worth comparing the findings of this and other contemporaneous vocational literacy projects to see if the unique cultural history of Iran did in fact make it easier to revive literacy among the masses. The results obtained in Iran were much better than those obtained in other countries in Africa, South America, and other parts of the Third World. But that was the kind of luxury study the UN was not interested in.

There were many other examples of how Ashraf was zealous in backing useful projects. For her friend Majid Rahnema, she obtained funding for another unique pilot project that cost millions; it aimed to find the best ways to plan and stimulate rural development. Rahnema was given the power to take over a sizable area of western Iran and bring in volunteers and a few key experts to study everything from building methods to education and health care in the hopes of setting up a model for use elsewhere in Iran.

Several other related studies were going on at the same time through the Pahlavi and Bou Ali Sina Development Universities. Sadly, the brilliant people who were running these had different patrons, and there was rarely any real cooperation. The Free University, which Hoveyda encouraged and set up, was also involved in rural health care research. The separate elements never bonded; that reflected one of the Shah's weaknesses.

Ashraf was also building through her Imperial Social Services Organization a series of clothing factories to produce cheap but serviceable clothing for the masses of people throughout the country. However, most of her business activities had nothing altruistic about them; a housing development for the better off and other investments of many kinds were meant to bring maximum financial return. As was the case with representatives of other princes and princesses, her aides would appear when contracts were to be signed between Iranian and foreign interests and demand a percentage to allow the agreements to go through.

As did Empress Farah, she absorbed into her organizations officials who were her friends or friends of friends. Ashraf was also given credit for pushing her friends into government jobs. It was claimed that a former escort, the handsome and personable Parviz Raji, became the Shah's ambassador to Queen Elizabeth because of her influence. Raji had also done a good job as assistant to Premier Hoveyda for some time, so the premier probably backed this appointment as well. Raji was very much a ladies' man; I was amused to hear one young scion of a leading Tehran family explain that he admired Raji for he was known to have screwed nearly every girl in Tehran.

While she was always helping friends, on occasion, Ashraf's quixotic nature made her vicious. When there was time to think about what she'd done, she would try to make it up to those she'd hurt. One example of this took place when I was up at the ski resort hotel at Dizin one weekend. Ashraf arrived to find only one room available; the hotel had heard only a short while earlier that she was coming, and the general clientele of the hotel was too well connected to allow the staff to kick them out abruptly. Ashraf apparently didn't mind the two upstanding young men in her party sharing her room, but she had two other relatives with her, and they were each to get a room. Somebody must be asked to leave, she insisted. When the receptionist finally found two unsuspecting American visitors whom he sent to a small hotel in the village, she was satisfied. The next afternoon, feeling guilty, she invited the Americans to have tea with her.

Ashraf behaved like the eastern potentate of popular conception. When she saw something she liked, she wanted it. That had been a tradition of not only royals but also of high officials in Iran for centuries. People locked up their daughters and even their best horses when princes and governors traveled. Even in my time in Tehran, mothers would tell me they would never allow their daughters to get involved with members of the royal family.

As a woman, I felt some sympathy for Ashraf. The ambivalent attitude of Iranian men I have spoken of is one factor. The legacy of the long years of women's humiliation by the conservative male hierarchy meant that the Iran in which she grew up and later lived as a public figure was a country where men instinctively insulted women who tried to break out. What horror she must have felt at Tehran University in the thirties when her father took her, her mother, and sister to stand at a public ceremony without the traditional veil. The eyes of the men there must have expressed their feelings as they gazed on the women. Perhaps it was that day that she decided to get a bit of her own back on them.

Princess Shams, the elder sister of the Shah and Ashraf, was never associated with drugs. Christianity was her fad, and she had a fanaticism about germs and hygiene. The Pearl was the name of the candy-floss palace Frank Lloyd Wright had designed for her; it was close to that of her mother's. She took elaborate precautions to protect her beloved dogs from picking up germs from visitors. She tried to avoid shaking hands unless it was absolutely necessary. After formal engagements, she would be led to a washroom to clean her hands thoroughly.

Her conversion to Roman Catholicism, although kept a secret most of the time, must have been one more irritant to the Muslim clergy of Iran. She was a staunch patron of the Italian Roman Catholic missions in Iran, which steadily expanded its education facilities for Iranian and foreign children alike. She had also converted her husband, Mehrdad Pahlbod, by all accounts. He came with her to the Italian church in downtown Tehran on Christmas Eve each year to celebrate midnight mass. The marriage of their daughter to a young American ended any credit this section of the family had with most of the devout Muslim community.

The Shah's ill-fated full brother, Prince Ali, had a son of the same name from his French-born wife, who was at one time in the running to become crown prince of Iran. It was when the Shah had no son by either of his first two wives; this was one of the ploys being considered to allow him to keep his beloved Soraya. But Ali's mother was the daughter of a Polish-born wholesale butcher in Paris, and she was not considered to be the kind of distaff blood for an Iranian monarch.

Gholam Reza was about the dullest of all the royal brothers and sisters. His name was big in sports, but he was really only being used by friends with ambitions to take over sports in Iran to gain them prestige and money. The budgets allocated to activities such as sports in Iran were always tempting to officials. Any federation chief and his cronies could rely on being able to subsidize themselves considerably with them. In fact, most of these jobs went to retired generals or courtiers. They always promised sportsmen and athletes many benefits that rarely materialized. The shocking betrayal of promises to the athletes who took part in the Asian Games held in Iran in 1975, and had been promised homes at the Olympic village built for the occasion was typical; the village was kept as a conference center.

When I met Gholam Reza the few times I did, I was astonished at how boring he was. His conversation suggested he had only the most superficial knowledge of sports, and he appeared to have virtually nothing to say on any other subject. This dullness extended even to his sexual life according to women gossipers. His second wife, the attractive Princess Manijeh, was said to have had to teach him how to kiss her when they made love for he had never considered even that nicety before satisfying himself with his first wife.

Opposition groups in Paris claimed they had beaten up Gholam Reza after he fled Iran to take up residence in his flat in the French capital. They said they lured him onto a balcony by shouting loyal slogans to the Shah and then asked if a delegation could come up and speak with him. He was said to have agreed, and when they got into his flat, they beat him thoroughly and urinated on him before smashing up as much of the place as they could. It was easy to imagine that Gholam Reza was stupid enough to have fallen for the trick. The urinating was apparently in revenge for the similar treatment alleged to have been meted out by SAVAK agents to dissidents in Iran. It was common knowledge in Tehran that they had done this into the mouth of one of the religious leaders. Again, this was the gossip one heard at the time.

The next brother, Abdul Reza, was an enthusiastic hunter and conservationist who spent much of his time hunting in different parts of the world and bringing back trophies for his collection. He too had vast business interests, but his influence in protecting Iran's wildlife and setting up an environmental protection department was at least one achievement to his credit. The brains behind this work was his friend, Eskandar Firouz (brother of my friend Narcy), a princeling of the former Qajar Dynasty. Firouz worked out most of the details and made the plans with foreign and other Iranian conservationists. They drew up an excellent law that safeguarded huge areas of land and forest, and they controlled hunting to a remarkably effective degree. Here was one of the advantages of having a rubber-stamp parliament. Prince Abdul Reza was able to persuade the Shah that these protection measures were necessary, and the law went through.

Firouz also prepared plans for a superb environmental park outside Tehran, which would be the key to persuading Iranians to understand and conserve their natural heritage. This project had been approved by the Shah, and work had begun when the troubles burst.

Some idea of the fickleness of relationships between the Pahlavis can be gauged by the fate that befell Eskandar. His friend Abdul Reza had for a time run into bad waters with his brother, the Shah. In 1976, they became friendlier again, and the reconciliation led the Shah to ask his brother a favor—he wanted him to stop inviting the former Qajar prince Mohammad Firouz, father of Eskandar, to his home on the Caspian Sea for the big annual party he hosted each summer. He didn't like the older Firouz, a former foreign minister and man of strong opinions. In spite of his close friendship with the younger Firouz, Abdul Reza agreed to the Shah's request. This led to a gradual deterioration of the relationship between the prince and Eskandar.

When Jamshid Amuzegar, who was a friend of Firouz, replaced Hoveyda as premier in 1977, he promised him that he would ensure he received the full budget for his work in the future; Firouz had always been dogged by budget cuts while Hoveyda was in power. But Abdul Reza had apparently decided to deliver the coup de grâce to his erstwhile friend because Amuzegar was ordered, presumably by the Shah, to replace Firouz. This was a tough blow for that really hardworking official.

Apparently, the Shah's youngest sister, Princess Fatimeh, liked Firouz and appreciated his work. She promptly visited the botanical gardens Firouz was still in charge of and was photographed with him for television and the press. But that wasn't of much avail; he never did get his old job back. That's how things went in Iran. Personal malice seemed to get the better of so many otherwise good people.

Fatimeh was the youngest of Reza Shah's children. She was pleasant and considerate when she came to Farahabad to bring friends to visit or to just come to see the horses which she loved. She was married to General Khatami, head of the Shah's air force and a brilliant man at the job. Khatami met a tragic end in a hang-gliding accident over Dariush Dam near Shiraz. I had met the handsome young man who had been brought to Iran by the daredevil general to teach him the art of hang gliding. He was a Frenchman who was supposedly the world's expert in the sport. I had watched him give a friend of mine lessons one day when the general was obviously too busy to take instruction. I was reminded of Leonardo da Vinci and his early experiments in flying as I watched my friend soaring through the air. Quite terrifying!

There were rumors that Khatami had been murdered, but those close to the family completely discounted them. Witnesses said he had disregarded pleas not to risk jumping off in the strong wind; he met his end when he was blown into a mountainside. When I encountered Stephan, the French instructor, shortly after the incident, he told me that he had warned the general not to fly free over the Dariush Dam because of the treacherous crosscurrents of air that were always there. "He didn't listen to me and so, *adieu!*" The Shah was so angry that one of his most valued generals and the husband of his sister had killed himself in such a foolhardy way that he refused to allow an official period of mourning for him.

Between Abdul Reza and Fatimeh were two other brothers—Mahmud Reza and Ahmed Reza—who were less well known to the public than the rest. Mahmud was chiefly interested in business and was involved in countless companies. He did appear at many parties and was the center of a lot of gossip because of his adventures with young women. One particular incident with a Scandinavian girl working at a Tehran hotel seemed known by the whole town. She gave him a disease, the stories said, and he was very angry with her. The girl herself hotly denied it. The town enjoyed hearing about it all! Ahmed was also a successful businessman, but rumor tied him up with drug trafficking in particular. He was virtually unknown to the public.

One saw little of the Shah's nephews and nieces. Princess Ashraf's son Shahram was to be seen from time to time at parties, as were Abdul Reza's two bright children, Kamyar and Sarvnaz, who completed their studies in the States. Prince Kamyar, whom I knew well due to his keen interest in horses, came to the Imperial Stables often after he had returned to Iran from university. He loved the horses and was especially interested in polo.

When his uncle, the Shah, told him he would give him two horses so he could play polo, he asked me to pick out the ones I thought would be the best for him. Kamyar disappeared later for military training in Britain while Sarvnaz stayed in Tehran only for a few months working with television and writing occasional articles for the English language press before she returned to work in the States.

CHAPTER 3

The Empress

Kambiz Atabai, my boss at the Imperial Stables at Farahabad, gave me my first ideas of what sort of a person Empress Farah was. Kambiz was exasperated because she had commented during a discussion he'd had with the Shah to which she was listening that she didn't see any purpose in keeping on the stables if they were using up money.

How stupid! I thought. The horses at the stables represented a nucleus of good specimens of Iranian breeds and a foundation for developing breeding stations for all kinds of riding horses. I thought the Empress's comment was simply another one in a series I had heard from upper-class Iranians about fields in which they were ignorant and in which they had no interest. Iranians seemed to feel it was incumbent upon them to express an opinion on everything that existed or happened; one television man told me in all seriousness that he didn't believe in horse racing and was against organizing it in Iran. "We don't need it," he told me while admitting he had never sat on a horse or seen a horse race in his life. Another chimerical Iranian expert.

But I later realized that Empress Farah's comment was in line with her sincere belief that court expenditures should be confined to necessary state protocol and projects that could benefit some section of the ordinary people, not just a privileged few. Not long after that, she heard we planned to set up a Pony Club to encourage children and young people to ride. She gave the money for the club and stables as the center of the organization. It ended up as did nearly everything else in the horse world as a new facility for the richer section of the community.

Empress Farah sent the royal children to ride there. As well, many children of foreigners and the well-to-do Iranian children got the chance to enjoy the equestrian sport at the club over the years. It certainly hadn't been Empress Farah's idea that it should end up only for the elite, but having no interest in horses herself, she wasn't around to check up on it. She was a tremendously hardworking consort for the Shah, a woman who preserved her interest in ordinary human beings. She took everything she did so seriously that she didn't have enough time to check on every detail outside areas such as social welfare and the cultural field in which she was most enthusiastically involved.

She was born on October 14, 1938, in Tehran. She was an only child; her father was a captain in the Imperial Iranian Armed Forces, and her grandfather had been a diplomat serving as the Iranian ambassador to the Romanov Court in St. Petersburg, Russia. She was devastated when her father, to whom she was very close, died when she was just nine. Her life changed dramatically when it was evident that there was not enough money for her mother to maintain the large family villa in northern Tehran; they moved to an uncle's apartment.

The influence of two women in her life strengthened her great quality, humanity, which preserved her from being submerged by the pomp and splendor of the court and enabled her to create an oasis of positive achievement in a country full of sterile flops. The women were her mother, Farideh Diba—a strong, typically matriarchal Iranian mother with a finely balanced mixture of religious faith and good sense—and Sister Claire, a French nun who was a teacher in her school who spotted something special about the rather shy Farah Diba and took an unusual personal interest in her.

I met them on different occasions. Madame Diba, as she was known, was very faltering in English, so I learned little about her on the social occasions where we met briefly. But the women of her own age ranging from social butterflies to serious women with some social conscience always expressed great respect for her.

Sister Claire came to visit at the invitation of the Empress. I noted that she was a Frenchwoman of very strong character and was unusually worldly for a nun. She acted as the Empress's representative in many matters in Paris after she was returned to France following a parent's complaint about a child hurting herself on a school outing. As I spoke with her, I noted how her strength of character must have influenced the young girls she loved so much.

Farah went to school in Tehran at the French Jean d'Arc school and finished high school at the Lycee Razi, so she was fluent in French. Her family was not affluent, so she applied for and was granted state sponsorship to attend the *Ecole Speciale d'Architecture* in Paris. While in Paris in 1958, she attended a reception for Iranian students and met the Shah for the first time.

The following summer when she was back in Tehran for vacation, her uncle arranged with his friend, Ardeshir Zahedi, the Shah's son-in-law, who was in charge of the foreign student program, for her to again obtain financial support for continuing her education. He also hinted, "My niece has all the requisite qualifications for becoming His Majesty's wife." For at the time, the court was searching for a woman who could produce a male heir to the throne to marry the Shah. He had been almost forced to divorce Empress Soraya when she had failed to do so.

God's hand or fate, whatever you believe, was behind Farah Diba's arrival in Ardeshir Zahedi's office one summer day in 1959 to discuss finances for her studies abroad. Zahedi told his wife, Shahnaz, the Shah's daughter, about this girl who had greatly impressed him, so when the second interview took place, she was hiding behind a door and viewing Farah. The two decided to invite her to their home and introduce her to Mohamed Reza.

Farah was awed at the size and beauty of their home when she arrived for tea a few days later, and she was shocked when who walked in to join them but the Shah himself. It was love at first sight for them both, and the courtship ended in a royal wedding in the Marble Palace's Hall of Mirrors on December 21, 1959. Farah was twenty-one, and not having been raised to aristocracy, she had a lot to learn.

The Shah didn't want to make the same mistake he had made with Soraya, who was not popular in royal circles, so he appointed her a valet whose job it was to help her ease her way into the life of the court of Iran. He also encouraged her to maintain her friendships outside the palace. She soon learned what her limits were and about the pressure of palace life; she was expected to produce a male heir, and soon it was announced she was pregnant. She fulfilled her duty when Crown Prince Reza was born on October 31, 1960. When the Shah told her she had given birth to a boy, she burst into tears. What would have happened if the baby had been a girl?

After the birth of the Crown Prince, she was free to devote more time to other activities and official pursuits. She slowly became actively involved in government affairs when it concerned issues and causes that really interested her such as education, health, culture, and social matters. She pursued her interest in social work, the emancipation of women, education, sports, and art. She founded Pahlavi University, which was the first American-style university in the country, to improve the education of women. As queen, she became the most visible figure in the Iranian government and the patron of twenty-four educational, health, and cultural organizations. As well as supervising these organizations, she paid visits to the most remote parts of the country to gain firsthand information about the aspirations of farmers and ordinary people.

Her strong interest and involvement in the arts were responsible for Iran's cultural movements. She visited and held art exhibitions and performances that gave a new birth to the Iranian artistic community. She encouraged financially and supported many young talented artists through her endeavors, and she was the driving force behind many art museums and other projects to preserve and make public ancient and traditional Persian art and architecture.

I think that only those who lived in Iran during the boom decade could appreciate what an extraordinary role this woman played, what unusual opportunities she had as wife of the Shah, and just how she used the chances and the money at her disposal. Those who were associated with what she was doing or who were observant enough could see how pragmatic she was and the philosophy behind what she was doing. She strongly believed that if you just started laying the foundations for a healthy society even with limited resources, you stood a much better chance of getting one than if you waited until you could do everything at once. But in a man's country, it was always hard for a woman to get kudos for what she did.

In the Imperial Court of Iran, Empress Farah's strictly Western-style attitudes to privilege and behavior were not the least bit popular with the older courtiers or with some of the brash young men who spent their time ingratiating themselves with people in positions of power. They resented the way she criticized their extravagance, hit out at their sycophancy, and pushed aside people whom she felt didn't appreciate the glory of the Iranian monarchy and 2,500 years of history.

They were quick to point out that she was a commoner and had no right to make decisions on protocol and the way things were done around the Shah. However, several of Empress Farah's forbearers had held high offices around the court and government, and she had many well-educated relatives. One met quite a few of them, but like all families in Iran, they couldn't resist exerting pressure on one of their number who was in a privileged position.

Though Empress Farah stopped inviting any relatives who exploited her name to take unfair advantage in business dealings, she gradually found herself sponsoring them almost without realizing it. For one thing, there was a lot of talent among them. For another, in Iran, it was always so hard to trust people who were not close to you or beholden to you. Empress Farah finally perhaps decided it was worth being charged with nepotism if she could ensure her wishes were being carried out. Her sponsoring of her cousins, Reza Ghotbi, who did a magnificent job in developing Iran's national radio and television service, and Kamran Diba, who designed and oversaw the construction of the attractive Museum of Contemporary Art in Tehran, had paid big dividends. The risk could have seemed justified.

Unfortunately, the saying "Nothing succeeds like success" has to be qualified when applied to Iran because success there brings you as many enemies as it does admirers, and Empress Farah quickly found that out. How often I heard people from Princess Ashraf's organizations trying to decry what the Empress was doing in the welfare fields. And how often did officials of the Ministry of Culture and Arts, headed by the empress's brother-in-law Mehrdad Pahlbod, scorn to conceal their opposition to the often highly imaginative work her aides were doing in the field of the arts.

Experience showed Farah Diba that if she wanted things done her way, she had to have complete control over whatever she was doing. Princess Ashraf had taken on the mantle of fairy godmother in the social welfare and women's emancipation fields when Farah got to work, and the princess and her aides were angry at having some of their responsibilities usurped. Since there was no way two royals could share responsibility, Farah set up her own organizations. She had to do the same in cultural fields, for Pahlbod, backed by his wife, the Shah's sister Shams, was not going to work with his sister-in-law. His ministry was a bureaucratic quagmire that employed vast numbers of people who achieved very little. Like so many courtiers, Pahlbod felt a real devotion to the Shah and through culture sought out new ways of glorifying and flattering him and the monarchical traditions.

Soon, Empress Farah's private bureau was employing hundreds of people including a whole corps of social workers. People by the thousands took complaints there knowing that if they really were suffering from injustices, they would be assisted by the Empress and her organization. If the injustices were long standing, officials would be asked to deal with them; they knew the Empress would check that this was done. If the complaints were routine, they would be put into the pipeline like others waiting at ministries for sorting out. Any case of real distress would be ensured of help. All this was necessary because of the hopeless bureaucratic paralysis that seemed to have occurred in Iran as development spurted and institutions couldn't cope with the swollen activity.

At one point, Azizeh, my own *badji*, or maid, decided that I was not paying her, her daughter, and her cousin, who were working for me, enough weekly salary. I had been paying what I was told was a fair amount and gave them the small guesthouse on the property to live. She haughtily told me one morning that she would not be working for she was going down to see the Empress at her offices to complain about me and get the Empress to tell me to pay her more money. After all, I was working for the Shah, so the Empress would know I had a lot of money and could pay her more.

When I saw her that evening, I asked her how it had gone at the court offices. "Well, Khonume, the Shahbanou told me what you were paying was fair, so I guess we will stay here and work for you."

"Did you actually speak to Her Majesty, Azizeh?" I asked.

"Well, she was not there, but there was a secretary I talked to."

I wondered if she had actually gone to the court offices in the center of town.

There is no doubt of the wonderful contribution Empress Farah made to the welfare of the Iranian people in the social field. The hospitals she sponsored were all beautifully equipped; she ensured there were doctors with proper qualifications, and she made sure there were linkups with institutions in the West that could offer the best expert advice or help. And God knows, with the combination of sloth and mindless chauvinism there was in Iran during the years I was there, this was an almost incredible achievement.

She pushed on the development of training facilities in many welfare fields. She found people such as Shojaeddin Shaikholeslamzadeh, a young doctor who was able to create a rehabilitation organization that dealt with the horrendous problems Iran had after centuries of neglect. The problem of inbreeding, common even among urban families, meant there were thousands of young children with physical and mental deformities that could be helped. She set up a steadily more effective nationwide organization to find the cases, get them in queues for treatment, and provide the necessary aftercare. The orthopedic hospital she sponsored in Tehran was the best in the Middle East; it treated many injured Syrians and Egyptians after the 1973 war between the Arabs and Israel.

Her presence and support also removed certain bureaucratic obstacles when she pleaded causes brought to her attention that she believed in, to the Shah or the government. This was the case with her campaign against leprosy. She had heard about the disease as a child and had read stories of people being driven out of society, banished, and exiled because of it, but she had no idea that it was rife in Iran.

Early in her life as empress, she was approached by the Lepers' Aid Association and asked if she would accept the position of president. She readily accepted; she knew she could do more than sympathize with these unfortunate people. She decided to visit the leper center in Tabriz (there was also one in Mashhad). She was deeply shocked when for the first time she saw ashen, disfigured faces and distressed eyes. The more moderate cases were housed in dormitory-like buildings, but the others were relegated to little, dark rooms that smelled dreadful. When the caregivers threw small cakes to the afflicted as if throwing bones to dogs, she was appalled. "How could you? How dare you? They're human beings!" she cried out. These attendants were afraid of catching the disease. She learned that Iranian and foreign doctors as well as nuns were working in these two centers but that not one Muslim religious member of the clergy helped.

She initiated studies and research, and by the end of the seventies, those in the medical field who had been so afraid of the disease were realizing that it was not as contagious as once thought and that it was curable. Early detection and admission to hospitals was implemented with much duress.

It was almost impossible to integrate those who were cured back into their villages because the disease inspired such fear in rural communities, so she asked the Shah to grant a site on one of his properties to establish a village especially for cured lepers. He gave the charity a large piece of land in Gorgon Province, where a community was developed that included hundreds of houses, a fifteen-bed hospital, a primary school, a cinema, a police station, restaurants, factories, a joinery, storehouses for agricultural products, wells, vegetable gardens, and so on.

The village was so successful that the integration took place the other way around—the inhabitants of neighboring towns came to work there or to take advantage of the cinema or restaurants. History did not leave enough time to build another town like Beh Kadehs, but in twenty years, her organization managed to make Iranian hearts respond to the fate of leprosy sufferers and those who had been cured.

Her example encouraged people in other areas of the administration to embark on more scientific programs. The Special Education department of the Ministry of Education developed a nationwide program of classes for handicapped children and even started programs for gifted children in Tehran. In many other specialized fields, contacts were made with foreign institutions thanks to generous funds always allowed, and steady advance was being made in setting up a host of organizations and operational networks for special care. I mention this because it is the kind of activity the press outside Iran never mentioned. Big strides were being made in some areas in Iran.

Enlightened as all this work was in providing help for the handicapped and oppressed in one way or another, it was only marginally important in ensuring votes or mass public support. As is well known in the West, it is the much larger, able-bodied, active section of the population that has the real power to decide whether you are doing a good job; it is their verdict that counts. The selfish materialists that most Iranians were didn't believe they received such a good deal from the state organizations; they didn't mind very much if a legless beggar had to wait for treatment, but they didn't want to do that themselves if they had a cold. They mirrored the arrogant attitudes of their ruling class, which felt that as the cream, they were entitled to live as such. So much of Farah's work went unappreciated by the public as did that of not a few other sincere and capable officials.

It was probably the failure to allow for the exaggerated expectations of the new urban middle class that led to the downfall of the Empress's former protégé Shaikholeslamzadeh when he rose rapidly to become the Minister of Health. His arrival in the office coincided with the preparation of the much-heralded medical insurance program. Like so many other projects in Iran, this was launched during 1977 without adequate preparation. On paper, everything looked all right. The doctors were to do their part, reluctantly, it must be admitted, but Shaikholeslamzadeh had softened them up by barking angrily about their lack of conscience and what plans he had for coercion if the profession didn't cooperate.

The insurance firms arranged to deduct premiums from salaries, the prescribed 8 percent. The money was deducted smoothly enough, but getting treatment proved more difficult. The doctors and the pharmacists did their best to foul it up, anxious to get their own back on the officials with whom they hated dealing and on Shaikholeslamzadeh, who had become a very bumptious character by that time. They were also losing money because the government program was not as lucrative as was their private work. The public, neither knowing nor caring why, got angry about the holdups. The doctors saw their chance and thoroughly exacerbated the situation. One result was that the government and the Shah by then under pressure from a restive people saw a chance of giving the public a sop and finding a scapegoat for themselves. They arrested Shaikholeslamzadeh and his two chief aides and put them in jail on embezzlement charges. Most people who really knew him conceded that it was unlikely that Shaikholeslamzadeh, a successful man in most senses of the word, was the kind to steal. But in Iran, everyone hated a loser, so everyone let him go to slaughter without a word.

I learned about Empress Farah's social work only through the press and dinner-party talk. But I did get a chance to see her operating in her cultural world, which was always punctuated by museum and gallery openings and arts festivals to which one could go as a guest or a paying member of the public. Actually, the first time I saw her was at a polo match; I was able to sit in the Royal Horse Society seats very close to her. I had heard she had had facial surgery, but I was not prepared for how beautiful she looked when I saw her. But close up, I saw just how thickly made up she was. She was such a pretty girl at the time she married that one wondered why she had interfered with her looks at all. I had often been told the Shah had married her because he was conscious of his own shortness and wanted a wife who could correct that deficiency in his children. Perhaps he wanted her to look a certain way too. Photographs of Farah during the early days of their marriage do reveal a quite marked facial likeness between her and her predecessor, Soraya. Perhaps it was that that goaded her to change her face a little. Soraya was undoubtedly a ghost hanging around the palace.

The Shahbanou didn't attend very many sports events with the exception of tennis matches, which she loved, and the odd equestrian event, which the Shah loved. Seeing her at art shows and theaters, however, was to see a woman very much at ease. While her deep humanity gave her the enthusiasm for her social work, her devotion to the arts was a passion.

The Shah was virtually dead to the arts as was the rest of his family. So it must be a bittersweet memory for Farah to ponder the way he had begun to take an interest in her achievements during the last two years of their reign. He was so impressed by the crowd of Western arts personalities such as Nelson Rockefeller who came to the opening of the Contemporary Art Museum. It was designed with a look of traditional Iranian mud architecture from the outside and had a beautifully laid out complex of galleries. He opened the country's first carpet museum, and soon after that, he began to openly endorse the Shahbanou's passion.

The arts museum was a wonderful tribute to the Empress's faith in her cousin Kamran Diba, who provided the design conception and got the best help available in executing it. Kamran, who was brought up with Farah as a brother, studied town planning and architecture in the States. He returned to Tehran with an English wife, and his early commissions showed his talents.

Surrounded by friends educated and formed in Europe, Empress Farah seemed convinced that any revival of Persian culture must go hand in hand with an awareness of living a Western culture in particular. That's why she started the Shiraz Festival of Arts in the lovely, southern city, the capital of Fars Province and famous for its wine, roses, and the poetry of Hafez and Saadi. A lovely city it was—until the boom, when people started knocking down the old houses and the narrow streets became jammed with polluting traffic. Farah's idea was that the festival would show young Iranians what was going on in the arts in the rest of the world. She envisioned a permanent theater and art workshops.

Her cousin Reza Ghotbi and the most truly cultured man I met in Iran, Farrokh Ghaffari, who worked for him, were the inspiration and organization of the festival. In the eleven years it was held, it drew many of the big names in avant-garde theater and other performing arts. They were well paid of course, which may have been the principal attraction for them. All but a few of them were intrigued by the mixture of vitality and animosity they found among younger Iranians. The students would gather around the famous names at informal gatherings at night and would listen to them attentively. They would often roar with applause at the end of performances. But at public discussions the next day, they would ask long, aggressive questions that ended up as denunciations of the artists and the West itself.

These young male Iranians always sported long, black hair and beards as a gesture to their past and a symbol of intellect. It seemed a fitting adornment as they vented their frustrations on the visitors. By the time the 1976 festival came around, visitors including me saw that something of Empress Farah's hopes were being realized. The audiences were almost entirely young people. Most of them were still desperately resisting acceptance of the forms and ideas of the Western arts they were watching. They spent more time discussing Iranian theater and music, which was playing an increasing role in the program; there was no doubt of the stimulus they were receiving.

The critics preserved an ambivalent attitude toward the event. They were all guests of the festival, for Tehran newspapers refused to pay the expenses of their reporters when they traveled except on rare occasions. They were not accustomed to paying. Ministries and contractors always flew or drove reporters to see their projects. Tehran journalists would not leave the comforts of the capital for the primitive provinces, which were to my way of thinking much more civilized than the capital was in many respects. Big crowds of top Tehran society always flew down to Shiraz for the opening and closing days of the festival, which Farah attended. Many of them were her friends, and their ice-cold aloofness and often arrogance were a startling contrast in most cases to her determined warmth.

The society girls taken on as hostesses for the visiting stars and foreign critics usually managed to infuriate their charges by their manner and dilatoriness. The service at the Cyrus the Great Hotel in Shiraz, where guests stayed, was always pathetically handled by management and bemused local boys whose parents in most cases had lived in tents when they were young.

It was pure entertainment sitting and people watching in the elegant foyer of the hotel, which had hosted prime ministers and secondary guests who were not invited to sleep at the famous tented village at Persepolis during the Persian Empire's celebration of 2,500 years thrown by the

Shah. Elderly impresarios from New York and Paris were looking for their tardy guides, and famous names from music and theater were trying to get tickets for each other's performances without much success; they complained about that vociferously. Local boys who fancied their chances were trying to chat up foreign women, a British critic was trying to pick off a young man of his fancy, and the rest of us were desperately trying to get a drink of any kind.

At a restaurant, a waiter brought us white wine instead of red; he said, "It's all the same—only a different color" and poured it. He may have been right. When a UN expert surveyed Iranian wineries for the Ministry of Economy, he reported that some of those in Shiraz should be preserved for museums because nowhere else in the world could such centuries-old methods still be found in use.

The festival in 1977, my last visit, was not an outstanding festival, but there were some intriguing highlights out at Persepolis and the nearby tombs of the old Persian kings at Naqsh-e-Rostam. Maurice Bejart, the Brussels-based pioneer in the modern ballet world, premiered a new work that was much more movement than dance and that had some rather lewd passages I thought. Among the crowd who watched it the night the Queen was there was Manuchehr Khosrodad. Later at the Isfahan Horse Show, I heard him inveighing against the festival and in particular Bejart. "I would shoot Farrokh Ghaffari [the festival program director]," he said. "These people are fouling Iran." He said that given the chance, he could put on a really good festival with good music and other entertainment; it was the kind of fatuous remark Iranians made without self-consciousness. He really believed he could have done it.

Many of the local Shirazes came to see these avant-garde shows along with the students and the art buffs. They soon became bored and started laughing and chatting and then wandering off before the end. For the rest of us, much of the interest lay in the ancient backdrop and striking atmosphere of the occasions. We sat in the moonlight gazing up at the towering cliffs out of which the famous tombs of the Achaemenid kings had been hewn more than twenty centuries before; the carvings depicting the dead monarchs and inscriptions recalled their greatness. Their presence was strong.

A few nights later, I scrambled among the ruins of Persepolis following the dramatic unfolding of a bloodthirsty and often grotesque performance of a Greek tragedy put on by Andre Serban and the La Mama Theater

Company from New York. It moved from tableau to tableau, rape vying with battle scenes in a tour de force that gathered remarkable force there among the floodlit columns of the ancient palaces. The going, however, was tough. Many people fell, and most people scraped their shins on rubble in the dark as we staggered around following the cast as it doubled back and forth among the pillars. We contented ourselves with the knowledge that this was a once-in-a-lifetime event.

At the end, we waited outside the ruins for the Empress to leave before we piled into our buses and cars for the thirty-mile trip back to Shiraz. The floodlights shone on the great stairway built so long ago by Darius the Great, and Farah was a regal figure coming down the stairs with her entourage. One got a taste of the scene of those early days when every Now Ruz, the first day of spring and of the Persian New Year, the great king received representatives from all over the empire.

In the early days of the festival, a little mud village stood opposite the ruins; the villagers used to come out and cheer the Empress. But the village and a small hotel at which countless travelers, including many of the famous, had stayed, were removed so that it wouldn't offend the important guests at the Shah's 1971 celebration. One could be excused a wry smile when one looked at the expensive tents, which had housed the heads of state, that stood rotting in the place of those simple village homes. Though one had to admit that officials had done their best to organize a cooperative for the local people near this site. It had been built so visitors could see what the government was doing, but it wavered on inefficiently in the way so many things in Iran did.

The 1971 festival will figure in the annals of the history of drama for its centerpiece, the latest of famed director Peter Brook's experiments in ritual theater. Cooperating with him was Ted Hughes, one of the Western world's leading poets. They spent several months along with several other well-known theatrical names rehearsing in the garden of a lovely, old nineteenth-century house in Tehran and later in Shiraz. Nobody ever revealed how much Brook received to make Iran the base for this research into ancient ideas and experiment in the use of sound rather than language.

There was always criticism of the festival's expense. It certainly must have cost a fortune to bring some of the great names there. In different years, it hosted people such as Stockhausen, John Cage, and Xenakis, bywords in the world of new musical sounds, Yehudi Menuhin, Arthur Rubinstein, Pendereszki, Cathy Berberian, and other greats in contemporary arts. They performed at Persepolis, the fine old Shiraz bazaar, and in the lovely, old gardens of the southern city.

The festival at which Brook performed was a memorable occasion. It opened with a performance by the Greek Xenakis of a new work written specially for the event. To the amazement of the vast crowd there, it depicted the Greek assault on Persepolis more than 2,000 years earlier. There was a chauvinistic Greek for you! Fortunately, a fierce dust storm blew up, and very few people were able to see anything of it. In the end, they all rushed back to their homes and hotels.

There was more fun later in the week when Farah came to see Brook's play performed. When the actors arrived at Naqsh-e-Rostam, the second locale, to set the stage for the Empress's arrival, Brook was refused entry to the site by the officer in charge of security. The festival officials had given SAVAK a list of the actors and little men but not the big chief himself. This led to a walkout by the whole company, which refused to perform until their director was allowed entry. Farah demonstrated just how clear minded she was. Her entourage urged her to flounce away at the insult, but she knew how the Shah would react if the news got around, so she sat in a darkened bus for a couple of hours until Brook and his troupe were persuaded to return and begin the performance.

When she received Brook afterward, she contented herself with making only one reference to her feelings. "Some people might wonder which of us is the queen, Mr. Brook," she said. Her restraint so impressed the hardened foreign critics there that they made little of the incident. If they hadn't and Farah had walked out, it would have been the end of the festival and so much of her work.

The local press, which had been planning its attack on the festival for a long time, found a way to get at Farah. Though they knew better than to recount the incident in a way that hinted at an affront to their empress, they tore the play, players, festival, organizers, and everything to do with the event apart as much as their limited abilities were able.

It had not escaped the notice of their colleagues and festival officials, however, that the most vociferous of the critics were driving around in chauffeur-driven Mercedes-Benzes that were not supplied by their newspapers or the festival itself. They turned out to have been paid for by the Ministry of Culture and Arts, which employed many of them in spare-time capacities anyway. That was to provide them a little extra comfort while they did their wrecking job. Cultural Minister Pahlbod hated the festival; he was forced to attend its opening and closing and see how well rival officials were successfully usurping his functions. But the critics went too far in their naiveté. The Shah read what they wrote, and even he, trivially vindictive as he could be at times, was appalled and publicly said so; the attack backfired.

The critics' attitude, like that of many of the writers and students who packed the discussions each morning of the festival, was a mixture of chauvinism and frustration. Their Iran had managed without the West for centuries, and they resented the West influencing them then. Yet they knew they should be taking note of what the rest of the world was doing. They were always upset by attempts to introduce the man in the street to Western ideas. They didn't mind a group from the States or Germany announcing on stage to an audience that included the Empress that they wished to express their disapproval of Iran's "fascist regime," but when a performance spilled over into the street and women in *chadors* (full length black veil) saw it, the newspapermen turned it into a scandal.

The inadequacy of the press was apparent when the Empress inaugurated the first of the planned series, Festivals of Popular Traditions in Esfahan in 1977. This was almost exclusively Persian in content, an attempt to revive and analyze the popular entertainments of Iran from traditional storytellers to religious drama performed by villagers. It should have been dear to their hearts, but they passed it off as just another event. It certainly wasn't just that. For one thing, it was the first event on which the two rival organizations, the National Television and the Ministry of Culture and Arts, cooperated with one another. At Shiraz, the ministry supplied a few classical musicians to perform late at night in the candlelit paradise of the garden of Hafez's tomb, but that was virtually it. Here, officials of the two bodies actually sat down together and worked out a program of performances and seminars that seemed to satisfy everyone who attended it even though privately, officials of the two organizations swore afterward that they wouldn't work together again. They didn't really mean it; preparations for the second festival were well advanced when events caused its cancellation.

The foreign scholars, many of them well known, who had gathered for the discussion side of the festival, were entranced by the event. For one thing, it gave new prestige to their fields of study ranging as they did from tribal weaves and marriage customs to rural domestic utensils and ancient beliefs. The Empress planned to make it the launching pad for a special research institute that would finance a lot of their work. Iran had so many people of its own working in these fields too that it excited them. Everyone felt that here at last was a positive step forward in the much-delayed campaign to assess and revive Iran's true culture.

In this incomparably beautiful Iranian city that was the capital of the famous Safavid king Shah Abbas the Great and his successors in the sixteenth and seventeenth centuries, the famous Nawsh-e-Jehan square was closed off for the opening ceremonies of the festival. Pale floodlights picked out the lines of the famous towering royal mosque, the perfectly shaped dome of the small Lotfollah Mosque, and the Ali Qapu pavilion, from which the Safavid kings watched polo and other entertainments in the square below. Farah sat in a specially built dais to watch a parade of traditional entertainers, wrestlers, snake charmers, dancers, musicians, acrobats, sweet sellers, and colorful groups from the tribes march past.

The next day as we wandered the great square, they were all there entertaining the ordinary Esfahanes, who loved the whole thing. This was the first time in all the years that I could remember seeing crowds of ordinary Iranians enjoying themselves like crowds at carnivals and fairs in the West. They also loved the religious dramas, the *ta'ziehs*, which were almost the only traditional theater Iran had. Some semi-professional actors performed in these, but traditionally, villagers played all the roles in these tales, which centered on the fate of Hossain and Ali, who died in the battles for the succession to the prophet Muhammad and who are revered by Shi'ites all over the world.

Ruhozi, a kind of knockabout comedy performed at weddings and similar occasions, was also featured. There had been a series of these from different parts of Iran at the previous year's festival. I watched crowds of ordinary people flock to these and roar their heads off, and the same feeling came over me when I wandered Esfahan's square amid the happy crowds.

On the final night of the festival, a composite program of entertainers performed for Farah on the portico of the *Chehelsotoun* Palace not far from the great square. Twenty columns adorn the entrance to this spectacular pavilion, whose walls are replete with paintings of court and battle scenes dating back to Shah Abbas's days, but the name *Chehelsotoun* means "Forty columns"; the other twenty are reflected in the pool.

A team of dervish musicians from Kermanshah, a Kurdish city in western Iran, strummed away almost mesmerizingly rhythmical. Iran has untold treasures in these traditional groups that were just being revived by the

Empress's organizations in the last year or two of the regime. Two musicians from Peru played haunting flute music that whispered away into the tall poplars in the gardens. As she went to talk to the South Americans at the end of their performance, we saw that she was wearing an alpaca shawl, the kind of gesture she was always trying to make. At the opening, she had worn a long gown with the patterns of the *qalamkar*, a traditional Esfahan textile.

All the reporters who followed the Empress around were there full of their importance and proud of their job. Farah knew them all by name and looked after their welfare; her patronage made their careers. She had no idea that a year later when she carried out what was to be her last official engagement in public as the Empress, none of them would be there; no longer did they want to be even associated with her. A foreign journalist who did go told me he would never forget her thin face, worried eyes, and the way she had to force herself to smile until the enthusiasm of the girls of the nurses' training home she had founded carried her away. Nor would he forget the smile she gave him as she left. He felt it to be a personal gesture in the circumstances. She must surely have been hurt by this show of disloyalty on the part of her personal press corps though she must have been well aware of her compatriots' special weakness in that respect. The day after she left the country, the staffs of the hospitals and other institutions she had founded or transformed erased her name from their titles.

I know for a fact that many of these same people loved her and were grateful to her for what she had done, but it was natural for them not to take risks and try to switch their support to the winning horse whoever that was. It was a sensible move for protection to the Iranian way of thinking.

Loyalty and gratitude were two qualities she demonstrated all the time she was empress. One could recount dozens of instances of this one heard about. If people in her party on her journeys in Iran or abroad became sick, she ensured they were treated and never failed to enquire how they were the next morning.

My friend British reporter James Underwood, who covered so many of her activities, had firsthand experience of her sense of concern for those who served her. Farah did not like injustice especially if it involved people she knew. On one occasion when she heard James was in trouble over something he had written about her, she sent for the cutting, confirmed it committed no fault, and had her office call off the Ministry of Information hounds who were badgering him. The incident demonstrates what reporters had to suffer from the officious bureaucracy.

On the last day of an arduous trip around the great central desert area of Iran during which Farah had helicoptered and driven from village to village over four or five days in high temperatures, the tired reporters had been forced to change a lunch venue at a local inn because officials had invited the Empress there. When they rushed back to get their bags, which had been left in the inn, they were barred by security. Roloff Beny, the well-known international photographer from Canada, was preparing a book on Iran. He had left his teddy bear mascot in his bag. He turned to Underwood and said rather acidly, "Teddy is lunching with the queen. He's such a snob you know." James duly quoted that in an amusing piece in the newspaper on incidents of the trip. The head of the Queen's office at the time, Karim Pasha Bahadori, hated Roloff Beny because Farah was very fond of him and the Canadian had used this to outflank Bahadori on official occasions. He read it and thought to himself, *I'll get this Beny for disrespect.* He apparently contacted the Minister of Information and told him there was a story in the paper that said, "Her Majesty lunched with a doll!" That caused one heck of a hullaballoo.

The ministry's busybodies, afraid of Beny, decided to blame James. His publisher got a call saying he must not write for the newspaper in Iran any more. "The Empress is very angry," publisher Farhad Massoudi was told. Since James had been told on a dozen occasions before that he must never write in Iran again, he was comparatively unconcerned. Massoudi was very upset, however. Fortunately as it turned out, Beny had recounted the whole story to his ambassador, James George, at dinner, and George was due to have an audience with the Empress that week. He told her what had happened, and she quickly stopped the matter.

More than two months later, she caught sight of James among the crowd during a concert interval at the Shiraz Festival. On the way back into the concert hall, she excused herself from the party, which included ministers, and greeted him. "Mr. Underwood," she said, "I want you to know from me personally that I was very angry when I heard what these people did to you earlier this year. Everyone knows you have always been very sympathetic in your reporting and there was nothing at all wrong with what you wrote." It was an accolade the Englishman relished.

Several months later, Iran had a new government. At a concert she attended with the Shah at the lovely old Golestan Palace, where the Shah and she had been crowned, she happened to catch sight of James again. And in the interval, as she relaxed with the new premier, Jamshid Amuzegar, and other ministers, she sent for him and talked briefly with him in front of them. She knew that would show the new officials that he was definitely somebody and they were not to pester him afterward. That was another of her ploys to help people she respected.

One heard of many other examples of Farah interceding to try to right wrongs. "I cannot go against the laws of the land," she told an Amnesty International representative enquiring as to how she could help political prisoners. "But if you let me know of any cases of persecution of the families of political prisoners, I can do something."

She was realistic about these problems when talking to the foreign press. During the 1971 festival, she received many of the foreigners in private audiences, and on the final night, she talked to them all at a party in the garden of the Bagh Eram, the former home of a Qashqai family in Shiraz, that the royal family used as their residence when visiting the south. Farah tried to explain to them the problems of achieving democratic processes in a society that had never known even the beginnings of them. She tacitly conceded she would handle the younger opponents of the regime differently, but she pointed out her constitutional position and the limits of her power. The Western reporters obviously felt these things were pretty irrelevant and that a Westminster-style government should be ushered into Iran immediately. But they thought she was surprisingly honest about the problems the society faced. Hers was not the mindless insistence that nearly everything was perfect and that foreigners didn't understand, which was the stock reply of most Iranian officials.

One Farah-sponsored project in Iran showed even the most casual visitor that she really did mean business when she tried to help young Iranians cope with the modern world. The organization called the Center for the Intellectual Development of Children and Young Adults was run by one of Farah's closest friends, Lili Amir-Arjomand. Up-to-date libraries based on an American pattern were built in well over a hundred large and small towns throughout Iran. These were in effect cultural centers providing not only books but also classes in numerous subjects ranging from graphic arts to filmmaking. They were individually planned to appeal to the minds of young people in areas in different stages of development; in Tehran, they were more sophisticated in their approach, while in small, remote towns, they were designed to awaken the awareness of children to the elementary possibilities of the modern world.

While the Ministry of Education was still using bad translations of foreign textbooks, the center got down to the job of writing its own books and other literature in the light of Iran's cultural history and needs. Among the people who devoted themselves to this was Firouz Shirvanloo, a bright young graduate from Britain who had been jailed on charges of being involved in the 1965 plot against the Shah. Farah rehabilitated him as she had several other brilliant former opposition stalwarts. He and his team got to work to make a long study of the different regions of Iran and assess the cultural background of children there. Then they charted their program, and the center's books and other activities were geared to it. Comfortable and bright, air conditioned, staffed by well-meaning people, these library clubs were oases for the children and even many grown-ups who were allowed to take out books in the small towns. Most of the other facilities provided by government or local authorities for the public in Iran had previously been primitive, skimpy affairs. These centers gave people new expectations and a feeling that the authorities did after all respect them.

After the first few years of the center's work, the National Iranian Oil Company and other governmental institutions became much more generous in helping Farah fund the project. Hoveyda himself was always willing to help, and he did a great deal to back the Empress's work when he could. They seemed to be very much in accord on the need for young people's minds to be stimulated as an essential preparation for the Great Civilization the Shah was always talking about.

But others hinted that Farah didn't know what she was doing in setting up these newfangled Western-type institutions; they contended that they would give children dangerous ideas. Perhaps they did, for the children and young people all over Iran certainly joined in the revolution with endless enthusiasm. Farah and her aides were not to know the regime itself would prove to be so unable that it could not accommodate the rising expectations and the inevitable unrest when the very first crisis came.

If you knew older Iranians, you would understand why they resented Farah. Most of them set much greater store in positions and titles rather than achievements. Many of the older scholars and officials were startled by the way Farah and her young, Western-educated art advisers managed to accomplish things that they themselves had been putting off for years. Of course she had the tremendously privileged position of being the Shah's wife and had access to large amounts of money. But she also seemed to be able to suborn many of the old colleagues of Culture Minister Pahlbod, who obviously hated her for it.

Being Iranians, many others resented her just because she was successful. One way Pahlbod and his aides could get at Farah was by holding up the visas for the foreign experts she wanted to bring out to advise her on her museum and other projects. That they did gleefully quite oblivious to the bad reputation it gave Iran in the eyes of the UN and other international bodies. It also created problems for the experts themselves, who were busy people and found it difficult to reschedule visits to Iran.

I recount these details because I think Farah's activities show what was possible in Iran despite the problems posed by its real backwardness and the country's vast size. They also show just how sincere she was and how much she achieved. Iran was by no means the barren cultural desert or the haven of neglect of public welfare that the unfriendly Western press would have us believe, and Farah could take a big share of the credit for that.

She had absolutely no business interests, but she did make every effort to support makers of Iranian goods and any Iranians with talent. She wore mostly Iranian-made dresses if possible made with Iranian materials. She paid more than the price demanded for paintings by Iranian artists just to encourage them, and she sponsored their exhibitions abroad to try to give them prestige. All this in addition to doing her utmost to show herself a proper consort for the Shah and to help put his grandiose aims into a more realistic and human framework.

Unlike the rest of the royal family, she showed genuine interest in people and their problems and discussed with foreigners objectively about the difficulties Iran faced. She was a great asset to the Pahlavi Dynasty.

On the day she was crowned Shahbanou by the Shah, she said, "When he crowned me on October 26th, 1967, the king made me feel he was crowning all the women of Iran." She was always a women's rights advocate and did much for the women of Iran during her reign.

I feel deep sympathy for her today. Facing her is permanent exile from the land whose people she genuinely loved and served throughout her reign. The Islamic fanatics sentenced her to death because she introduced so much of the Western world to Iran and fostered the arts, which outdated theologians insisted were forbidden by the religion.

The people of Iran had lost Western arts and artists with the fall of the Pahlavis, but the Islamic government has now begun to make the museums, arts, theater, and many other cultural institutions readily available to the people again; that I know would please Farah Pahlavi.

CHAPTER 4

The Prime Minister

I didn't see much of Amir Abbas Hoveyda, the Shah's ill-fated premier throughout my time in Iran. When he occasionally turned up at parties, he was always very good humored with a word for everyone he knew or to whom he was introduced. He was a cultured and brilliant Brussels- and Paris-educated man who for thirteen years until his dismissal in 1977 had the unenviable job of trying to keep the Shah, his tough taskmaster, happy while goading his slothful administration into some kind of action. As an Iranian who had spent most of his young life abroad, he was as startled as many foreigners were by the unpreparedness of his compatriots for even the initial stages of a modern society.

He set a new style in prime ministers for that country of stuffy officials. Instead of the formal dark suit and tie that officials had always worn in public, he always wore softer shades. He always sported an orchid in his button hole sent to him each day by his lifelong friend and for a brief period his wife, Leila Emami. He was usually puffing a pipe as he carried his shining walking stick in his hand. He was the first premier to wear an open-necked shirt without jacket on hot days and on trips to the provinces. He was much more approachable than were any of his predecessors or ministerial colleagues. There was no doubt the ordinary man appreciated him during his heyday. True to form, however, they turned against him when they realized he was on his way out. His execution was received with exultation by the same people who only a couple of years earlier were applauding him with gusto.

He spurned the traditional big, official limousine and drove himself around in a small Paykan saloon, the locally assembled Hillman Hunter, which was the Iranian national automobile. If he flew in for an official visit and there was a Mercedes-Benz waiting, he would insist on taking the wheel himself to deflate the formal image. There is no doubt that this was a sincere effort to make Iranians feel that they had human ministers and that officialdom was concerned about them.

Having appointed so many officials who showed their arrogance and feelings of superiority in their dealings with the public when he wasn't breathing down their necks, he knew the limitations of his fellow citizens in their steadfastness and loyalty. Perhaps he wasn't so shocked when many of his appointees scrambled to join the Khomeini bandwagon when they knew the writing was on the wall and helped throw him to the wolves.

He was an unusual Iranian whose upbringing had been largely outside Iran. His father was a diplomat who spent many years in the Arab world, and much of Amir Abbas's schooling was in Lebanon, where he learned Arabic and French. He desired to attend university in France and went there to do so in 1938, but the Nazi occupation of that country led him to move to England, where he sharpened his command of English; he completed his higher education in Brussels. His ability to speak several languages including Persian, French, English, Italian, German, and Arabic helped him climb the political ladder later in his life.

His father was a dabbler in spiritual matters and was certainly deeply interested in Bahaism, the faith Iranian Muslims regarded as the most heretical of all because its progenitors had broken away from their native Shi'a faith. Hoveyda was constantly accused by his enemies of being a secret Baha'i himself, but he seemed far too easygoing in his general habits to have been a devout adherent of a strict faith such as Bahaism with its teetotalism and other taboos. He was basically a nonreligious man.

He was very close to his brother Fereydun, who was for several years head of Iran's delegation to the UN and who later wrote several novels of intriguing originality. Fereydun was a leading expert on the cinema, and after Amir Abbas's death, he wrote a book about his brother.

When Amir Abbas came back to Iran after working with the UN High Commission for Refugees, he worked with the National Oil Company before joining the government of his close friend Hossain Mansour. When Mansour was assassinated in 1965, Hoveyda took over the reins of power despite his real distress. It was an important moment for Iran.

The Shah was launching his ambitious development plans designed to give Iran a renaissance. If the hapless rural population were to accept these meekly and be carried away on the current of moves such as land reform regardless of their abilities to cope, the growing industrial communities and the rising middle class required some more-dexterous handling. Hoveyda provided that. He played off different groups against each other to prevent any single one becoming too powerful, and he subtly induced a modern approach in general social attitudes at least to the rights of the individual especially the young. Unfortunately, SAVAK wouldn't allow this new liberty to break through the hidebound restrictions of free speech. Hoveyda brought in young technocrats to key positions whose sophisticated approach to life followed his. They enjoyed status and incomes that attracted back to Iran more of their kind.

Many other bright young men from the best families found it just too difficult and boring to tackle dull, day-to-day jobs in ministries and cope with the mores of a minor officialdom not yet out of its medieval torpor. But they at least returned to Iran to set themselves up as designers, architects, restaurant proprietors, fashion boutique owners, or in other positions that didn't cause them to lose face by having to argue with people of lesser social status. Unfortunately, in an upper class and official society as small as that of Iran's, they set standards that were copied by the technocrats who stayed working for the government. Hoveyda found himself presiding over a lavish bureaucracy that required heavy financing to ensure its members' standard of living.

Parties became more significant events than meetings; a peek at a senior official's daybook would show more references to family occasions than to official meetings. Officials who didn't want to fit into this social pattern found themselves slated for demotion or dismissal because they threatened the peace of mind of the boss or the majority of their colleagues. Hoveyda had a tough task trying to get this unwieldly administration of pampered senior men and the mass of largely benighted junior officials to press on with development plans. He knew best of all their shortcomings, but it was impossible to tell the Shah frankly that the material just wasn't there to carry out his grandiose plans at more than a funereal pace.

The Shah just wasn't capable of understanding the ramifications involved in managing an economy in conjunction with a society like the one being created. Worse, he had no idea of the true character of his people especially once they had achieved a little status. Hoveyda was between the devil and the deep blue sea. While things were going well, it wasn't too bad a job, and he had a knack for giving the crowds who listened to him a sense of euphoria. But he lacked the right people around him to preserve the kind of relations with the main groups of the society that could have helped him gain more support.

Among those who had big influence on Hoveyda was Parviz Raji, longtime friend of Princess Ashraf who later became ambassador in London until he was dismissed when Bakhtiar came to power. Raji was a supercilious character sensitive to any sort of criticism and certainly not closely in touch with the Iranian public. People like him helped keep Hoveyda insulated against the reality of Iran. Hoveyda thus seemed led to believe he could manage without those who were critical of him, and that led him to take less notice than he should have of intellectuals and others with an understandable sense of self-importance. They became his enemies instead of his supporters; that led him to stay loyal to obviously useless officials for far too long. His governments were invariably reshuffled rather than subjected to radical change. Some names of course were the Shah's nominees and had to stay. Others perhaps SAVAK had insisted on. But Iranians insisted that some of the people were just friends Hoveyda was sentimental about or were even nominees of his mother, to whom he was utterly devoted, which is just another instance of the matriarchal society.

People wondered how men like Agriculture Minister Mansur Rouhani, who was openly accused of corruption in society throughout most of his several years of tenure in office, kept his job so long. There was a story that the Shah had made Rouhani pay back money that had disappeared. Another minister, Nasser Golesorkhi, who was responsible for natural resources, allowed his brother to obtain the monopoly concession for export and sale of walnut wood and banned all imports at the same time. Golesorkhi also had an unenviable reputation as a womanizer. There were many other instances of Hoveyda's indulgence as far as his ministers were concerned. Thus people accused Hoveyda of condoning the widespread corruption among his officials to further his own interests as premier. He allowed the people's interests to suffer because he knew that greasing palms was the quickest way to get things done in Iran and he would get the credit for the achievements with the Shah.

Hoveyda was in reality more of an idealist than that. I believe he genuinely wanted to make Iran a great power and have his compatriots hold their heads up in the world. But he took a gamble that he could achieve that by driving the corrupt system down the road to the future while trusting that the introduction of a technological society would kill the opportunities for theft and create a natural meritocracy.

Hoveyda used to shake his head at foreign visitors and tell them how he was astonished at the primitiveness of his fellow citizens. That was presumably why he felt he had to rely on the technocrats he really trusted to do so much. But even he probably wasn't aware of how they began to carve up the takings for themselves under the system of non-accountability in which Hoveyda's administration worked. When time ran out on him, Hoveyda had to carry the can for all they did.

There were plenty of signs that he was wary of those younger technocrats who were not entirely dependent on his patronage and who thus could become rivals for his own post. He kept from high office people such as Manuchehr Ganji, a brilliant international lawyer who returned to Iran to become dean of the prestigious faculty of law at Tehran University, and Hushang Nahavandi, who was head of Empress Farah's private bureau when the revolution came.

In 1977, Court Minister Alam begged the Shah to replace Hoveyda because in the country's dire financial situation due to the falling price of oil, a drop in industrial production, and national electricity grid failures, he had abandoned the budget and imposed a spending freeze. That caused industrial and defense projects to be postponed or canceled. Alam had wanted him to appoint Hushang Ansary, who had good relationships with the generals and senior clerics and was as well a consummate negotiator who would not hesitate to maintain order in a time of liberalization. The Shah, however, chose Jamshid Amuzegar, a talented economist who came across as officious, haughty, disdainful, and out of touch with the common people; that turned out to be a grave mistake. He asked for the resignation of his longtime friend Asadollah Alam, Court Minister of eleven years, who he knew was ill with cancer, to give the position to Hoveyda.

No one who lived for long in Iran or who knew Hoveyda failed to experience deep regret over his execution. He had personally remained free of corruption, but he had turned a blind eye to many of the activities of the security men because he had no power to influence them. If he used them at times, it seemed to be largely because he knew they were a calculated risk to preserve plans that were not jeopardized by those who opposed him. As I have said, the corruption he appeared to tolerate, was considered a necessary evil in a prosperous, free-enterprise Iran. The end, he felt, would justify the means.

The Shah was advised that by arresting Hoveyda as a scapegoat for the ills of the crumbling regime, he would slow the revolution's momentum. In September 1978, he was put under house arrest; the Shah assumed he would be tried and freed. That did not happen.

Once the Shah fled the country, Hoveyda was arrested by the revolutionary forces. There was nobody to protect him. The only real sympathy for him as he awaited death came from a few close friends and officials outside Iran who appreciated his problems and his worth. Everybody else turned on him, even those he had sponsored and established. There was almost a feeling among Iranians of having been purged when he was tried and executed on March 15, 1979.

CHAPTER 5

Two Generals and the Master of the Horse

When General Nader Djahanbani wanted to invite his friend Shah Mohammad Reza Pahlavi to come to see his newly completed Spanish-style home just outside Tehran, he made it a memorable occasion. He was keen on show jumping having openly boasted to me only a few years before that even though he had just started jumping, he would become good enough to compete internationally. Not the most modest guy!

He decided that only the best was good enough for his king. He invited Eddie Macken, at the time the world's leading rider, to come and compete in a little show he organized for the afternoon of the visit. He never divulged the fee he had to pay Eddie, but one can imagine just how much it must have been. Having bought a racehorse breeding farm for more than $2 million in Ireland not to mention some thoroughly expensive horses, Nader had connections there, so he had flown Macken in from Dublin.

He planned to lay on a dinner fit for a king after the show. Where else would you get that but from Maxim's in Paris? The order was placed—"Fly out dinner for fifty," Nader ordered. The caviar, which could be found on the spot, was freshly brought in from the Caspian almost warm from the sturgeons' bellies. Then of course it was properly chilled.

What a scene greeted the Shah and Empress when they arrived and sat on the terrace in front of the swish, paneled, discotheque with its lovely furnishings and bar Djahanbani had built at one end of his splendid, grass-covered ménage.

Against the background of the majestic Alborz Mountains to the north stood the palatial, Spanish-style home of Nader and his beautiful wife, Farah. Its vaulted tiled roofs were echoed in the stable block to the east of the emerald stretch of turf, which must have cost nearly as much to maintain as it did to lay in the dry Iranian climate.

To the west, a small stand was packed with guests mostly from the Iranian horse world. The most prominent members had been invited to ride in the competition against Macken. But they were not invited to dinner; not even the Djahanbanis' close friends, Fereydun and Elian Elghanian, members of a prominent Iranian Jewish family, were given an invitation to the posh affair. The guests were mostly relatives including Nader's cousin Princess Manijeh and her husband, Prince Gholam Reza, the Shah's oldest half-brother, and a few other royals.

When he strolled around the spread with his host afterward, I wondered what the Shah thought of it all. The tiles for the house and stable roofs had been imported from Spain, the wood paneling in the high-ceilinged rooms was from Britain, the metal grillwork around the windows came from Germany, and the black marble and the gold fittings for the bathrooms came from Italy. The furnishings were elegant, and Nader's wife had chosen traditional red and black Turkoman carpets for the floors in a flash of inspiration and nationalism.

There was a big swimming pool in the courtyard for the Djahanbanis and their guests. Away across the green lawns was another pool for the horses, which were housed in stables with thick, rubber-matted floors for the animals' safety along with a beautiful sitting room, tack room, and pharmacy. Smaller than the Shah's stables they might have been, but they were far more impressive. A training track for the horses ran around the property. The fences for the jumping show were decorated with flowers and shrubs. The riders lined up in military uniforms and red coats made a stirring sight.

It's good that Iranians have a sense of humor to go along with their sense of elitism though; this was an occasion when events did not match the grandeur of their setting. Host Djahanbani himself jumped badly on his two mounts. The Shah's other great friend Manuchehr Khosrodad was run away with, and Master of the Royal Horse, Kambiz Atabai suffered a fall. The mount of champion Macken also jumped slothfully, and he failed to make a clear round. It was left to the Shah's own *djelodards*—stable boys—and me to take the top three placings and snatch the trophy to the chagrin of the other riders but to the pride and amusement of the Shah.

Could the Shah have been so naive as to have imagined that Djahanbani could have afforded that sumptuous place and all the rest of the show on his income from his holdings in Air Taxi, the group that had a virtual monopoly of private-hire flying in Iran? It was common knowledge in Tehran that Nader's father, the distinguished Amanollah Djahanbani, who had represented the country in many international dealings including the Baluchistan border problem, was an honest man who took only his salary throughout his life. He had many other sons besides Nader among whom to divide any wealth he had after he died. People pointed to Nader's position as a top general in the air force and his handling of the purchase of the new F-5 Freedom Fighters the Shah acquired for his air force and nodded knowingly. Did the Shah never suspect any link between sudden wealth and the handling of these contracts by his men? Nader was one of many, but few were as unthinkingly ostentatious about it as he was. Nader in fact typified the attitude and behavior of members of the royal family and those closely connected with them. They felt that the connection qualified them as exceptional people and that the rest of society had no right to question anything they did.

In Nader's case, the Shah's indulgence toward his friend was first demonstrated after he had disobeyed an order that had resulted in the loss of an F-5 and its crew. Djahanbani had flown his squadron of new fighter jets from the US, and during a refueling stop in Turkey, he had been given a radio message telling him to delay his departure to Iran because of bad weather. He was however, so anxious to get his planes home and receive congratulations that he pretended he had not received the message and set off for Tehran.

Unfortunately, one of the planes flew into the side of a mountain on the way in thick clouds, and two men were killed. Though he was arrested when he arrived at the air base in Tehran, his friend the Shah interceded and obtained his release. Since His Majesty's brother-in-law General Mohamed Khatami, the husband of his sister Fatimeh, was head of the Iranian air force, one supposes that was not too difficult to arrange. But Djahanbani was barred from flying military aircraft himself, a cruel blow. He was made chief of air force training instead. The mishap failed to deflate his ego, and he remained supremely arrogant and cold toward all but a few close friends and quite unable to make contact with inferiors.

I felt Nader's coldness the first time I met him. It was at a horse show in which he had competed. When he rode into the ring in his air force general's uniform on an almost pure-white Turkoman stallion, the sight of him almost took my breath away. He had inherited his blond hair, blue eyes, and fair looks from his Russian mother; he stood out among this race of dark-haired, dark-eyed people. He was known as the blue-eyed general.

All changed when he started to jump his horse. At that time, he was one of the worst riders I had ever seen. He was introduced to me after the show. He looked at me with those steely blue eyes and informed me he'd been jumping for only a few months but intended to win the national championship. I said casually, "I wish you the best of luck!" thinking to myself he'd never make it. I had underestimated the determination of this man of iron. He soon afterward went to Ireland, paid nearly $100,000 for one of their top jumpers, and after a tremendous amount of perseverance finally achieved his ambition in 1977.

He and his wife had only one daughter, Goli, a pretty girl who was terrified of horses. In spite of that, which was obvious to all the rest of us, her father forced her to ride in shows until she left to study in the US.

It was through Prince Gholam Reza, who was married to his cousin, that Djahanbani angled for power in areas in which he was interested. Gholam Reza was chair of Iran's Olympic Committee and was being pushed by his henchmen to take over all sports in Iran. Nader wanted to be chief of the horse world, but his route was blocked by his friend and my boss, Kambiz Atabai, whose father had been Master of the Royal Horse before him.

Relations between the two men began to deteriorate when Kambiz realized that his friend was trying to push Prince Gholam Reza into demanding the presidency of the Royal Horse Society from the Shah. Kambiz moved swiftly; he persuaded Court Minister Asadollah Alam to suggest to the Shah that the Crown Prince should become the society's patron. That would keep Gholam Reza out, for no two members of the royal family could be involved in any single organization. The Shah agreed to Alam's suggestion, and Atabai breathed again.

The breach between the two men widened when one day, Kambiz and his father walked into the royal stable yard to see Djahanbani beating a stable lad with his whip. Nader had the privilege of keeping two horses at the stables, and the lad had been tardy in bringing out a horse for his girlfriend of the time. He was ordered to remove his horses from the stables; striking imperial servants was not accepted at the palace, and the general obviously realized he would do best to concur and end the matter there. The horses were taken away, and thus he began construction on his picture-book country home.

Among Nader's women friends during my stay in Iran, there was only one who must have caused his beautiful wife, Farah, any real concern—the beautiful Golnar Bakhtiar. She was the daughter of Teymour Bakhtiar, the founder of SAVAK and its head from 1956 to1961,who was killed it was said by the Shah's men after he had turned on his old chief and begun forming an opposition from his exile in Iraq. Goli, as she was known, was Iran's top woman rider, not that that meant much. When she became friendly with Djahanbani, she took over the stables at his out-of-town property and moved her own horses in there. The main house was not yet built, so Farah was not on the spot, but she was livid about it.

When I accompanied the Iranian team to Beirut to jump against the Lebanese, I noted that Goli and Nader had adjoining rooms. That didn't seem to worry the others in the party, so I didn't comment on it either. Later, Goli accompanied Nader and a group of other friends to Ireland to buy horses. In Ireland, Goli found just the animal she wanted. Since they didn't have a great deal of cash with them, Nader suggested that Goli give him her cash so they could spend it on fun and that he would pay for all the horses with his line of credit from Tehran.

I ran into them at a party shortly after their return from Europe but before the horses had arrived. I told them I had heard they had bought some very special horses from Ireland. "I have bought the best horses you can imagine," replied Nader with total arrogance. "They will make the horses you have at the Imperial Stables look like nothing." The most expensive, he told me, was a horse called Oatfield Hills, which I knew had won many international prizes the previous year.

"I won't tell you how expensive," he said. I knew the British horse press had put the figure of £55,000 on the horse, which had been bought by some Middle Easterner, but I wasn't sure it was Djahanbani until then.

Goli told me about the young horse, Windsor, she had chosen. She had complete faith in Nader at that time and looked up at him with goo-goo eyes as she added that she hadn't anything like the kind of money Nader had.

Whatever the truth was about the deal the couple had made about money and horses, it broke up their close friendship. According to Goli, Nader told her when they got back that he intended to keep Windsor for himself and that he would pay her back the money she had given him. That did not suit the competitive Goli, so she promptly went to his stable and removed all her horses and tack. She ended their relationship that day with a cold finality that was amazing for all to see. Farah Djahanbani was delighted. She made sure that once they were hosting shows at their swank spread, Goli never set foot there and was excluded from all the parties they threw.

Goli decided to concentrate on her riding. Did this influence her to marry a much older but very wealthy man, Serge Bezrukeh, who was at least in his late fifties and with a daughter her age? When she agreed to marry him, she received three top European show jumpers of her own as a wedding present from Serge. They were estimated to have cost about £70,000, but I don't remember Goli ever winning a good competition on them.

Nader Djahanbani's ambition and arrogance were seemingly endless. Only a few months before the collapse began, he finally managed to get the position he had long sought—chief of all sports in Iran. He started out well; he tried to put some zip into the organization. But when the unrest worsened and his employees went on strike for more pay, he told them publicly and contemptuously that they would achieve nothing by striking and were not important in any way. That helped formulate the charges against him of "destroying sports institutions" when he appeared for his trial after the revolution. The officials of the sports bodies all rushed to provide evidence against him.

Nor could he resist the temptation to exact revenge on Kambiz Atabai. He told the Shah that to allow Atabai, a court official, to be head of the Football Federation as well as the Equestrian Federation was psychologically bad. He tried to persuaded the Shah to take the job from Atabai, who, to give credit where it is due, had backed an old friend and other bright, young soccer officials in Iran so well that they managed to develop the game effectively enough to reach the later stages of the World Cup.

All the Iranian riders I knew believed they would be able to win anything they wanted once they had good horses; they hadn't the patience to really learn how to ride well. General Manuchehr Khosrodad, who headed Iran's paratroop and Special Forces, was a much more modest man than was Djahanbani, but he also succumbed to this temptation in the end. He acquired an experienced horse from France that failed to improve his record.

Manuchehr, having no wife at the time, could quite cheerfully be seen with girlfriends on every occasion. But as is the Iranian way, he found the lure of a married woman irresistible. For much of the time I knew him, he was constantly seen with Danny, the French wife of a doctor friend, and there was no doubt of the admiration and friendship these two people felt for each other. He had a daughter by his first wife, but I frequently heard people making the kind of jokes Iranians enjoyed about him. "Manuchehr, the man who can't get it up" I heard his friends comment laughingly on several occasions when he walked into a show ring. The truth of that we may never know; it wasn't the sort of thing he would have bragged about anyway. But his friend, Danny's husband, never seemed to mind the obviously close relationship between the two. Indeed, I twice saw her faint at parties—she seemed to be prone to such attacks in stuffy atmospheres—and on each occasion, Khosrodad jumped around solicitously while her husband remained unperturbed.

A couple of years before the end, Khosrodad married Mahin Nazemi, the sister-in-law of a friend and secretary to Kambiz Atabai. He flew her himself to Mashhad to be wed at the shrine of Iran's most revered saint, Imam Reza, who must have smiled sardonically in his coffin if he knew how Khosrodad would meet his end soon afterward at the behest of Muslim priests. This marriage was the most extraordinary on again–off again affair ever. One week, they were together all lovey-dovey, and the next, they were separated. It became too delicate a matter for people to dare ask them about each other when they were alone.

There was no doubt about Khosrodad's physical courage and his rare honesty among the generals and the people around the Shah. He lived modestly; his only excesses in the public eye were his prodigal use of the aircraft and helicopters under his control for flying his friends about. As a busy man, he had to fly almost everywhere just to do his job of course, and most of the time, he was taking friends on what were business trips anyway.

He had sprung to fame by his handling of the riots of 1963 in Tehran, when the land owners and the clergy opposed the Shah's plans for land reform. This was the Shah's move to clip the wings of those sections of the population whose main power and wealth was derived from their possession of vast areas of land and the people who worked on them.

A mere major at the time, Khosrodad led the troops who put down the uprising in central Tehran, when the opposition sent mobs of rioters into the streets. Khomeini was the spokesman at that time against land reform; he ironically contended that taking personal property was against the teachings of Islam. He changed his mind on that when he came to power himself. Many people died during that unrest, but Manuchehr Khosrodad was promoted overnight.

When he became chief of the Special Forces, he was given the job of making a deal with the American firm of Bell Helicopter for the machines and the technical know-how to prepare his department. When asked by the Bell people what he wanted in return for making the deal, he was said to have told them he sought only the best helicopters and training available. Didn't he want some money? Never! He would not take *bahkshish*!

The Bell operation in Iran was huge. Hundreds of American personnel were sent to Iran, and many Iranians were hired and trained to be pilots at the cost of about $100,000 per pilot. My children's nanny dated one of the pilots in training, and I remember having a discussion with him one evening when he came to pick her up.

"How is your training going?" I asked Ali.

"Oh, it's going pretty well, I guess. I had a bit of a problem today with my American instructor. We were practicing landings, and he kept telling me I didn't have enough RPMs on the rotors. I couldn't see what difference it made. Five thousand or forty-five hundred, what's the difference?"

"Probably a foot or two," piped in my husband who had been listening. "You would be below ground level if you didn't have enough RPMs, and that would be a crash!"

Manuchehr was an excellent pilot himself. In the States, he was often asked to demonstrate his prowess as a pilot, and at games such as firing missiles against a competitor, he was a hot shot. During the summer of 1976, he spent little time riding and training his horses as he was preoccupied with trying to break world records flying helicopters. He made several new marks in flying higher and descending faster than any other man, and his accomplishments went into the Guinness Book of Records.

Manuchehr did surprise me when we went to Beirut with the Iranian show-jumping team. A round of parties for the two teams took place the first two days. I was shocked to find the first evening that the riders who worked at the Imperial Stables were not taken along to these parties. When I mentioned this to Khosrodad, he said they were only poor peasants and would be out of place in the homes of wealthy Lebanese. "You are just too democratic for our society," he told me. At that time, he was in charge, for team captain Kambiz Atabai had not arrived. When Kambiz arrived, he ruled the men should go to the parties when I mentioned this to him. Khosrodad told me afterward without rancor, "You have westernized your boss. Before you came, he would have agreed with me. I congratulate you on having won the battle." He never broached the subject again, and I learned too that he never bore a personal grudge.

I had already found out what an excellent sport he was on the first occasion we met. I had no idea who he was as he rode into the ring at an international competition between a team from Iran and another from Soviet Armenia that I was judging. He broke an international rule by riding into the ring on a horse for the jump-off that was different from the one he had ridden in the first round. The first horse had been a bay, and the second one was a gray, which showed he had done it innocently. As the judge, I eliminated him and told him to leave the arena. I explained that a rider must ride the same horse in the jump-off that he had ridden in the first round. He merely told me what he considered an even more important fact: "This is Iran," he called out airily, wheeled his horse around, and rode him through the starting point toward the first obstacle. But I was not cowed. As he jumped the first obstacle, I reached for the hammer and gonged the bell loudly to signify he was eliminated from the contest.

The hullaballoo in the jury box, where my fellow judges were all Iranians, was deafening. "You can't eliminate him!" "No, no!" "Do you know who that is?" The noise subsided to silence as an angry, red-faced rider rode up to the jury box.

"What do you think you are doing? Don't you know who I am? You can't eliminate me! I want to know the reason for your ringing the bell!" he demanded.

"General, I told you when you saluted the jury that you must ride the same horse in both rounds of the competition. It's an FEI rule. I am sorry, but you are eliminated."

"You listen to me," he replied firmly. "This is Iran, and we don't have such a rule here." They certainly didn't—there were no Iranian show-jumping rules at that date.

"General," I replied firmly, "this is an international completion. I must eliminate you. Now would you please leave the ring so we can continue?"

Khosrodad was beet red, and my heart was palpitating. Silence reigned in the jury box. Without another word, he turned his horse and cantered out of the gate.

The Soviet riders won the Iran-Soviet Friendship Cup that day, a fact that didn't calm my nerves when I saw General Khosrodad walking toward me in the jury box at the end of the competition. I was alone and marking up the official results on the FEI card. I didn't suppose I would be jailed for this act of *lèse-majesté*, but I have always hated verbal confrontations.

"You know that you humiliated me today!" Khosrodad roared at me. "I cannot stand for that! You had no right!"

"*Timsar*," I replied using the Persian word for his rank, "this was an international competition. I could not let you ride a different horse in the second round. What would the Russians have said? They would certainly have protested, and you would have looked even more foolish."

"But you see," he said, "my first horse went lame, and I couldn't use him again. I had to jump for my country, so what else was there for me to do?"

The argument lasted only briefly. His mouth suddenly began to crinkle at the corners, the crow's feet around his eyes deepened, and he began to laugh. "Well," he said, "I had heard rumors that you stood your ground, and now I have found it out for myself. You were right. I knew it. But I had to try, didn't I? I am sure we'll get on well, you and I."

He was right. We never had trouble with each other again. Military men have their duties. Manuchehr Khosrodad carried out his and was an honest human being.

The third of the Shah's men I got to know well was Kambiz Atabai, another very complex character. His family's origins were humbler than were the others, but his father had risen high in the court through his qualities of reliability and loyalty. Kambiz had instincts acquired from his father's example and tried hard to be humane and fair in his work as a high official of the court. But he was a child of the court, brought up in its influence, and he never learned to fully accept the need to be more democratic in the steadily socializing Iran.

I saw Kambiz nearly every day at the Imperial Stables and was able to see the immense pressures on him. First, there was the desire to serve the Shah faithfully and well. Then there was the need to live up to the demands of the court minister and his own father, another longtime court servant but an unsophisticated man from a generation that knew nothing of the modern world. Then there was the need to handle official colleagues who had their own interests at heart and felt that by downplaying yours, they would automatically help their own. In addition were the other members of the royal family whose interests had to be taken note of. Then came the officials who were patronized by the different princes and princesses and who wished to feather their nests at the expense of others including Kambiz. Finally, there came the need to ensure a reasonable public image in times when it was becoming fashionable for all officials to display they were conscious of their responsibilities to the country. In truth, the priorities were in that order. I enumerate them, however, to help people understand how any fairly senior Iranian official had to be both very shrewd and perspicacious if he wished to succeed or even simply keep his post.

Court officials had to contend with the pressures put upon them by the court minister, who at the time was Asadollah Alam. Every senior official in the court was conscious that he worked directly for the Shah, and they tried to be more Catholic than the Pope as it were; they felt less answerable to authority than did the officials of the government itself. They enjoyed privileges that helped make them immune to authority; these included a 5 percent income tax rate, half of that for the rest of the population, and the right to import automobiles for free. They had medical treatment and other care provided long before the rest of the populace too. No wonder they felt superior.

You couldn't help developing a great deal of sympathy for an official such as Kambiz Atabai, who was in his early thirties when I met him. He meant well in most things he did, but having been brought up in the court, he was part of its mores and intrigues. He also came from a tight tribal group of Turkomans from northeast Iran, and he suffered as did so many Iranians in a country where nomadic tribal life still suffers today from the effects of long inbreeding and the complexities derived from a tight social structure.

His father, Abolfath Atabai, was a stableman at the court when the Shah's father, Reza Shah, came to power. That Shah took a fancy to him, and he became the old king's personal groom, a post that finally led him to become Master of the Royal Horse and later the controller of the court's purse strings. When Reza Shah was exiled in 1941, he counseled his son, Mohammad Reza, to listen to Atabai, who knew so much about the day-to-day running of the court and the country's affairs.

One problem he had, concerned other members of the Atabai tribe. Reza Shah's first child had been a daughter he had with a Qajar princess from the old regime; this girl had married an Atabai, who rose to become a general. The three children of this marriage called themselves princes or princesses, and like all the other relatives of the Shah, they received a regular stipend. This trio never failed to remind Kambiz when they got the chance that they were the Shah's nephews and nieces and that he was simply the son of a stableman from their tribe.

I saw Princess Hamdamsaltaneh, the Shah's oldest half-sister, one day when she came to see Kambiz, who had the job among so many others of dealing with the problems of lesser members of the royal family. I was sitting waiting in his outer office when she arrived in a great rage. She was an extraordinary sight. I had heard that her eccentricities had led to her not being invited to court functions any more, but I wasn't prepared for this spectacle. She was garbed in a tattered, old, three-quarter-length mink coat that was worn at the elbows and the cuffs. She carried an equally battered, old crocodile skin purse, and her old Oxford shoes were worn at the heels. The incongruity of this outfit on a sister of the Shah was heightened by the immaculateness of the uniformed officer who marched in after her. But her face was much less lined than one would imagine in a woman of over sixty, and there was a decided similarity in her looks to those of her brother. She was in regal rage anyway. She marched straight into Kambiz's office and began to harangue him in a shrill voice for several minutes. I don't know if he had mistakenly docked her allowance or whatever, but he sounded very apologetic. She came out and marched straight off with her escort.

Kambiz had been sent abroad to school, Sandhurst in England, with a military career in view, but he really didn't relish the military life and asked for a transfer working for the court; that was one way to be released from the army. His father stepped aside as Master of the Horse to let him have the job, and his son decided he would try to develop horse sports as a stepping stone to fame and fortune.

At the onset, he had the right person to help with this job in Louise Firouz, the Virginian wife of a princeling of the former ruling family, the Qajars. Louise had already sought out and formed a stud farm of the miniature horses that roamed the mountains of northern Iran. She named them Caspian horses for the area in which she discovered them. There were only a few of these left, and Louise's search undoubtedly saved them from extinction. The reliefs of small horses on the walls of the ruined palaces at Persepolis carved nearly 2,500 years before had excited her interest in the horses. There was a distinct connection between the head structure and other features of the little animals she found and those on the reliefs.

Louise also spent a lot of time in Turkoman country, and her technical knowledge of and experience with the native horses was considerable. Kambiz turned to her to get the outline of the Royal Horse Society he planned. They started registering purebred horses of local breeds and preparing a studbook.

But Louise was a woman and a foreigner to boot. The irascible old colonels and other denizens of the Iranian horse world couldn't stand for a woman making plans for them, and no foreigner could possibly know anything about Iranian horses they thought. Boy, did they stir it! The relationship between Kambiz and his chief aide never really had a chance in those circumstances.

Basically, however, Kambiz was a decent man. When Louise's husband's business ran into trouble, he accepted a suggestion that the Royal Horse Society should buy their farm and allow Louise to stay on with her husband to run it as a riding school and stud farm for the Caspian horses. But he had not sufficient strength of purpose to kill the disputes that arose between Louise and his aides, and the scheme floundered. The Firouzes found another home.

Atabai did buy the farm for the society, but a succession of instructors from abroad also ran into too much trouble with his aides. One, an international polo player, was attacked by grooms with shovels at the instigation of one of the aides. The farm was a real showplace, and while the Firouzes were there, it hosted some wonderful horse shows sanctioned by the Royal Horse Society. All the local clubs came to compete in the beautiful grass ring surrounded by bleachers.

When Kambiz and I met for the first time at the Imperial Stables in early 1972, I could tell he was taken with my horsemanship and knowledge of the equine. It was a brief but pleasant encounter, so I wasn't surprised when he called me one day after we had settled in Tehran to ask me to come to see him at his office. The result of this meeting was that I eventually became an employee of the Imperial Court of Iran and The Royal Horse Society. He thus had a second foreign woman for whom the old colonels would complain and cause trouble.

During my tenure, the Royal Horse Society became the sole importer of saddlery, which I arranged to be imported from the States and England, and had the only tack store in the country. I personally opened a business that manufactured horse blankets and saddle pads that were sold in the shop. The society also controlled the country's import and export of horses.

If Kambiz didn't like you, as Louise found out after they quarreled, there was no way you could make money from horses. This crushing of those who don't go along with you was a tradition with Iranian senior officials. He found it impossible to resist doing that in spite of his hankering to be liked that often made him more human. The attitude of elitism the monarchical system engendered really came out in him in the last year of the Pahlavi regime. A new, $40-million racetrack financed by a gamblers' syndicate from Hong Kong was opened, and to publicize membership, the foreign officials threw open the doors of the members' floor to all kinds of foreign and local people.

Kambiz turned up there one afternoon in his riding clothes and was horrified to see people of all kinds in short sleeves, jeans, and other casual attire. He promptly sent for the officials and ordered that jacket and tie would be obligatory in the future. Downstairs in the public enclosure, he was equally horrified to see hordes of children running around with their parents. He promptly banned all children under fourteen from the track. Many of the women in that enclosure were in chadors; ordinary Iranians were fascinated to watch such a spectacle though there was more-casual racing of Turkoman horses at Ghargoushdare outside Tehran and in the Turkoman Steppes.

The original estimates for the cost of the track, stands, and other facilities was around $10 million, but as was the case with most projects in Iran, a combination of delaying tactics by contractors and inflation swelled the projection several times. But the investors pressed on because they were expecting a return on their investment, a big share in the casino gambling operations throughout Iran. This would have been a really lucrative business given the way Iranians liked to gamble. In the end, they were left with something of a white elephant. Club patrons received permission to bet in 1978, but the crowds were small to begin with. Hope revived for at least some return on their big outlay when the mullahs decided betting on horses was an acceptable form of wagering based on the Quran.

The racing project owed its origins to the idea of a group of sportsmen connected with the Imperial Country Club. Australian Ron Dabscheck had launched a similar project in Indonesia; he was hired, and negotiations began. Financing was brought in from Hong Kong to complete the joint venture.

During the first season the track was in action, it did prove to be a real hit in spite of occasional postponements because of riots and the animosity once again of the older Iranian horsemen. They knew nothing about running such a big, modern facility but were damned if they would let foreigners do it if they could get their hands on it.

One old, irascible colonel went on television as media controls were lifted to attack Kambiz Atabai and denounce all the foreigners working at the track as tricksters and charlatans. But just as the new freedom gave him his chance, it also gave ordinary Iranians theirs. A zealous TV interviewer, who went to ask ordinary people what they thought about this wicked new Western thing in their midst, was told that they thoroughly enjoyed it. "There's so little for the ordinary man to do in Iran—it's a godsend," one said. The campaign against the track floundered, which only went to show that if officials who really were trying to do good in Iran had not been so secretive, they may have gotten the public support that would have defeated their denigrators more easily.

The racetrack was one of Kambiz's greatest achievements along with his organizing of soccer and equestrian activities. Even though show jumping and riding remained the preserve of the rich, they were very popular. He managed to get rich, young business people to buy and back soccer clubs, and his international youth soccer competition was a great model. But the alienation of the press and public was evidenced by the wave of anger he faced when Iran failed to get into the semifinals of the World Cup. To have gotten to the final series of games in Buenos Aires and not winning something seemed synonymous with failure to the naive Iranian public. They blamed the defeat on the fact that a court official had control of football.

Kambiz's story shows so much of what was wrong in Iran. He frequently defeated his own purposes because of his tendency to listen to people who wanted to discourage him. Unlike many of his senior colleagues, he didn't literally despise ordinary people, but his court upbringing made him afraid of them. He was trusted by the Shah and his court minister, so he was given responsibility. He in turn would give responsibility only to those he could trust to serve his interests and do what he wanted. Many of his plans failed to take off because of his inability to find the right people to execute them.

Goli Bakhtiar and Nader Djahanbani

Manuchehr Khosrodad and his girls

Manuchehr competing at a horse show

Manuchehr in his helicopter

Kambiz Atabai and Manuchehr Khosrodad at horse show

CHAPTER 6

Tehran's Social Scene

Only a few people in Tehran were lucky enough to receive an invitation to the Shah's palace. But there was another home in the city to which an invitation implied that you had the necessary social status to be regarded as being in the in crowd. That was the elegant mansion of Jamshid Khabir, an erstwhile chamberlain to the Shah's brother Prince Abdul Reza, who hosted the city's ambassadors and top society at regular weekly at-homes as they were called and sumptuous black-tie parties that had European and other Western visitors wide-eyed with wonder.

The large, modern house of stone and marble had been built in the foothills of the Alborz Mountains on the northern edge of Tehran, only half a mile from the Shah's palace at Niavaran. When you walked in through the front door, you were in for a surprise; the house was built on a slope, and you found yourself looking down into a great hall with several huge crystal chandeliers and Doric marble pillars that would have been a feature of older European houses.

I remember my first invitation there. The door opened, and I heard lilting Persian music and hands beating time to it. The scene from the balcony at the top of the stairs descending into the hall was breathtakingly brilliant. The chandeliers bathed it in a glow, reflecting on the diamonds, emeralds, and sequins of many of the dresses in the besuited and begowned crowd of perhaps a couple of hundred people crammed below. In front of a small group of traditional musicians, a circle had been cleared where several women guests were stepping and whirling in the lively, rhythmic *Baba Karam* folk dances, which were a feature of nearly every Iranian party of this type. The swish crowd beat time to the music, and every now and then, one of the men would jump in to join the dance.

As I handed my fur wrap to the maid, I thought whimsically that if it got mixed up with one of the countless others piled up in the cloakrooms, I wouldn't come out worse off. I wasn't yet used to the magnificence of the Tehran social scene, where mink and diamonds were commonplace possessions for well-to-do women. Toward the end of my stay, even a visit to one of the fashionable food stores would present me with a fashion parade. The new rich wives would put on their best furs and jewelry just to buy meat for their parties; it was unforgivable to be seen plainly dressed outside your home.

At the bottom of the stairway in the hall, we were greeted by the host, a rotund, jolly man in his sixties whom everyone in the social world seemed to love dearly, and his wife, Marina, German-born and very much an elderly Marlene Dietrich type. We had been introduced to them by some of their closest friends, and that was enough recommendation to have them open their door to us whenever we felt like dropping in.

Marina's family had lived in Iran when she was young, and it was there she met and married Jamshid. She spoke a slow, deliberate English with the most excruciating accent, so she wasn't the most rewarding of dinner-table companions, but like Jamshid, she was totally lovable. And this couple did far more to make foreigners love Iran and Iranians than did the whole of the country's Foreign Ministry.

Seated on a sofa surrounded by acquaintances was a frail old woman I knew was Fifi Ala, widow of Hossain Ala, former court minister and envoy to Washington. Although she suffered from an illness that affected her balance, she loved her evenings out, and friends were always ready to bring her to important social events.

Her British-educated son Fereydun had done a magnificent job in forming Iran's first real blood bank in the mid-seventies. Before that, blood had been supplied by agents who kept whole bands of poor people in food so they could siphon off their blood regularly and sell it for big sums. The blood for the public hospitals was frequently not checked at all, so before Ala got to work, accident victims must have frequently received blood from people suffering from one disease or another. This practice had been featured in a brilliant film by a bright, young Iranian filmmaker, Dariush Mehrjui, which had been banned from public showing by the censors at the insistence of the doctors' association in Tehran.

It was indicative of the Shah's indifference to matters of public interest that when he was asked to allow its showing, he merely replied, "If what he says is right, then let it be shown. If not, don't show it." He obviously never inquired further about the film for it was never shown. Yet we knew what it depicted was true, and so did most of his compatriots.

One's heart always lifted too at the sight of Safieh Firouz, the nearly eighty-year-old *grand dame* of Tehran society who came from the famous Nemazi family in Shiraz, whose representatives live all over the world but who had married a Qajar prince when that dynasty was still in power. He had adopted the name Firouz to differentiate himself from the many other descendants of the old royal family many of whom were *bacheh kholfati*, children of housemaids or concubines. The Qajar royals had so many children by different women that scores of people claimed descent from them.

Safieh was still addressed as princess by most people, and her wit and culture combined with her gorgeous, mostly traditional Iranian gowns and exotic silver Turkoman jewelry fitted her title perfectly. Her daughter-in-law, Iran Ala Firouz, was a splendid figure too in her own adapted traditional dresses made of native fabrics. Iran had just produced the first detailed book on Turkoman jewelry at a time when things Iranian were coming very much back into fashion, and Safieh always displayed her collection of the beautiful silver pieces with pride. Her brother, Mohammad Nemazi, settled later in the US, where he set up a foundation that raised money to build and equip the excellent Nemazi Hospital in Shiraz. It was through her son, Narcy Firouz, and his wife, Louise, that I was fortunate enough to get to know this great woman.

Safieh Khonume, as she was known to everybody, hosted fabulous lunch and dinner parties at the lovely, old, Persian-style downtown home where she lived with her husband, Mohammad, a former foreign minister and soldier who belonged to the very top echelons of the old Qajar royal family. Lovely, old, Qajar-period paintings and other Iranian art filled the place. She always served traditional Persian food, many different kinds of rice and stews, called *khoreshts*, that took hours to cook and were uniquely tasty, and delicious sweets we Westerners had never seen before.

Iranian dinner parties were buffets; guests meandered out to eat on the terrace or in the cool, tree-shaded garden where lights illuminated the foliage and reflected off the clear blue of a swimming pool in summer. Guests would position themselves in strategically favorable spots in the many reception rooms during the cooler months.

As the women were serving themselves, many of the men would stand idly opposite I noticed gazing at the women's suspended breasts peering from their low-cut gowns as they bent over the tables. Even elderly Iranian women went in for revealing gowns. Whenever I took young male houseguests to a swish party, they were startled by the way women in their sixties would often dance seductively up against them. The young men's gaze was held fascinated by the ancient breasts leering at them so provocatively.

The younger women had to be wary about their jealous husbands and often dressed more conservatively. But the more beautiful appeared confident that they could get away with anything, and any of the scores of upper-set parties in Tehran every week was a feast for the eyes of all men. Some young women known for not being too chaste would risk pneumonia even on winter nights to ensure their charms were brought to the attention of the wealthy men as much as possible. I found out there was a strong sense of a pecking order among the upper-class women based not on age but on social status. I never learned the nuances of this social standing in Iran, but those women knew, and those who regarded themselves as the absolute cream didn't like it if women just below them on the social scale received any kind of precedence. Social climbers, however, found there were ways into the drawing rooms of the really top set. Helping their favorite charities was one, and going in for dress designing or selling foreign fashions was another.

A regular at many of these posh parties who was in this category was Shamsi, an acquaintance who packed her solid curves into Paris dresses while leaving a pretty big proportion of her generous upper structure on show. With the aid of Paris beauty houses, she contrived to look a glamorous forty instead of the sixty she was. Shamsi's husband made a lot of money in business, and she used it to set her on the road to fame in Tehran society.

Her parties were lavish affairs; she would strew white flowers in her gardens and float roses in the pool. Carpets filled bowers beneath the buds and shrubs to provide a Thousand and One Nights atmosphere. When the International Women's Club or some other body wanted to hold a charity party, Shamsi was ready to foot the bill. We legged it across the lawns from bars around the pool to tables loaded with caviar in another corner. The buffet tables could obviously have borne the weight of elephants considering the massive amounts of food on them. Musicians and dancers lulled us into feeling we really were in the exciting Orient and not in the middle of a sprawling urban mass of nearly 3 million. But when Shamsi ran for office in the International Women's Club, she stood no chance of getting in. And when Empress Farah's mother, Madame Diba, came to a charity fashion show Shamsi had paid for, Shamsi wasn't seated at the same table with the organizing committee even though the evening wouldn't have been possible without her.

It was not unusual for older Iranian women with money and husbands to take a handsome young man as a companion, and it was common for many of the wives of prominent bankers and other officials to be seen constantly with young friends. Surprisingly, in most cases, the husbands didn't seem at all concerned. They went on living in the same houses with their wives, and that gave society the impression that the relationships between the older women and the young men were entirely platonic. While many people pooh-poohed this idea, I wasn't so sure in some cases. Just as older men often liked to be seen with young girls as a boost to their vanity, I think the older women liked the cachet they got from their young beaux.

Life was much harder for wives with less-sophisticated husbands or moving in lower official circles. They had to be very covert about their liaisons. In Tehran, women sometimes rented an apartment or a room to pass an hour or two in the afternoon with young lovers. These Iranian gals explained to me the factors leading to this phenomenon. The principal one, as far as the women were concerned, was their early marriages to much older men in many instances. Their husbands failed to interest them physically after a time, and their husbands began to lose interest in tiring sexual activity with their wives once they had a son. Men considered that the main reason for marrying, and they rested on their laurels once they had achieved it. Young wives naturally got restive.

The practice of *sigheh*, a contractual marriage of convenience for a limited period, still continues in Iran. The man has to make financial provision for the woman when the contract is finished, but that is all. The children of *sigheh* marriages seemed to be accepted by society, but the families of the official wives always claimed superiority over them.

Top society weddings were other occasions in Tehran that I recall with wonderment. Have you ever seen a crowd of women in Paris, New York, and London gowns with not a single hair or toenail ungroomed and not a single piece of paste jewelry among the glittering gems on show? I didn't believe it possible until I attended one of these wedding parties at the Royal Tehran Hilton in 1975. The Kouros family had taken over the grounds of the hotel for the occasion, and the sight was unbelievable. The bridegroom's father was a senator, and his wife was quite favored in high society. Young princes, ministers, and anyone who had a position in Tehran's top social echelon were there. The family hosted three gigantic wedding parties in the same number of years, and the bills for flowers alone would be in the scores of thousands of dollars each time. People contended that the family could have spent $250,000 on those three weddings alone.

The last of them in 1978 was at their magnificent, new, traditional-style mansion in the foothills of the mountains, one of scores of fairy-tale homes that were being erected in the fashionable north of the city. These houses ranged from enormous Swiss chalets to Victorian gothic palaces; many took portions of styles from a score of different types. Furniture was nearly always imported at great cost. Pictures and antiques became popular, and smaller dinner parties at new homes often included tours of the houses. Sometimes, they were of exquisite taste, but more often than not, Westerners were astonished at the gaudy decorative taste.

Persian party

Author with friends Judi Summers (L) Susan Khaki (R)

CHAPTER 7

Life as an Expat

Iran was the first Persian Gulf country to discover oil in 1908. The British team of William D'Arcy gained the rights to make explorations in 1901 and found oil seven years later. Great Britain signed an agreement to have the rights to this black gold. Of course the French, then the Dutch, other European countries, and finally the United States all wanted a part of this rich find.

The inexperienced and uneducated Qajar shah in effect almost gave away the rights to extract the oil and develop the petrochemical industry. When the Pahlavis took over the country, the deals with the international companies became more advantageous for Iran. Due to the huge industry that developed, many foreigners came to take care of business. As time went on and many more industries were brought to the country, more and more expatriates came to live in Iran especially to the capital, Tehran. By the early 1970s, there were over a hundred thousand expats living a life of carefree comfort and luxury. I was one of these privileged people.

When I first arrived, I needed to find a suitable house for our family. We were staying in the luxurious Hilton Hotel high up in northern Tehran overlooking the sprawling city. I had met several American women who had been in Tehran for some time, and they advised me to look into one of the communities where large numbers of foreigners lived an American-type community life. But I wanted to assimilate myself into the Iranian way of life. My husband's company gave me a car and driver along with a list of rental houses. I spoke little Farsi, and my accent was obviously not good; when I would tell the driver the name of the street we were looking for, I always had to repeat it many times.

"Couche Marjan," I would say.

"Couche Murjer?" my driver would ask.

"No! Couche Marjan!" I would reiterate.

That would go on until he would finally give me a street name that sounded nothing like the way I pronounced it, but it would be the one we were looking for.

I looked in the foreign communities but found nothing I really liked. Most of the houses were three bedrooms with small entertaining areas and no garden. After over two weeks of searching, I finally found the house we would live in for our time in Tehran. It was a big stone and marble house with five bedrooms. It had very large living, dining, and entertaining areas as well as a reception room with a fireplace and a den I used as an office and TV room (TV was black and white and only shown certain hours of the day). The kitchen and pantry area was large though old fashioned, and it was painted fuchsia and pea-green, not my favorite colors though I knew I would have a *badji*, a maid, to do the cleaning and cooking so I wouldn't have to spend much time there. The house had a huge walled garden, swimming pool, two patios, a guesthouse for the help, and a beautiful view of Mount Damavand to the north from the upstairs balcony. It was perfect!

When I showed it to my husband, Don, he liked the house and said it was within budget, but he was not so sure about it because it was at the end of a very small *couche*, street, in the strictly Iranian district of Chala Harz. But when he found out that our neighbors on each side were generals in the Shah's army, he knew we would be safe there.

We had barely moved our rental furniture and few things we had brought with us into the house when the gate bell rang. I opened it and saw a small woman in a black chador with several gold teeth. "I you *badji*," she said. I had no idea where she had come from. She showed me a letter of recommendation in Farsi, which I couldn't read. Luckily, the driver was there, and he told me that it was a good reference. So in my pigeon Farsi, I worked out with her that she would become our maid, live in the little gate house, and receive the equivalent of $25 per week. How lucky could I be?

Parvin, as she called herself, was a pleasant little woman who kept the house clean and tidy with her broom and dustbin and cooked delicious Persian meals. All was going along very well until one afternoon she told me she was going to pray at the local mosque, something she did most days. But that day she did not return. I expected she would come back the next day, but no Parvin. When I questioned some of my American friends, they said that would often happened with the *badjis* and I should probably look for another maid.

When I spoke to the wife of the general who lived next door, she told me there had been a problem at the mosque on the day Parvin had disappeared; the mullahs and people who were there praying had been arrested by SAVAK. She said she might know someone and would send her to talk to me.

The next day, a rather tall, thin woman also in a black chador and with gold teeth was at the gate. I negotiated the same arrangement I had had with Parvin and was satisfied. The following day, she was at the door with all her worldly goods, a teenage daughter, and a young son about the same age as my four-year-old. The little house would be full. She was a far better cleaner than Parvin had been and turned out to be an amazing cook. Her daughter began to help her, and her cousin, Zahra, who also moved in, helped out whenever she was home; she had a morning job somewhere else. I had three helpers and a friend for my son. All was well.

Upon our arrival in Iran, we contacted the Firouzes, who in their characteristic manner welcomed us with open arms. I was commandeered by Louise to help her children and their friends with their riding as an instructor, a job that I did most willingly. We got together with Ali Reza Soudovar, who was the first Iranian to import foreign horses for show jumping in Iran, and had a series of horse shows through the summer and fall. By the end of the season, we had all the local clubs competing with the exception of the Imperial Stables. We had sent an invitation there each week, but Mr. Atabai refused to let his team compete in these unofficial competitions.

The Imperial Stables, which was the personal stable of the Shah, had a riding team that was supposed to enter local horse shows as a representative group of his stable. Mr. Atabai was the Master of the Horse, and so all the decisions lay with him. He declined all the invitations; it seems that at the time, the Imperial Stables had a dearth of good horses, and he refused to enter competitions where there was not much chance of their winning.

Ali Reza Soudovar and I became friends due to our common interest in show jumping. As there were no rules or regulations for show jumping in Iran, we pooled our ideas to develop some. We used the FEI (*Federation Equestre Internationale*) rules with some modifications to suit the Iranian situation.

When the winter arrived and there were no shows, Ali Reza and I spent time together compiling an Iranian show-jumping rule book. We finished that in March, and I had already started working at the Imperial Stables. We felt that these rules along with a translation of the FEI rules should be the foundation of the Iranian competitions. I mentioned our work to Kambiz one morning while we were riding, and he was surprised and impressed that we had done that. He asked to see the results of our work with the intention of sanctioning it if he felt the regulations were applicable.

We set up a day for a meeting the following week. Ali of course arrived about an hour late, but it didn't really matter because most of the time I had been waiting in Kambiz's office, he had two telephones to his ears and at least four other people in the office all talking at once. When we got to our proposal, he agreed wholeheartedly to have the new rules translated and printed in a booklet form in English and Farsi.

Kambiz asked me to stay on for a few minutes after Ali Reza had left; he had something to show me—a rather large office with one desk, a chair, and three filing cabinets. "This," he said, "is your office. I would like very much for you to plan the horse show season for us this year, and I feel you should have proper place to do this. We will supply you with secretarial help and anything you need. I thought that perhaps a couple of days a week, after you have finished your work at the stable, you could come in here to work. I would like to make you Chairman of Show Jumping for Iran because I really want to make the sport into something here."

"I hardly know what to say, Kambiz. As you know, I don't want a full-time job. I will do as much as I can, but please don't expect too much." I felt I was being buried in a snowdrift.

I recalled the telephone call I received from Kambiz months before asking me to come to see him at the Imperial Court complex on Pasteur Avenue, where he had his office. The following day, I took a great deal of care with my appearance as I was sure that something big was about to happen. I very nervously drove downtown; the traffic in Tehran made traffic in Paris or Rome look very tame.

By the time I arrived at the Imperial Court offices, my hands were dripping with perspiration and I was five minutes late. I scurried up the one flight of stairs and down the long hall to enter the waiting room of his office; I was panting slightly. A number of people were waiting in a tiny anteroom. I walked up to the desk of Parvin, Mr. Atabai's secretary, to announce my arrival, and she just looked at me bewildered.

"You don't know how busy Mr. Atabai is today, Mrs. Rose. He has four people to see before you, and he must leave in half an hour for a meeting. I don't know how he will ever find the time. But please sit down and wait."

I picked up the English newspaper to see what was going on in the world; I read the usual bold headlines about the Shah on the front page with smaller print informing the readers about other members of the imperial family. A bustle about me brought me to the present. "He is coming out now, Mrs. Rose, but he will not have time to see you as he is on his way uptown to a meeting at the palace."

The door opened and out came Kambiz Atabai. He was tall for a Persian, and he had a thick head of black and slightly wavy hair. His slight figure was beautifully turned out in a deep-blue, silk, hand-tailored suit from Paris most likely, immaculately polished shoes, and an Yves Saint Laurent tie. "Oh Mrs. Rose! I had forgotten about you. I must go up to the palace now. Do you have your car?"

"Yes I do," I replied slightly confused.

"Good, Good. I will get my driver to drive your car behind us, and you will drive up with me so we can talk as we go."

Five or six people were following us out the door of his waiting room all trying to have a word with him before he left his office. I was whisked through the corridor and down the stairs by my escort while these people followed behind asking all kinds of questions and giving messages ranging from a reminder about a dinner appointment to a request for permission to order more hay for the Imperial Stables.

When we were outside, the driver was given my car keys and I was ushered into a small beige Mercedes-Benz. I was quite curious as to what the conversation would entail, but as we started up toward the north of the city, we passed only pleasantries and asked after each other's health and family. I was beginning to feel that I had come downtown for no reason at all when he finally broached the topic to be discussed.

"As you may know, her Imperial Majesty has given some land at Farahabad and is about to build a stable for a riding club geared toward the development of junior riders in Iran. I, as the Master of His Majesty's Horse and secretary general of the Royal Horse Society, am asking you if you would consider taking this stable on and running it along the North American lines. We of course would not expect you to do this job all on your own and would want you to hire an assistant from the United States, Europe, or wherever."

"I thank you for the compliment of offering me such a job, but I don't think I could accept such a responsibility. You probably know that Mr. Bozorghmeyer offered me the job of running the stables at the Imperial Country Club, but I refused him."

"Yes, I had heard that, but why did you not want the position?"

"With three small children and a husband, it is an impossibility. I am sure that you can understand. My riding activities throughout my life have been mostly amateur, and I have followed this field because I love it. I can't see why I should turn my pleasure into my profession."

We then discussed the acquisition of the Imperial Stables' new German show jumpers. It seemed that Kambiz's father, Abolfath Atabai, who was one of the Shah's closest advisors and treasurer of the Imperial Court, had gone to Germany to buy some carriage horses because the eight white horses that had been pulling the imperial coaches were ready for retirement. When he was in Germany, he had bought five show jumpers as well. A few people had imported foreign show jumpers the previous year, and those horses proved quite successful in the competitions, so he decided that His Majesty should have some European horses as well. And his own son, who had been educated at Sandhurst in England, was very keen on show jumping and wanted it to become a noteworthy sport in Iran.

"You see, Mrs. Rose, my father spent quite a bit of His Majesty's money on those horses, so I am embarrassed to admit that we cannot ride them properly. We need help. Actually, I need help because His Majesty will want to see what we are doing with these new horses very soon, and I don't want to make a mess of the whole thing. Would you be kind enough to ride the one that is supposed to be for me and tell me what you think?"

"I'd enjoy that. It'll be fun to ride a good horse again, but I really can't promise you anything. I'm certainly not fit, and I haven't done any serious riding for quite some time."

"I'm sure you can help. Could you go down, say, how about tomorrow morning? I'll tell the people at the stable that you'll be there ... at what time?"

As I had nothing in particular to do the next day, I agreed to go to the Imperial Stables the following morning at about ten o'clock. The conversation was ending as we drove into the gates of Saadabad Palace, the working palace of the Imperial Court of Iran. The guards acknowledged Mr. Atabai with a cursory glance and opened the gate for the car to pass through. Kambiz said his farewells as his door was opened by a man in a palace guard uniform. He rushed off to his meeting; my car was parked not ten feet from the front door of the palace. I got in, drove to the gate, and relished the bow I received from the guard as he opened the gate for me.

I was not surprised when I received a call from Kambiz's secretary one day as I was working in my office; he wanted me to see him. My friend Arab Shehbani, who was a close friend of the Shah, had mentioned to me that I would be given a contract for the volunteer work I had been doing at the stables and the Royal Horse Society.

"Good morning, again, Gail," Kambiz greeted me as he had seen me at the stables earlier. "Would you please read this while I sign these few letters?" he asked as he handed me three large white sheets of paper titled "Contract between Mrs. Gail Rose and the Imperial Court of Iran." The contract stated that I would be an employee of the Imperial Court of Iran; I would be the trainer of the Imperial Stables of the Shah and the director of show jumping for the Royal Horse Society and the Iranian Equestrian Federation. As well, I would be the trainer of the Iranian national show-jumping team. I was to work whatever hours would be necessary to discharge my duties in accordance with the operational requirements of these positions. The interesting thing about the contract was that the salary I was being offered was exactly the amount Don and I had decided would be fair when we had discussed the subject one evening.

When I had finished reading it, he called his secretary to have her hold all calls. It was obviously important to him because Iranians very seldom held calls.

"Well, what do you think?"

"First of all, I'm overwhelmed. I really don't want a real job, and you know it. I feel that you have tricked me into this. I'm happy as a volunteer, and actually, when you consider the amount of money you're offering me, I think I would rather work for one *rial* [the Iranian currency] a year. The other thing is that I have committed myself to spending two months in the United States this summer, and I can't take on a job one month and leave for two months' vacation the next."

"I'll give you more money if that's what you want, and as for your summer off, that is no problem. Please, Mrs. Rose, we really need you to help us, and I cannot allow volunteers at His Majesty's stable—it is just not allowed. I have spoken to His Majesty himself, and he is in favor of your doing this work. You know this is quite an honor. We have had other people here to try to teach us about show jumping, but none of them stayed. Either they did not like us or we did not like them. We had a Frenchman about three years ago. He went away in disgust. Last year, we had a German come to hold a clinic. He was to stay for six weeks, but he left after just two weeks. But you understand us. You seem to have a certain key that makes us like you and respect you as well. You have been helping out at the stables for just about six weeks, and I know that the boys who work with you would do anything for you. You are what we need."

"Listen, Kambiz I really have to think about this. You are giving me a great compliment by offering me this contract, but I don't know that I can fulfill it."

"You can't turn down an offer from His Majesty's court. That is not allowed. You are a guest in this country, and he and I want you to take this job. Just think of it as a formality in an informal relationship. I know you can do it. As a matter of fact, I have stuck my neck out to get this contract. Won't you please sign it?"

Sign it I did. Who could refuse? As I drove home to my little family that afternoon, I couldn't believe what I had done. The ways in which my life would be complicated were nowhere in my thoughts. In retrospect, my ignorance makes me laugh. How could I have believed that the fun and amusement I had been having would remain static? We all know that financial commitments alter everything beyond recognition. If I had realized that, I certainly would have had second thoughts, but then, I would not have attained the sense of fulfillment and the excitement that were to become a part of my life during the next years.

Two weeks later, Kambiz came into my office at the stables after we had finished the riding for the morning with an envelope in hand. "I have something for you, Ga*eels*"; he always pronounced my name with a long *e*. I put the envelope on my desk. "Well, aren't you going to open it? It's your first paycheck," he said.

"Oh thanks, Kambiz." I left the envelope on my desk.

"You need to open it so you can see how much it is," he told me with a slight smirk.

"I know how much it is. I signed the contract against my better judgment, so I know what it will be."

"Still, please open it while I am here. I want to make sure they spelled your name correctly."

I slit the envelope with the silver letter opener on my desk and took out the check as well as an accounting of it. I couldn't believe it; I was in total shock—my salary was double the amount we had agreed upon, and I had been given two months' pay retroactively for the time I had been working. Smiling, I gave Kambiz a big hug. "Thank you so much! I can't believe it! I'm in complete shock. Now I'm really going to have to work hard."

The first morning after I returned from my vacation in the US one summer, I was awakened by a rooster's loud crow. I couldn't imagine there would be chickens nearby. When I went downstairs for my breakfast, I questioned Azizeh.

"Oh Khonume, I was given some baby hens by my uncle while you were away. I knew it would be good for us to have fresh eggs."

"But Azizeh, hens do not crow."

"Well, Khonume, that's the thing. They were all hens, and then one morning, one of them had become a rooster. It was the will of Allah, a miracle. We have to keep him now."

And keep him we did.

My friend Skip Link, a US army sergeant who stayed with us for a time, decided it would be a good idea to fill the swimming pool with trout for the winter. He suggested we buy small ones, feed them during the cold months, and then have a fishing party in the spring. Don thought it was a great idea. The trout were duly put in the pool, and the children's responsibility was to feed them every day, and they seemed to enjoy the job. The trout grew to a good size, and when the weather began to warm up, we planned our event, but that was to the children's consternation; the fish had become pets.

Our guests arrived for our fishing and cookout, many with their own fishing poles. We had a large crowd of expats and Iranian friends. In the afternoon, we heard camel bells; nomads would come to the city to sell their camel dung for spring gardening. I didn't want any of the very smelly fertilizer, but I had them bring the camels into the yard to give the children camel rides. All the fish were caught and cooked on the grill, and a good time was had by all.

One morning as I was driving along a narrow, one-way street in Tashrish, a small Paykan truck came out of a side street and smashed into the driver's side of my car. I screeched to a stop and jumped out of my car.

"You're going the wrong way!" the little man with a scruffy beard screamed at me as he ran over to my car.

"I am not!" I yelled pointing at the one-way sign that was going in my direction.

"It was going the other way yesterday," he said with assurance.

A little policeman in his white cap sauntered up in no hurry. He listened to us and finally said, "Khonume, he is right. Yesterday, it was going the other way, so they must have changed it during the night. It is your fault because this man didn't know the direction had been changed. And you are a woman!"

He wrote out a ticket and gleefully handed it to me. He said I would have to go to court the following week; the date and court address were on the ticket. The truck driver and I exchanged insurance information, and he said, "You'll have to pay it all. It's your fault."

When I recounted the story to Kambiz at the Imperial Stables the following morning, he thought it was quite amusing. I was not amused because I would have to retain a lawyer to take to court with me as I felt my Farsi wasn't good enough to defend myself in an Iranian court of law.

"Don't worry," he said. "I'll contact the judge, and you'll be fine. Go yourself. You don't need a lawyer."

"But my Farsi isn't good enough to go before a judge. And the policeman will say it's my fault."

He asked me for my summons; he wrote something on it and handed it back to me.

The following week when I timorously entered the dingy courtroom, I saw that my adversary had two people with him; I thought at least one was a lawyer. The policeman was smirking at the side of the judge's bench. The truck driver and his two companions were called to the bench and asked to give their side of the story. They talked so fast that I could hardly understand what they were saying.

I was called up; the judge questioned me in very precise language so I was able to understand, and I answered in my halting Farsi. The policeman was also questioned though I knew he was siding with the other driver.

The judge banged his gavel and said, "Aga Ramirez is charged with failing to stop at an intersection."

The case was over. I didn't know if it was my superb presentation or the fact that the judge had been forewarned that I worked for the Shah. My first and only brush with the law in Iran had ended well.

When we had first arrived in Tehran, Don's company supplied him with a car and driver from the local taxi station and charged it to his living expense account. That proved to be quite expensive, so we decided to buy a car and hire a chauffeur who could do other things for us while he was not driving one of us around.

We quite liked Kiani, a driver at the taxi service; he spoke good English, which Don needed, so we broached the subject of his becoming our personal driver. He was only too happy to do that as he would have a much better salary and his hours would be more consistent than they were at the taxi company. We hired him, and his first job was to find a suitable car to drive Don, the sales manager for Iralco (Iranian Aluminum Company) around town. His choice was a used white Mercedes sedan with beautiful brown leather seats and an excellent radio. I don't remember the year, but it was in mint condition.

One week, I drove with friends to the Lahr Valley with the children to camp out. Don was unable to come until Thursday afternoon after work, so it was decided that he would have Kiani drive him to the area where we planned to camp in the Mercedes. We had been camping in the valley at the bottom of Mount Damavand before, so he felt that he and the driver would be able to easily find us and that the Mercedes would make it to the campsite because the dirt road in the park was good.

We were waiting for him as we fished for brown trout in the river when one of the park guards rode up on his small bay Kurdish horse. Kurdish horses are small in stature, about fifteen hands tall coupled with a coarse head, but they are very strong and have great stamina. I have no idea how he knew where we were, but somehow, Don, who spoke no Farsi, or perhaps Kiani had explained where we would be and directed him to find us at our campsite.

"The *agha* is down by the river crossing, and his car is unable to move. He told me to get you to drive down to pick him up there," the guard said.

I got in the Paykan I had driven up the mountain road; I left the children with our friends and their kids. It took about a half an hour to get to the place where the beautiful white Mercedes was marooned. Kiani didn't know what was wrong, but he told us he would work on it. If he couldn't get it repaired with the help of the mechanic in the little village, he would get a ride back to Tehran and we would figure out what to do on Saturday, when the new week started. If he had to leave the car in the village, he would make sure someone would watch it for us.

We had a wonderful time hiking, swimming, and eating trout cooked over an open fire. We slept under the dark sky with the brightest stars I had ever seen; they were coruscant. The constellations were so easy to pick out, and it was a great learning experience for all the children. We were sad to leave the enchanted valley surrounded by the magnificent mountains, but back to Tehran we went on Friday evening.

Kiani arrived Saturday morning without the Mercedes, so Don rented a car from an agency around the corner. Apparently, the transmission had gone bad; we had to figure out how to get the Mercedes back from the mountain village two hours away. Kiani spent most of the day trying to arrange a tow truck to pick up the car to no avail.

However, there were great advantages to working for the court; when I told my boss, Kambiz, about the problem, he said, "Don't worry, G*aeel*, I'll tell Abrahimi at the garage to get the car picked up, and we can have it repaired for you at the court garage."

It took several days, but in due course, Mr. Abrahimi called. "Khonume Rose, your Mercedes needs a new transmission, but don't worry. I will have it fixed by next week."

About ten days later, I was at the Imperial Stables riding when I saw our beautiful white car drive into the yard. I rode over; the head mechanic was at the wheel.

"*Salam, Agaye Abrahimi, gorboneshoma.*" I addressed him with thanks.

"*Ruz baher, Khonume,*" he replied. "I brought your car myself because I wanted to drive this beautiful vehicle. Would you consider selling it to me?"

I explained that we really didn't want to sell it, but I thanked him for the compliment and for repairing it.

Every time I saw him after that, he offered to buy the Mercedes; finally, when we were ready to leave Iran, I sold the car to Mr. Abrahimi.

In the 1970s, Tehran was a big city that comprised many small villages in its environs each with its own administrative center, police force, and group of small shops. Chala Harz, where we lived at the end of a dead-end couche, was quaint and old world and was just north of Hoseini Ershad

Mosque. The people in our neighborhood were all Iranian, and most of the families had lived there for generations. The bakery where the *nun-e-barbari* was baked freshly twice each day and which also provided us with *nun-e-lavash* and *sangaque* was just around the corner from the house. Each morning, Azizeh would rush out the gate in her black chador looking like a hovering crow to get the fresh *barbari* that we all loved to have with our breakfast of fresh-squeezed orange juice and hot tea.

As time went on, she would take my tow-headed children with her on the errand, and finally, when Helen and Denis spoke enough Farsi, she would send them up the street for the bread on their own.

"Aren't you afraid those beautiful blond children of yours will be kidnapped going out into the street alone or robbed of the rials they are carrying with them to pay for the bread?" my friends would ask me.

"Of course not," I would answer. "Ours is a very safe village. The policeman and all the shopkeepers know them well. There would never be a problem."

And for the five years we lived in Tehran, there never was. We felt extremely safe and were looked after by the people of our small village as if we were their treasure.

Though they were expensive, there was a steadily growing number of bilingual schools in Tehran, and you could opt for courses entirely in English if that's what you wished for your children. In the early seventies, an outburst of chauvinism led to a threat to the bilingual schools by Ministry of Education officials, but that soon dissipated, and by 1978, there was even the first boys' boarding school with an entirely British curriculum.

Different foreign communities also had their own schools, and places in these were available to the children of nationals of those countries married to Iranians and even to Iranian families if they wanted. In the early seventies, the Shah's twin sister, Princess Ashraf, founded the Ashraf Pahlavi School that was bilingual from kindergarten through eighth grade. My children attended Ashraf Pahlavi, and I was extremely satisfied with the education they received.

The rapid expansion of activities by the different cultural centers added to new museums being opened, and greatly expanded opera, ballet, and musical programs made life much easier in general in Tehran. During the three or four years before the revolution, the Iran-America Society, thanks to a series of quite brilliant directors, was an exciting place for anyone with cultural interests. It drew literally thousands of young Iranians to its exhibitions and entertainments to see what contemporary Western arts and thinking were. At the same time, it provided a theater for Iranian artists and performers to showcase their talents.

On my birthday just a year after we had arrived in Iran, my badji, Azizeh, came to me with a small box in hand. She, her children, and her sister had purchased a gift for me. I was quite embarrassed, and in the Persian way, I tried to refuse it. "*Naher, Azizeh, nemitunam*," I exclaimed several times until I finally felt I had used enough *taarof* to accept the object.

I opened the box and saw a beautiful gold necklace with six coins attached to a delicately curved bar that hung from the chain. I was flabbergasted; I knew it was a very expensive gift. It was a Muslim religious token similar to the cross worn by Christians; because Azizeh and her sister were very devout Muslims, the gift had a very special meaning to them.

Shi'a Islam, which is the religion most Iranians follow, is based on the Quran and the message of Muhammad. Ali, Muhammad's closest relative, is believed to have been divinely appointed as the successor of Muhammad and the first *Imam*. The religion also extended the doctrine of *imami* to Muhammad's family and individuals among his descendants whom they believed possessed special spiritual authority and other divinely ordained traits. The *Imams* are believed to be the spiritual and political successors of Muhammad. Each coin on the necklace given to me by Azizeh and her family had the name of one of the five most important *Imams* plus one for *Allah*. I was extremely touched by this gift and wondered why it had been given to me.

"You must wear it always, Khonume," Azizeh said. "Everyone will think you are a Muslim, so you will be treated much better and be kept safe by the *Imams*."

I thanked them effusively and gave them hugs and kisses on both cheeks. I wore my *tala*, gold, as it was called, almost always and found that it did come in handy much of the time especially when I was shopping. In Iran, nothing sells for the price displayed; there is always the game of bargaining before purchasing anything. Shopkeepers love this back-and-forth bantering; they consider customers who do not bargain complete fools. I had learned the custom early in my stay and always thought I had gotten the best of the deal until I began to go to the shops wearing my *tala*.

"*Khonume, Musalemi?*" The man behind the fruit counter in the village asked me if I was Muslim the first time I went out wearing my gift.

"*Bali, Agha.*" I answered in the affirmative.

"*Behbashid, Khonume nemitunam.*" He apologized for not having known that I was Muslim.

When our bargaining began for the delicious blood oranges our family loved so much, I was shocked to hear that he wanted half the price I had paid two days previously. My *tala* helped me, and from that day on, I found I could almost always get things for much less than I expected to pay.

When I drove out to Nowruzabad, the country home of my friends the Firouzes, I would pass by Ghargoushdare, the Tehran racetrack. I was shocked at first to see the horses tethered to stakes in the desert covered head to toe in felt blankets. The theory was that these blankets kept them warm in winter and cool in the summer. When I began my position as the trainer at the Imperial Stables, I was surprised to find that in winter, our horses were wearing the same heavy felt blankets. They were too heavy for the majority of the winter days, and they were made of a rough material that I thought most unsuitable for these valuable horses. I asked Kambiz if we could order some blankets from England where the Lavenham Company made what I thought were the best blankets. He gave me the okay, but when I had ordered ten and he saw how expensive they were, he refused to allow me to order more.

When the horse community found out about the beautiful blue and gold blankets we were using on some of the horses at the stables, everyone said they wanted some just like them. So I had the idea that I could start a small blanket-manufacturing business myself and thus be able to have blankets for all the horses at the stables and then sell them to the ever-growing group of people in the horse world. I knew that Kiani, our driver, had grown up as the son of a tailor, so he was enthusiastic about my plan. He would be able to do the sewing in the many hours he was not chauffeuring us, and he would make a commission from me on every piece completed.

The two of us went to the main bazaar to purchase supplies. It took several weeks to encounter just what we needed, but we did. We set up deals with the merchants who would keep the items we needed on hand. Next, we found a small hole in the wall to rent in south Tehran quite close to the stables where we would put the two-pedal sewing machines that Kiani was able to purchase quite cheaply from a friend of his father. The English blankets were the pattern for our Iranian horse blankets; it was easy for him to make them.

We started production first for the Imperial Stables' horses, which Kambiz had agreed upon at a discounted price, of course. We soon had so many orders from horse owners that we had to hire another sewer as Kiani couldn't keep up. As we made those initial blankets, we realized there was quite a lot of wasted material, so I designed a saddle pad that could be made from the scraps.

I took the orders, which were all done in custom colors. Kiani and his helper would manufacture the items, and then, the items would be delivered in my trusty Paykan. Business boomed, and when the Royal Horse Society opened its shop, we supplied all the blankets the shop sold.

It was always a delight to go shopping in the Grand Bazaar in downtown Tehran, which is known to have been an area of trade for more than a thousand years. Despite this historical legacy, much of the bazaar had been constructed within the last two hundred years although the oldest walls and passages are most likely four hundred years old.

The main entrance is a beautiful arch of blue mosaic tile, and the ceiling, also of intricate tile work, is extremely high with small openings through which the dancing sunlight shines. From the main entrance, one passes on to a labyrinth of passages with small shops on either side that go on for many kilometers and are covered by brick domes with small windows to let in the light. There are many architectural styles that were applied haphazardly over many hundreds of years.

A bazaar is a type of marketplace, but it also fulfills many other functions such as banking, finance, politics, and religion. The Blue Mosque is at the entrance of the bazaar and is at all times filled with people praying, discussing politics, and making financial deals. Three times a day, the recorded voice of a mullah is heard shouting the call to prayer from the tall minarets.

The trade is in sections, so shopping for a particular item is easy. When Kiani and I were looking for our materials for the horse blankets, we spent hours searching through the area that sold fabrics and all items to do with tailoring and sewing. It was a huge section with hundreds of shops selling these materials and thus it took us many days to find what we needed.

There were too many areas to list, but my favorite places to shop were the copper section, which sold beautiful copper pots and lamps, the antique section, where one could find delightful collectibles from ancient times, and the carpet section.

The majority of foreigners would purchase carpets at the shops on Ferdowsi Avenue where the mostly Jewish dealers spoke English and it was more difficult to bargain the prices down. I bought my carpets in the bazaar and was able to buy some spectacular antique carpets for a song. I found that it was not uncommon to be pinched on my bottom when leaning over to have a closer look. It seemed the carpet salesmen could not resist a little fun with the foreign women.

Azizeh and her family stayed with me until the day I left Iran. Unfortunately, that day turned out to be a terrible drama. She covered herself with her chador and walked up and down the small *couche* crying and moaning as if she were being tortured as the movers were loading our effects into the van. I tried to comfort her, but it was to no avail.

Late in the afternoon, when the house was cleared and we were ready to go to the Hilton for our last night's stay, she and her family left hugging us and crying as they went. It was only when we went into the living room to pick up the few things that we were hand carrying that I discovered Don's 35 mm camera was missing and the antique gold, aquamarine, and pearl necklace that had been in the family for three generations was nowhere to be found. It was the only experience of thievery I had had while living in Iran. I just hoped she was able to sell the items for enough money to add to the generous departing stipend we had given her!

Author with Iranian team
L to R Ezat Vodjdani, Manuchehr Khosrodad, Kambiz Atabai, Ali Rezai

Camels in the garden

Author at Persepolis

CHAPTER 8

The Diplomatic Scene

Tehran abounded with diplomats during those Golden Years. I was lucky enough through my husband's business connections and the many people I met through my position at the Imperial Court and the Royal Horse Society to have been invited to many ambassadorial parties. These were held on an almost daily basis during the season—September to May. The social scene was a whirlwind during the seventies. If we weren't being entertained at the embassies, there were private parties, and of course it was necessary to reciprocate. During our last year in Iran, I counted only twenty-five days that we were not either out being entertained or entertaining at our house in the evenings.

The Saudi Arabian ambassador bought an impressive mansion for around $4 million in 1976. Shortly afterward, the Iraqi envoy paid nearly $6 million for another house roughly the same size and not far away. The Iraqis bought their residence from a former mayor of Tehran, who had built it during his time as the boss of city hall with a lot of help from taxpayers' money the gossips alleged. It had ceilings with plaster friezes, the patterns of which matched specially woven carpets on the floors of the two main reception rooms.

The Saudi envoy, Ibrahim Bakr, was among the big embassy entertainers. One party he threw at the Hilton when a couple of Saudi princes and the oil minister at the time, Shaikh Yamani, came for talks with the Shah sent me staggering. There were mountains of caviar, and we could have swum in the drinks laid on for the hundreds of Iranians who came. It was horrifying though amusing to see the way the Iranian women chased the two handsome Saudi princes around the gardens; they seemed to have some special charisma for them. Young women whose sense of propriety I had always admired worked themselves up into a lather over the Arabs, who admittedly were very handsome, their swarthy features a contrast against their billowing white robes.

Shaikh Nasser al-Sabah, Kuwait's representative to Iran, was a nephew of that country's ruler. He was another great party giver but on a more conventional scale. He and the British ambassador were the only envoys allowed to use Rolls-Royces by special permission from the Shah. Shaikh Nasser served only Arab food at his receptions and never drank. He observed religious periods such as Ramadan meticulously and took great pleasure in inviting close Christian friends to join him and Muslim colleagues in fast breaking in the evenings. He was no bigot; his polish and humanity endeared him to everyone. He spoke French fluently and became dean of the diplomatic corps in Tehran after ten years as envoy there. He always gave parties in honor of arriving and departing diplomatic colleagues, which almost exhausted the social set. Perhaps more important, his tact and popularity contrived to mend many fences between the Iranians and the Arabs.

Foreign ambassadors in Tehran frequently complained about the absence of meaningful contacts with the ministry. None of them seemed able to get direct answers to their queries from undersecretaries and protocol officials presumably because everyone was afraid of making decisions without approval of the minister. The latter had to be sure he in no way upset the Shah in any decision he made. Being an ambassador in Tehran was a thankless business if you didn't enjoy the compensations on offer—the fabulous social life and traveling about the wonderful country to regions each with its own cultural identity.

Britain's longtime envoy in Tehran, Sir Denis Wright, took long journeys through the country, which resulted in a coffee table book and helped inspire him to add to the historical data on Iran with a book on earlier British travelers in the country. His long stays away from the embassy upset his officials, but he was on fairly close terms with the Shah and Court Minister Alam, so it didn't really matter.

His successor, Peter Ramsbotham, was an enormous success in Tehran. He and his wife restored the embassy to its former important place on the social scene, put its administration on a healthy footing, and delighted the rapidly expanding British community. The Brits were upset when the next envoy, Anthony Parsons, a first-class diplomat who did a great job for Britain's commercial and other interests, turned out to have a decidedly antisocial wife. She hated the large diplomatic parties and did no more entertaining than was necessary.

The German ambassador and his family became special friends due to their interest in horses. Georg von Lilianfeld was an accomplished rider and had competed in Europe when he was younger. He had served as a censor of radio programs in Germany's Foreign Office before the Nazi defeat in World War II. He then joined the West German Foreign Office and held positions in African countries and the States. He was appointed ambassador to Iran in the late sixties and arrived with a wife, who unfortunately was unable to socialize due to a mysterious health problem, two sons, and two daughters. He quickly assimilated himself into the Iranian way of life and social scene. His daughter Charlotte, who was about ten when I met the family, became one of my students when I was teaching the Noruzabad children during my first few months in Iran. We became good friends; his house was only a short drive from Chala Harz, where we lived, so I would often take my children to swim with his, who were a few years older but happy to play with them.

We spent a lot of informal time with the family. Georg would host two or three official embassy parties each year, which were usually held in his beautifully landscaped gardens in the spring and fall because he didn't like to spoil his skiing time in the winter and the family would travel abroad in the heat of the summer. He was an extremely popular member of the ambassadorial group in Tehran, and we were all sad to see him leave for his new appointment in Spain at the end of 1974.

Sometimes, a bachelor envoy or other senior diplomat would help give his country a special glow in the smart, romantic world of Tehran high society. When Canada sent the personable young Kenneth Taylor to Iran, his wife, a scientist, couldn't join him for the first year, and he found himself positively engulfed by young Iranian women. I saw half a dozen of them trying desperately to outlast each other at one of his parties in the hope they would be the one to grab him, and his staff were looking slightly distraught at having to try to outlast them. Finally, his wife arrived to save him from the continued threat of a fate worse than death. Taylor successfully whisked six American diplomats, who were not at the embassy the day the Iranian students stormed the walls, out of Iran with a brave and clandestine plan. The remaining eighty or so were kept as hostages for 444 days.

The American embassy never enjoyed the same status in the social set as did the British thanks to a series of unexceptional envoys. One ambassador's wife was reportedly a dreadful bore unless she had taken a few drinks. Another stayed in her bedroom, the gossips said, along with a cat, which refused to leave the residence after being attacked by crows that nested in the trees around the house.

When Richard Helms, the former CIA boss, and his wife, Cynthia, moved in, things became different. An outgoing couple, they managed to attend as many social engagements as the other envoys did in spite of Helms's much heavier responsibilities in the Tehran of that time. The American community loved the Helmses because they took an interest in them. At the same time, they had an envoy who had access to the Shah whenever he wanted. They knew how and who to entertain, and Cynthia's genuine interest in all things Iranian including a surprisingly competent grasp of the language made them quite the most successful American ambassadorial couple.

One evening when my husband and I were at a dinner party at the ambassador's, he had a call and had to leave all his guests, for it was the Shah who needed to speak to Richard as soon as possible about an urgent matter. The Shah relied greatly on Helms's advice; he had been instrumental in placing him on the throne after the Mossadeq fiasco.

From translating stories to arranging evenings discussing tribal rugs, Cynthia identified beautifully with Iranians and their country. Richard's charm and sense of humor earned him personal friends in many places. President Ford's defeat in the 1976 election deprived the US of the services of a really first-class envoy. We were not to know at the time that it was also going to help bring about the collapse of the Shah.

Helms's successor, Bill Sullivan, had no experience in and little knowledge of the Middle East when he came to Tehran. In the Far East, however, he had presided over the embassy in times of war in Indochina and Korea and was experienced in the kind of guerrilla warfare Carter perhaps envisioned for Iran. The Iranians liked him, but like the British envoy, he was saddled with a somewhat antisocial wife.

Sullivan himself had a difficult job of course. He was representing a president who was pushing the Shah to become more liberal, so his relations with the palace were obviously more distant than those of his predecessors. The fact that he didn't know what was happening in the month or two before the final stages of the revolution was shown by his presence at parties he wouldn't have bothered attending in ordinary times. There were so few opportunities to meet fellow envoys and officials during that time that he presumably had to go to try to hear any tidbits of information. Ultimately, Sullivan was the one who persuaded the Shah that he must leave Iran in January 1979. He had been a hopeless and uncaring ambassador.

How could anyone have foreseen how pathetically the Shah would collapse? Oilmen and others with twenty years of close association with Iran and its officials were taken by surprise. The second surprise they got was the fact that Washington couldn't grasp the fact of the Shah's personal disintegration, which was clear enough in Tehran, and appreciate its implications. Many people seemed convinced when the White House didn't act that Carter and his officials had already decided to replace the Shah with opposition liberal leaders. If that was the case, there was a bit of miscalculation involved concerning the dangers from the Islamic revolutionaries, wasn't there?

German Ambassador Georg von Lilianfeld with friends

CHAPTER 9

Nationalities and Religions

World War II brought an influx of Poles who had been taken prisoner or sent to labor camps by the Soviets. When they were released, they were allowed to immigrate to Iran. Many of these Poles then left for Europe to fight in the war though most of the women and children stayed behind. The women found Iranian husbands in many cases. One met them at the parties for they seemed to have chosen their husbands well. The two bloods seemed to mix well for the children were some of the most handsome I have ever seen.

The Russians were at one time a sizable community, but many left for the US and Australia after World War II as did a big proportion of the Armenian community. The Russians left forever, but the Armenians left behind relatives and in numerous cases returned to combine businesses in the US or Europe and Iran.

Reza Shah had trusted his Russian professionals. One of them had designed his downtown palace. This man, named Markov, had helped raise two Russian brothers, Serge and Boris Bezrukeh, who both made fortunes, one in Iran and the other in Europe. Serge, as he was known, was a delightful character who in his late fifties surprised everyone by snapping up the wayward horse-riding beauty Goli Bakhtiar. He was a partner in the construction business with General Nassiri, the chief of SAVAK, an association that threatened to cost him dearly after the revolution, but happily, he survived.

He was a generous man who had contributed money and helped house many old and destitute Russian women. Some of these women came from aristocratic families but had no money left. Some of them had married Iranian men years before when there was little protection for wives and all the husband had to do was say, "I divorce you" three times and it was done. More than twenty of these women lived in an old house in what had been a fine neighborhood at one time. They had been supported by the Russian Orthodox Church, but in the early seventies, the church lost its priest and the house fell into disrepair. The dwindling community of women found the costs of keeping it up beyond them.

The UN Women's League, an organization of wives of officials in Iran, went to work to get money from the UN refugee body for them; they were told they could get money only if it was sponsored by a member of the royal family. It was arranged through the women's minister, Mahnaz Afghami, to have Princess Ashraf become the patron of the project. Once there was royal patronage, funds were handed over and an old school behind the Russian church was bought to house these women. With his own funds, Serge Bezrukeh adapted the building to suit the Russian women, and a Russian priest was found for the church; he kept his eye on the old people, and they were thoroughly content.

Among the Russian exiles were also many Iranians who had lived in the Caucasus before the Bolshevik Revolution. The most colorful of these were undoubtedly the Zolghadr brother and sister, Ali and Soraya, or Zorik as the latter was known to all. They had been evacuated from the Crimea with their parents during the revolution; a British warship took them to Malta with little but the clothes they were wearing. Fortunately, an uncle was the Iranian ambassador in Paris, and they were able to live with him in France.

Ali joined the army and became a phenomenon—a foreigner who was given a commission with the French Foreign Legion. He later returned to Iran with his father and joined the Iranian army. The stories told about this larger-than-life character are legion. One of them I like was of when he fell for a barmaid in the only bar Tehran claimed in the thirties and forties. It was in the Ferdowsi Hotel—all ferns and antimacassars—run by a couple of Russian women with a firm hand. No waitress of theirs was allowed to leave with a customer. Told that, an incensed Ali was said to have gone to his barracks, found one of the few armored cars the Iranian army possessed at that time, and driven it to the hotel. In he went, grabbed the girl, and took her away.

When I knew him, Ali was in his sixties and still a handsome man with a commanding appearance and a powerful, aquiline nose. He would open bottles of champagne with a sword presented to him by the Shah's father. One swish of the weapon and the neck of the bottle was gone. Hassan Arfa, one of the Shah's most distinguished generals, referred to his bravery in battle in his book about the wars against the Kurds. Few things upset Ali; good company was all he sought, and everyone loved to be with him. His parties were always fun and attended by all sorts of interesting people from court officials to merchants. When the revolution came, he was running a restaurant he had bought several years earlier serving the fine food and drink he loved.

His sister, Zorik, ran perhaps Tehran's best restaurant. She had married a Russian Cossack colonel at age eighteen, divorced him pretty quickly after they had a daughter, and worked in the Foreign Legion offices in Paris for many years. She finally decided to return to Tehran, where most of her family was living. At that time, she was fifty. After a brief spell working for a bank, she opened Xanadu, a restaurant that quickly became a landmark in a city that had very few truly good restaurants. Everyone who was anyone frequented Xanadu. The international groups of embassy people were seen there frequently as were many high court officials. When the Equestrian Federation had dinners for foreigners visiting Iran, there was no other place suggested to entertain them. Zorik was to be seen at the restaurant most nights entertaining friends with caviar and other good things. Like Ali, she enjoyed entertaining and helping people more than anything. For ten years, she gave free lunches to the score of old Russian women in their nearby home. A couple of them would come down each day pushing an old perambulator that would then be loaded with soup, rice, and some Russian delicacies at the kitchen door.

In summer moonlight, Xanadu's small garden was a paradise for discerning eaters. The food, mostly European with a leaning toward French cuisine, was always beautifully served by tuxedoed waiters on white linen tablecloths. After the revolution, Khomeini's Guard took over, so Zorik decided she'd be better off going to visit with her daughter in Paris.

Her cashier had to write in expenses for buying potatoes so he could pay her enough from the takings to have her hair done before she left.

Zorik's restaurant served a few Russian dishes; it was said that you could find better Russian cuisine in Tehran than you could in the Soviet Union. Another restaurant that specialized in it was Leon's Grill, which was run by an Armenian who had studied the culinary arts in Moscow. I'll never forget eating caviar blinis in his garden on summer nights. If you have eaten fresh Caspian caviar as distinct from the much-traveled variety we eat in the West, you will know what I am talking about—it's superb. Even without the vodka Leon's served in carafes frozen in ice, I'd love to have a few grams now.

Iranian vodka was excellent. It was made in the Russian pattern by Armenians who brought that skill from Russia when they moved to Iran. Most experienced drinkers rated it almost as highly as Russian and Polish vodka. Some cheaper brands were the favorites of truck drivers and people of that kind; it had a special taste, but the half dozen or so leading brands were very smooth. Etadieh vodka, my favorite, won the gold medal at the 1975 International Vodka Convention.

In that dry climate, a vodka lime—vodka, fresh lime, and water or lemonade, soda, and fresh limes was a magnificent freshener. It was the natural successor in modern times of the sherbets, such as the *sekhanjebin* made from cucumber or melon, vinegar and syrup, which had been traditionally drunk. You could still find these sherbets in many homes, and when I was riding on hot summer mornings at the Imperial Stables, Khanlahani, our office manager, would bring to the ring a pitcher of it for me and a crystal glass. It is the most thirst-quenching drink I have ever had.

Persian wines were a little on the rough side until the new Pakdis Winery, with largely foreign expertise, came on the market. The launching of the new wine was accompanied by a heavy spending campaign designed to put its rivals out of business. Hotel food and beverage people found it worth their while to stock only Pakdis, and even supermarkets took other brands off their shelves. The company was given permission to sell at twice the price of other brands.

When the owners of one leading competitor turned up in Tehran and told the press that the mayor of the city of Qazvin, where they made their wine, had sealed their premises on the grounds they were unhygienic, the then sizable wine drinking community in Tehran, smarting at having to pay much higher prices, reacted furiously. It was pointed out in fact that the Pakdis plant was not yet in proper working order so that the wine it was selling at such high cost under its label was unlikely to have been produced there. After a considerable brouhaha, the prime minister ordered the opening of the seals on the closed winery, and the hotels and restaurants that had been influenced by Pakdis had to return the other brands to their service. It was a rare triumph for public opinion in Iran.

The soft-drink makers years before had fought a similar battle against each other. Each had collected the others' bottles and broke them up and played numerous tricks on one another to hurt the others' business. The Armenian family that owned the Coca-Cola franchise in Iran did not hesitate to play a trump card against the Pepsi-Cola family, the Habib Sabets, who were Baha'is, members of the sect hated by the Muslim clergy. They let it be known that Pepsi was made by Baha'is, so religious cities including Mashhad and Qom would not allow a bottle of Pepsi into their precincts. Countless Muslims refused to drink it too, except in really hot weather when other drinks were perhaps in short supply. Allah would not have expected them to go thirsty.

The Armenians were the backbone of the musical world in Tehran until Empress Farah and her cultural organizations along with the Ministry of Culture and Arts extended their activities. They also played an important role in Iran as bankers, doctors, teachers, and other professionals. They had survived numerous ups and downs; the period of revolutionary unrest and uncertainty was just another downer for them. Although the very wealthy Armenian business people were badly hit, they did not suffer as much as the Jews did. Inevitably, an anti-Israel regime such as Khomeini's continued to damage Jewish interests and made life difficult for Iran's Jews.

The Jewish community has been with Iran for at least 2,000 years. The first Jews were said to have been sent to the foot of Mount Damavand, the highest peak in Iran and only about forty miles from Tehran, by the Assyrians. To them it was said that Damavand was the end of the known world and that was the place for Jews! The ruins of an ancient Jewish settlement can still be seen near the foot of the mountain. Tehran Jews often asked to be buried in the cemetery there. When I walked among its old stones one day, I was surprised to come upon new graves with small bottles of rose water on them.

Still living in the Isfahan area are the descendants of some blue-eyed, fair-haired Jews who are believed to have come from a region north of the

Black Sea that converted to Judaism centuries ago. Shiraz, in the south of Iran, however, is the original home of the main community of Jews, who came into the country several centuries before the Arab invasion.

Habib Elghanian, one of the leaders of the Jewish community, was from a Shirazi family. These Jews were always loyal Iranians in spite of having experienced considerable discrimination under the Qajars. Jews were allowed to ride only donkeys in the streets, not horses, for example, a century ago.

Elghanian and other Jewish industrialists like him played a big role in Iran's development. They set up big, new industries that helped keep pace with rapidly rising consumer demands and created thousands of jobs. The Shah's considerate treatment of them helped to bring in a lot of foreign Jewish investment and along with that non-Jewish funds too. Many Iranians told me that had the Shah not treated them well and encouraged more Jewish links, his economic dreams would never have begun to take shape. Many prominent former Jews converted to Islam during the nineteenth century; some of the best-known modern Muslim families had once been Jewish, and there was no doubt their sentiments were back with their own kind in recent times.

The Assyrians in Iran were fewer in number than were the Armenians and played a less-important role. They were divided between Nestorians of the old church of the East and Catholics and often seemed to be at odds with one another. Their main communities had always lived in western Iran near the Iraqi and Turkish borders; early American Presbyterian missionaries worked among them, and the missionaries earlier in the twentieth century came to play a prominent role in developing educational services in Iran.

The school for girls they founded in Tehran developed under a series of devoted principles into the big, new liberal arts Damavand College that was built on land given by the Shah on the northeast edge of the city. One of the principals of the school, Jane Doolittle, retired and continued to live in Tehran into her eighties; many of the girls she taught revered her. She shared a house with an Iranian Jewish missionary whose family converted to Anglicanism and who taught for many years with the Christian Mission to the Jews in Iran. During most of the time these women taught, Iran was a backward country with very few really rich people and masses of poor. The wealth of most of the Iranians was in land, not money, anyway. Miss

Doolittle was sent to teach in Iran in 1922, riding in a ratty, old car over the rough roads from Baghdad.

In pre-revolutionary years, the Christian communities developed an ecumenical center in Tehran and were very active in the tremendously tolerant religious climate. They established meaningful contacts with some Muslim leaders. While most of the Christian missionaries in Iran were content to carry out their mission of service to their God by good works, a few were interested in converting people. Under the Shah, that was possible. Now, it can obviously be done only in secret.

Unlike Christians, Jews, and Zoroastrians, the Baha'is don't predate Islam in Iran. Muslim zealots point out that they had much more influence under the Shah in the court and government than did any of the other minority groups. There was no doubt that during my time in Iran, Bahaism was attracting new converts in Iran. The failure of Islam in general and Shi'ism in particular to update themselves for the modern world made many people look for a reasonable alternative. While more and more young people opted for agnosticism and atheism, the older people in this land were religious. Mysticism was as commonplace as cinema going is in the West, so they still worshiped the religion of their choice.

People needed a proper alternative if they regarded themselves as thinking people. Bahaism, with its simple rules and clear division of good from evil, echoed traditional Zoroastrian ideas and appealed to Iranians. The Muslim clergy's hatred of the religion had led to widespread killing of Baha'is in Tehran and an attack on their main temple even though Baha'is lived circumspectly but freely until the unrest began in 1978.

The Sabets I mentioned previously were the most prominent Baha'i family in business and society. Like quite a few subscribers to the religion, Habib Sabet, a self-made former trucker, was of mixed Muslim and Jewish origins. He made millions through his business activities. His two sons were regulars at the top-set parties. Habib himself gradually moved out to Europe because of official badgering inspired by the press's nagging about his wealth. One of his follies was to build a reproduction of the Petit Trianon Palace in France as his Tehran home. It was an absurd extravagance that led to further public criticism and insinuations that unscrupulous business practices were the foundation of his wealth.

Another Baha'i who was constantly accused of furthering the cause of his coreligionists was the national airline boss, Mohammad Ali Khatami. One of Iran's first pilots, he nurtured the airline by the ruthless beating down of private competition. He appeared to have great influence with the Shah, who backed him against the complaints of the tourist and hotel industry, which wanted charter flights and other facilities. Khatami resisted these so the airline could continue to make money. He was said to have told the Shah that Iran's international prestige would benefit by Iran Air being able to compete with the top Western lines, and Mohammad Reza Pahlavi was sure to fall for that one.

Poor Khatami was murdered at his home during the unrest of 1978. A group of men came to his door, dashed in when it was opened, and shot him. The government said it was suicide, but nobody believed that. Equally, nobody was sure whether his religion or his tough business methods had prompted the attack.

One might have thought that Muslims would be wary about Zoroastrianism, the original Iranian religion, but that was not so. The Zoroastrian community in Iran had dwindled to such small numbers and had few important figures in the administration or industry that it seemed to pose no threat. Even the return to Iran of several thousand Parsees, as the Indian Zoroastrian community were know, did not worry Muslims in spite of the fact that the Shah was constantly harping on the greatness of the Achaemenid and Sassanian Empires, which were inspired by Zoroastrianism, rather than the glories of Muslim times.

The clergy were angered, however, by the Shah's decision to change the calendar in Iran to date back to the beginning of Cyrus the Great's empire 2,500 years before and to dispense with the Muslim *hegira* date, which Iran had observed for centuries. The decision of Sharif Emami to go back to the *hegira* date with the Shah's approval when he took power in August 1978 was one of the crucial ones that led to the Shah's fall. A ruler who had kept power by a combination of force and psychological domination of a comparatively primitive people could not afford the loss of face involved in this surrender of a principle of his policy. The ordinary Iranian saw it as a clear signal of his losing his grip on things.

CHAPTER 10

Iranian Men

I have met Arabs, Turks, French, and the overestimated Italians frequently in North America and abroad, but none of them is as concerned with ego and physical matters as is the Iranian man. The desire to look splendid is inborn in the Iranian. The ancient Greeks were staggered by the style in which the Achaemenids dressed for war and the luxury in which the officers lived in their tents. Cutting your cloth according to your coat was never an Iranian characteristic, and nothing would stop the average Iranian man from obtaining the best if he could get his hands on it.

For foreigners living in Iran, protecting the "face" and prestige of the people you worked with became second nature because the Iranian sought perfection as far as his image was concerned and he couldn't live without feeling he had it. In the days when women had no rights, they knew they had to respect those feelings or suffer the worst consequences.

However, as Iran came more in contact with the Western world in the twentieth century, women began to find a little more identity of their own. Husbands who had been in the West looked for some signs of personality or character as well as the other marks of suitability in their wives. By the time women began to be educated, upper-class Iranians looked for education in wives too.

The situation became dangerous for women who forgot their gender and behaved as if they were men's equals. Tehran was full of women who had become incautious and were divorced by offended husbands. Many of them were career women seeking consolation for loneliness in their jobs, and in most cases, their male colleagues resented them greatly. Several times, foreign men told me of the contemptuous and often downright obscene way Iranian men talked about these "liberated" women when they were not around.

But many men became proud of the abilities of their educated wives and found them useful aids to promotion especially when they were well connected. But tradition dies hard, and they also hankered for the dutiful, harem-type wife who would minister to their comfort and submit to their desires in the docile way they expected, which these new, modern wives were not wont to do. The solution was to find younger wives from another class to marry as *sigheh*, temporary, wives in secret and go to when they felt the need for their traditional kind of succor. Sometimes, that was discovered and divorce or other problems arose, but other times, original wives never found out or never divulged the fact if they did. They presumably felt that they had the superior position anyway and that that was sufficient consolation.

I knew of several cases of this when I was in Tehran. The one that caused most talk among the foreign community was that of Hassan Arfa, the distinguished ambassador and soldier, author of several books, and a pillar of the Iranian and foreign communities. His known wife, Hilda, was British born. She had met her husband in Monte Carlo when she was dancing with the Diaghilev Ballet in the twenties. He was a handsome young Iranian officer whose father kept a house there. The ballet company tried to dissuade her from marrying Arfa but failed. The general used to tell us the story of how he sat in a tearoom watching the famous ballet master entreating Hilda to stay, the afternoon she decided to marry him.

Hilda came to Tehran when it was still a very primitive city and moved into the family home several miles outside Tehran. She would recount stories of how she used to ride into town for an embassy party on a donkey. When I met the couple, she was an entertaining woman of eighty and he was around seventy-six. There was no doubt of his adoration for her at that time. When Hilda died unexpectedly, he seemed heartbroken. He built a beautiful tiled mausoleum on the grounds of their beautiful, rustic home where she was buried.

So Hilda's many friends were stunned when within a matter of weeks, a new Iranian mistress of the house appeared at Larak, as his home was known. What's more, she was already Mrs. Arfa, around forty, with three grown-up daughters claiming the name of Arfa too. It turned out she had been his wife for more than twenty years! "How could he?" the European and American wives demanded. Had Hilda known? The answer to the second question nobody seemed to have; she had obviously never discussed it if she did. Amazement increased when friends of the general, who claimed they knew, said he had taken the second wife to Ankara and Islamabad when he was ambassador in those two cities. Hilda had accompanied him as the official wife, but he was visiting the second wife in other quarters from time to time.

Many of Hilda's friends stopped visiting the General at Larak, but he was unperturbed. He invited those who still kept in touch to an annual ceremony outside the mausoleum on the anniversary of Hilda's death and wept as he recalled their happiness together, and he was utterly sincere about it. He had been born in another period when men of his class were expected to take on young successors to their first wives. In his case, he had taken the pretty sister of a man who worked on his farm; that way, she would not affect his first wife's world.

If the second wife had known her place and remained out of sight when Hilda was alive, she also had the ability to cope with her new role when she became mistress of the house at Larak. Those of us who recognized the General's honesty and integrity in not trying to disguise anything about his marriages and then giving this comparatively uneducated, simple woman the same respect he had given his first wife were delighted when she carried out with tremendous composure her duties as wife of a man still active in public life. She learned to dress for state receptions and embassy parties and to entertain the General's friends at dinner and regular Friday lunch open houses as though she had been born to it.

The General thoroughly enjoyed the new people she brought to their home too. Their daughters attracted young men from rising middle-class families who respected the name of Arfa, and they were soon married off to husbands with prospects. The General was in his mid-eighties when the revolution came; he remained active riding his horses and as I found out enjoying normal marital relations with his wife. They were an admirable couple.

Not so lucky in love was the husband of Nahid Motamed, one of Iran's leading socialites and zealous workers on women's committees. She was in town one day when she saw her husband's car go by, and her curiosity was aroused. She followed him and saw him enter an apartment. She waited a short time before knocking on the door. When she asked to see Dr. Motamed, the woman replied that she was Mrs. Motamed and asked if she could help her. Knowing Nahid, a rather overbearing, extremely forceful, and outspoken woman, I would love to have been there to see what happened next. All I know is that she was said to have thrown her husband out and to have had nothing to do with him anymore. It said something about the attitudes of women that some of her friends told me they thought she had been wrong to do that. They said that he was deeply attached to Nahid and that she could have given him the chance to decide where he wanted to stay.

Many men married second wives openly without breaking with their earlier wives. Nader Djahanbani's father, another distinguished public figure, did that without leaving the Russian-born wife he loved and without diminishing her status in any way. There were also two other offspring who were treated with some respect by the rest of the family; we surmised they could have been the old man's children by a *sigheh*.

The younger men tended to change their wives to the same pattern as young Americans, however. They divorced as soon as frustrations grew too much for them or they met someone they thought they liked better. Even when happily married, they enjoyed flirtations and passing affairs. Iranian wives didn't worry much about them, and male society saw them as a symbol of a man's virility. In many cases, the girls were just for show, designed to demonstrate to the rest of this male-dominated society that the man was a real man. Others were taken on as emotional symbols with which to castigate wives with too much character. Whenever husband and wife had any disagreements, the girlfriend's name was introduced as a foil between them; this was a very common phenomenon in Iran.

Foreign girls, especially blondes, had a special cachet among Iranian men. They could always find a rich lover if they knew how to dress and could move in polite society. Iranians always allowed foreigners more freedom of behavior than they did themselves, so they accepted these blond Europeans and Americans in public at least as equals. The men had special relations with foreign women. They discussed things with them in a much franker fashion than they did with their own women, who had been brought up to accept a certain place in the social spectrum and to concern themselves with only marriage and money. That often left discussion of the more personal and intimate side of a relationship as the preserve of foreign women. The only time a good wife had to worry was when her husband reached his forties and began to feel middle age coming on. He would then begin to look hard at young girls, and if one really fancied him and was faithful, he would begin to think actively of divorcing a wife his own age and marrying the young girl.

My friend Mahnaz was offered $1 million by her husband, Ali, if she would give him a divorce. He had had many open affairs with young foreign and Iranian women and had found one he wanted to marry. She refused.

"Mahnaz, why would you turn down such a sum? Not only would you be free of him, but you would also be rich."

"Are you kidding? He's offered me a pittance considering all the money he has from his many businesses. I love my way of life, and I love to spend his money. I'll never give him a divorce. I'll continue my life as is. He can have all the affairs he wants."

People used to say the Shah enjoyed some girls of lesser repute who got in with his courtiers, but that was mere gossip. One high-class call girl in Europe recounted a story about being invited to Tehran for a client through Iranian friends; it turned out to be a royal occasion. She was whisked out to an apparent hunting lodge where after a long wait she heard a helicopter flying in. She looked through the window and saw many people bowing and scraping to the man who descended from it.

It wasn't until he entered the room that she suddenly realized it could be the Shah though she never really knew. A girl of some intelligence and charm, she tried to chat the man up, but he wasn't interested. They perfunctorily performed their business, and he left walking quickly past the fawning minions and back into the helicopter.

If you think that is extraordinary, you're mistaken. The vast majority of Muslim men treat their sex lives in the same casual way. Those who were educated abroad learned that there was another attitude, but they usually found it too late to readjust. Muslim women seem to have learned to accept this limited sex life.

Some marriages between Iranians and foreign women broke up, but the number of successful marriages of this type far outnumbered the broken ones. Scores of thousands of students had married Westerners while studying abroad and had become fairly westernized in their attitudes about marriage as a result. Sometimes, mothers-in-law and other family members willfully tried to break up marriages with foreign wives because the men had been betrothed to cousins or to daughters of a friend before they left for school, and the family wanted that honored. Years ago, it could be difficult for an American girl arriving in Tehran to stay with a typical or even well-off family. But the 1970s saw a wide change in values and attitudes; the Western way of life began to spread and to be seen as a viable existence that did not necessarily break up the family.

More and more young men moved out of their family homes with their wives when previously the custom had been for married children to stay with parents until much later in marriage. And it required only a limited amount of tact on the part of the foreign wife for her to get on well with her in-laws. Of course much depended too on the husband. If he reverted too quickly to the traditional Iranian habit of leaving his wife at home while he went out each evening, trouble would brew, but most Iranians who had lived in the West and married there preferred a Western type of relationship.

The man who didn't mind his wife walking around in shorts in the street back in the States would object quite suddenly to his wife wearing a dress that revealed even a little too much of her neck. She had probably worn the dress several times before, but he had said nothing. Slightly out of sorts, her husband would take it out on her. Even a too friendly conversation with a close male friend of the husband could cause a scene, but the wife had merely to remain cool and the whole thing would blow over. An Iranian husband just couldn't stand too much common sense in his marriage and a wife. Whatever else she was, she could never really get bored.

To get back to Iranian male attitudes, I often heard foreigners remarking on the way young men walked around hand in hand even in the main streets in Tehran and warmly embraced each other when they met. They felt there were homosexual undertones to that, which was nonsense. Muslims have always shown their affection for their friends in this way. They greet good nonMuslim friends with the traditional cheek-to-cheek embrace too. The actual planting of the lips on the cheek they reserve for really warm friends.

When Iranians were homosexual, one learned from friends, it was because of a functional need to have some form of sex in a society in which girls were unobtainable for many young men. Money could seduce many poor youths; that was a legacy of the former feudal society where 90 percent of the people lived in hopeless poverty and sexual favors were a desperate means of gaining benefit of one kind or another. Wry as it sounds, evidence of men's preference for the opposite sex was demonstrated by the fact that as women became freer, they still wanted virginity in a wife, so they would have dalliances with their own sex.

Many men were constantly seen running their hands over their flies as if concerned about whether it was still there. One Iranian woman friend told me laughingly after we had watched a court official doing this on a public occasion that the fact that Iranians loved to wear tight trousers was to blame for the gesture; she didn't mind talking about it at all.

Nor I found out later were Iranian women modest about discussing their husbands' prowess or lack of it among themselves, and some of the dirtiest jokes I ever heard came from them. In public, however, they preserved a meticulous propriety. Even though Iranian men were reputed to be neither skilled nor enthusiastic lovers, Iranian men loved women. I never had so many gallant things said to me in my life, and flirting was a way of getting problems solved through any official of your acquaintance.

The idea of women was a charm to most Iranian men. Though the new middle class found it hard to change their attitudes toward sisters and wives, they were always excited by the appearance of a liberated female. Foreign girls had such a good time in Tehran because the guys didn't have to worry about their brothers or fathers coming after them later.

CHAPTER 11

Women

Helen Bakhtiar, an American who had married a son of a tribal khan, had come to primitive Iran between the two world wars. She and her husband started the first nurses' training school in Iran. He was a pioneering character himself having been sent with his tribal siblings to the States as their guardian and then deciding to study there himself.

In their early days at home in Iran, they traveled extensively so Helen could get to know the country and its customs. They traveled considerable distances by many means of transportation, even by camel. Once they settled down and started their nursing school, they had a family of sons and daughters who were all educated in the States.

One of the sons, Jamshid, or Jim, was a well-known football player for the University of Virginia. After graduating, he went back to Iran to teach psychology at the Pahlavi University in Shiraz during the seventies. His sister, Shirin, worked in public relations for the National Iranian Oil Company in Abadan in southern Iran. She was quite a renowned artist and poet as well; she usually sallied forth in traditional-style tribal gowns with many layers of gaudy colors when she had exhibitions of her paintings or readings of her poetry. She had exhibits of her works shown as far away as Vienna. Her search for more and more truth, as she put it, led her on a trip to India during which, at about age fifty, she met a young Indian in his twenties. She divorced her Iranian husband, who was on his deathbed anyway, changed her name to an Indian one, and married the young guy. Besides being little more than half her age, the husband was only half her size!

Naqi Khan Gharagozlou, a US-educated physician who was a member of the leading tribe in the Hamadan area, married an American girl who had been a librarian at Johns Hopkins University when he was a student there. He swept her off her feet and brought her back to live in Varkhaneh, a mountainous village outside Hamadan, where he had grown up.

The Gharagozlou tribe had been brought from Central Asia (Turkey) to northwest Persia by Tamerlane in the late fourteenth century, and the tribe owned hundreds of small villages in this area. This particular Gharagozlou preferred the anonymity of his home village to the life of the capital, Tehran, and he, his wife, and their children lived in this remote place. It was there that Mary Gharagozlou, one of their daughters, whom I knew well because we were both associated with the Royal Horse Society, grew up. She was a tomboy; more exactly like a typical tribal boy though her mother's feminine hand was there to ensure she learned some of the graces too.

Mary learned to ride as well as any boy and developed an interest in the tribal people that led her as daughter of one of the khan's immediate family to feel a great responsibility for them. She was sent away to Europe for her education and married the son of a Swiss ambassador, but that marriage did not last long. She was soon back in the tribal areas of Iran, where she met the love of her life, the handsome, dashing Majid Bakhtiar, head of the Bakhtiar tribe, who was several years her senior.

They married and led a delightful life in the days before Land Reform and other measures weakened the power and influence of the tribal chieftains. Majid and his family owned hundreds of horses including some the sturdy, little Bakhtiari Mountain breed, but the pride of his herd were the purebred Asil—Arabian—horses that had been in southern Iran for more than a century and maybe much longer.

When they first moved to his home in Khuzestan, Mary insisted on taking her two favorite horses, which she had bought at exorbitant prices, with her, but Majid objected. "Maryjun, I have the best horses in Iran in my stable. You don't need to bring down your coarse, little, mixed-breed Kurds with you. You will see."

"Majid, I have superior horses I have trained myself. I must bring them with us."

"Do as you wish, my love, but you will see when we get to Andimeshk that my horses are the superior ones. I will give you any one you choose."

When they arrived with Mary's mixed-breed horses and she saw Majid's Asil horses, she said, "Majid, how can you call these horses? They're goats!"

He naturally was incensed at the comment, but as time went on and she learned what wonderful horses they were, she wanted to bite off her tongue. They hunted gazelle with long legged, silky haired *salukis* (dogs) on the plains, *mouflon* (Uriel sheep) and ibex in the hills, and raced their horses against the sheikhs of Arab origin that were mixed with the Iranians in that part of the country. Life had more than a little medieval splendor about it.

Perhaps it was the teaching of an American mother and her early life in the mountainous tribal area that gave Mary the intense interest she had in the welfare of the ordinary tribespeople. Her life with Majid Bakhtiar whetted her appetite for this as well. During the 1960s at the time of the Shah's Land Reform, she was put in charge of tribal affairs and reported directly to General Hossain Pakravan, the head of SAVAK. The government wanted to settle the nomadic tribes who it was thought were too independent and destabilizing to the central authority of tribal affairs. To be able to do that, she divorced Majid, who did not want her to be involved; however, they remained very close. She did her best to resist this new policy pointing out that the nomads provided the country with its meat and that if they were forced to settle, their sheep would die. She traveled by jeep, horse, and camel in regions that no other official would contemplate visiting. During the tribal famine, she was instrumental in saving the Bakhtiar by supplying them with wheat and flour. At the time of the Qazvin earthquake in 1962, General Pakravan put her in charge of the relief program.

Mary went off to work with the Qashqai tribe in southern Iran. There, she heard of violent treatment meted out to a tribal boy by the gendarmerie. As there were Gharagozlous in the court, Mary had a complaint passed to the Shah. The commander of the gendarmerie, General Oveissi, the same man who had been banished from Iran by the Shah years later, was admonished. He never forgave Mary, who paid for that. When she went to work among the Baluchi pushing a project for badly needed water and agricultural assistance, Oveissi had her accused of causing unrest, and she was sent back to Tehran and kept under house arrest for some time.

It happened about this time that the court decided it needed to have better relations with Iran's most powerful tribe, the Bakhtiar. Majid was lured more and more to Tehran and the delights of court life. He softened and began to enjoy the social life of the city. While he and an Armenian friend were visiting the Caspian resort of Ramsar, the Armenian bet him that he could not land his plane on the beach at night. They left a party one night, both drunk according to others there, to take up the plane and attempt the landing. The plane disappeared. No one was certain what had happened to it until Majid's body was washed up on the beach a few days later. The body of his companion, who was a close friend of Princess Ashraf, was never found. The princess was genuinely grief stricken by her friend's death and mourned for a long time; Mary was devastated by the death of her one true love.

Upon Majid's death, Aga Khan Bakhtiar, his younger brother, became the new chief of the Bakhtiar tribes. He was the head of the National Iranian Oil Company and gave Mary control of one of Majid's former stables on the southern edge of the Bakhtiar Mountains, which had been one of Majid's and her favorite homes. She inherited a handful of horses in the former stable of hundreds of Arabians that had survived the African horse sickness that more than a decade earlier had swept through the Middle East and killed off most of the horses of Iran.

She received no money from Majid's extensive estate, but Agha Khan Bakhtiar was one of the most important officials on the board of the Royal Horse Society, so Kambiz Atabai, the secretary general, took over the funding of the stable and the breeding operation she set up there. Mary worked extremely hard on the place as her dream was to get the Persian Arab horses recognized by the World Arab Horse Organization. She spent years checking the pedigrees of the horses with the sheikhs of the area, verified them, and finally got her little stud farm accepted and recognized by the association.

I went down to help her a few times as the Royal Horse Society wanted to make sure that the inspection, which would be made by the committee of the WAHO, all of whom were Westerners, went well. It was an adventure to get there. I flew to Ahwaz and was picked up by

Ali, Mary's driver, in an old, rattletrap Land Rover. We drove for what seemed hours over the brown desert road and finally came to the Karun River, where we stopped at a dock; a small ferryboat was awaiting us. I was aghast when I realized that we were about to drive the vehicle onto this dilapidated ferry. When we arrived on the far bank, we again got in the Land Rover and drove for another duration over sand tracks in the desert not seeing a person, animal, or tree.

"There it is!" said Ali as he pointed to what looked like an ancient *caravanserai* in the distance. We drove through the gate into a beautiful oasis where fruit trees and flowers abounded. Mary's home was a small, domed, square building decorated in the true Persian desert style. The floors were covered with colorful tribal carpets; there were large cushions and camel bags for seating and a low table where one would squat sitting on the stuffed camel bags as seats for the meals.

She spent winters in the balmy climate of Aghili, as the place was called, living in this simple mud house caring for her horses, riding through the desert, and receiving visitors from different parts of the world from time to time. Every spring, she would drive the horses with her men over the Karun River to the nearest railway station some thirty or so kilometers away at Andimeshk. There, she would put them on a train to transport them through the high Zagros Mountains, and drive them again for more than a week across the Borujerd Plain to her girlhood summer home near Hamadan, where they spent the summer.

It was a thrill knowing Mary Gharagozlou. She was completely Iranian in many ways, almost chauvinistically so. But her upbringing by an American mother and her years in Europe gave her an ability to relate to Westerners that most of her compatriots lacked. As I sat with her, camped under the stars with her, and rode with her across the plain in spring or autumn when she migrated with her horses, she told me things about Iran and its tribespeople that demonstrated her deep love for both. The men would cook rice and stew, and there'd be melon and hot, sweet tea afterward. I'd sigh contentedly as I burrowed into my sleeping bag and went to sleep.

In the spring, the plain was a carpet of wildflowers. It was the same all over Iran in the spring. Even the desert areas would burst out briefly with little forget-me-not type flowers and skimpy green shrubs.

The cavalcade of ridden horses that surrounded unridden mares and foals would traverse dirt trails and skirt mud-built, fortress-like villages from which children and women in bright blue, yellow, red, or green tribal dresses would watch us pass. These were Lors, a people who once had a reputation for being fierce bandits. The protected villages were a reminder of only twenty years before when traveling that way, Mary told us, was dangerous if you didn't have arms and men to protect you.

Iran's tribal women never wore veils as did their urban counterparts. They looked at us with an open gaze. The people there had long been settled in their own areas, but farther south, in early spring and late autumn, you would run into the nomadic tribes moving from winter to summer pastures in the Bakhtiar Mountains. Several hundred thousand tribespeople still made their nomadic treks every year in spite of the inducements there were to settle. Electricity had reached many of the villages, and there were schools, but old habits die hard; it will take many years before the nomads of Iran all settle. The gendarmerie did a magnificent job over the years in bringing law and order to all these areas; we could camp out in the length and breadth of Iran without fearing attack when I lived there.

Mary rode like a man, and the tribal men had great respect for her. Among the Qashqai and Baluchi, her name was sufficient introduction for you. Men fell easily under her spell; she seemed to have had brief but numerous affairs with them. Once when she and some friends from Tehran went to a Qashqai tribal wedding—a colorful and unusual thrill with dances, horse races, and a host of entertainment—she stayed behind as the fiancée of the tribal chief's son. A few days later, however, she was back in Tehran, and it was all over.

Shortly before the revolution, she moved her stud farm to a new, more convenient, and permanent site near Shiraz and the spring and autumn drives were no more. She continued to breed more of the unique Asil horses, which were in danger of being lost forever when she took over the care of the little group at Aghili.

Perhaps the most stoic American wife I met in Tehran was Kay Khalvati, the wife of an irascible Iranian colonel who was thoroughly unpredictable to put it mildly. Kay was just passing thirty when I knew her, and her husband must have been more than twenty years her senior. Sohrab, her husband, had already married and divorced two foreign wives before he met her.

Kay had come to Iran to stay with her father, an architect, who joined an Iranian company after being sent to Iran with the Point Four aid program. She stayed on to have a disastrous love affair that made her turn to the drug crowd for solace according to her friends. She was on the verge of suicide when Sohrab met her, felt great sympathy for her, and married her. They embarked on a stormy relationship that kept their friends goggle-eyed as they watched Sohrab often go berserk in public. There was no doubt that he was deeply fond of Kay and that she had come to love him, but his violence began to drive her back to drugs and drink. One incident seemed to give their friends a lot of satisfaction to talk about; after Sohrab had become violent with Kay at a nightclub one evening, she went home. When he returned to his house, he saw all his dress uniforms lying in the street cut to ribbons!

As time went on, Kay, an intelligent, attractive girl, found the strain too much for her. Sohrab's daughter from his first marriage, a pretty girl in her early twenties, had married none other than the head of the feared SAVAK, General Nassiri, who was in his sixties. Stories of Kay's drinking had reached his ears, so he persuaded Sohrab to separate from her. That didn't last very long; their son, Yousef, a talented but temperamental boy, wanted his mother home again, and his father couldn't handle him anyway. He brought Kay back home, and they managed to continue to live violently but without threats of a new break.

Sohrab's behavior in public had led to a deep dive in his fortunes by the mid-seventies, and he was in danger of losing his job as riding master at the Imperial Country Club. But the marriage of his daughter to Nassiri restored his position because Nassiri was a powerful man nobody dared annoy. It was said that Sohrab had a part in engineering his daughter's marriage. It was common knowledge that Nassiri's first marriage to a beautiful childless woman was at an end when Sohrab went to a luncheon at the Officers' Club one day. He knew that Nassiri would be there, so he took with him photographs of his attractive daughter. He showed them to the General and suggested he should come to meet her over a glass of tea. The General did, and Sohrab apparently did the rest.

The girl was quite agreeable to the match, and when she gave birth to a son after a little more than a year, it was no wonder Sohrab was in high good humor. To have an heir had long been Nassiri's sole unachieved ambition.

Sohrab had another friend in Amir Ali Shebani, the head of a Soviet-built steel mill near Isfahan. Shebani was a horseman too, and when Sohrab had problems at the country club, Shebani had Sohrab appointed sports adviser to the steel mill and had him come and develop a riding club there. Once a year, Sohrab would invite European riders of international repute and Iranian riders to compete in a show-jumping contest at the club built near the mill way out in the desert.

I used to go down with my team of riders from the Imperial Stables to compete. The show was held at night under floodlights. What an extraordinary scene it was with flags of the countries represented flapping in the wind as the band played in the ring. In the stands on one side of the ménage sat the mill's Soviet experts with their wives and families while Iranian officials, workers, and friends sat on the other side.

It was difficult to believe we were miles from anywhere in this barren part of Iran. The scene within the island of light could have been in a stadium at the center of any city in the world. The foreign riders rubbed their eyes in disbelief. So they did during the show when the Soviets, deprived of any entertainment other than their cinema, applauded almost hysterically for the winners no matter Iranian or foreign.

We would all be whisked off to a lavish party at the boat club nearby. Apparently, a big supply of water had been found under the rock and sand there, and a huge artificial lake had been made where small sailboats and canoes were seen adding a marine atmosphere to the desert. We dined and danced in the open while the lake and the huge swimming pool glittered in the lights. This event continued for three days, so when we left to go back to Tehran, we were sated and exhausted after a desert sojourn of food, drink, and fun that could have been put on only in Pahlavi Iran.

Sohrab's world was to collapse around him when the Shah in an astonishingly naive move fired Nassiri and appointed him to be ambassador to Pakistan; that meant Sohrab had lost his protector. When Nassiri was brought back to Iran and jailed, Sohrab had a distressed daughter, and when his only son committed suicide, he and Kay were grief stricken.

Sohrab Khalvati was typical of so many Iranians I knew. He was basically a kind man and did many things to help people. He felt tremendous sympathy for Kay, and I think he genuinely loved her. But he couldn't cope with the new egalitarian attitudes in Iran. He loved his country and his Shah, and he hated anything that hurt either. He shouted and screamed at people he thought had forgotten their place. He wanted Kay to be someone he knew she was not. He ranted and raved at her so much that she lost her nerve. He was a confused man who found it difficult to adjust to the new world he was living in. Fortunately, the Khalvatis moved out of Iran in good time; even being related to Nassiri would have been an anathema to the revolutionaries of Iran. He and Kay spent their final years in California.

One of the toughest American wives I met in Iran was certainly Louise Firouz, who married Narcy, a prince of the previous Qajar Dynasty, when he was studying in the States. When I met them, they were living at Nowruzabad, their beautiful farm just outside Tehran, but they also had a city house on Damghan Avenue in the city. She was an accomplished equestrian from Virginia and decided to set up an equestrian center offering riding lessons for children; she had three of her own and wanted them to be able to socialize with others.

She was having a difficult time finding suitable mounts for these children, so she decided to go to the remote Turkoman area by the Caspian Sea; she had been told she could find ponies there that were small and narrow enough for her purpose. What she discovered was a small breed of horse that was said to have been one of the oldest equine breeds in the world. They were believed to have descended from small Mesopotamian horses that had disappeared by the seventh century AD. This rediscovery of these beautiful, perfectly conformed miniature horses with docile personalities became her legacy. This little horse measures about nine to twelve hands—three to four feet at the withers—in height, is as short as a pony, but has the temperament, stride, and jumping ability of a horse. It also has an Arabian horse's facial shape and finely proportioned legs. Genetic testing has linked the Caspians, as she called them, to horses of ancient Persia demonstrating that they were the precursors of the Arabian and other breeds. Today, the Caspian horse is on the list of most-endangered animals; the estimated global population is less than two thousand.

Louise set up a breeding farm at her riding school at Nowruzabad with seven mares and six stallions and named the breed the Caspian horse, which became a part of the heritage of Iran. She also helped found the Royal Horse Society, which had been set up to protect and improve Iranian breeds of horses.

Louise and I became very good friends while I was in Iran, and she introduced me to many interesting people and places. She helped me learn to love and appreciate the beauty of the country and people. When I had first arrived, I couldn't believe the brownness that seemed to be everywhere, but I learned to realize how lovely the different shades of brown were with the change of the seasons. In the spring, the mountains seemed a light shade of chartreuse, while in the autumn, they became a light mauve. Each day, the color change from morning to evening was a wonder. She introduced me to Kambiz Atabai, who later became my boss at the Imperial Stables. We worked together for the Royal Horse Society through which I also became friends with Mary Gharagozlou.

I accompanied Louise on several trips to inspect and buy horses for the Royal Horse Society. These trips were always fun and very interesting as we traveled to many out-of-the-way and primitive spots in Iran. On one trip, we learned there was a very special Arab stallion owned by a sheikh who was in Kurdistan near the town of Dezshapuz not far from Sanandaj on the Iraqi border. After two days of driving across the desert and over mountains and spending the night in a small caravanserai near Sanandaj, we were on the Iraqi border being shown the beautiful white stallion of ancient pedigree when we heard shouting and shots. We were beside the Tatun River, which at that point was the actual border between the two countries. I looked up to the rooftops of the small, one-story huts and saw *chiliques*—mercenaries who fought for whichever side payed them most that month—firing across the river, where a group of soldiers were trying to cross into Iran. Needless to say, we got into the Jeep and hightailed it back to Sanandaj.

The following morning at dawn, we tentatively drove back to try to purchase the stallion from the sheikh. Along the way, we saw a train of packhorses and mules wending their way down the barren, stony hillside to our right. We pulled over to watch. As they came close to the road, we saw that two of the horses were lame. On closer look, we saw they had bullet holes in their shoulders. When we questioned the Kurdish man who was leading the pack, he told us they were bringing tea and silk across the border—obviously smuggling—and had been attacked by bandits on the way. We knew there was quite a lot of smuggling in the area, but we were surprised to actually see the activity, which kept many families in funds with which to survive.

The owner of our prospective horse proved difficult to deal with. Why should he part with his best horse for the few thousand *toman* (a toman was worth 1,000 rials) we offered him? He invited us into his small house to have tea while we bargained for the stallion. After an hour or so of squatting on beautiful Persian carpets drinking tea, we ended up buying the horse as well as two mares from his herd, that I would keep at the Imperial Stables as brood mares for our program. All three of the horses were from the Wadne Kersan strain, famous for their will to perform, power, and stamina. This was the same strain of the Persian Arab Mary Gharagozlou had inherited from her husband, Majid Khan. We of course had spent more money than we had hoped, but we did get three horses for the budget Kambiz had given us, so we were sure he would be pleased.

We went back to Sanandaj to arrange for transport, which we found in the center of town near the bazaar. The driver of the open truck refused to go to Dezshapuz to pick up the horses, so we had to go back to tell the sheikh that he would have to ride them to Sanandaj, which would take a couple of hours. While we waited for them to arrive, we had time to do some shopping in the bazaar, which sold beautiful, handwoven, colorful Kurdish print materials and shawls that were colorfully hand embroidered. I also bought a small Kurdish carpet with animal designs in shades of brown, gold, and rust.

The horses arrived; they happily loaded them from a bank on the side of the road into the open truck that would carry them to Teheran. I never got used to this primitive way of transporting horses, but they arrived safe and sound.

In the mid-seventies, Narcy's construction business was accumulating debts at an uncontrollable pace due to the inflation caused by the hike in Iran's oil prices, so Nowruzabad and the Caspian stud farm were sold to the Royal Horse Society. At that time, Louise found temporary stabling for what horses she had left near Hamadan, but eventually, she and Narcy bought a piece of land in the Turkoman Steppes near Gonbad-e-Kavus and the village of Gara Tepe Sheikh, close to the Turkmenistan border. There, they built a small farm where Louise would spend a big part of her year way out in that remote part of the Turkoman Sahra looking after the farm. She lived there alone most of the time sleeping in the tack room, the only living accommodation. It was an attractive room, however, with sporting prints and an open fireplace. A cluster of small village houses a few hundred yards away was the only other sign of life near her, but she did have a shoal of dogs to protect her if needed.

She would summer her horses a long day's drive away in the foothills of the mountains where the summer grass was lush. She slept through the pleasant, dry summer nights on an uncovered wooden platform to avoid insects and small animals. There were leopards in this area, but they didn't trouble her as they had plenty of other quarry.

In winter at her small farm, she heard wolves howling regularly at night. Sometimes, they would tear a donkey apart, so she would go out with the men of the village to try to shoot them. I heard her telling stories of wolf attacks at dinner parties in Tehran with everyone listening wide-eyed and wondering how she survived in the north.

Goli Bakhtiar was an Iranian woman with gusto. I knew her through the horse world and always admired her good looks and desire to win in the horse shows. She was the daughter of Teymour Bakhtiar, a very controversial man in Iran during the Pahlavi reign. He had been educated in Beirut and then at the Saint-Cyr military academy in France. He rose rapidly in his military career after the fall of Reza Shah. As a close friend of Prime Minister Zahedi, he was promoted to military governor of Tehran and became modern Iran's youngest three-star general. He was made head of the newly formed security service, SAVAK in 1956. In 1961, the Shah began to distrust Teymour, and he was fired.

He went into exile from where he retaliated by establishing contact with Iranian dissidents including Ayatollah Khomeini. From Iraq, he broadcast anti-regime propaganda on Iran Free Radio, which he established. On August 12, 1970, he was assassinated while out hunting. Rumor was that Mohammed Reza Shah was quoted as claiming the assassination was a personal success, but it has never been proven that the Shah or his regime had had anything to do with it.

Goli had a beautiful white stallion named Shabdiz with which she won a great number of speed classes in the horse shows. When she was selected to go with the Iranian team as a member to an international competition in Beirut, she was told she could not take her stallion because the Lebanese would not allow foreign stallions into their country.

One day about six weeks before the team's departure, Goli, the beautiful *femme fatale* with marvelous features, striking black eyes, luscious, long black hair, and a figure to match, came to me as the trainer and asked confidentially, "Gail, you know how badly I want to take Shabdiz to Lebanon. What would you think of my having him gelded? Would he be able to jump in Lebanon in six weeks?"

I was shocked. Iranians never wanted to geld their horses; to them, it was a crime to take away their manhood. I had heard in gossipy conversations the comment, "Watch out for that Goli—she'd cut off anyone's balls!" And she wanted to do that to her horse! I explained to her that it was not such a serious procedure but that she should check with our resident veterinarian for his opinion. He agreed with me, and poor little Shabdiz had his balls cut off so he could go to Lebanon. It was a good thing too; she and Shabdiz were the biggest winners on our Iranian team.

Goli always stuck up for her rights. One example was at the Aryamehr Cup, the only horse show of that year that the Shah attended. She refused to salute the Shah as was customary before starting the course. She rode into the ring, waited for the start bell, and rode on. She believed the Shah had arranged the assassination of her father, Teymour, and she would not bow to him.

Goli had a long-standing affair with the head of the air force, General Nader Djahanbani. They rode together first at a stable in Tehran, where they kept their horses, and later, she kept her horses at the beautiful stables Nader built at his country home in Karaj. They were almost inseparable. Nader's wife seemed oblivious to that, or maybe she didn't really care.

One summer, Nader and Goli took a trip to Ireland with their friends, the Elghanians. They were all looking to buy show jumpers to bring back to Iran. They had a whirlwind trip looking at and buying several horses. While in Dublin one day, Nader went off on his own and bought a beautiful diamond bracelet for his wife, Farah. Somehow that evening, Goli found the box and asked Nader about it; she thought it was for her. When he told her he had bought it for Farah, she threw it into the toilet and flushed!

Ultimately, the affair broke up, and Goli married the delightful and very rich businessman Serge Bezrukeh. They seemed very happy and were able to leave Iran just before the revolution.

Goli and Serge Bezrukeh

Loading stallion in open truck

Mary Gharagozlou

Smuggler on Iraq border

Chiliques (mercenaries) on Iran/Iraq border

Stallion and owner

CHAPTER  12

The Drug Scene

One morning when I arrived at the farm of my friend Ali Reza Soudovar, I saw an uncommon number of cars in the driveway. He was the son of the man who had the exclusive right to import and sell Mercedes-Benz vehicles in Iran, and through a holding company, he owned a significant part of the parent company. Ali had all the funds he needed to support his horse business. We had been friends since I had arrived in Iran, and from the beginning, I would often go out to his place to help him with one horse or another. Even after I began working at the Imperial Stables, I would find time to visit often. I thought Ali and his young brother Mohammad were probably having one of their all-night parties. That wasn't my scene, and I didn't want to walk in on one so I went in through the kitchen to get my riding boots I had inadvertently left the day before.

Morad, the servant, greeted me and quickly added, "Something terrible has happened, Khonume. A friend of the master's has died, and everyone is very sad. Go on in. Agha will tell you."

The eyes that looked up at me were mostly red and filled with tears. I couldn't imagine what could have happened. I solemnly greeted the ten or so people who were in the room and went across to where Ali was sitting.

"My God, Ali!" I exclaimed. "What has happened to put you all in such a state?"

"Sit down," Ali said. "Maybe it will help to tell somebody about it and get it off our chests. Everyone here knows and trusts you to keep quiet, so we'll tell you what happened."

He asked one of the girls if she didn't agree. She nodded. "Yes, Ali, it's a good idea. We all know Gail; she is a good friend and will help us decide what we should do."

They told me about the party they had all been to the night before at Princess Ashraf's palace. It had started out as a quiet party with a little music, a little talking, and a leisurely dinner. As usual on such informal occasions at the princess's home when she wasn't there and only members of her set were present, most people were smoking something or other. Some were using opium, others heroin or hash. And of course there was beautiful white snow—cocaine—which everyone loved.

It had been a casual, congenial, and uneventful get-together until someone noticed that an attractive, fair-haired girl was out cold. Nobody knew how long she had been lying that way on the cushions, but when her boyfriend, a young official from the Foreign Ministry, tried to revive her, she didn't respond. He began to panic and started slapping the girl. This didn't work either.

Another guest, a notorious young homosexual, said he knew how to wake her up. He grabbed a lit cigarette from one of the others and put the red end against the girl's breast. There was a sizzling sound and a bad smell. Suddenly, others of the younger set there, all high on drugs, scented fun. They all rushed over and began to butt lit cigarettes into the girl's breasts. Soon, her clothes were ripped off, and they covered her body with burns. She still lay there unconscious. Her boyfriend, who seemed to have lost all control, began to beat her head. It was then that the soberer people there frantically moved in to drag the frenzied mob away from the girl. They wrapped her in a blanket and drove her to a hospital.

At the hospital, the hysterical boyfriend made up a story that they had been in an auto crash and the girl had been knocked out by hitting her head on the windshield. The doctors found she was dead; as the law demanded, they informed the police. The boyfriend was arrested, an automatic procedure when a driver was involved in a fatal accident.

The question put to me by the group that morning was whether they should go to the police and tell their story of what happened at the party or keep quiet and forget the incident. I was so shocked and sickened by the story that I couldn't answer.

One of the girls said, "The fact is that it's murder, for that's what it was, at the home of Princess Ashraf, who was not even there. If it were to come out in the papers or even just be hinted at, there will be dreadful trouble for the princess and the whole royal family. Think how it would affect people's thinking toward the Shah if it became known that there were parties at the princess's where there were drugs. There were so many people there from important families too. This would also give a bad impression." She seemed confident that the boyfriend's family would get him off and that his friends should do nothing.

The whole story filled me with such horror and disgust that I didn't feel qualified to say a word. But they looked so pathetically anxious to hear what I thought; I searched my mind for something to say. "I guess I would sit tight and wait to see what happens. Leave it to the families of the boy and the dead girl to report and ask questions. You guys were just innocent bystanders and probably should keep out of it until you're approached. If it comes down to a court case, you will all have to testify, and then the fur will really fly."

They did wait. The radio and television later that day reported that a girl taken to the hospital with head injuries and covered with cigarette burns was pronounced dead on arrival. Soon afterward, at the insistence of the girl's family, a case was opened against the boyfriend. It caused a big scandal, but the affair was not publicly tied to any party at the princess's home. When medical evidence was produced that the girl had died from a drug overdose before the burns and other injuries were inflicted, the matter was quickly dropped. Further attempts by the family to revive charges against the boyfriend as a result of promptings by the girl's friends failed; those who wanted the matter hushed up were too powerful.

If it had been an isolated death among the young society drug crowd who had parties at the big houses in the posh Niavaran neighborhood, one might have forgotten all about it, but it wasn't. People told me of others who had died or whose health had been permanently damaged. When one of the two attractive daughters of the Shah's friend Felix Aghayan died in her room one night, the gossips quickly reported that she had been at one of those wild parties the evening before. We didn't know at the time that her other charming sister, whom we all used to meet at the ski hotel under her father's charge, would also die from the effects of drug overdose within two years.

A discotheque Princess Ashraf had a share in was one of the most notorious drug exchanges in town. It seemed general knowledge that members of the court sold the stuff they brought into the country under cover of diplomatic credentials there. Nobody could interfere with them because it would have been very difficult and dangerous to prove that court officials were trafficking in drugs; a mafia-type clique in that society stood firmly together.

However, occasional evidence was exposed to the world. One member of the court, a prince of the earlier Qajar family who was a landscape gardener for the royal palaces, was held in Switzerland when a suitcase full of drugs was found in his possession. What made the incident worse was that the man was a member of the Shah's entourage when the ruler visited Europe at the time. But he was quickly released through diplomatic immunity channels and returned to Iran without having to pay for his crime.

What infuriated the public about these escapades was the fact that the government was dealing very firmly with drug smugglers who didn't have these connections. The press regularly ran stories about smugglers who were apprehended and received long jail sentences or were executed.

There had traditionally been a constant flow of drugs into the country from neighboring Afghanistan; it was the preserve largely of the Turkoman tribes that spread across the border. The two or three hundred mile long brick wall built by the Sassanians 1,500 years earlier to keep out invaders from the northeast Iran was covered by earth; it had served as a road for the smugglers in this thinly populated region for centuries. However, when the gendarmes clamped down and put up a blockade, it led to constant running battles. The smaller drug traffickers from Tehran and other parts of Iran began to help the big-time smugglers bring in drugs, tea and other contraband. Iran had its own tea, but it was not of high quality, so there was a heavy demand for illegally imported Indian tea.

In Tehran and other towns, the police also kept watch on and constantly raided the opium dens frequented by ordinary people. While the upper class smoked and chewed freely at their swank parties, the rest of the public was forced to take their pleasures more and more furtively. The opium dens frequented by men from the office-worker and truck-driving class were in several of the poorest quarters of Tehran. The men sat around smoking and drinking glasses of strong tea, chatting fitfully, and sitting mostly on the floor. My friends told me that these places were being protected; that probably meant the local police chief had been bribed or was getting his own supplies through these places.

This information made me smile to myself as I recalled going to the home of a well-respected senator in a fashionable northern suburb of Tehran. The host had had no compunction in inviting us to join him in his opium den downstairs after dinner. There were other Iranian officials there, and they didn't turn a hair either. I remember it so well because it was one of my first small Iranian dinner parties. Those I had attended previously were usually huge affairs with up to a hundred guests; one either sat around or stood drinking anything from tea to whiskey and ate fruit and the small cucumbers beloved by all Iranians until a buffet dinner was served at around 11:00 p.m. On those occasions, you left for home right after eating.

This party was a hastily arranged affair by the senator, who had business with my husband and a delegation of American businessmen, and he decided they should be his guests at home rather than at a restaurant. I learned about it only as I was relaxing at home waiting for my husband to return. The phone rang; a woman told me I was invited too and that my husband's car was on the way to collect me. I was still in my stable clothes, and it was 10:30 at night. I frantically showered and threw on a long, soft pink dress of Persian design that a local dress designer had made for me. I had just pulled my long, straight, brown hair back into a bun and was swiftly applying my makeup when our maid came into my room to tell me that Kiani, our driver, was at the gate waiting for me.

Upon arrival at the senator's impressive mansion, I was ushered into a huge, marble-floored hall to be welcomed by the hostess. Dinner was a bit of an ordeal because I didn't eat much by Iranian standards, and since this was a sit-down affair, I couldn't hide that fact from my hosts. As well, I was seated between the senator and the president of my husband's American company and was expected to translate; the senator spoke no English, and Don's boss spoke no Farsi. As I thought we were about to get up from the table, the senator said to me in Farsi, "Ask Mr. Reynolds if he would like to have an after-dinner smoke of opium."

I was really shocked because I had heard that many of the high officials had their own private opium dens but had never seen one.

"*Nemitunam!*" "I can't!" was my reply.

"What did he say?" asked Louis Reynolds.

"Nothing," I said.

"Why can't you ask him, Khonume Rose?"

"Because it is not a question I want to ask my husband's boss. Smoking opium is illegal in the States, and I just can't ask him."

"What did he say?" Louis wanted to know what we were talking about.

"Nothing."

"I know it wasn't nothing, Gail!"

"Ask him, Khonume!"

"All right. The senator wants to know if you would like to smoke opium with him."

"I certainly would!" was his reply.

We descended a flight of stairs to a room in the lower level of the house that had not one stick of conventional Western furniture. I was familiar with such traditional Iranian rooms but had never attended a smoking session in them. I saw beautiful cushions made from tribal carpets and woven camel and donkey bags. The floor was covered with layers of beautiful Persian carpets laid one on top of the other. In Iran, carpets signify wealth.

My hostess and I waited outside for a minute or two while the men put on their smoking pants. When we entered, each of them was wearing a pair of black, silk, pantaloon-type trousers. They sat in a circle on cushions, and we were motioned to join them. Once we were settled, the door opened and a servant carrying a charcoal burner entered and placed it on the floor in front of our host.

"*Tariaq mikeshid, Khonume?*" the senator asked me; he wanted to know if I had ever smoked opium.

"*Ta allan, nakheir, Agha,*" "Not yet," I answered.

I had seen pictures of men sitting around smoking this product of the pale, mauve poppy that once was grown all over Iran squatting around a brazier with porcelain-bowl opium pipes to their lips, but I hadn't dreamed I would ever try my hand at it. Among upper-class Iranians of our host's generation, opium smoking had been a daily pastime. I remember my surprise when I learned that an opium bowl and pipe were components of the royal regalia in the days of the Qajar kings, who vacated the Peacock Throne in the early twenties after almost two hundred years of rule. Smoking the drug had been as common to the court and landowners, women as well as men, as alcohol is among Westerners today. Old people looked upon it as the fountain of youth that kept them from getting older.

The servant stoked the small brazier filled with white-hot charcoal. He pulled out of his pocket a traditional opium pipe, an egg-shaped porcelain ball attached to a wooden, flutelike pipe about eleven inches long by a brass fitting.

At the senator's instruction, I explained that it was an old Iranian custom to smoke opium after dinner.

"I've smoked a little pot, but I've never had the chance to try any of this stronger stuff. What's it going to do to me? Have you ever tried it?" my husband's boss asked me.

"No, I haven't tried it. I don't really know what it does to you, but I'll ask the senator."

The senator explained that it didn't hurt to smoke it as long as one didn't become addicted and smoke it all the time. It was great psychological drug that helped clear one's mind and made one's thinking clearer. As well, it was an effective medicine that would take away pain and relax muscles. One could have the most stimulating conversations while under its influence.

All of the Americans save my husband seemed fascinated. I could tell that they all wanted to try it, but I could also tell that each one was afraid to be the first.

"I'll try anything," said one. "It'd be fun, but I don't know whether I should, as I have to take a plane early in the morning," another said. And so the discussion went as the servant was stoking up the fire and cutting up the pencil-thin piece of dark-brown opium.

"Don," ordered one of my husband's superiors, "you're the one who lives here and is supposed to know all about Iranian ways, so you must be the first to try. Then you tell us how it feels and maybe the rest of us will try it too."

"I'm sorry, sir. I've just given up smoking cigarettes, and I don't want to smoke anything," Don replied firmly. "I'm having a hard enough time as it is."

"Well then, I guess that leaves it up to your wife to be the guinea pig. If she tries it, we'll all have a puff."

"Frankly, I'm not too keen to try," I said. "I've tried grass and hash, but I hate the stuff. It makes me feel terrible the next day, and I have to get up early tomorrow because I have a busy day at the stables."

"Oh come on. You have to be the one." They all began needling me.

My Persian hostess said she smoked it all the time. She would be the first to toke and would show me how to do it. "You will see that it is not at all like hash!" she said. "I promise you that you'll like it. Come on, have a try."

She showed me how to take the pipe in my lips and blow out until the little blob of opium stuck to the porcelain bowl just under the tiny pinhole began to bubble from the heat of the piece of red-hot charcoal that was being held about half an inch from it by long, thin tongs. She told me that when the opium bubbled and a vapor formed, I was to suck as long and hard as I could and to hold the opium vapor in my lungs as long as possible so the vapor would enter my bloodstream. I watched her do it, and I watched the senator take a small blob about a quarter of an inch thick and continue smoking and heating it until it had all but disappeared from the side of the pipe.

I could put it off no longer. It was my turn. All eyes were on me. I held the pipe in shaking hands and put my lips cautiously on the smooth wooden stem. I pursed my lips; the senator held the small piece of charcoal near the blob of opium. I began to blow out slowly; I expelled the air from my lungs twice before I began to see bubbles on the brown opium.

"*Mikeshid, Mikeshid!*" ordered the senator, so I began to suck in. I was shocked by the sensation of the smoke entering my throat and lungs; it felt soft and cool and medicinal all at once and not at all like tobacco, marijuana, or hash. It was like inhaling a billowing cumulus cloud. I blew out again and drew in my breath; I continued until there was just the tiniest brown stain on the bowl where the opium had just shortly before been.

"How does it feel? How does it feel?" everyone asked me.

I waited a moment because I was beginning to feel a weight lifted off my shoulders, which had been sore from riding six horses that day. My head was slowly lifting off the top of my neck. My whole body felt totally relaxed.

"It's fantastic! I feel like me, but I feel so relaxed and yet in complete control. I don't know how I'll feel tomorrow, but I feel great at this moment."

And so the pipe was passed around to the five foreigners. Don still refused to try though I did my best to persuade him. Mimi, the senator's hostess for the evening, started another pipe and began passing it so that there were two going. Everyone agreed that a feeling of confidence came over them after the drug took effect. The men began talking about the business deal they were trying to make with the Iranian government. They were able to ask the senator questions without being at all inhibited, and he gave them the best answers and advice he could.

We smoked and talked into the wee hours. No one seemed to get tired at all. As we were leaving, which we did together, we agreed that if given the opportunity to smoke opium again, none of us would hesitate. When I got home and laid my head on my pillow, I fell asleep almost immediately.

Whether any of the others had the opportunity I will never know. As for me, I was quite surprised when the following week I was at a party and one of my friends asked me, "*Tariaq mikeshid?*" "Did I smoke opium?" Having heard my affirmative reply, she told me to follow her. We entered what I thought was one of the bedrooms to find it was an opium den that was almost a replica of the senator's den. I recalled that I had been asked the question many times before but naturally had always replied no. After that first time, a whole new world opened for me. It was amazing that I had lived in Iran for over two years before being introduced to the secret of the Persian social set. From then on, I could instinctively tell when I went to a party whether there was an opium den in the house. If there was, I more often than not went to have a toke or two during the evening.

I did enjoy the sensation, and I suffered no ill effects the following day. I certainly could not become addicted to something that I had the opportunity to partake of only a couple of times a month, and often, months went by when I did not have the opportunity at all. Opium was strictly a social thing for the people I knew, and there was certainly no smoking alone. Often nowadays, when I am feeling upset, tired, or sore, I wish for a puff of opium.

It was not until the late 1950s that opium became illegal unless bought by a carded addict. Many of the older clergy if not all smoked because they felt it brought them nearer to their maker. It is said that hallucinations can occur through excessive use of the drug, and nonbelievers contend it was the cause of many apparitions Iran's holy men have seen.

Opium was freely available for older people. It had been in use so widely until it became illegal that the government, while trying to discourage its use and making some attempt to provide treatment, had to accept the fact that many older citizens had become addicted to it and it would have been too cruel to cut off their supplies. Generally, anyone over age sixty could buy a gram of opium at a drug store. It had to be signed for, and the individual's birth certificate had to be shown. People could also register with the government narcotics bureau as an addict. They received cards they could present to get their rations.

If you haven't been associated with drug takers, it isn't always easy to tell when somebody is really gone on the stuff. I remember how surprised I was to realize that my friend Ali Reza Soudavar was that way. I'd heard the gossip but had dismissed it since I saw him so often and he'd always appeared pretty normal to me.

Toward the end of my time in Iran, he decided to leave; his father had wanted him to take over his business as the sole agent for Mercedes-Benz in Iran, but he didn't want that. He asked me to look after his stables while he was away. When I went to get his last-minute instructions the day before he was to leave, I learned the full extent of his addiction.

I was shown into his office and saw him shaking badly. His hands were bent like claws making him look almost deformed. I hadn't seen him for a couple of months—I had been skiing in Italy—so I was shocked.

"Ali, what's the matter? You look terrible!" I blurted out.

"I feel terrible too," he said miserably. "I've been having a bad time with drugs."

"What do you mean drugs?"

"You know that I'm a heroin addict." He sounded almost irritated that I'd asked the question. I told him I'd heard gossip but hadn't believed it.

"The heroin's the reason I bought a place in Ireland. I've tried three cures here in Iran, but they didn't work. And the stuff here is so easy to get that I'm always tempted. I'm going into hospital in London, and then I'll stay in Ireland."

The doctor he was going to was the wife of a British diplomat who had developed a system combining acupuncture and electronic stimuli while living with her husband in China. She was having considerable success, and the fact that she had agreed to take him as a patient had given Ali the will to do something about himself.

He opened a magazine that lay on the table in front of him and pulled out two pieces of aluminum foil. One piece he folded into a trough about six inches long, and the other he rolled into a cone-like straw. He pulled a 35 mm film container out of his pocket and popped off the top. He poured a little of the contents, which were brown crystals, onto the trough. He took the trough in one hand, put the straw with the narrow end in his mouth, and lit his cricket lighter, which he held with his free hand under the trough containing the brown stuff. I saw the crystals start to melt and a vapor rise from them. Ali bent his head down so that the aluminum cone protruding from his mouth was directly over the melting substance. He began to inhale the vapor.

I watched in silence as he went through the procedure and finally asked, "What is that stuff, Ali?"

"Don't you really know?"

"No I don't."

"It's brown sugar."

"What's brown sugar? You're talking to a dumb Canadian you know, Ali."

"It's heroin. We can't get the refined stuff here in Iran, but this stuff does the job just as well. It's really terrible for you. Don't ever try it."

"I have no intention of that, Ali."

We sat and talked for some time, but Ali gradually began to get bleary eyed and finally almost fell asleep. He had refilled the little trough many times during the course of our visit. I finally took my leave and went home.

As it turned out, Ali didn't leave Iran the next day or the one after; it took him some weeks to get himself together to leave. During that time, I saw him almost every day. I was able firsthand to see what a danger heroin was to the human system when its use was abused. Ali got thinner and thinner, his hands became more and more deformed, and he finally seemed unable to walk properly. He was completely different from the man I had met four years earlier.

It seemed Ali was into all kinds of drugs. I recalled one afternoon when I had arrived at his place just in time to sit down to one of his houseman Morad's sumptuous Persian lunches with Ali and a few of his friends. I was exhausted; I had been out late the night before and had been working at the stables since five in the mourning. I knew that Ali and his pals were prone to taking pills, so I broached the subject with him.

"Ali, I'm really exhausted today. You don't by any chance have something that would wake me up? I once took Ritalin when I was driving for twelve hours, and it was super. Something like that might just give me what I need to school this horse of yours for you and drive home without falling asleep at the wheel."

"I have something that will work. I'll give it to you after lunch."

"I don't have any uppers, but I have this stuff which is better anyway," he said when I walked into his office after we had eaten. I shut the door behind me and walked over to the desk where he was seated. I looked at what he had in front of him; I was puzzled. His hands were on a small picture frame that seemed to have a cartoon in it, and on the glass was a little pile of white powder.

"What is it?" I queried a little scared because I knew what it must be.

"It's coke. Have you ever done it before?"

"You've got to be kidding. Me? I thought only drug addicts took that stuff. I really don't want to try it!"

"Don't be so stupid! It won't hurt you. All you do is take a little sniff. I'll show you how, and you'll feel marvelous. You won't be addicted to coke. I'm your friend. Do you think I'd give you something that would hurt you?"

"'No, no. I'm just frightened to try it."

"It won't hurt you. Here's how you do it."

He rolled up a $100 bill he just happened to have in his desk drawer. With a razor blade that had one edge taped, he chopped the white crystals into two thin lines of powder. "You put this straw up to your nose, close one nostril with a finger, and then inhale the line of coke as deeply as you can into your nose."

"I don't think I can do it," I said shakily.

"Don't blow out or you'll blow it all away. It's easy. Let me show you." He bent his head to the little frame using the money straw and sucked a line of powder into his nostril.

"You do the other line. I'll make another one for you because you need two to really have the effect."

I still hesitated.

"Don't be such a chicken. Just go ahead and snort it. It won't kill you. I'm still standing, and I've done it lots of times."

I did as I was told. The sensation in my nostril was like making a dive into a pool and having the water go up your nose. It hurt and itched, and I wanted to sneeze.

"Don't sneeze because you'll just sneeze it all out. Keep sniffing in while I make you another line. It's a strange sensation to the nose the first few times, but after you get used to it, it feels great. Here you go. Take this one in the other nostril."

I again obeyed and experienced the same sensation in the other nostril. My eyes began to water, and I pressed my upper lip to stop the sneeze that was about to come. Suddenly, I felt as though I had just had ten hours of sleep. My head cleared, and I felt very wide awake. I could conquer the world!

On my way home from Karaj that evening after having ridden two horses for Ali, I still felt exhilarated. I thought I could very easily become addicted to cocaine. My nose was still running a little, and its tip was slightly numb as was the back of my throat, but I was wide awake and aware—so aware. It was a clear evening, and as I approached Tehran from the west, I saw the cone of the high Damavand Mountain a frothy pink in the reflection of the sunset behind me. That mountain will remain a symbol of cocaine to me until I die.

I had enjoyed my first experience with cocaine, and Ali knew it. After that, he would often offer me a snort to tide me over or just for the fun of it. Occasionally, he would bring out his little cartoon frame with the coke piled in a corner, a razor blade, and a red and white plastic straw after we finished lunch. I certainly didn't become addicted to coke, but I had access to it whenever I wanted. One day, Ali asked me if I would like a supply of my own.

"It isn't something that I really must have, no thanks," I replied. "And I'm not about to spend money on something I don't really need or want. Why do you ask?"

"Well, Mahmadi has a new supply, and if you want some, just go into his room. He's feeling generous today."

Mahmadi, his brother, was a known heroin addict. When young, he had suffered from cancer of the spine and had begun to take the stuff to relieve his pain while studying in New York. He was caught with drugs in the US and jailed. His father, fortunately, was owed some favor by the Shah, and he appealed to him to have Mahmadi extradited. He promised he would punish his son himself. Mahmadi was brought back to Iran, but his punishment seemed to have been overlooked.

When I walked into Mahmadi's room, he was sitting cross-legged on a low bed. In front of him was a clear plastic shirt bag bulging with what I realized must be coke.

"Hey, man, do you want some coke?" he queried. "Just look at this stuff! It's the best!" He seemed absolutely delighted with his stash. "Do you know how much this is worth?" I had no idea. "Well, there's about fifty thousand dollars' worth of straight, pure, uncut coke in this bag." I was astounded. He took a film container on the bedside table and dipped it into the bag. He capped it and threw it to me. "That's a little bonus from me for all the help you've been giving us here. We appreciate it. Any time you run out of the stuff, just ask me and I'll get you some more."

"I imagine this will last me for quite some time," I said as I looked in the phial to see that it was completely full of white crystals and rocks of cocaine. I was a little frightened that I was about to take drugs home to my house and most probably use them. What was this Iran doing to me?

Ali Reza Sudovar went to London to take his cure. Once he finished his treatment, he went to Ireland, and everyone who saw him commented on the new lease on life he had apparently found. We were all looking forward to seeing him when he sent a message to say he was coming to Tehran on a visit to renew his passport. On the way, he stopped in London at a hotel where he had often stayed. In the morning, a maid found him lifeless in bed. They said he had died of a heart attack. It was a cruel blow of fate.

Going back to the hotel may well have been his fatal move. Some of his friends in London said it was known there that he used dope; they thought somebody probably told a pusher that he was around. They thought Ali might have tried a whiff of something just for old times' sake and taken a fatal dose, but there was never any proof of that.

Ali and Mahmadi were charming people, but money was their downfall as it was for many other young Iranians who were given unbelievable amounts by their newly rich parents. How often did I hear indulgent mothers and fathers saying that they wanted their children to enjoy the best things in life while they were young and could really appreciate them? It was a fatal indulgence in hundreds of cases. I went to parties in the smart homes in north Tehran at which scores of handsome young men and beautiful young girls were ruining their lives nightly by smoking and sniffing different drugs. That reduced the girls' sensitivity to their vulnerability in this male-dominated society, and they soon found they had damaged their marriage prospects irrevocably. They then threw caution to the winds and gave themselves up to lives of debauchery.

Smoking hash was common among the foreign community in Tehran. I had an English friend whose French wife was a bit of a hippie who enjoyed smoking marijuana before she came to Iran. She had been told that if you visited some of the many beautiful parks in the city, hash dealers would approach you. Marijuana was not available in Iran, but hash was plentiful. She sent her husband to Farah Park, which was close to their house, to get her some. The poor man went down many times and sat on benches for hours but was never approached by dealers. She was getting anxious that he hadn't been able to find her any when one day they stopped by the side of the road to buy some pickled walnuts sold by venders at almost every corner. When he was paying for them, the little old Persian fellow asked, "Do you want some hash too?" So he finally found his source.

It was only in the last couple of years that some real progress was made in developing treatment facilities for addicts along with tightening control on some smuggling routes. The government built hospitals in different areas in the early seventies to treat addicts. Some were opened up one Iranian New Year, before their staffs were ready presumably, because the Shah had ordered that they should be hastened and because the Ministry of Health at the time had not honored its pledge to the UN officials. Most of the nurses and doctors didn't have proper training in the field of drug abuse, so their effectiveness was limited right up until the revolution.

Mount Damavand

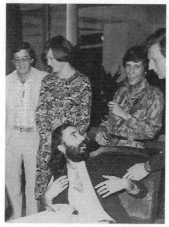

Ali Reza Soudovar and friends

Old man smoking his opium

CHAPTER  13

The World of the Press

In the seventies, Tehran had two English-language morning papers until lack of advertising closed them a few weeks after the revolution. The competition between them allowed foreigners to get much better insight into what was happening in Iran. Advertising rates were almost as high as in the Western industrialized countries at the peak of the boom. The salaries paid were high too in relation to most countries where expatriate British and American journalists found work, so there was usually plenty of talent around.

Social columns were popular with Iranians, who had never had them until the English papers began them in the sixties. Business and social activity reached almost frenzied proportions in the early seventies, and the English papers in Iran began to chronicle it. Clever officials realized that a word or two of praise in the gossip columns was worth a whole article in the political or business sections. Since they had traditionally bribed reporters to write nice things about them or had paid the newspapers to print articles the officials wrote themselves, the public had become very skeptical of what they read about politics or business, so the new social pages became the place where the true politics could be discovered.

There were many independent articles on development projects albeit pretty superficial in many cases. There was more praise than objectivity, and any criticism usually aroused furious denials by the officials involved. The reporters enjoyed the sporting and cultural occasions because of the lavish hospitality that usually went along with them. In the last few years of the Pahlavi regime, piles of caviar and gallons of champagne flowed at receptions thrown by every kind of organization from ministries to banks. Undistinguished indeed was the senior official or businessman who failed to appear in the social columns.

My friend James Underwood, an English reporter, seemed to switch between the two English dailies with bewildering regularity. He had a prodigious memory and could rattle off the most difficult foreign and Iranian names in his column every day. He was often critical in particular of official intolerance in the social columns and elsewhere. Though fired more than once and told frequently by the Ministry of Information officials that he should not write in Iran any more, his tact usually rehabilitated him quickly. If he'd been an Iranian however, SAVAK would probably have beaten the hell out of him, he admitted. They were always nervous about touching foreigners for fear of the Shah's wrath if the country's image was affected.

David Frost was encouraged to make a film on Iran in return for a gigantic sum of course! He got a bit of "imperialitis" during his filmmaking thanks to the helicopters and other lavish attention he was given when filming. An American archeologist acquaintance told me how Frost had arrived at Malyan, the site believed to be the center of the area where Cyrus the Great was born in southern Iran, and was thoroughly petulant when the archeologist in charge wasn't there at the hour they were to meet. "Tell him to phone me immediately!" Frost snapped as he stomped angrily back to his chopper and flew off, though there wasn't a telephone within miles of the place.

Many small specialist publications were of very low quality, but they survived because advertising rates were very high and they were outlets for people whose only way to get their interests put across was by paying the proprietors of these small magazines to publish their opinions. The Tehran *Economist* was a bilingual paper owned and run by a former Communist who expressed his independent points of view frequently and thus spent a considerable period of time in prison due to the content of his publication. *Echo of Tehran* was essential reading for embassy and business people in the early seventies. This publication had many troubles with officialdom; their writers and editors spent time in prison as well.

Kayhan International was the prestige paper for Iranians, but its rival, the *Tehran Journal*, was often more interesting and daring though it was largely staffed by foreigners and was hampered by a skimpy budget. But both covered the local scene fairly adequately. Their particular appeal lay in the fact that many Iranians who had left home to study in Britain or the States early in life spoke and read English better than Farsi, so the English-language press thus had a readership of natives and expatriates.

The pertinence of the English-language papers was that they were read, or so it was widely believed, by the Shah every morning. People felt that if they got publicity in the *Kayhan International* especially, the Shah would be sure to read about them. That's why they were sensitive to criticism in it as well. If he did read these papers, the Shah was probably doing so to find out the world news in the language in which the international agencies had put it out. Iranians are notoriously bad translators, and no doubt the Shah found it safer to rely on the original English version of the stories.

Although few of the writers on these newspapers knew more than superficially the fields about which they were writing, the coverage of both the English-language papers made them far superior to their counterparts in most non-English speaking parts of the world. When the foreign influx had reached its height, their circulations went into the twenty thousands. Advertising revenues must have been phenomenal, but distribution remained poor because it was in the hands of local people who refused to change their habits.

One time, I flew to Shiraz on a 7:00 a.m. flight from Tehran that brought in the newspapers. The trip took one hour. I asked at the hotel if they could give me a copy at 9:00 a.m. as I sat down for breakfast, and they told me the papers were not delivered to them until 11:30 a.m. I asked why that was and learned the local distributors had an agreement not to collect the papers from the airport or start distributing them until 10:00 a.m. No pressures from Tehran ever changed these procedures. The local representatives remained impervious to complaints; "It's an agreement," they said, and no power on earth seemed to be able to influence it.

Kayhan International had been founded a few years after the *Tehran Journal* by a group of serious-minded Iranians who felt that they and the world needed to know what educated Iranians were thinking. The man appointed as the publishing company's president, Mostafa Mesbahzadeh, was a former Mossadeq supporter who was brought back to Iran and rehabilitated through the intervention of Court Minister Asadollah Alam. Mesbahzadeh came from the region around the Persian Gulf port of Bandar Abbas, where Alam's name until recent times meant as much if not more than that of the Shah. I was told that Alam, through the court ministry, put up much of Mesbahzadeh's share in the company. It really became a gold mine in spite of the widespread fiddling by many of the executives when the boom came and advertising rates went up to the same rates as in the West.

Mesbahzadeh always tried to please Alam, who got him for instance to sponsor a horse show in conjunction with the Royal Horse Society, where I was in charge of show jumping. His fawning manner with Alam was very obvious, but Alam was to die in 1978 before unrest in Iran really steamrollered and when the press obtained its freedom. Mesbahzadeh either permitted or couldn't stop his staff from turning on the Shah and all that Alam stood for. He made his escape in good time to avoid retribution from the mob for his serving the Shah's interests.

By the end, the newspapers were really powerless to influence policy even if they had wanted to. The printers were pro-Khomeini, and the editorial staffs were either Khomeini men or leftists to a man; they were in control. No moderate opinion was given a hearing.

In the early seventies, the Shah decided to close many of Tehran's smaller publications because they were it was suspected taking money from foreign sources and their criticisms were felt to be irrelevant and unnecessary in a society that was going along so well in His Majesty's opinion.

It was true that Iranian journals observed no rules in their personal attacks on officials they didn't like and usually chose vulnerable targets rather than those who had the power to hit back. Libel laws didn't exist, but money could always ensure you had nothing bad written about you or earn you unjustified praise from a grateful publisher. The stories one heard about the owners of some of the smaller publications were so scurrilous that you wouldn't have believed them if you didn't mix freely with Iranians and could see for yourself that it was possible they were true.

It was reputed that the proprietor of a weekly called *Farman* had founded his fortunes in the early days of his publication by writing stories about families or individuals that were shown them before publication and then usually being paid not to publish them. He later earned the Shah's approval by helping negotiate with restive Kurdish chieftains and getting them to behave; he had married into a prominent Kurdish family and had obtained their confidence. His efforts were a valuable service to his country, and he was rewarded with a seat in parliament and other favors.

My curiosity about the family was aroused when I met his eldest son, Bahman, who took over his father's seat in parliament and was a seemingly successful public relations man when I arrived in Iran. Portly Bahman, in his early thirties, had a lovely and talented wife and two children; he seemed on top of the world at that time. He came to all the horse shows and was the honorary commentator at most of them.

But by the time I left Iran, his reputation had become so unsavory he had lost not only his seat in parliament but also his wife and business. Allegations of minor fraud over a long period led to Bahman finally being stripped of his Majlis seat he had taken over from his father. The speaker told him he could not be a candidate at the government-controlled elections because of his deteriorating reputation, and that was the end of his political career.

After that disgrace, his attempts to build up a false reputation for himself became more insistent than ever. The fact that he was still to be seen, in spite of all the stories, talking to top officials at social functions led people to give him the benefit of the doubt over a long period. So Bahman didn't find it difficult to obtain a suite at the Royal Tehran Hilton in which to set up a new business. The manager there saw him every day with top officials and ambassadors, so when Bahman delayed payment, he decided discretion was the better part of valor. The hotel was actually owned by the court through the Pahlavi Foundation, and it gave Bahman plenty of time.

Meanwhile, Bahman seems to have decided to go for a quick picking perhaps to get the bill paid before it screwed up his other activities. The top carpet dealers in downtown Ferdowsi Avenue one morning received telephone calls from the Hilton telling them that a Mr. Bahman was buying carpets for the president of Zambia and asking them to bring only their finest wares to his suite at the Hilton. These smart businessmen did that, but they had run up against somebody smarter that time. When they rang up Bahman at his suite a few days later, he had given up the suite, and he and the carpets were gone. The Hilton manager seemed as surprised as they were. The carpet men went to the press, and their story appeared in the big-circulation Persian paper *Ettelaat* with a description of Bahman as chubby and bespectacled. The following day, a publication wrote that it knew of only two Bahmans in town who could answer that description and there was no doubt which one it was.

I could never find out what happened next, but Bahman, disappeared for a brief spell and then emerged smiling and apparently unassailable. One court official insisted that Bahman had actually been in jail and was later bought out by his family.

I saw from closer at hand another purloined and chimerical deal Bahman executed, and I couldn't help admiring the smooth way he got himself the chance to drive around Tehran for a month in one of the world's most unique automobiles.

Jim O'Donnell, a big, congenial American who had taken over the name and patents of the famous old Stutz Bearcat car, brought one of them to show at the Tehran International Trade Fair in 1975. He had made only ten of them; he had sold two to movie stars, one to King Hussein of Jordan, and a couple more to sheikhs in the Arab Emirates. Each of the cars was almost completely handmade in O'Donnell's small workshop. The one he brought to Tehran was a very handsome silver-gray with a soft-blue interior of real leather seats and dyed mouton carpet. When I saw the car, it really took my fancy, but the price tag of $50,000, which was a lot in those days, didn't.

I was a little surprised one evening when I went to the Hilton for dinner and saw the Stutz parked just outside the front door. Inside, I saw Jim O'Donnell sitting with none other than our friend Bahman. When I asked Bahman where he'd been, he stood up, kissed me on both cheeks like a long-lost friend, and said airily, "I've been busy with government matters. Then by a stroke of luck, I met Mr. O'Donnell here. He wants to sell his beautiful Stutz to the Shah. What do you think of that?"

"It seems you have not been idle," I replied saucily. "It's probably just the kind of car His Majesty would like—one of a kind."

When Jim asked if I really thought the Shah might look at it, I told him just how enthusiastic the Shah was about cars. I knew about the 1927 maroon Rolls-Royce limo I had seen in the imperial garage. It was a beautiful car in mint condition, and it was the first vehicle bought by the Shah's father, Reza Shah. The store the Shah set by it was shown by the fact that he had turned down an offer of over $1 million for it. I had heard that from Kambiz Atabai, my boss, who was in charge of the garage. Rolls-Royce had a multimillion-dollar collection of their own cars, and the only one example missing was of the model and year of the Shah's. The Shah's reply to the offer was that if the car was worth $1 million to Rolls-Royce, it was worth that much to him, so he wouldn't sell. He wanted it for himself.

"That's what I've been telling Jim," Bahman said. "It's exactly what I've been saying. Right, Jim?" Poor Jim didn't have a chance to answer; Bahman went on. "I'm going to take the Stutz personally to show it to Princess Shams. The point is that if she wants it, the Shah will want one too, so you Jim, will be able to sell two, this one to the princess and another specially made to the Shah. What do you think of my plan?"

"Sounds just like you, Bahman. You always have something going. I must run now. Nice to have seen you. See you soon." I waved goodbye quickly and was off to join my friends for dinner.

A few days later, I talked with Jim again; he was very excited about the prospect of selling his car to Princess Shams. He told me that he had gone out with Bahman to her beautiful Pearl Palace the day before and had met her.

"'Really?" I was astounded for I had heard she was out of the country.

"Yes. We drove the car out and parked it right at the front door of the palace. Bahman went in and came back out with the princess and some man, very distinguished. I think it was her husband. They didn't speak English, so I didn't talk to them, but Bahman introduced us. I sat in the back seat with the man while Bahman drove the princess around her estate. Afterward, the three of them went into the house for some time. When he came back out, Bahman said that she really liked the car and would let him know in a few days."

"Well, I hope you sell it, Jim." I said. "But I'd be careful of Bahman if I were you."

The next time I saw Bahman, I couldn't resist needling him just a little. "Have you sold the car to the princess yet, Bahman?"

"No, unfortunately not because she is allergic to the mouton carpet. But we are going to build her another one, and hopefully, the Shah will purchase this car we have here now. Jim is leaving tomorrow for the States and has hired me as sales manager of his Iranian operation."

"Congratulations!" I said, but I wondered what the operation was other than selling the car.

For the next month, Bahman was seen driving around the streets of Tehran in the Stutz Bearcat. I always wondered how he managed to not get it banged up. He had not yet been able to get the ear of the Shah, but he assured Jim every day that it was imminent.

From a friend who worked for Princess Shams, I heard that Bahman had taken Jim to the palace while the princess was indeed away on vacation and had shown it to the housekeeper and butler; he had them pretend to be the princess and her husband. I wondered how he would con Jim into believing the Shah was really looking at the car.

I should not have doubted Bahman, though, for he flaunted the car so often in the face of Kambiz Atabai that the latter was forced to take the car into the court garage for the mechanics to look at. The Shah himself went to see it one day while he was riding at Farahabad. He wasn't overly impressed, but he did say that if Mr. O'Donnell wanted to give it as a gift, he would greatly appreciate it. He would personally pay the import tax on the car rather than have Jim do that. How generous of him.

Bahman was of course unable to give the car as a gift without the say-so of Jim, so he took it away from Farahabad, where it had been housed for about three weeks, and again began driving it on the streets. Kambiz was a little upset that the car was not being given as a gift; he thought that the Shah should have whatever he wanted, and Kambiz, his personal assistant, wanted to give him what he had shown him. So he began to turn some wheels that would put a spanner in the works for Bahman and perhaps get the car for the Shah.

Bahman was stopped by the police while driving the car because it did not have the proper import duty sticker. The vehicle was impounded and eventually ended up in the garage of the Imperial Court again, where I saw it one afternoon. Eventually, O'Donnell got wind of what had happened. He came back to Iran to claim and ship the car back to the US.

Nearly everybody you met in Tehran society had stories of Bahman's exploits from his student days in London up to the previous evening. Many claimed he was a SAVAK agent; the German community became convinced of that after one of their companies dispensed with his public relations services they had been using. The following morning, officials descended on their offices to check the papers of every expatriate employee, and those whose residence permits were not in order were immediately ordered out of Iran.

The break in his marriage came after Shayesteh, his wife, had been caught shoplifting in a London store. Unfortunately, Bahman advised her to plead diplomatic immunity as the wife of an Iranian member of parliament, but Bahman was no longer an MP at that time, and the immunity would not have been allowed if he had been anyway.

The sad upshot of this was that the London newspapers printed details of her case because they thought she was the wife of a member of Iran's parliament. Had she just pled guilty and paid up, nobody perhaps would ever have known.

Back in Tehran, Bahman's family was furious about her escapade. Shayesteh's sister Mahin was married to Bahman's brother, so before long, both sisters were divorced. Friends of the two sisters said that they had been divorced because of Shayesteh's disgrace, which offers another insight into Tehran's upper class.

A more sympathetic character I met in the Tehran press scene was Luigi Ghisletta, a reporter for *Kayhan International*. In spite of that Italian name, Louis, as everyone called him, was a chip off the old British block except in his dealings with the opposite sex; then, the Italian side was stronger. Louis had arrived in Iran in the early sixties as the husband of a beautiful young Iranian girl who was the niece of one of the Shah's closest friends, Hossain Fardoust. Fardoust had been sent to school in Switzerland with the Shah and at one point was in charge of his friend's security.

The Iranian girl was Louis's third wife though he was barely thirty when he came to Tehran. He had married twice in London, where he had come into the world as the son of a waiter at Claridge's who rose to become that famous hotel's banquet manager. As a child, Luigi claimed, he met Winston Churchill, who ate late at night at the hotel, and developed a taste for the statesman's favorite dish, steak tartar.

Luigi was still a young-looking man when I met him in the early seventies. He was already married to a fourth wife by that time, a young Armenian girl more than twenty years his junior. He had some magnetic appeal for young women that wasn't apparent to all of us. When the crash came, he was already preparing for his fifth wedding to a girl again more than twenty years his junior. He had gone through a spell of heavy drinking and come out of it but leaving behind his youthful looks. Nonetheless, his new love absolutely doted on him in spite of the fact that like all her predecessors, she hated steak tartar but was forced to eat it many evenings from Louis's fork. Winston Churchill died without knowing just how he had influenced the lives of so many attractive young women with his eating habits.

Luigi was only one of a colorful band of expat newspaper people I encountered in Tehran. Most of them sat through the revolution working for foreign news agencies or just helping the mass of foreign reporters who flew in to cover the events. That way, they could at least pay the rent, and somehow, it had always been easy to survive in Tehran. The Tehranis accepted foreigners with all their foibles and treated them as virtual equals.

That ability of foreigners to survive in Tehran was perhaps best exemplified by a British woman reporter who had wandered in there after working in San Francisco, various parts of Africa, and other out-of-the-way parts of the world. She was one of the most generous souls I ever met, but she was unfortunately afflicted by an obsession with crude, worthless men she could never control.

One of her boyfriends in Tehran was a young Iranian Jew who regularly made her pregnant. When complications set in after one mistake, she was advised to go to Britain for treatment. That she did leaving the boyfriend with her flat and a note to her employers telling them to pay him her salary so he could put it in the bank and the checks she had given for her rent would be honored. None of us would ever have trusted an Iranian like him to keep his word on such a matter. The guy of course spent the money; he also sold all her carpets while she was away and spent that too. When she returned, she was jailed immediately for having written a bad check, which in Iran at that time was a crime punishable by prison.

The world of the press and the reporters was a very colorful part of the society in Iran during the regime of Mohamed Reza Pahlavi.

James Underwood with Sulu Rose

Princes Shams' Pearl Palace

CHAPTER 14

Industry

In the late sixties, the Shah called on Louis Reynolds to talk about the building of an aluminum smelter in Iran. The Shah was collecting vast sums for himself and his country from the oil revenues, but he was at that time fully aware that the oil would not last forever. He wanted to industrialize the country to diversify its sources of revenue.

Aluminum was the metal of the future, and Reynolds was a good, solid company that was willing to go into Iran with an operation that would within a few years of production commencing be turned over directly to the Iranians. Louis talked a good story, and so did the Shah. Reynold didn't have to put up any money initially, for its 25 percent share in the Iranian Aluminum Company, Iralco as it became known, and the Shah didn't have to start paying for his technical know-how until the plant began production. Each thought he had made the best deal. It was not until production began and the Iranians failed to begin paying for their know-how that Reynolds decided it wouldn't put in capital for the 25 percent interest. Instead, they decided to put nothing in and just retain a 14 percent interest in the company.

My husband, Don, and I arrived in Iran just two months before production began at the smelter built in Arak, about 150 miles southwest of Tehran. Don was to become the marketing manager, a rather pretentious title in a company that had nothing other than aluminum ingots and billets to sell. In actual fact, his job was to teach the newly returned from exile Qajar prince who was to be the sales manager how to do his job without letting the man realize he was being trained. That was the role of so many foreign experts in Iran at that time. Most Iranians had such egos that they felt they were qualified to hold any job no matter in what field as the result of a degree either genuinely or falsely earned.

Roqnehdin Kadjar—he used that spelling—as this particular paragon was called, was the son of the last of the Qajar shahs before Reza Shah replaced him. He had been raised in Europe having left Iran when a babe with members of the family who decided to accept exile rather than risk the humor of the feared Reza Khan, as the monarch was known before he took the throne. Roqneh had landed a job with Alcan, the Canadian Aluminum Company, in Switzerland when he finally graduated from college in his early thirties. Like most Iranians, he had taken years with his college education to have plenty of time to play before he had to settle down to a proper job. In Switzerland, he married a very attractive Swiss girl who treated him with the princely respect he felt he deserved.

During the years he worked with Alcan, he became involved in the international sales of electrical equipment, and being Iranian, he was asked to handle the Middle East as part of his territory. Before he could visit Iran, he had to regain his Iranian nationality, and when he got to know the country, he fell in love with it.

When he saw the advertisement for a sales manager with Iralco, he promptly applied. He left no stone unturned in his efforts to get the job; he contacted members of his family in Iran to use their influence on his behalf. Through Roqneh, Don and I met many of the former princes and princesses of the old Qajar Dynasty. I had been taken aback when we had first attended these Qajar parties by the number of princes and princesses with whom I was hobnobbing. I thought it was illegal for them to use their titles publicly under the Pahlavi Dynasty, but they clung to them in private.

When the plant started production, Roqneh was terribly impressed with the fact that he was selling not only to the domestic market but also abroad. At that time, total annual Iranian consumption of aluminum was close to 14,000 tons, but the plant was producing 40,000 tons of aluminum ingot. Like all Iranians of his status, he refused to make calls on customers. He would sit in his posh office and receive customers who wanted to buy some of this new commodity from the Iranian makers.

One night at a dinner party, he told me, "It's really wonderful to have these uneducated men from the bazaar come to my office and beg me to sell them some of our aluminum. Many of them remember when my father was the shah, and they bow and scrape to me as if I were still a part of the ruling family."

To them, there was no difference between the Pahlavis and the Qajars. Thus he sat selling to the domestic market and yet not caring what these people were doing with the metal. He condescended to sell to them only because the Iranian government had stopped all imports of aluminum to protect the company.

Meanwhile, Don went into the field to see the primitive plants where foil, pots and pans, and other aluminum products were made. He became familiar with the managers and owners in the industry. During the years we were in the country, he expanded the domestic consumption to 150,000 tons of metal by advising and cajoling the leaders in the field to bring in new presses so they could expand their businesses and push the sales of the finished products. Importation was once again permitted by that time to help fill the gap as business expanded. Plans were made for a smelter that would produce an additional 150,000 tons.

Aluminum became a multimillion-dollar industry during the five years Don was there developing the markets. It came as a bit of a shock to him when Roqneh said to him the day we were leaving Iran, "You know, Don, I'm sorry I was unable to teach you that the salesman's job is in the office, not mixing with *hoi polloi*." This was so Iranian. Don felt a bit of a failure in relation to his training of Roqneh.

From the start, of course, there was a great deal of trouble with the Iranian metal. The people who had been importing the metal to Iran were naturally irate when their livelihood was taken away from them to protect the government-owned project. Industrial sabotage took place in the cast house, where ingots were melted and poured into billet form that was used in the extrusion presses. The supposedly tightly protected pots were pouring out billets with rocks that would jam and break the purchasers' dies. That created a desperate situation because the dies were for the most part imported. At that time, there was no die caster in Iran who could make the sophisticated dies needed for the presses, and each die cost upward of $3,000. There were complaints from every major maker of aluminum goods in the country. It seemed that the quality of the metal itself was good but the rocks that somehow got into it were ruining their production rates.

Roqneh cared little for the manufacturers' problems. He blamed the cast house in Arak and did nothing about the complaints. It lay in Don's hands to pacify these customers. He was happy to do that, and in the process, he made many fast friends. He became known among them as Mr. Aluminum. Even the Shah said to me at the stables one day, "Your husband is Mr. Aluminum." That was a bit of a surprise.

When complaints came from the Japanese, who had been sold poor billets, the Iranians refused to make good what they had sold, and as a result, Iralco gained a very poor reputation in the international metals market. But that did not affect the company a great deal at that time because there was such a shortage of aluminum that companies all over the world were begging for it.

Don and Roqneh had many serious arguments because Don tried to make good the poor metal that had been sold in the country. When he took back a whole shipment of billets on one occasion, Roqneh blocked the move and had it sent back to its purchaser. The latter telephoned in a rage to Don, who again told the purchaser to send it back to Arak. It eventually ended up in the yard at the plant, where it sat collecting dust while the Iranian experts tried to figure out why there were so many inclusions in the billets. Roqneh threatened to refuse sales to this customer, who had just put in a large aluminum electric cable plant. Fortunately, senior government officials took up the matter and insisted that because the angry customer's plant was supplying cable for government projects, it had to be kept operational.

It was never learned who actually was putting the rocks and scraps into the molten baths of metal, but even with strict security, the problem continued until the government lifted the ban on imported aluminum billets and ingots.

When the Shah first talked to Louis Reynolds, he had promised that the new super dams he had built in Iran would ensure a surplus of the electric power that was so essential to the production of aluminum. Yet it was only a year after production started that the power allotted to the plant had to be cut for a brief period during August, when the country planned to celebrate the beginning of the Pahlavi Dynasty with spectacular fireworks and decorative lighting on all government buildings and monuments. The electricity was needed, it was explained, for the week of the celebrations. The plant could shut down partially for that period and could start up again when the power would not be needed for the lights.

What the officials did not realize was that it was a very expensive matter to let a line of smelter pots shut down and restart them. The metal freezes in the pots when the electricity is cut off, and then, when they are restarted, they must be completely emptied of the frozen metal. That took pneumatic hammers and many days of work. Such a cut in power would cost the company hundreds of thousands of dollars.

This first shortage of power worried the company's executives, but they didn't know to what extent the shortage would affect them. By the end of 1975, only half the pots could be supplied with electricity because power was needed for so many other projects; it meant that the company was producing only half of the metal it should have been putting out. Naturally, the financial loss caused a lot of criticism.

Other problems added considerably to costs. Iran had no minable bauxite from which the alumina needed to produce aluminum was extracted, so it imported its raw material from Australia by sea. Congestion arose at the ports as government and private enterprises began importing every kind of material and merchandise; ships bringing in the alumina couldn't get in to land their cargo. The heavy surcharges put on for these delays meant that a consignment was costing the company $5,000 a day while waiting outside the port. One Iralco cargo waited fifteen days outside Bandar Abbas on the Persian Gulf, meaning an additional $75,000 for the cost of producing the aluminum.

There were not enough trucks nor drivers ready to risk their lives over some of the hazardous mountain roads of Iran that delivering goods to their destinations required. That also meant long delays for the consignments in dockyards after they were off-loaded. That gave some enterprising officials the idea of presenting a program to the Shah that could speed the off-loading process, and the plan seemed quite feasible. The Iranian government would buy 7,000 White trucks and trailers costing upward of $50,000 each. The White company would set up a training center in Iran, where in three to four weeks, drivers would learn to handle and maintain the vehicles.

Once licensed, a driver would sign a contract to make two trips a week for five years; at the end of that period, the government would give him the very valuable tractor-trailer. It sounded like a great deal; a group of three or four drivers could start up their own trucking company that would be worth at least $200,000 without having invested a nickel. It was felt that Iranians would naturally jump at the chance.

The trucks were paid for and arrived in the mid-seventies. Two years later, 4,000 of them still sat in the port facility. Why? Very few men could be recruited to take the wonderful opportunity being offered them. When I asked my driver why he didn't try this line of action when he was complaining bitterly one day about not having enough money, he simply replied, "That is not the life for me. To drive twice each week to Bandar Shapour and back would be too much. I would not have more than two days off, and I would be so tired then that I couldn't have any fun."

"But think, Kiani, of the valuable truck you would own at the end of five years," I said. "These trucks are huge and have so many modern conveniences like beds and stereos. You could take a buddy along, and then you would not be that tired."

"No! The roads are too dangerous. I would most likely be killed, and then the truck would be of no use to me anyway."

Others complained that the roads were too bumpy and it would be hard on their backs, and others thought it was too difficult to drive such a vehicle. The dropout rate for those who started the drivers' training program was very high. Iranians lacked any sense of dedication; in spite of their complaints, they would always opt for the easy life. In the end, exasperated officials had to bring in Korean, Filipino, and other nationality drivers to keep goods moving.

Some funny things happened as a result of that port chaos. I remember that on his return from a trip to the US, my boss, Kambiz Atabai, told me of the fabulous station wagon he had ordered for the Shah. His Majesty loved cars and was often seen driving himself incognito to or from the ski area an hour and a half from Tehran. The new station wagon had been ordered from General Motors with precise specifications. It was to have every extra that could be put on it, including bulletproof glass and steel. It was to be powder-blue, the color of the security force cars. Kambiz was very excited about the car because he personally had gone to Detroit to order it, and he could hardly wait for its arrival in Iran so he could personally present it to the Shah.

Many months later, I was in his office when he called in his driver. He handed him a bill of lading and a set of car keys telling him to make haste to pick up the new car at the port and drive it very carefully back to Tehran. I didn't think any more about the car until a few days later when I noted that Kambiz still seemed to be driving himself around.

One morning at the stables, he asked me, "Remember the car I told you about?"

"Oh yes. Has it arrived? I'd love to see it."

"Unfortunately not. Jafar got to the port, and they were unable to find the car. He has been there all week and no sign of it. It is somehow lost in all that congestion."

"I'm sure it'll turn up, Kambiz." He was too. But it didn't. The car was never found.

"What do you think happened to that station wagon you bought for His Majesty?" I asked him one day months later.

"It either got sent to one of the nearby states having been sold by someone connected with the port, or some stupid Iranians stripped it and sold the parts. You know that nothing is sacred here anymore. It matters not that it was something for the king of the nation. These stupid people don't care."

The laziness and dishonesty of ordinary Iranian workers led to the wholesale importation of foreign workers on every level from 1976 on. Drivers, clerks, and store men poured in especially from India and Pakistan. It was estimated that there could have been a million immigrants from the subcontinent alone, just before the collapse, to take jobs Iranians felt they could do. The Shah's impatience and the greed of the owners of industry and business sparked this gigantic influx of foreigners. Iranians had always looked down on the people who lived around them, and though the Indians and the Pakistanis were unassuming people who lived modestly, they began to be resented as much as the Westerners who lived in considerable luxury even when they were often only junior executives.

Permission to import even their own semi-skilled labor was a godsend for foreign companies. They were exhausted by the battles with Iranian officials and the hopeless outlook of the Iranians who worked for them. They felt they had a chance to complete their contracts without wasting a large part of their profits.

Of course in this helter-skelter development, the Iranians felt overlooked. How easy it was when the opposition began its anti-shah campaign to let the monarch be seen as the agent for all these foreigners who were eating up Iran's wealth. It redounded immensely to the credit of ordinary Iranians however, who though they mouthed threats and unnerved many of the foreign communities, hurt hardly anybody. Had Khomeini and his associates urged them to kill foreigners, I've no doubt that many would have done so, but the leaders of the Iranian revolution preserved an admirable firm line in repeated calls for no physical harm to be done to foreigners throughout the dangerous period.

It was not just Western countries that were busy in Iran. Indian heavy industry had a sizable stake, the Shah having developed a healthy respect for their standards. A Tehran-based Hindu family, the Hindujas, had close contacts with the court via Prince Shahram, and they won many lucrative contracts for Indian industry. Unfortunately, the prince's business methods helped stain the Hindujas's reputation somewhat toward the end.

The biggest Soviet project was the steel mill being built near Isfahan. Unfortunately, the process used was an old-fashioned one designed to allow the growth of auxiliary industries alongside it. A large satellite town was built with Soviet technical assistance near the site too. The concept of the steel mill scheme was probably more suited to the Iranian people's real development needs than were other industries that achieved much greater efficiency. Iralco was an exception rather than the rule by achieving its aims so quickly; many other industries employing the latest modern methods were working at only up to half their capacity even after several years.

The steel mill seemed designed to provide as much work as possible in conjunction with its growth especially in the development of the small-scale industries Iran was so short of in light of its labor's limited skills. But it just didn't really get moving on producing the steel it was supposed to produce.

The first time Don and I went to see it, we were struck by the awesome silence of what should have been a noisy, dynamic factory. We waited so long for the tour to start that we began to suspect they were afraid Don might see things were wrong, so we left.

It was only a few weeks later that the Iralco people asked Don to go down to the mill with another American expert to see if they could get the Russian quantum meter working. When they arrived, having taken several hours to negotiate the hazardous roads between Arak and Isfahan, they were informed that the man who was in charge of the quantum meter was away and that they would not be able to see it that day. They stayed the night nearby and went again to the mill the following day to be told another story. So they decided that was the end of it and they would go back to Arak.

The following week, they were again requested to go to the mill to see if they could get the quantum meter working. When they refused, pressure was brought through some high government official, so there was no way they could avoid going. When they finally were able to get in to look at the quantum meter, they saw a totally obsolete monstrosity that was the size of half a room. It was in very bad shape, and it seemed it had never worked.

The engineering expert worked for many hours and finally succeeded in getting it going. But it was then decided that the procedure for working the piece of antiquated equipment was so complicated that it would be better if the mill sent its samples of metal up to Arak, where Iralco could test them with their equipment and send the results back.

Nearly a decade after the mill began working, it was producing only pig iron and very few other types of steel. However amazingly, by 1978, this gigantic plant was producing 1.9 million tons of steel annually.

Another Soviet project was the machine tools factory planned to produce many types of sophisticated tools and parts that had not even been thought of in Iran up to that time. It was a specialized company that in this case was about ten years ahead of its time. But the government wanted a machine tool company, so that is what it got. The factory was built in Arak alongside the Iralco plant.

Many Russians stayed on in Arak to train the Iranians for the factory. They lived in the same complex of homes as did the American technicians for Iralco. It was a subdivision of American-type homes in the middle of the desert. There was some grass that had taken much longer than that of the Iralco plant to become established, and the stench of the camel dung used on it nearly drove the Americans and Russians mad.

The two nationalities did not readily mingle, but Jack, a good friend of ours who was Iralco's plant manager, became quite friendly with his counterpart at Machine Sazi. The Russian couple accepted invitations to dinner with Jack and his wife, but the Americans were never invited into the Russians' home.

The Russian plant manager came to Jack in great distress one night telling him his daughter was very ill. Jack was only too happy to lend the Russian his car to take the suffering child to the hospital in town just a few miles away. Jack knew that the Russians were not allowed to drive cars; they had the use of a car and driver during the daytime but not at night.

One morning a week or so later, another Russian came to Jack in his office to tell him that he was the new plant manager of the machine tool factory. A little confused, Jack asked what had happened to his friend. The Russian sighed and explained that he had been dismissed for improper conduct. When he was pressed, he admitted that it was because the poor man had borrowed the car of an American.

There are countless stories about the new industries being set up in Iran and of official and private attempts by the Iranians to avoid keeping their sides of agreements. There were agreements that went as projected, but they were in the minority. Iranians even at the top had a "What's mine is mine, and what's yours is mine if I can possibly do you out of it" attitude. There was sometimes an unmistakable admiration on the part of Iranians, who should have known better, for their compatriots who brought off the biggest cons or straightforward frauds. "That's a smart fellow," they would say.

The really hardheaded businessmen in Iran couldn't go wrong because profit margins were so enormous. They were reduced in 1975 when the new middle class of Tehran began to complain about the prices of consumer articles along with increase in rents and things such as municipal taxes. However, the reductions still gave Iranian businessmen profits that made them the envy of their counterparts elsewhere. Thanks both to Don's contacts with the Elghanian aluminum goods factory and my own friendship with his son, Fereydun, I got to know Habib Elghanian, the leader of the Iranian Jewish community, fairly well while I was in Iran. He was one of the victims of the 1975 government's campaign against industrialists on the profits question.

The profits on most merchandise in Iran up to 1975 rarely fell below 100 percent and was often as high as 200 percent on an item. Elghanian's plastics company had total control of the market and prices, and it was among those most seriously affected when the government insisted profits be cut drastically to respond to the public outcry on prices.

Companies were given three weeks to submit a list of their new prices to the Ministry of Commerce. There was a threat of prison if satisfactory prices were not agreed upon at the end of the period. Habib Elghanian, as chairman of the board of Plasco, just made the deadline with his price proposals. But three nights later, the police came to his home in the wee hours of the morning and took him away. His panic-stricken wife immediately tried to contact influential friends but found that the phone wires had been pulled out of the wall outside their house.

Afraid to leave the house, Mrs. Elghanian had to wait until daylight to let the rest of the family know what had happened. For three days, all efforts to find out Habib's whereabouts produced no results. Finally, son Fereydun managed to contact his riding friend Sohrab Khalvati and persuaded him to ask his son-in-law, SAVAK boss General Nassiri, where his father was. Fereydun finally learned that his father had been sent to the small town of Sanandaj in western Iran under sentence of banishment from Tehran following a conviction for profiteering.

During the three days he had been held in custody in Tehran, he had been submitted to frequent sessions of aggressive questioning before a summary trial. This was the way the government made scapegoats out of people regardless of their standing or of their loyalty or service to Iran. Some of the cynical officials who sniggered when they heard what happened to Elghanian stopped smiling when they were sacrificed in the same way later.

Elghanian appears to have been a model prisoner in Sanandaj; after two months in this cool city in the Kurdish hills, he was allowed to have his car and driver sent to him. Although he was not allowed to communicate directly with his businesses in Tehran, unlike one of three other top industrialists who suffered the same fate, he spent his time buying up land as speculation for the future.

One of his colleagues in exile, who was supposed to be incarcerated at the desert town of Tabas in eastern Iran, actually got himself moved into a private suite at the Hyatt Hotel in the city of Mashad, a few hundred miles away. From there on a private line he purchased, he conducted his business operations as if in Tehran until the Tehran newspapers published the news of where he was and what he was doing. The authorities sent him back to the desert.

At the end of six months, Elghanian and the others being held were told they could return to Tehran. He cabled his family to meet him at the airport the next day. As the plane landed in Tehran, his heart rose at the prospect of seeing his wife and sons again. He was on his feet the moment the plane landed, but the man sitting next to him put his hand on his arm and said, "I'm afraid you must sit down again, Mr. Elghanian." Habib was about to give him a smart reply when the man pulled out his police identity card. Habib was confused. *What do they want with me now?* He wondered.

After everyone else had disembarked, the man led Elghanian to the door of the plane. Below, he saw a police car and three officers waiting. He was handcuffed and whisked away to the crowded Qasr Prison, where he was put into a cell with common criminals. It took several days for him to find out that the crime for which he was being held was the engagement of a lawyer to clear the family name when he was told he was released in Sanandaj. He spent three more months in jail. When he was released, he was firmly told he should abandon any attempt to right what had been done to him and his family. This was SAVAK-controlled justice in Iran.

Habib continued his life as before; he ran the family business, acted as the spokesman for the Tehran Jewish community, and organized the dispatch of large sums to Israel. When Khomeini came back to Tehran, Elghanian backed the community's approach to the religious leader to express support for him when he took power.

I also learned just how easy it was for people involved in advising on deals to make money in Iran. Don had been asked to make a feasibility study on a sheet-rolling mill that would produce aluminum sheet and foil in which the Shah's eldest sister planned to invest. After a lot of hard work, Don realized and recommended that a hot-roll system would be best and that the most advantageous place to purchase such a system was the US. But one of the princess's friends and advisers had other ideas. He was at that time Iran's ambassador to Italy and had a close association with the owner of a company there that specialized in installing turnkey, cold-rolling mill operations.

One afternoon, Don phoned me to say he was having dinner with an Italian who wanted to talk about the rolling mill. He said that he thought he had something that would convince Don the operation should use the Italian system rather than the US system.

Over dinner at the Hilton, the Italian exposed his hand. He offered Don $100,000 if he would recommend that they buy the Italian equipment. He certainly had something; he said that people in higher positions were taking large amounts and that the mere pittance he was offering Don would never be noticed. I think Don wanted to punch him in the nose. He was a Reynolds man down to his toenails, and the fact that the guy had the audacity to think someone with such connections would be open to a bribe infuriated him. But he controlled himself. When he got home, he told me, "I have to talk to the Iranian managing director about all this pressure building up. It stinks!"

When he told his friend Bahman, who was the CEO, he laughed. He knew that there was too much at stake for the ambassador and others to let the project go anyplace except to the Italians. IDRO—the Iranian Development Organization—would purchase the Italian cold-rolling mill. With this *fait accompli*, Don's recommendation for the hot mill was accepted for the second phase scheduled for two years after the project began.

In addition to the royal family, nearly all the top establishment had big interests in different businesses and industries. Officials such as the SAVAK boss Nassiri had interests in many construction companies. With his influence it was easy to obtain contracts that earned vast profits. One of these companies got the contract to build the new security prisons that would be under his control. The general was paid handsomely to run them and earned plenty building them.

One time, the Shah ordered a new regulation banning government officials from holding interests in private business. It went on the statute book all right, but it never took effect. Indeed, the situation worsened toward the end. It seemed that half the population of Tehran was engaged in private-enterprise import businesses as the mania for consumer goods and luxuries such as foreign foods grew. I had virtually nothing to do with business, but even in my isolation from what was going on, I saw an incredible race for money. Even the so-called liberal opponents of the Shah were coining it in their businesses. That's how Iran was near the end of the Pahlavi reign.

Aluminum fabricating shop

CHAPTER 15

The Last Days

The majority of Iranians including the Shah didn't understand the mechanics of a Western-style society. The fact that the structure of Iranian society had been virtually unchanged after so many years of complete isolation from the West prevented the formation of a genuine meritocracy that could have utilized the best brains and experience among Iranians.

Officials from the upper class could not stand those of a lower order being promoted over them. Young graduates returning from the West could not stand the attitudes of the older men who controlled the universities and government departments. The struggle to have modern ideas accepted was too protracted for the limited stamina of most of them.

I will detail how the administrative setup in Iran worked. The Majlis was the lower house of the Iranian legislature from 1906 until 1979, while the upper house was the Senate. This was created by the Iranian Constitution of 1906 (Iranian calendar year 1285). Under the rule of the Shah, many noteworthy bills were passed including the Oil Nationalization Bill and the Family Protection Bill, which gave women many basic rights (though women were not allowed to vote until 1963) as part of the reforms under the Shah's White Revolution. All bills had to be ratified by the Majlis and approved by the Senate before going into effect.

The Court Ministry ran the affairs of the Shah's court and took no orders from the central administration. Even if the Shah had ordered that it should, its officials certainly did not do more than pay lip service to the order. At best, it tried to keep its relations polite with the country's government. However, having worked with court officials, I was often appalled at how arrogantly even minor ones told administrative departments who raised questions of governmental policy vis-à-vis court projects that Hoveyda, the prime minister, had no authority over them.

Empress Farah's private bureau, a ministry unto itself, did work in association with both the Court Ministry and the government, but executive decisions were the responsibility of Farah herself as far as could be seen. The fact that she had the Shah's ear each day meant she could manipulate policy in favor of what she wanted to do. Her sound, friendly relationship with Hoveyda meant this probably irritated him less than did the autocratic attitude of the court itself.

The Ministry of Culture and Arts remained under the personal control of Minister Pahlbod, the Shah's brother-in-law. He survived every government reshuffle until the name of the royal family was dragged through the mud by the opposition in mid-1978. He lost his job after well over a decade in the post when that happened. As far as could be seen during Hoveyda's tenure in office, he had no control over what was done by this ministry.

Both Princess Shams and Princess Ashraf ran big organizations with attendant business sections that avoided any interference from outside officials. Many of their administrators worked as well in the Court Ministry, so they had its protection against any attempt by the central government to control them. There seemed to be no queries, at least in public debate, on the budgets of these virtually autonomous organizations when they were approved by the Majlis.

In 1961, the Shah founded the Pahlavi Foundation, which looked after the royal family's investments; it held much of the wealth he had inherited from his father. The foundation, a nonprofit organization, held the majority of the Shah's investments including the Omran Bank, luxury hotels, all the casinos in the country, and many large land holdings.

The absence of public accountability in the upper echelon of society enabled people with budgets at their disposal to patronize their families and friends as far as jobs were concerned. Disgruntled young technocrats who couldn't or wouldn't get on with other officials persuaded their patrons to give them projects of institutions where they could indulge their individuality and talents. Under the umbrella of a prince, princess, the Court Ministry, or any other organization that would finance them, they would indulge in esoteric research supposed to help future planning or projects that took years to come to fruition.

What Iran needed from all its people who were educated abroad or in the country itself was practical teaching and administration with plenty of attention to work in the field. Unfortunately, that didn't often occur due to the social-status norms of a backward society. For those who couldn't find themselves a high-falutin' title under the umbrella of the court or some other patron, the central government had its Plan Organization. This was a jungle of departments crammed full of people who had graduated from universities in the West and were between the ages of twenty-five and fifty who spent their days arguing and drinking tea. They would be called upon periodically to develop plans for some area or other. They would be secunded to jobs in different areas of the administration, where they would have a special title and a project that as often as not faded away. They then returned to the Plan Organization building for more tea and discussion.

The Shah's plan to invite international organizations to hold their conferences in Iran to help polish his image with the outside world was good; it provided jobs for many of these Western-educated people. From human rights to sewage disposal, the conference subjects brought in international civil servants and experts of all kinds for up to a couple of weeks of junketing and tourism interspersed with talk sessions. All the relevant senior officials threw parties, delivered papers, and perhaps with an eye to the future tried to impress the UN and other officials with their abilities in the fields under review.

One should not get the impression that nothing was being done in Iran. The private sector was developing at a colossal rate, but in the public sector, the development was only on the surface to a large degree. What made it go was the fact that officials at all levels could take a cut out of all government money being spent on providing new facilities. If they didn't build or equip anything, they couldn't expect their percentage or in the lower echelons their tips for facilitating things for contractors. Indeed, the frenetic rate of building of hospitals, schools, roads, and other amenities gave visitors to Iran the impression that this was one country where everything was being done for the people. In many of the new factories, the equipment was the most modern that could be acquired.

However, when it came to staffing, the situation in these new institutions was generally pathetic. They were mostly showplaces—an establishment that looked impressive on paper but was thoroughly inadequate in practice. A public hospital would have two or three local doctors who made more money from private practice than they did from their government jobs; the standards for technicians and nurses would be abysmally low. In the private hospitals, which turned out to be money-minting vehicles for their partners, standards were somewhat higher, but most people couldn't afford them.

It was the same everywhere. Because of the lack of training facilities, unqualified people took a great proportion of the jobs. Their inability to properly carry out their duties held down the pace of work and brought about stagnation. Since they got paid anyway, they had no incentive to improve themselves. A few devoted officials together with UN experts carried on the battle to create proper training facilities in practical fields, but the backwardness and lack of aptitude on the part of young people whose elementary schooling was so pathetically bad meant there was precious little material to work with.

SAVAK, the Shah's security organization, was another section of the administration that operated autonomously and infiltrated all areas of life in such a way that it became a weapon for the Shah to fragment any move to construct a real public opinion. By doing that, it suffocated the incentive of those with a social conscience and left the people with virtually no champions and no voice to let the Shah know what they thought and what was wrong.

SAVAK wasn't just looking after the security of the realm. Most of its ill treatment of political prisoners was meant to humiliate them, not to pry out information. That's why its bestiality became almost unlimited; those who carried out the tortures and humiliations had carte blanche to do so as long as they liked, unless a prisoner relented and was willing to publicly admit it, thereby giving SAVAK its justification.

Even after some semblance of accountability to the Shah and the public was established in the late sixties, the people, including those who had the power and standing to complain about SAVAK's excesses, were so cowed by its previous viciousness that they failed to recover their will to fight it.

Western newspapers always made much of the torture of political prisoners, but SAVAK's arm reached out to controlling the days and nights of the great mass of Iranians through a combination of intermittent thuggery and the use of psychological pressures so that life was stifling for the people.

An understanding of the social administrative setup in which Iranians lived and worked, helps us understand how corruption found such fertile soil in Iran as development raced on, and how corruption spread to the ordinary man like the garbage collector and the servant, who by the middle seventies would refuse to work if he didn't receive regular perks.

SAVAK was called in to deal with people who stepped out of line by saying or writing original thoughts. Higher up the ladder, the Shah dismissed any senior official or officer who showed initiative beyond the basic guidelines of the command structure. As was well known, the Shah controlled promotions of all officers in the military over a certain rank; that was one reason his army collapsed in the final days of the revolution. By then, the Shah had lost his ability to think and act decisively, and no officer could act decisively without his backing. Officers of real talent and integrity had come to be regarded with suspicion. Unless they were in the Shah's immediate circle, they never got key positions. In the ministries, SAVAK officials, not the ministers, had real control. On the economic side, the Shah was more closely in touch with matters, and the very intricacy of the subject meant the security men played a less-significant role. But in cultural and press areas, the SAVAK had a tight hand on everything; they appeared to be accountable to nobody.

Every published word and inch of film was censored. Only the queen's office and the television, which was controlled in its earlier years as a relatively small organization by its director, who was Farah's cousin, had sufficient sway to be able to put on original performances or make concession to modern ideas. Television lost much of this freedom toward the end.

The general population had emerged quite suddenly from the captivity and hopelessness of the old feudal system into a world in which at least some of their number, shot up to wealth and seeming freedom that only land holders and bandits previously had. In the cinemas and on television, they began to see a glittering world. When foreigners began to arrive in big numbers, they saw that these outsiders enjoyed a freedom of spirit as well as seeming riches that they naturally felt a wealthy country like theirs should surely be able to give overnight to its people. When it couldn't, they began to resort to every game in the book to get a bit extra for themselves. They cheated and jostled one another for the perks. Honesty seemed to be an undesirable quality in anyone who wanted to succeed.

Though the Shah paid public tribute to his religion, he and many of his officials pursued a determined policy of humiliating the clergy and the simple faith of the common people. Those of the clergy who cooperated were left alone; the brutal treatment meted out to those who objected to changes that they felt contravened Islamic principles led many wise, old religious leaders to compromise and remain silent to save what they did have left.

When the boom first came, the public and especially the young, didn't worry too much about the fate of the clergy. One reason for that was the way modest mullahs lived. They would beg in tattered robes, their shoes worn through or their feet in plastic sandals. They were seen as something for young, self-respecting Iranians to be ashamed of. With the cinemas, discotheques, and snack bars where boys and girls could mix freely, and the arrival of other symbols of a carefree secular existence everywhere, the mournful Shi'ite religion lost much of its appeal. Less sensitive officials too, often treated the clergy with contempt. The mullahs were seen as part of the mass of illiterate nobodies who were of no concern to those who had good jobs and responsibility in the new Iran. One symptom of this was the way non-Muslim guests of officials were taken into the sacred shrines, regardless of the feelings of the devout, who normally packed them. In Islam, holy places were and are barred to nonbelievers.

My fair-haired husband and I were taken to the shrine of Iran's most Holy Saint, the Imam Reza, in the holy city of Mashhad, when we accompanied the Crown Prince and a party of officials on a sporting engagement there. The shrine had been unceremoniously cleared for the prince. We followed at a respectful distance. I was given a chador, a full-length veil, to wear as every woman must cover herself in these places. But when we came out, the crowd recognized me as well as my husband as Westerners and began shouting angrily *"Farangi! Farangi!"* "Foreigners! Foreigners!" Somebody pelted us with tomatoes. Our feelings of triumph at being able to see this holy of holies were seriously diminished by the sense we had hurt people's feelings.

The Shah gave up consulting religious leaders on important matters. Mullahs who questioned his wisdom and the way the country was going were handled roughly. One rarely saw religious representatives at government receptions; drink on the other hand flowed copiously. Pork, of course forbidden to Muslims, was openly served in different forms. It was well known that court officials and their associates had been studying the possibility of setting up vast pig-breeding farms in which to invest. They thought that once other meat became in short supply as consumption rose at such an astronomical rate, the people would have to give up their antipathy to pork if they were not to starve or become vegetarian. They wanted to be the first to profit.

Another aspect of the Shah and his officials' ignoring the religious leaders' feelings was their continued support for Israel. The Shah's government nominally supported the UN resolution calling for Israeli withdrawal from Arab land, and the Shah paid lip service to the idea of a Palestinian homeland sometime in the future. Yet Iran continued to supply Israel with oil, and the Israeli business stake in Iran continued to grow.

As time went on, the Iranian public changed from its general support for the Shah, to animosity to what he was doing, and it started mainly with the young. The toing and froing of students at universities abroad enabled student groups in Iran to have closer contacts with outside organizations. Strikes at universities and other institutions of higher education were better organized. The lighter hand that rested on human-rights activists, in the belief that Iran had reached a stage that they were not so dangerous, enabled closer contacts with them.

Corruption was reaching new heights by 1976, and inflation was really biting. Land holders and other profiteers became crazy with greed, and customs officials were taking cuts uncontrollably on the gigantic import trade. Other officials were filling their pockets. This corruption made the cost of every activity abortively high.

The young people began to find a new sympathy with the community. The bazaar merchants who had originally controlled so much of the economy and business found that the new, slick bankers had taken control of that from them. Older officials and statesmen who had been pushed aside began to get together and talk more about what was happening. Some of the technocrats who had constantly been bypassed by the Hoveyda government began to express their disapproval of the corruption more openly. More articles began appearing in the periodicals in which Western values' effects on Iran were being questioned.

It would be hard even now to say just when the signs of something brewing first showed itself to Westerners living in Iran. It is really only with hindsight that one can recognize the symptoms. The advent of Carter and the naming of Iran among the countries where he was to press for improvement in human rights was a factor, but one suspects this was much more a signal to the opposition groups outside than the somewhat cynical intelligentsia and business community in Iran.

But the Shah put on such a strong face. It seemed he was in such tight control that none of us thought we were in for anything more than a period of unrest, perhaps a new outburst of terrorism. Imperceptibly, without most of us being aware of it, change was coming. The success of the Shah in providing opportunities for so many educated young people to return conversely added to his problems. They could not see why the Shah and his government did not look more seriously at ways to democratize the system without going too far. They felt especially sensitive to what the thousands of young professional foreigners flooding Iran thought of the lack of civil liberties, in a country developing physically at such a rate. Slowly but surely, the wheels were grinding into action to provide the institutions and the programs to help the general Iranians come up to date.

Hoveyda was probably right when he said a few more years could have brought Iran to a point that enough would have been achieved for people to recognize that they were progressing to where they wanted to be. But it was too late. The Shah and his administration's failure to make the people have faith in them, left the door open for other forces to steal the Iranians' imagination.

When the movement began, it snowballed. Average people and the masses of the young adopted Islam for political purposes. It brought to the surface the resentments of the intelligentsia and other thinking Iranians against the Shah's arrogance. They particularly hated the way he lectured the Western world on its faults when they could see the mote in his own eye so clearly; that embarrassed them intensely. Everybody sniffed a chance of a change in the wind, and in keeping with Iranian tradition, they switched horses at the first sign that the one they were riding might be carried away with the current. They could not believe it when the Shah made mistake after mistake. He dismissed the government of Jamshid Amuzegar, who had proved to be no different than the other technocrats in being unable to communicate with the people as the troubles swelled. The rest of the technocratic structure disintegrated. They began to leave. The brain drain became a flood again.

In Amuzagar's place, the Shah appointed Jafar SharifEmami, head of the Senate and of the Pahlavi Foundation and a man who was supposed to persuade the religious leaders and try to bring them back to sanity. The arrests of ministers and other officials were a waste of time. Nassiri's departure from his job as chief of SAVAK a few months earlier had demonstrated that the Shah was losing his grip; everyone saw he was panic-stricken. But it was—let's face it—all his own fault. First, he had the opportunity to be the most benevolent dictator the world had ever known. He had the money; he had twenty years of great wealth with which he could have established a paternal, progressive regime that could have drawn his people into the twentieth century without too much of a shock.

If it were true that there were Iranians with enough political skill to have formed a viable government as an alternative to the Shah, it is also true that Iran was still too backward and disorganized to have supported a democratic system that would have survived for long. The country was still divided by regional and tribal loyalties, and many people felt more tribal than Iranian. They had been Bakhtiari, Baluchi, Qashqai, Turkoman, and members of other tribes for centuries. The Shah's success in giving all these groups a sense of belonging to one country enabled them to identify with one another when this first challenge to him since 1963 came along. The opposition, most of it organized abroad, would have had little hope of moving them on this occasion however, had it not hit on the one common denominator that had earlier held them loosely together—their sensitivity to their religion.

It was around the time when Ayatollah Khomeini became the rallying point for all the opposition forces that the Shah seemed to finally lose his nerve. Did he suddenly realize his mistake? That by sending Khomeini into exile in 1963, he had made a fatal move? Had he also realized the administration in Washington had decided to sacrifice him having confidence that the liberal opposition, not the mullahs, would replace him?

Used to relying on the US embassy for advice and help when faced with difficult problems, he must have felt forlorn that the US was pushing him into a region in which he had no experience. The British were no longer of any significance in this kind of crisis. He must have already begun to suspect the French were playing a clever game—they were said to have asked his approval for giving Khomeini a visa but were making no effort to make the Ayatollah honor the guarantee of no troublemaking that was said to have been a condition of his visa.

The Shah had also lost his two close friends through untimely deaths in the previous months. Asadollah Alam, his court minister for a decade and a man on much better terms with the religious leaders than he was, and oil company chief Manuchehr Eqbal had been the Shah's lifelong advisers. How he must have wished they were there in those last few months.

He had already dismissed most others who could have helped him. Nassiri, his SAVAK chief, was a man of incredibly steadfast loyalty to the Shah. One can only believe that an obsession led him to go to such lengths to put down all forms of opposition. However, his system had not united the technocrats; it had used them and allowed them to prosper. Their reaction of quitting when dropped was totally human. When the military government was appointed, it showed how far the Shah's collapse had gone.

By the time the Shah left Iran, he had done a great deal to complete the task his father, Reza Shah, had entrusted to him—turning his country into a modern secular state and giving it some of the prestige it had enjoyed in Safavid, Sassanian, and Achaemenid times. The son's personal failings had caused the job to remain unfinished. He had none of his father's understanding of human beings.

The revolution of 1979 provided Iranians plenty of food for thought. It was inspired in no small way in my opinion by their dissatisfaction with themselves, not just their rulers. Many who never went near a mosque to pray marched in the demonstrations calling for Khomeini and an Islamic Republic. They wanted to show their disgust with the Shah and the way Iranians were being forced further down the road into the quagmire of corruption and dishonesty. They wanted a cleanup and saw this as the first real hope of achieving one.

These people were certainly not anxious to see an Islamic Republic run by religious fanatics, but having been brought up Muslim, they preferred the title Islamic Republic to People's Republic, which smacked of communism; fifty-odd years of the Soviet Union as a close neighbor had made Iranians instinctively wary of leftist movements.

The mass of uneducated workers and peasants went all the way with the Islamic revolutionaries and Khomeini. The Ayatollah a rallying point for many, became a saint for them; they were ready to die for him, and many of them did when he called on them. They turned against the foreigners who had brought in millions of dollars to carry out development projects that the Iranians themselves were unable in their state of backwardness to do themselves. The foreigners were now working all over Iran in addition to Tehran itself. All the Iranian companies were looking for foreign helpers; their efficiency had helped bring in more work and more money.

The Shah made a big mistake by trying to turn his people back to their old Persian ways as distinct from later Iranian traditions. The Achaemenids he worshiped so mindlessly were ahead of their time. Like the Shah, they had tolerated minorities as long as they toed the line and paid lip service to the greatness of the Shah and the empire.

Parades of protesters on the streets openly insulted the Shah and the royal family. The appearance of communist banners led to the declaration of martial law. The press, hastily freed, turned on the Shah's men savagely. The army was accused of vicious killings. On Friday, September 8, 1978, the morning after martial law was declared, protesters swarmed to Jaleh Square in east Tehran. The military was called in, but the protesters kept pushing toward the military line until the military was forced to open fire. On Black Friday, as it became known, many people were killed or wounded. For a moment, people held their breath. Would it, they asked, stop the unrest? It didn't. The rest is now history.

The country went on strike with the condition for lifting the ban on work, being the departure of the Shah. He seemed to believe that he could survive if he could set up a government made up of opposition liberals, but they too insisted on his departure. For too long, he wouldn't budge. Any last sympathies for him among the business and middle-class professional people disappeared as they saw their livelihoods disintegrating. If the Shah had gone early, there might have been a squeak of a chance for him or at least for the monarchy. The idea of him handing over to his son had been suggested, but Iranians, to virtually a person, soon became anxious to get rid of Mohammad Reza Pahlavi.

By the beginning of 1979, the political unrest had transformed into a revolution that on January 16 forced the Shah to leave his beloved country.

The Shah with President Carter

INTERLUDE

The Shah

The Shah and his entourage left from Mehrabad Airport on the morning of January 16, 1979. All the week before, life at the palace had been frantic with the packing of the royal family's valuables and personal belongings. One of the Shah's most-trusted valets had been sent in a small charter jet to Geneva, where he reportedly deposited the Shah's valuable papers in banks. The flight was kept secret, and it has never been revealed what the papers were.

The Shah had been growing irritable and anxious to leave Iran. He felt betrayed by his people and his allies in the West. The unbreakable bond he always believed had connected him with his subjects was torn asunder; the reality of the people's anger could not be ignored. The Queen, who wanted to save the monarchy and protect her son's chance at the throne, suggested that the Shah leave and let her stay as a symbol of his presence. He wouldn't agree to that; he had become increasingly dependent on her presence and support.

What was not known to the world was that the Shah had contracted a rare lymphocytic blood disorder, Wald Enstrom's disease, in 1973; it was said to be serious but treatable and even curable. He had a team of French and Iranian doctors who treated him secretly; even Empress Farah was kept in the dark at his command. Because he kept himself extremely fit with exercise, running, playing tennis, and riding, his doctors felt that his prognosis was fairly good. He also had a strong personal and psychological character that worked in his favor. His doctors didn't use the term *cancer*;

they thought the disease was only chronic at the time but could become malignant, which it had by the time of his departure.

At the airport, reporters were told that His Majesty was embarking on a vacation and would be returning soon. In the morning before leaving the palace, he met with some of his servants and friends and offered them a chance to accompany him; few accepted the offer. In spite of the pretense that he was leaving on a holiday for recuperation, most everyone knew his was a one-way trip. Two of his close friends with whom I was also good friends, General Manuchehr Khosrodad and General Nader Djahanbani, refused to go with him thinking that they would continue to serve their country as loyal Iranians. Fortunately, my ex-boss, Kambiz Atabai, accepted the offer.

The Shah arrived at Mehrabad Airport before his new prime minister–designate and had to wait for Shapour Bakhtiar, who had been delayed due to the bad traffic caused by the strikes called for by the revolutionaries. He had fought against the Shah for three decades, but he had been the best choice to lead the government at that time. The sad moment of the Shah's departure brought tears to the eyes of Shapour, and the Shah told him, "I hope you will succeed. I give Iran into your care, yours and God's."

Bakhtiar and General Badrei, the commander of the Imperial Guard, followed the Shahbanou and the Shah onto the plane to say their farewells. Neither man would survive the eventual terror of the impending revolution.

The teary-eyed Shah went to the cockpit and piloted the plane during takeoff and for the first hour of the flight. He was worried that they might conspire to take him somewhere other than his planned destination, Egypt. His initial plans had been to go to the United States, but a few days before departure, President Carter had called asking him to stop over to confer with President Sadat and get his visas for entry into the United States that would be waiting for him in Egypt. Unbeknown to the Shah, a number of other countries had also been contacted about offering visas or asylum and virtually all had said no.

The stay in Egypt was short, but President Sadat went out of his way to make the Shah feel not just safe but also royal. After a week, the royal family set out for Morocco, where they were able to stay only a few weeks as King Hassan was under pressure from religious circles to ask the Shah to leave.

Until a few hours before he was to leave, his next destination was unknown. No country was willing to provide the Shah a visiting visa let alone asylum. The government of the Bahamas agreed to give him and his family temporary tourist visas. It was hoped that the family would be able to finally go to the United States because the Shah wanted his children to go to school there. Again, bad news. Things needed to be more settled, Carter said, though the children would be welcome to pursue education if the proper security arrangements could be made for them through a private security company.

England had been another place the Shah and his family would have liked to settle, but after her election, Margret Thatcher was warned against allowing the Shah into Great Britain. Mexico finally agreed to issue visas to him and his family. While he was in Mexico, his health deteriorated, and he needed an operation that could be done safely only in New York. Henry Kissinger, David Rockefeller, and a litany of prominent Americans argued that the Shah must be allowed in on humanitarian grounds. The pressure put on the Carter administration was incessant. On the evening of October 22, 1979, a Gulfstream aircraft landed at LaGuardia airport carrying the Shah and his group. It had been a hard decision for President Carter, but he believed the promise of the Iranian revolutionary officials that they would protect the American diplomats in their country in the event the Shah was allowed to come to the United States for medical reasons.

As the Shah was settling in to his hospital room, students were meeting in Tehran to plan a response to the US decision to allow the Shah into the country. On November 4, 1979, the students climbed the walls of the American Embassy and took diplomats and other staff hostage.

The Shah's hospital stay after an operation and therapy for cancer was not pleasant. It was not just the medical treatment that was a problem; as well, it was the critical news he saw on television, the shouts of the demonstrators he could hear, the fact that his telephone was bugged, and his belief that his room was bugged.

On November 30, he was discharged from the hospital, but again, his destination was not his first choice, Mexico. The Mexican government was afraid their diplomats in Iran might also be taken hostage if they let him in. From the hospital, he was taken to LaGuardia, where he boarded a US Air Force jet that flew him to Lackland Air Force Base in Texas.

The Shah and the Empress were taken to two small rooms that had all the trappings of a prison. The Shah was exhausted and slept, but Farah did not. She wanted to know if they were prisoners and if they would be handed over to the mullahs. Three hours later, they were transferred to a small, three-bedroom bungalow that was usually used for visiting officers. They spent two weeks at the base.

He was then told that they would be going to Panama, where President Royo had agreed to give him asylum. He would stay on the island of Contadoro in a house owned by a successful businessman. There was not much chemistry between the exuberant dictator and the shy, arrogant monarch, but they did get on. Royo called the Shah a *chupon*, an orange bereft of juice and flesh. "This is what happens to a man squeezed by great nations," he said. "After all the juice is gone, they throw him away." The Shah needed another operation, that time to remove his spleen.

On January 15, 1980, one day short of a year after the Shah's departure from his beloved country, Panama's President Royo received an official extradition request for the Shah from Sadeq Gotbzadeh, the Islamic Republic of Iran's foreign minister. It stated that the Iranian regime would not tolerate any longer the presence of the deposed Shah of Iran, a tyrant and criminal, on Panama's soil. President Royo wrote a note to the Islamic Council a week later stating that Panama was considering the extradition request and would abide by international law and hoped that in return, the government of Iran would follow Panama's example and release the American hostages. The release of the hostages was predicted on the arrest and extradition of the Shah, but that step was opposed by Kissinger and many powerful Americans. Around March 20, the Shah received word from Kissinger that he should leave Panama immediately. At the time, the Carter administration was making every effort to keep the Shah in Panama, but that was not to be.

A private jet was chartered from a company suspected of having ties with the CIA. It was finally time for the Shah to accept Sadat's open invitation to return to Egypt. He arrived in Cairo on March 24, 1980. When he saw Sadat, he commented with tears in his eyes, "I've done nothing for you yet, you are the only one to accept me with dignity." President Anwar Sadat had a full military guard awaiting the arrival at the airport.

Shortly after he arrived in Egypt, his spleen was removed; it was found to be full of nodules indicating localization of cell lymphoma. In early July, he underwent surgery again, that time to attend to a sub-diaphragmatic infection, and a liter and a half of pus was drained from his body. There was little hope of recovery. On the morning of July 24, 1980, Mohammed

Reza Pahlavi, former Shahanshah Aryamehr, died in the presence of his family. Iran's once visionary king of the Great Civilization was gone.

The Shah and his regime were not all bad. During his time on the throne, he accomplished many things that were for the good of his country and his people. He maintained a pro-Western foreign policy, and his was the strongest military country in the Middle East, which kept things there relatively safe and calm. His national development program, the White Revolution, modernized Iran; among many other accomplishments, it redistributed extensive land holdings of the wealthy and the mullahs to millions of small farmers, emancipated women and gave them the vote, nationalized the forests and water, and established profit-sharing plans for workers. During his reign, adult literacy programs were begun, thousands of new schools and universities were built, and sanitation and development corps were established. He wanted the best for his country, so he expanded road, rail, and air networks and supported great industrial growth. He loved his country and subjects and believed he had an almost mystical reason for being their king.

Casualties of the Shah
and the Revolution

Ayatollah Ruhollah Khomeini made a statement that during the Shah's reign (1963–1979), "60,000 men, women, and children were martyred by the Shah's regime," and this number appears in the constitution of the Islamic Republic. In fact, researchers have found that there were only 3,164 dead among the anti-shah movement during his time on the throne (1941–1979).

During the revolution itself, the Martyrs Foundation (established after the revolution to compensate survivors of fallen revolutionaries) could identify only 744 dead in Tehran, where most of the casualties were supposed to have occurred, and the coroner's office counted 768 dead.

On January 9, 1978, a protest in the city of Qom prompted by a libelous story that had been published about Khomeini was the first major protest of the revolution. It was at first reported by the opposition of the Shah that 300 had been killed when in fact only five people were found to have died in the protest.

In Tabriz on February 18, 1978, a protest against the rule of the Shah drew troops and tanks from nearby bases. The opposition claimed that 500 demonstrators were killed, but the official count in a recent pro-revolutionary review stated that the total was 13.

The clash between government and protesters that was said to have enraged anti-shah forces and eliminated any hope for compromise occurred on September 8, 1978. The Shah had introduced martial law and banned all demonstrations, but thousands of protesters gathered in Tehran. The Shah's security forces shot and killed demonstrators on what became known as Black Friday. Clerical leadership declared thousands had been massacred, but the number turned out to be eighty-two based on the report from the coroner's office. The reason for such a small number of casualties is that the Shah had been unwilling to massacre his subjects to save his throne; he gave instructions to "do the impossible to avoid bloodshed."

During 1978, many propositions were brought to the Shah's attention. A martial law commander proposed bombing Qom, an air force general offered to kill thousands of protesters to quell the disturbances, a SAVAK general had bloodthirsty plans to put an end to the demonstrations, and the head of Iraq suggested the execution of hundreds of mullahs, but the Shah vetoed all those plans. Iranians thought they would have great, new lives if they ousted the Shah. They were mistaken; they got Ayatollah Ruhollah Khomeini.

Ayatollah Ruhollah Khomeini

Ruhollah Khomeini was born on September 24, 1901, in the little town of Khomeini just forty kilometers south of the city of Sultanabad-Arak on the banks of the Qom River. He was raised by his mother, Hajieh Aga Khonume, and his aunt; his father was murdered five months after his birth.

Ruhollah, which means "spirit of God," began to study the Quran and Persian at age six and continued his religious education at school and with the help of his relatives. He attended a Muslim seminary in Esfahan as a young man and finished his religious education at a new seminary in Sultanabad-Arak, which he had entered at age seventeen. He wore a black turban, which denoted that he was a direct descendent of the prophet Muhammad. On graduation, he was given the title of Sayed Ruhollah Musavi Khomeini.

Toward the end of 1921, he was continuing his studies and began to teach in Qom; there, he was welcomed by Ahmad Shah, the ruler of Iran. He married a fifteen-year-old girl when he was twenty-seven. He had only one wife; they had two sons and three daughters.

He continued teaching and studying Islam until he was appointed an Ayatollah, a supreme religious leader, in the Iranian Shi'ite community in the 1950s. He became a leading scholar of Shi'a Islam, teaching political philosophy, Islamic history, and ethics as well as Islamic law. Though he was not politically active, his writings revealed that he firmly believed in political activism by clerics.

In 1962, he launched a campaign against the Shah's regime for conflicting with Islamic values. In January 1963, the Shah had announced his White Revolution, a program calling for land reform, nationalization of the forests, and the sale of state-owned enterprises to private interests. Also included in this reform were electoral changes to enfranchise women and allow non-Muslims to hold office, profit sharing in industry, and a literacy campaign in the nation's schools. Khomeini regarded these initiatives as dangerous and denounced them vociferously.

Under the Shah, Iran became the first Muslim nation to recognize the State of Israel, and more important, he maintained good relations with Arab nations. This prompted Muslim extremists and especially Khomeini to hate the Shah.

In June of the same year, Khomeini delivered a speech in which he denounced the Shah as a "wretched, miserable man." After that, Khomeini was detained in Qom and put under house arrest until August, when he was released.

In October 1964 in a speech at a huge gathering in Qom, the Ayatollah denounced the Shah as well as the United States and Israel, and he was again arrested. That time, he was driven directly to the Tehran airport and sent into exile, where he stayed for fifteen years.

His first destination was Turkey, where he lived with the family of a colonel in the Turkish military intelligence. To the annoyance of the SAVAK officials who were sent with him, Khomeini enjoyed the Turks and Turkey too much. It was finally decided that he should be allowed to go to the holy Shi'a city of Najaf in Iraq. When he had arrived in Turkey, he had not a penny on him, but when he left, he was a millionaire having been sent large sums for his cause and having received more from Iranian visitors.

On November 14, 1965, his supporters arranged his ceremonial entry into the Holy City. It was his first visit to the "den of snakes" as it was called; he had hoped to go there as a seminarian, but he finally arrived as an exiled cleric plagued by the animosity of the Shi'a clergy of Iraq, who viewed him as a rival and threat. "This *Sayyad* has created havoc in Qom. We must be careful not to let him do the same in Najaf," the clerics were reportedly saying.

Relations between Khomeini and the Iraqi government were not good. He let it be known that his plan was for a government for life, and as Islam had ruled for five centuries, it was the duty of Muslim rulers to return to it and practice it once again.

While in Najaf, he began to realize the value of the media. "Islamic rulers must have a radio program for the introduction of Islam in which the clergy can tell the truth about Islam," he stated. He broadcast his anti-shah doctrine on Iran Free Radio, which he had established with the help of Teymour Bakhtiar and donations to his cause. He fed his propaganda not only to Iran but also to the thousands of Iranian students across the world. He somehow managed to become a cause célèbre among young people though their outlook on life was light-years from his. He spread his pronouncements to the wing of student opposition until the revolution of 1979. Khomeini regularly sent his messages by radio and on tape recordings distributed to students and dissidents around the world.

The Iraqi government began to pressure Khomeini to curtail his activities at the request of the Iranian government, but he had already decided to leave Najaf rather than tone down his anti-shah statements. He traveled to Kuwait but was denied entry when the authorities realized he was the Shah's archenemy. From there, he traveled to France, where a supporter bought a house for him in a town outside Paris. The French government granted Khomeini a visa on the condition he would not stir up trouble. They checked with the Shah, who felt it was safer to have Khomeini in France than anywhere in the Middle East. However, Khomeini did not comply with the conditions of his entrance to France. With the superior (compared to those in Iraq) French telephone and postal connections, he flooded Iran with tapes and recordings of his sermons sent there illegally.

Many Iranians were euphoric thinking about the coming revolution and piled into the movement hoping to gain power in the aftermath; they ignored the fact that Khomeini was the antithesis of all the positions they supported such as women's rights. Though it was clear he was not a liberal, it was perceived that he would be only a figurehead and that the power would eventually be handed to secular groups.

The Shah left Iran on January 16, 1979, and Khomeini waited only ten days to make his return after years in exile. On February 1, he returned to Tehran in a chartered Air France Boeing 747. The welcoming crowd was so large that he was forced to take a helicopter after enthusiastic crowds overwhelmed the car he was in.

He was the undisputed leader of the revolution and had become what some called a semi-divine figure. When asked by a reporter how he felt returning to his home country, Khomeini replied, *"Hich!"* "Nothing!" He made it clear he would reject the government of Prime Minister Shapour Bakhtiar, who had been appointed by the Shah; he said, "I shall kick their teeth in. I appoint the government. I appoint the government in support of the nation."

PART II

Turbans

CHAPTER  1

The Revolution

To the Iranian masses, Ayatollah Ruhollah Khomeini was not an ordinary man. He had become a living symbol of hope for the millions who wanted a leader who would personify their aspirations, restore their spirituality, and bring freedom, independence, and justice. His view was to set the reincarnation of a society that had not existed since the death of the prophet Muhammad in the seventh century. Those who awaited his arrival were looking for a better future—and not necessarily only in spiritual terms.

As he stepped off the plane, the atmosphere was frenzied. Cries of *"Allah-o- Akbar"* went up, and the chant *"Khomeini, O Imam!"* was sung by school children to welcome him. The term *imam* is used to describe a prayer leader in most Muslim countries, but in Shi'a Iran, the title was reserved for the twelve infallible leaders of early Shi'a, so to ordinary people, it carried awe-inspiring connotations. As he stepped off the plane, he was asked, "How do you feel today on returning to Iran after such a long exile?" "I feel nothing," he replied. How could someone who had spent fifteen years in exile and return under these unbelievable conditions feel nothing?

While in exile, he offered a vague utopia designed to maintain the unity of a wide spectrum of leftists, liberal democrats, and Islamist opposition groups, but once back in Iran, his tone began to change. He knew he had to prepare himself to take over the apparatus of the state very quickly; he had to establish his position without alienating those who had helped the revolution.

His first act was to appoint a provisional government; within two days of his arrival, it was agreed that the best man for the provisional prime minister position was Mehdi Bazargan, an Islamic modernist whose democratic credentials were widely accepted. When he accepted the position, he reminded Khomeini of his commitments to democracy and modernization.

Khomeini held a press conference on February 5, 1979, to introduce the new prime minister of the provisional government; he said Bazargan had been chosen regardless of his party's political affiliations. In his speech, Khomeini stated,

> This is not an ordinary government. It is a government based on Shari'a [the religious law of Islam]. Opposition to this government means opposing the Shari'a of Islam, and revolting against the Shari'a and revolt against the government of the Shari'a has its punishment in our law … it is a heavy punishment in Islamic jurisprudence. Revolt against God's government is revolt against God. Revolt against God is blasphemy.

With that pronouncement, he set the tone for the new regime. Iran had just emerged from arbitrary imperial rule, but it seemed it was about to experience a new, divinely inspired autocracy. From this edict would flow the arbitrary arrests, executions, floggings, confiscation of properties, and abrogation of women's rights that would bedevil the new regime and begin to erode its legitimacy.

While the direction Khomeini was heading was lost to most Iranians, the country now had two governments. Bakhtiar, the Shah's appointee, had refused to merge with the Khomeini government. Two days after Khomeini's speech, large rallies in Tehran and other cities demonstrated support for the Bazargan government. The following day, Bakhtiar staged an unsuccessful counterdemonstration in support of the constitution.

Most of the liberal and nationalist opposition who might have supported Bakhtiar had decided to support Khomeini believing he would bring genuine democracy to the country. And by that time, most of the Shah's erstwhile supporters among the middle classes sensed the way the wind was blowing and evaporated into silence or exile.

The military was still holding its ground with the moderate chief of staff General Gharebaghi; it kept in touch with Bazargan and Bakhtiar while the American Embassy, hoping for a smooth transition, used its influence with the military to support the moderates. The revolutionaries feared the pro-shah element.

On February 8, 1979, a division of the armed forces, namely the air force, descended on Rafeh School, which Khomeini had taken as his headquarters, to declare their allegiance to the revolution and its holy leader. The next day, the Imperial Guard attacked air force bases at Doshun Tape and Farahabad, and fighting quickly spread to the rest of Tehran. Police stations and army barracks were attacked by guerilla organizations and revolutionaries, and crowds looted arsenals.

Bakhtiar tried to resist the inevitable and had the military governor impose a curfew on February 10 that was to commence at 4:30 p.m. and continue until 5:30 a.m. The plan was to arrest anyone caught breaking the curfew. Unfortunately, that did not work because the population of Tehran was at that point mobilized and armed. Khomeini quickly instructed his followers to ignore this curfew, and he declared he would proclaim *jihad* against any army units that did not surrender to the revolutionaries.

Guerrilla units attacked the Imperial Guard, took over the American Embassy, the Evine Prison, the national television and radio stations, and numerous government offices. The following morning, the Supreme Military Council declared its neutrality in the political dispute and ordered all military personnel to return to their bases. Sporadic fighting continued throughout the city, but the revolution—and Khomeini—had triumphed. As the leader of the Iranian Peoples' Movement, he announced,

> In the name of God, the Merciful, the Compassionate Heroic Muslim people of Iran, first I would ask you not to allow rioting and unrest to take place. I would remind you that our revolution has not yet achieved complete victory over the enemy and I would request you, my dear brothers

and sisters, to cooperate with the interim Revolutionary Islamic Government.

For a short while, the moderating voice of liberals among the revolutionaries prevailed over the hotheads, and despite his militant temperament, Khomeini was concerned about bringing what he had unleashed under control. He spoke of the need for vigilance and action to complete the revolution. He appealed to the population to preserve Iran's artistic, scientific, and industrial heritage and to be kind and compassionate to captives as the Islamic tradition required.

But those who challenged the Shah's rule drowned out moderate voices; those who had suffered humiliation or had lost family members through execution or torture wanted revenge. Pressure from these groups as well as demands from extremists and Islamic radicals, that all leading members of the Shah's regime should be executed, gave Khomeini the sense that he might lose control, so he decided to show he could be ruthless.

He began to hold trials and executions to avenge the "129 martyrs of the revolution." He put one of his old supporters, Sadeq Khalkhali, who became known as "Judge Blood," in charge of a makeshift courtroom he put in a classroom of the Rafeh School. The executions took place on the rooftop of the school; on the evening of February 15, my friends General Manuchehr Khosrodad and General Nassiri were shot along with two other of the Shah's generals.

The trials and executions continued nonstop for several weeks. Horrified protests from Bazargan members of the provisional government and international organizations ended these executions for about three weeks, but by April, they recommenced with the execution by firing squad of the Shah's longtime Prime Minister, Amir Abbas Hoveyda. In a short time, over 200 more of the Shah's senior officials also saw their end. "Our belief is that criminals should not be tried and must be killed," was Khomeini's justification for his brutal acts.

For about a month after Khomeini's return, the country was in limbo. In most of the cities, a military-type government had gone into effect. The Ayatollah ordered people to be in their homes by nightfall. He also instructed the nation to go to the rooftops at 9:00 every night and scream, "*Allah-o-Akhbar!*" "God is the greatest!" It was an ingenious way to raise the volume of fury and discontent. More than any other, this tactic revealed how effectively the Ayatollah was able to play on the religious emotions of the masses.

The coalition had begun to organize in order to ensure Khomeini's hegemony during the post-revolutionary period. It consisted of a small circle of clerics who were close to the Ayatollah and who had been responsible for Khomeini's welcoming committee when he returned. It had a big hand in organizing the logistics of and keeping order during the huge street demonstrations, and it owned Rafeh School, where he would make his headquarters.

The Islamic Revolutionary Party (IRP) operated on every level of society from government offices to almost all city quarters as well as some villages. In the streets, it wielded power through organized gangs of thugs that became known as Hezbollah, the Party of God. The Hezbollah attacked demonstrators who challenged Khomeini, offices of newspapers critical of the new government, and the premises of any opposition organization. At first, it was said that Hezbollah represented the will of the people and that the Revolutionary Council had nothing to do with them, but as time went by, it was admitted that they were the shock troops of the IRP.

The komitehs, Islamic committees, that sprang up around the country were also allied with the IRP. They were based on the social structure of the religious community and were organized by the mosques and the Society of Militant Clergy. They were armed and saw it as their main task to keep order and security and to act as the regime's ears and eyes. They were responsible for many arbitrary arrests, executions, and confiscations of property.

The paramilitary Islamic Revolutionary Guard, which was to protect the revolution from destructive forces and counterrevolutionaries, sprang up within weeks of Khomeini's return on his direct instructions and was directly responsible to the Revolutionary Council.

The first job of the Islamic Republican Party was to make sure that the referendum planned for March would yield the desired results. The people would be asked to choose between a monarchy and an Islamic Republic though Khomeini and his clerics maintained a discreet silence on what form of Islamic government they favored. The enthusiasm for the revolution and the question to be put to the people meant that the result Khomeini wanted would be a foregone conclusion. Women were encouraged to participate in the referendum as their support was needed, though in voting for the Islamic government, they were putting their rights at the mercy of the clergy. As we now know, the new government did indeed take away those rights.

In a radio broadcast, Khomeini stated, "Soon, a referendum will be held. I am going to vote for an Islamic Republic, and I expect the people to do the same. Those who are opposed are free to vote accordingly." The referendum results were for the Islamic republic.

A great deal of dissention and confusion in the governing of Iran marked the next few months. There were still large numbers of uncalled-for arrests, torture, and executions. Bazargan had difficulty getting anything done, and Khomeini stayed in Qom, from where he tried to rule the land.

When on October 22, 1979, the Shah was allowed into the US for medical treatment of his advanced cancer, Khomeini angrily complained that this was a provocative act by the Americans. On November 4, radical students charged over the walls of the US Embassy in Tehran, occupied the building and the grounds, and took ninety hostages; that was too much for Prime Minister Mehdi Bazargan. When he was unable to persuade Khomeini or the Revolutionary Council to evict the students and release the hostages, he realized his impotence and tendered his resignation; he soon fled the country.

With Bazargan's departure, the revolution had triumphed over reform. The members of the Revolutionary Council asked Khomeini what should be done next, and he said, "Nothing. You go and run the country. The people will carry on with their own duties."

CHAPTER  2

The Government of the
Islamic Republic of Iran

The structure of the government of Iran is similar to that of many Western countries, but it is much more complex in its organization. The main differences are that Iran is an Islamic theocracy and that one man, the Supreme Leader, has ideological and political control over a system dominated by Islamic clerics.

The current Supreme Leader, Ayatollah Ali Khamenei, succeeded Khomeini on his death in 1989. The supreme leader is responsible for the general principles of the tune and direction of Iran's foreign and domestic policy, is the commander in chief of the armed forces, and controls the Islamic Republic's intelligence and security operations; he alone can declare war and peace.

As well, he has the power to appoint and dismiss the leaders of the judiciary, the state radio and television networks, and the supreme commander of the Revolutionary Guard, the *Sepah e Pasdaran*. His power is spread throughout the country by his 2,000 representatives, who are sprinkled throughout all sectors of the government as his clerical field operatives. These representatives are more powerful than the president's ministers and have the authority to intervene in any matters of state on behalf of the Supreme Leader.

The President is the second-highest ranking official in Iran. He has a high public profile, but his power can be almost nil because the constitution subordinates the entire executive branch to the Supreme Leader. He is responsible for setting the economic policies. He has nominal rule over the Ministry of Intelligence and Security though in practice, the Supreme Leader dictates all foreign and domestic security. Under him are eight vice presidents and a cabinet of twenty-two ministers who must be confirmed by the Majlis, the congress.

The Guardian Council comprises twelve jurists, six of whom are appointed by the Supreme Leader while the head of the judiciary appoints the remaining six, which in effect are recommended by the Majlis. This body reviews all legislation passed by the Majlis to determine its constitutionality. If a majority of the council decided a piece of legislation does not comply with the constitution or the standards of Islamic law, it can strike it down or return it to the Majlis for reconsideration. The council supervises elections and approves all candidates for election including the president; it answers only to the Supreme Leader.

The Majlis, the Congress, is the legislative body whose 290 members are elected every four years. It drafts legislation, ratifies treaties, and approves the budget, but all bills it passes must be approved by the Guardian Council. Surprisingly, the parliamentary sessions are open to the public and its deliberations are broadcast and published.

The Assembly of Experts is the deliberative body empowered to designate and dismiss the Supreme Leader. Its eighty-eight members are elected for eight-year terms, but all its "virtuous and learned" members must be approved by the Guardian Council and the Ayatollah. It must meet for two days every six months. Similar to the Vatican's College of Cardinals, it elects the Supreme Leader and will periodically reconfirm him. It is the most obscure of Iran's many governing bodies.

The Expediency Council's thirty-four appointed members mediate disputes between the Majlis and the Guardian Council and serves as an advisory body to the Supreme Leader, which makes it one of the most powerful bodies in the country at least in name. Its decisions usually side with the Guardian Council's decisions.

The judicial branch of Iran's government is controlled by the Supreme Leader; he appoints the head of the judiciary who in turn appoints the head of the Supreme Court and the chief public prosecutor. The public courts deal with civil and some criminal cases though a Revolutionary Court tries crimes against national security, narcotics smuggling, and acts that undermine the Islamic Republic. As well, there is a Special Clerical Court; it functions independent of the regular judicial courts and is accountable to the Supreme Leader only; decisions made by this court are final and may not be appealed.

Pasdaran-e-Engelab-e-Eslami, as the Iranian Revolutionary Guard is called, has unprecedented power in the country. This branch of the military was founded after the revolution on May 5, 1979, by Khomeini. The regular military, *Artesh*, defends Iran's borders and maintains internal order while the Revolutionary Guard is intended to protect the country's Islamic system and assist the ruling clerics in the day-to-day enforcement of the new codes and morality by preventing foreign interference as well as coups by the military or deviant movements.

Its establishment served notice to the population and the armed forces that the Khomeini regime was developing its own enforcement body. The revolution needed to rely on a force of its own rather than using what they thought were the Shah's tainted military. Since its inception, the Pasdaran, an ideologically driven militia, has taken over a more assertive role in virtually every aspect of Iranian society, and some say that its political power has even surpassed that of the Shi'a clerical system. The Pasdaran was intended to protect the revolution and assist clerics in the enforcement of Islamic codes and morality. Though it operates independently of the regular army forces, it is considered a military force; it consists of ground, naval, and aviation troops and controls Iran's strategic missile and rocket forces. It is a decentralized force with thirty provincial corps, one for each province, and two central corps in Tehran.

Originally, Khomeini declared that the military forces should remain nonpolitical, but the constitution names the Pasdaran "guardian of the Revolution and its achievements," which in effect is political. Its members have influence in the political world of Iran. Former President Ahmadinejad was a member, and nearly a third of the Majlis, ambassadors, mayors, provincial governors, and senior bureaucrats are all members.

On April 30, 1980, under the arm of the Pasdaran, Khomeini established the Basij, a people's militia. It is a volunteer paramilitary organization with branches in virtually every city, town, and village in Iran. Khomeini declared that "a country with 20 million youths must have 20 million riflemen or a military of 20 million soldiers; such a country will never be destroyed." The Basij was open to those who were nineteen to forty-four years old including women. It was actually formed as a civil defense force, but in practice, it became a grassroots intelligence organization made up of young boys between ten and sixteen.

Propaganda in schools and intensive media campaigns encouraged people to join the Basij. During the Iran-Iraq War, hundreds of thousands volunteered including young children and unemployed old men some of whom were in their eighties. These volunteers were swept up by the Shi'a love of martyrdom and patriotism of the war effort. This group is best known for its employment of human wave attacks that cleared minefields and fought in the war; tens of thousands died in the process. By the spring of 1983, the Basij had trained 2.4 million Iranians in the use of arms and had sent 450,000 troops to the front.

At the end of the war in 1988, most of the Basij had left the service and reintegrated into their lives after many years on the front. At that time, those still active in the service were busy monitoring activities of civilians. They set up street inspection stations in urban areas to intercept drug smuggling and potential insurgency and to enforce the rule that women were to wear the *hijab*, the women's head covering. They arrested women for violating the dress code and youths for attending mixed-gender parties or being in public with unrelated members of the opposite sex; they seized what they considered to be indecent materials such as satellite dish antennae and other electronic devices.

The organization was established on college campuses to fight "Westoxification" and possible student agitation against the government; it did break up the student riots of 1999. It mobilizes as an emergency management service in case of earthquakes or other natural or human-made disasters. There had been significant rivalry between the Basij and the Pasdaran, but in 2008, the Basij was incorporated into the Pasdaran ground forces, and the two are basically one now.

The Quds Force, sometimes described as the successor of the Shah's Imperial Guard, is a special-operations unit that handles activities abroad and is also under the wing of the Pasdaran.

The involvement in Iran's economy by the Pasdaran began during the presidency of Ayatollah Rafsanjani. Reconstruction of Iran's economy, which was in terrible shape after ten years of war and revolution, was one of his main priorities. The Pasdaran had the manpower to engage in reconstruction activities, so they were given a slice of the pie; over the next twenty-five years, the Pasdaran became Iran's largest economic force.

They currently dominate most sectors of the economy—from energy, construction, and telecommunications to automobile manufacturing as well as banking and finance. They are linked to hundreds of companies that appear to be private in nature but are run by veterans. Their economic influence activities encompass a broad network of current and former members rather than a single official or centrally administered organization.

The Pasdaran and the Basij have benefited from international sanctions and Iran's isolation, which hurt their domestic and foreign business competitors by increasing business costs. The ability to tap into state funds and its relatively vast independent resources has provided them a decisive advantage. They were awarded hundreds of no-bid contracts in addition to billions of dollars in loans for construction, infrastructure, and energy projects. Overall however, they, like the rest of the country, have felt the heavy burden of the sanctions and thus supported President Rouhani's nuclear negotiations despite some of their objections and criticisms. The Pasdaran and the Basij have been accused of widespread corruption, which has been the Iranian way for over 200 years no matter which regime was in power.

CHAPTER 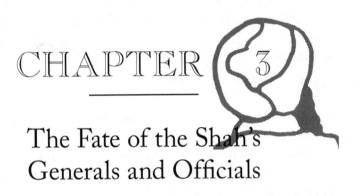 3

The Fate of the Shah's Generals and Officials

One day in late January 1979, I was collecting the mail from the box at the end of the drive. I flipped through the stack of letters and found one that had been sent from Morocco. *Morocco? The Shah is in Morocco*, I thought. I couldn't get back to the house quickly enough; I wanted to open the letter.

It was a two-page letter from my dear friend and ex-boss Kambiz Atabai. He wrote that he had left Iran with the Shah and his family on January 16. He said that he had been reluctant to leave but that his majesty had insisted he go along. Luckily, his wife, Avid, and their two boys had left Iran before things became really bad.

He was in Morocco with the Shah and his family, his own father, and several other courtiers of the Pahlavis. King Hassan had been most gracious in inviting them when things in Egypt, where they had first gone, had become tense. He sounded very sad to have left his beloved country and said that the Shah was very depressed and not in good health. He didn't know how long they would be there; he said he would call me when he got the opportunity.

Several weeks later, the phone rang. It was Kambiz. He said that they were on Paradise Island in the Bahamas; they were very comfortable, but he did not know how long they would stay there. He said he would keep in touch to let me know what was happening. Did I mind if my phone number would be used as a contact for people who needed to get in touch with him? No problem, I told him. I would be only too happy to help.

He had called me in the summer of 1978 to ask if I knew of any equine property that would be good investment for the Imperial Court in the US or Canada. I had called my dad in Canada and talked to some people in Virginia about what might be available, and then out of the blue, a friend in Florida called to tell me the Tampa racetrack was for sale. I called Kambiz, and he asked me to get as much information as I could. I knew very little about racetracks or big investments, but I said I would do what I could.

About that time, I heard that Ron Dabscheck, who had brought the investment money from Hong Kong to Tehran to build the racetrack there in the late seventies, had moved to Jacksonville, Florida, so I called him. He thought it would be a great deal; he said he would be happy to help out as there would certainly be a way to make some money on the deal! Through another friend, I arranged for Ron and me to meet with George Steinbrenner of the New York Yankees; he owned the Tampa track. I flew to Jacksonville, where Ron met me at the airport, and we drove to Tampa for our appointment. We spent several hours meeting and touring the racetrack, which hasn't changed much from that day till this, and got the price, about $12 million. George promised to send me all the financial and legal documents I would need within a few days.

I called Kambiz to get the address where he wanted the information sent—no faxes or internet in those days—and said I would forward the papers as soon as I received them. It was October by that time.

"I hear on the news that there are a lot of demonstrations and marches against the Shah happening there. Is it true?" I asked Kambiz.

"Oh, there has been a bit of trouble, but it isn't really anything to worry about. The average age of the dissidents is about seventeen. They are really only student riots, and His Majesty's people have it all under control," was his answer.

When I received the information on the Tampa track, I immediately sent it on to Iran, but that was the end of it all because by January 16, 1979, the Shah had left his country.

Kambiz and I kept in touch over the next few months. I was never sure when he called me if he was in New York or with the Shah at one of his places of exile.

The phone rang one day just before I went to the barn to teach a riding lesson. I was about to leave it but for some reason decided to answer. "Is this Gail Rose?" I was asked by a heavily accented voice I was sure was Iranian.

"Yes," I answered tentatively.

"You know your friends Fred and Elian? They need help. They want to leave Iran, so I was told to call you to let you know." He hung up.

I would be late for the lesson, but I immediately called the contact number in New York.

"Hello," a female voice answered.

"This is Gail Rose. I have a message for Kambiz."

I told her that Freddy and Elian Elghanian wanted help getting out of Iran, and she said she would relay the message.

A few weeks later, Freddy called. "Gaily, Gaily! Thank you so much! We're in France, but we're coming to the States soon, so we'll be in touch. We'll be going to New York, where we have family. It's amazing how it worked out. Thank you for your help."

"Freddy, you are so welcome, but I did nothing but make a phone call. I'm so glad it worked. My love to you both. We'll talk soon."

Several months passed before Kambiz called me to see if I would go to New York to meet him. I had been planning to take the manuscript of my first book, *All the Shah's Men*, to an agent there anyway, so I said I would meet him the following week. "You will not recognize me, Gail, when you see me. I have aged. My hair is totally white!"

I took the train from Richmond and arrived in time to meet him at our arranged place, Tiffany's. I recognized him and thought he was just as handsome though more distinguished with his wavy, white hair. We walked up Fifth Avenue chatting about the past in Iran. We kept it light and laughed a lot. We stopped at a small sidewalk café to enjoy the lovely, warm spring day.

"I see you are carrying a briefcase with you. Don't tell me you have written a book and are bringing it to a publisher."

"How did you guess that?" I asked.

"I know you too well. I knew you would try to write a book. But I want to tell you that this is not a good time to write a book about your time in Iran. It is dangerous. This revolution, which surprised us, has tentacles all over the world. All of us, including you, who were a part of the Shah's court, are probably on a hit list. I am sure you heard that Prince Shariar—you knew him, Princess Ashraf's son—was assassinated in Paris last December."

I had known that but hadn't thought that I, a Canadian living in the States, would be in any danger. It frightened me. He explained to me that I knew too much about the stables and the Imperial Court to be ignored by the revolutionary regime.

Kambiz was kept very busy by the imperial family after the Shah's death, and when things finally settled down, he was put in charge of the Empress's New York office, a position he has continued to keep.

Manuchehr Khosrodad, who resembled the Shah in height, sharp features, and wavy, graying hair, was a very dear friend of mine while I was living in Iran. He would come to the Imperial Stables usually in the afternoons after he had finished his day as the general in charge of the Special Forces. Most days, I would hear his helicopter a few minutes before he arrived; I would have a *djelodar*, a groom, bring his horse to the ring so he could walk the couple of hundred feet from the helipad to mount his horse. He was usually late and would start his conversation with, "I am so sorry, Rose. I just lost track of time. I promise that when I come tomorrow, I won't be late."

"It's no problem, General. I am here at your service. Don't worry about it," was my usual reply though I had been waiting for over an hour and wanted to get home to my children. He was a delightful man with a big heart and always seemed to be in a good mood. I knew he was a special friend of the Shah because not just anybody could ride and keep their horses at the stables. And I knew he would be late the next time he came for training on his horse. He was a decent man who always made me feel comfortable whether it was during a training session with one of his horses or in a social environment. He and I became good friends, and he was one of my favorite people in Iran.

On the morning of February 17, 1979, I was in the kitchen drinking coffee and watching the news as usual. They were talking about the revolution in Iran, so I began to pay more attention. I could not believe what I saw on the screen—the bodies of four of the Shah's generals who had been executed by Khomeini's revolutionary court that he had set up at his headquarters in Rafeh School. As I looked in horror, I saw the body of Manuchehr on the far left of the picture, obviously naked with only a white sheet covering his lower extremities; he did look peaceful in his death thank goodness. It has been said that he stood bravely for his execution saluting the Shah.

The other general I knew personally was General Nassiri, who had been head of the SAVAK and whom I knew socially as his father-in-law was a friend; he lay with his eyes open. The other two generals, Mehdi Rahimi and Reza Najid, I did not really know but had seen them at various functions. I was in total shock and overwhelmed with sadness at the brutal executions by firing squad of these four men who had done much for their country and the Shah. They had not had a chance to defend themselves. All four had been convicted of "corruption on earth," and on confirmation of their sentences by Khomeini, they were taken to the school and shot. All of their property was also confiscated.

In his memoirs, the notorious Hanging Judge or Blood Judge as Khalkhali was named, recalled this.

> The first people I tried for their deeds were Nematollah Nassiri, head if SAVAK and Manuchehr Khosrodad, air force commander ... All the people who were sentenced to death by the Revolutionary Tribunals were the best examples of "corruptor on earth" and they were sentenced as such.

He wrote that a corruptor on earth was someone who had contributed to and had spread corruption on earth, and he believed that all the parliamentarians and senators, all governors, all the heads of SAVAK, and the police who held office after 1963 should be sentenced to death. He included all high-ranking military officials who were instrumental in the survival of the Shah's regime and those who were close to the Shah and his family. In summing up his actions, he claimed all the people he had condemned and who were executed in the early days of the establishment of the revolutionary tribunals and later in the Qasr Prison were all corruptors on earth, and based on the Quran, their blood was a waste. As it turned out in the first couple of months, over 200 of the Shah's officials were killed, and by the end of 1985, the number reached over 8,000.

I respected Manouchehr, but he showed lack of judgment at the end. The Shah and his friends had all begged him to leave Iran with them, but he felt his loyalty to the country itself was enough to save him. He was tough, however, and at his brief trial in the Rafeh schoolhouse, where so many of the officials were accused and executed, he was one of the first to die before the executioners' guns. He stayed courageously loyal to the Shah and his own principles up to the last moment. His last words were, "Long live the Shah!"

Manuchehr's nine-year-old granddaughter Shiraz Rimer wrote the following poem to his memory.

Once upon a time
There was a very brave general
He fought through night and day
Through snow and sun, ice and rain
To live or die
He would always pray to stay alive
But one poor day, they all died.

Nader Djahanbani, about whom I wrote in part I of this book, was a distinguished Iranian general and deputy chief of the Imperial Iranian Air Force. Despite the fact that he was executed in 1979, he is still lauded as the father of the Iranian air force. Along with General Mohamed Khatami, who was married to the Shah's sister Fatameh, he was considered to have modernized and strengthened the air force with advanced equipment including the F-14, which helped save Iran's infrastructure during the Iran-Iraq war.

He was born into a family with a long military history; his father was a general in the Cossack Brigade of Reza Shah Pahlavi, and his mother was of the Russian aristocracy. One of his brothers, Parvis, was an officer in the Imperial Iranian Marines, and his other brother, Khosro, was married to the Shah's daughter Shahnaz. As well, his cousin was married to the Shah's brother, Golam Reza. He was very well connected!

He and Khatami attained pilot training in Germany. After returning to Iran, Nader formed Iran's first Iranian aerobatic team, the Golden Crown. During the sixties and seventies, he was instrumental in acquiring F-4s, F-5s, F-14s, advanced radar systems, and the AIM-54 Phoenix air-to-air missiles all of which were credited with saving the country from the Iraqi invasion during the Iran-Iraq war.

When the Shah declared martial law in response to the mounting protests in 1978 and put military officers in charge, Djahanbani was not one of them because he had little experience with internal security affairs. As a result, when the Shah fled, despite the urgings of his family, his friends in the US Air Force, the Shah, and his sister-in-law Shahnaz, he refused to leave believing that there would be no retaliation against him. He thought that the powerful air force Iran had would be a testament to his loyalty to the country, not the Shah.

General Shapour Azarbarzin, Chief of Staff of the air force, had been Nader's rival for years; they just didn't get along. When Nader was promoted to a position superior to Azarbarzin's, he was furious. After the revolution, General Azarbarzin had his chance to crush his enemy. He began spreading rumors that Nader was aligned with General Amir Hossein Rabii, commander of the air force, and that they were plotting a coup d'état against the new government. He arranged to have an audience with Khomeini at which he reported the rumor to the leader as a fact. Khomeini subsequently ordered the Revolutionary Guard to arrest Djahanbani and his cohorts and have them tried by the infamous Sadegh Khalkhali. In return, General Azarbarzin was promoted to commander of the newly established Republic of Iran Air Force and given $1 million!

Djahanbani was arrested for association with the Shah's regime, corruption on earth, antirevolutionary offenses, and war on God. He was taken to the Qasr Prison and shot in the courtyard early the following morning. His last words were, "Long live Iran."

Despite the fact that he was killed before the Iran-Iraq War, much of what he did for the Iranian air force such as acquiring fighter jets, air-to-air missiles, and excellent training for air force students was credited with saving the country from invasion by Iraq and protecting areas of the country crucial for the new regime's survival. It was said that the report of one Iranian F-14 in the skies was enough for the Iraqis to pull out squadrons from the area. Today, the F-14 Tomcat is still the premier fighter jet of the Iranian air force.

Djahanbani had sent his wife out of Iran when the unrest began to build up. He had been seen around with a new girlfriend just before his arrest a few days after the revolution took control; he continued to ride his horses often with his friend Fereydun Elghanian and showed no sense of his impending doom. He was visiting some American friends when the revolutionary gunmen hunted him down and took him prisoner.

It was sad to see the last pictures of the once-proud Djahanbani with a label tied around his neck, unshaven and broken, that were splashed around the world as he stood to receive his sentence before the revolutionary tribunal. Theirs was simple revenge on a man who was not a killer, just an arrogant anachronism who was born to privilege and let it get to his head. General Nader Djahanbani was executed in the courtyard of the Qasr Prison in the early hours of March 13, 1979. When he was insulted by one of the guardians of the revolution, he had the courage to slap him in the face before dying.

The families and friends of many of the men who were executed in Tehran were afraid to claim their bodies. Djahanbani, however, had a spirited Russian aunt, Luba Kaminski, known to her Iranian friends as Helen Khonume, and she was not to be deterred by such fears. She went down to the school and brought her nephew home for a proper burial.

Author with Manuchehr Khosrodad

Kambiz Atabai on Roshan

CHAPTER 4

The Iran-Iraq War

Iraq's invasion of Iran in 1980 was a mistake and miscalculation by Saddam Hussein. He had made significant strides in developing the nation-state of his country, but the successful revolution in Iran worried him; he was afraid that Iran's new religious leadership would threaten Iraq's delicate Sunni-Shi'a balance and would exploit Iraq's geostrategic vulnerabilities especially Iraq's access to the Persian Gulf.

The war was multifaceted; it included religious schisms, border disputes, and political differences. Conflicts that contributed to its outbreak ranged from centuries old Sunni vs. Shi'a and Arab vs. Persian religious and ethnic disputes. And then there was the personal animosity between Saddam Hussein and Ayatollah Khomeini especially as Khomeini was bitter about his expulsion from Najaf in 1977, where he had lived during his exile. But the real reason Iraq launched the war was that it wanted to consolidate its rising power in the Arab world and to replace Iran as the dominant power in the Persian Gulf.

The southern end of the Shatt al-Arab, the Stream of the Arabs, or Arvand Rud, Swift River, constitutes the border between Iran and Iraq down to the mouth of the river where it discharges into the gulf. Control of this waterway and its use as a border had been a source of contention between Persia and the predecessors of Iraq since the 1600s.

Under Saddam Hussein's Baathist Iraq, the navigable waterway was claimed by Iraq, but after fighting between the two countries over the Kurdish problem was solved, the UN, in 1975, negotiated a treaty between the two countries giving Iran the deep channel that ocean-going liners could navigate. This border dispute was revived by the two countries in 1979 as the Baath leadership regarded the treaty as merely a truce, not a definitive settlement.

In September 1980, border skirmishes erupted in that central section near Qasr-e Shirin, with exchanges of artillery fire by both sides. A few weeks later, Saddam Hussein officially abrogated the treaty of 1975 and announced that the Shatt al-Arab was returning to Iraqi sovereignty. Iran rejected this action, and hostilities escalated. There were bombings and raids deep into each other's territory.

1980–81

On September 22, 1980, Iraq launched an all-out invasion of Iran that started an extremely costly and useless war. Iraqi MiG-23s and -21s attacked Mehrabad and Doshun Tape, air bases near Tehran, and many other air bases around the country. The aim was to destroy the Iranian air force on the ground. There was some damage to runways and fuel and ammunition depots, but much of Iran's inventory was left intact because its jets were protected in specially strengthened hangers.

The Iraqis were confident because the Iranians lacked cohesive leadership and Iranian forces according to Iraqi intelligence lacked spare parts for their American-made equipment. Bagdad became even more confident as it watched the once-invincible Imperial Iranian forces disintegrate as most of the highest-ranking officers had been executed. Iraq possessed fully equipped and trained forces. Against armed forces including the Pasdaran troops that were led by religious mullahs who had little or no military experience, the Iraqis could muster twelve complete mechanized divisions equipped with the latest Soviet weapons. With his military buildup in the late 1970s, Saddam Hussein had amassed an army of 190,000 men backed by 2,200 tanks and 450 aircraft.

Iran prevented a quick Iraqi victory by the mobilization of volunteers and the Pasdaran forces to the front. The new revolutionary regime recalled veterans of the old imperial army and enlisted its pilots. The Pasdaran and Basij recruited at least 100,000 volunteers, and approximately 200,000 soldiers were sent to the front by the end of November 1980. The troops were ideologically committed and fought bravely despite inadequate armor support. Iran's resistance at the outset of the invasion was expectantly strong, but it was neither well organized nor successful on all fronts.

Tehran rejected a settlement offer and held out against the militarily superior Iraqi forces. It refused to accept defeat and slowly began a series of counter offenses in January 1981, some of which were successful and some of which failed. In September, Iran gained its first major victory when it suppressed Iraq with cooperation between the army and the Pasdaran and retook the port of Abadan after a long Iraqi siege. Iranian forces were also successful in the Qasr Shirin area of Khuzestan in December and January 1982.

Despite Iraqi successes in causing major damage to expose Iranian ammunition and fuel dumps in the early days of the war, the Iranian air force prevailed initially in the air war. Iranian airplanes could carry two or three times more bombs or rockets than could their Iraqi counterparts, and Iranian pilots demonstrated considerably more expertise; they attacked Bagdad and key Iraqi air bases in the first few weeks of the war hoping to destroy supply and support systems.

One interesting attack the Iranians made on Iraq's oil field complex and Al Walid air base, where the T-22 and T-28 bombers were based demonstrated considerable expertise. The targets were more than 800 kilometers from Iran's closest air base, so the F-4s had to refuel in midair for the mission. Iran's air force flew mostly F-4s and F-5s as well as a few F-14s for reconnaissance. As time went on, a lack of spare parts for the planes forced them to use helicopters for close air support, which proved advantageous in finding and destroying targets and maneuvering against antiaircraft guns and portable missiles.

1982

A major turning point in the war occurred in March 1982 when Iran penetrated Iraq's lines, split their forces, and forced them to retreat. Within a week, Iranian forces destroyed a large part of three Iraqi divisions, and in May, they regained the port of Khorramshahr though with numerous casualties. After that victory, they maintained the pressure on the remaining Iraqi forces. Saddam Hussein withdrew from Iranian territory believing that Iran would agree to end the war and negotiate a settlement to withdraw its forces to Iran, but Iran refused.

In July, the Iranian clergy launched Operation Ramadan, which utilized human-wave attacks against the city of Basra by the Pasdaran and Basij hoping Saddam would be toppled by a coup. Tehran used these volunteers in one of the biggest land battles since World War II. The soldiers ranged in age from children age nine to men and women over fifty. Though they were all eager, they were untrained soldiers who swept over minefields and fortifications to clear a safe path for the tanks and heavy artillery. These attacks faced Iraqi artillery fire; in spite of immense casualties, they enabled Iran to recover the territory.

By the end of 1982, Iraq had been resupplied with new Soviet equipment such as T-55 and T-52 tanks, BM-21 Stalin Pipe Organ rocket launchers, and Mi-24 helicopter gunships, so the ground war entered a new phase. The Iraqi Combat Engineer Corps was efficient in building bridges over waterways, laying minefields, and fortifying their positions. The Iraqi military planned on using the Soviet-type, three-line defense tactics.

1983

Throughout 1983, both sides demonstrated their ability to absorb and inflict severe losses. The Iraqis flooded lowlands to stymie Iranian advances, but both sides had trouble using their tanks and carriers efficiently. Rather than trying to maneuver them properly, they tended to dig them in and use them as artillery pieces. Thus, they would be left stuck in the mud. Neither side seemed to be able to master the effective use of tanks.

Iran continued to launch human-wave offenses but with huge losses of its volunteers and soldiers. In February, using 200,000 Pasdaran and Basij troops backed by air, armor, and artillery support, they were able to break through Iraqi lines, but Bagdad responded with massive air attacks many by helicopters. More than 6,000 Iranians were killed in one day.

Fighting continued through the year by the end of which it was estimated that 100,000 Iranians and 60,000 Iraqis had been killed. Despite these losses, Iran held a distinct advantage in its attempt to win the war.

1984

Beginning in 1984, Bagdad's military goal changed from controlling Iranian territory to denying Tehran any major gains in Iraq. Saddam Hussein purchased new weapons from the Soviet Union and France and began using chemical warfare. Even so, Iran continued its aggression and captured parts of the Magnum Islands, where Iraq had oilfields of economic and strategic value. Saddam Hussein proposed a meeting between himself and Khomeini at a neutral location to discuss peace negotiations, but that suggestion was refused.

Between February 19 and March 1, in one of the largest battles of the war, the two armies clashed and inflicted more than 25,000 fatalities on each other. Iran lacked the equipment to open secure passages through the minefields, so it again resorted to the human-wave tactic. One European journalist reported that he saw tens of thousands of children roped together in groups of about twenty to prevent the faint hearted from deserting.

Iran made little if any progress despite these sacrifices. Within four weeks, the Iraqis reportedly killed 40,000 Iranians and lost 9,000 of their own men; by midyear, it was reported that 300,000 Iranians and 250,000 Iraqis had been killed or wounded in the war. Both armies showed little coordination, and some units were left in the field to fight on their own without officers. Difficult decisions that should have received immediate attention were referred by the commanders to their capitals for action. The war was becoming a stalemate.

1985

During 1985, both sides increased their targeting of population centers with bombs and missiles. The Iraqi air force's strategic bombing campaign was aimed at breaking civilian morale and disrupting military targets. Between March and June, its attacks were very effective. Opposition from the Iranian air force was almost nonexistent as the Iraqis hit air bases as well as other military and industrial targets all over the country.

The brunt of the Iraqi bombings fell on Tehran in an effort to crush the Iranian spirit while the antiwar feeling was at an all-time high. They were being hit on an average of twice a day; they were hit six times on one day in particular. The Revolutionary Guard barracks, Tehran's main power station, the Military Staff College, the Military College, the main army barracks, Tehran's train works, industrial areas, and military airfields were hit. The only major ground offensive occurred in March near Basra; though Iran reportedly used 60,000 troops, the assault proved inconclusive except for heavy casualties on both sides.

1986

In March, UN Secretary General Javier Perez de Cueller formally accused Iraq of using chemical weapons against Iran. UN experts who had been sent to Iran reported that Saddam Hussein had used mustard gas and nerve gas; of course, Iraq denied that, but evidence in the form of many badly burned casualties flown to Europe for treatment was overwhelming.

The Iraqis were unable to oust the Iranians from Al Faw, so they went on an offensive and captured the city of Mehran only to lose it again in July.

The rest of the year witnessed hit-and-run attacks by both sides while the Iranians massed about 500,000 troops for a promised final offensive that never occurred.

1987

In the beginning of the year, Iranian units began pushing westward toward Shatt al-Arab in their next so-called final offensive and captured the town of Duayja at the cost of 20,000 Iraqi lives and 65,000 Iranians as well as forty-five Iraqi planes.

Tehran launched several attacks to capture Basra; its push came close to breaking Iraq's last line of defense, but it was unable to gain a decisive victory.

By May, the war seemed to have reached a stalemate in the south though the conflict was intensifying on the northern front, where a joint effort by the Iranians and the rebel Iraqi Kurds surrounded an Iraqi town near the oilfields, endangering them and the northern oil pipeline to Turkey.

As the war continued, Iran was increasingly short of spare parts for damaged planes and had lost a large number of planes in combat. By late 1987, Iran had become unable to mount an effective defense against the resupplied Iraqi air force.

The Tanker War

The tanker war precipitated a major international incident. A great deal of the world's oil came from the Persian Gulf; 70 percent of the Japanese, 50 percent of West European, and 7 percent of American oil was dependent on tankers or pipelines transporting it to its destinations. In 1981, Bagdad had officially warned all ships that were heading to or returning from Iranian ports in the gulf to stay away or proceed at their own risk. Iraq attacked Iranian ports, oil complexes, and neutral tankers and ships sailing to and from Iran.

In 1984, Iraq expanded the so-called tanker war by using French Super-Etenard combat aircraft with Exocet missiles. Seventy-one merchant ships were attacked in 1984 compared to forty-eight in the three previous years. Iraq wanted to break the stalemate by cutting off Iran's oil exports to force them to the negotiating table, but their efforts to put Iran's main oil exporting terminal at Khark Island out of commission failed.

The new wave of Iraqi assaults led Iran to reciprocate, and its first attack against civilian commercial shipping was launched in April. Iran attacked an Indian freighter, a Kuwaiti oil tanker, and then a Saudi tanker that was in Saudi waters, making it clear to Iraq that if it continued to interfere with Iran's shipping, no gulf state would be safe.

Iraqi attacks on the tankers and civilian ships exceeded Iranian assaults by three to one. These sustained attacks cut Iranian oil exports in half, reduced shipping in the gulf by 25 percent, led Lloyds of London to increase its insurance rates on tankers, and slowed gulf oil supplies to the rest of the world.

When the Saudis shot down an Iranian Phantom jet intruding in Saudi territory, it played an important role in ending this tanker war. Iran and Iraq accepted a UN-sponsored moratorium on the shelling of civilian targets, and Tehran later proposed an extension to include all gulf shipping. Iraq rejected this unless it would include its own gulf ports. The moratorium was ignored first by Iraq and later by Iran, and shipping continued to be dangerous. The US and other countries became involved, and during 1988, the gulf was a crowded theater of operations.

1988

Four major battles were fought between April to August in which the Iraqis routed or defeated the Iranians. In Bagdad, the Iraqis displayed captured Iranian weapons amounting to more than three-quarters of its inventory and almost half of its artillery pieces and personnel carriers.

The war ended when Iran accepted the UN Security Council Resolution 598, which declared an August 20, 1988 cease-fire. It had lasted from September 1980 until August 1988, almost eight years. Though casualty figures are not certain, estimates suggest that there were 1.5 million war and war-related casualties. Iran acknowledged nearly 300,000 casualties, and the Iraqi casualties were estimated to be 375,000.

In the end, none of the issues that are usually blamed for the war had been resolved. When it was over, the conditions that existed at the beginning of the war remained unchanged. Although Iraq won the war militarily and possessed a significant military advantage over Iran in 1988, the 1991 Persian Gulf War reduced Iraq's capabilities so that there was parity between the two countries and conditions were similar to the way they were in 1980.

CHAPTER 5

Escaping Iran

As I mentioned earlier, Habib (Habibollah) Elghanian was a prominent Iranian Jewish businessman and philanthropist who was president of the Tehran Jewish Society and the symbolic head of the Iranian Jewish community. The wealthiest Jew in Iran, he came from families in the tailoring and grocery business. He quit school at age fifteen to work in a hotel owned by a maternal uncle. After completing his military service, he went into business on his own in the Tehran bazaar selling imported watches, and when the veil was abolished by Reza Shah, women's hats.

He and two of his brothers, who eventually moved to the United States, formed an import company in 1936. Haji Habib, as he became known, and his brothers imported watches, textiles, dishes and tableware, crystal ware, radios, and sewing machines all of which were in demand in the growing country.

In 1948, the company called Plasco, which they started, opened a small factory and began producing simple plastic articles such as combs and buttons, and the business expanded rapidly. In the early 1950s, they moved their factory out to the Karaj Road where many new factories were being built. By the 1960s, they were using fifty to sixty tons of polyvinyl and other plastic materials every day and producing a large variety of plastic goods including plates, dishes, bowls, water pitchers, shoes, sandals, and toys.

The Elghanians also invested in real estate; in 1960, they constructed the first high-rise building in Iran, the seventeen-story Plasco building on Ferdowsi Avenue. Unfortunately, the two top floors of the building caught fire, and it collapsed in January 2017. They also built the multistory Aluminum Building on Shah Avenue, which is still standing.

Habib employed thousands of people in Iran's first refrigerator-manufacturing factory and in his other successful businesses. He contributed to organizations feeding the needy and orphans of all religions and even built a mosque for his Muslim workers. He donated his first home to be turned into a hospital.

He visited Palestine during World War II and then visited frequently after the establishment of Israel as a country. In 1968, he and his brothers completed construction on the twenty-three-story Shimshon Tower, the first of four skyscrapers that make up the Diamond Exchange outside Tel Aviv. He himself owned other properties and made other investments in Israel. He arranged for the purchase of a large home in Tehran that became the Israeli Embassy.

Habib was in the United States in the fall of 1978 as opposition to the Shah was gaining momentum. Against the advice of friends and family, he return to Iran via Israel, where he had business to attend to. Having stayed out of politics, he believed he had nothing to fear. He had been arrested by the Shah's government when it launched a campaign to combat rising costs of consumer goods; inflation at the time was due to rapidly increasing oil revenues, growing government spending and investments, rising demand, and the increasing cost of raw materials and labor. To make an example of a prominent businessman engaged in the manufacture and sale of widely used consumer goods, he was arrested on July 27, 1975. We were all in shock when we heard he had been exiled to Sanandaj, a remote town in Kurdistan. He was eventually jailed in Tehran and finally declared innocent at his trial. He felt that he had paid his dues and would not be in any danger from the new regime.

He returned to Iran just a week or so after Khomeini had arrived in Tehran; he was looking forward to life as usual and planned to continue with his business interests, his leadership of the Jewish community, and his many charitable works.

Haji's son Fred and his wife, Elian, were two of my closest friends while I was in Iran. They were kind and understanding people to whom I could go for advice when I was having troubles understanding Iranian ways. Their advice helped me on too many occasions to count.

Fred loved horses and competing in show jumping, so we spent a lot of time together. They built a lovely, modern house and barn near Karaj, where I would go with my children on the weekends when there was not a horse show. Elian was the Jewish mother to all of us. Our children would play together in the beautiful garden, and she would always have plenty of food and drink for us. Haji didn't think that Fred's interest in horses was what he wanted his son to be doing, but he respected the fact that he was good friends with my husband, who was known as Mr. Aluminum. Don and I were often invited to the business dinners Haji would have for his executives and sales people as he wanted to have Fred's American business friend along.

Fred and Elian had sent their sons, Dariush and Danny, abroad for school when things began to become tenuous in Iran during the summer of 1978, so when the revolution happened, they were safely out of the country. Fred and his father felt that he, a businessman manufacturing electronic parts for products made in Iran, was in no danger.

After the revolution, they continued their normal lives at their farm just outside Karadj. Fred would go to his factory on Karadj Road in the morning and work until lunchtime, about 1:00, and drive home for a delicious Persian meal of *mast-e-khiar* (cucumber-yogurt soup), rice, *khorest* (stew), *nun-e-barbari* (bread), and fresh vegetables followed by fruit. After a brief nap, he would go to the stable where his horse would be ready for him to ride. He would often call his close friend General Nader Djahanbani, and they would ride out in the beautiful countryside for an hour or two.

Neither one felt he would be in danger as they were both doing the country, whether under the Shah or the new Islamic Republic, a service, and they were loyal Iranians. They loved their country and believed the regime would support industry and those running it as well as keeping members of the military who were loyal to the country in their positions. Neither had a fear.

On February 17, 1979, the sixty-six-year-old Habib was arrested on trumped-up charges of spying for the United States and Israel; the charges also included corruption, friendship with the enemies of God, warring with God and his emissaries, and economic imperialism. All that was simply ridiculous as he was a selfless servant of the nation, and from the 1950s until his incarceration, he was one of the few people who helped improve Iran's economic situation with all his heart. He was a true asset to the country and was one of few Iranians who used his credit with international banks for the benefit of Iran.

Many friends and influential people tried to intervene with the revolutionary government to get Haji released from prison as he was such a dedicated and important member of Iran's society including not only the Jews but as well the Muslims, the Armenians, and the Baha'is. He had done nothing but be an asset to the country, but the revolutionaries were too stupid to see what they were doing.

One influential doctor, Kamran Boukhim, who was head of the Jewish Community Hospital and the Tehran University Hospital, where many of the injured revolutionaries and students were treated during the protests and marches, had become friendly with many of the mullahs and leaders of the new Iranian government. He tried very hard to convince them that they should let Habib go. He was even able to get Ayatollah Teleghani to write a letter to the head of the Revolutionary Court stating that they must release Habib Elghanian, but due to the disorganized bureaucracy of that court, the letter never got to the right people.

On May 9, 1979, the one-year anniversary of his wife's death, Habib was tried in a twenty-minute trial and wearing his *tallit* and *kippah*, he recited "Shema Israel" as he was executed by firing squad. Even though the family and members of the Jewish community were able to get his unrecognizable body that night and bury him, the new regime prevented them from holding a memorial service or to mourn for him—they could only say *Kaddish*. The Iranian government repossessed every penny of the Elghanian family's holdings down to the smallest of their belongings.

He was the first Jew executed by the radical regime; shock waves went through the Jewish community that had lived in peace under the Shah. There was great fear among the Jews, so a delegation of their leaders went to Qom to meet with Ayatollah Khomeini. He decreed that no more Jewish people would be harmed since they were descendants of Moses, a holy man. Shortly after that, thirteen more Jews were executed.

Before the revolution, there were between 80,000 and 100,000 Jews in Iran. Haji's death prompted 75 percent of them to sell or abandon their assets and flee the country and by 2011 the census showed that the Jewish population was 8,756 then.

With his father in jail and his good friend having been executed, Fred became nervous that he too might be a target, but he didn't want to leave Iran with his father still incarcerated. He and Elian kept a low profile staying at the farm and minding their own business. The children were all abroad, Dariush in Ireland and Danny and Dianne in England. International phone lines were still working, so they talked to their children weekly.

A week or so after Habib was executed, Fred and Elian were sitting down to the midday meal when they heard shouting in the yard. Seven ragged Revolutionary Guards clambered through the doors with machine guns at their hips. They were held at gunpoint while the house was searched by the other gunmen, who when they entered the large play room with its pool table, huge TV, and extensively stocked bar, called to their colleagues to leave their prisoners and come have a drink!

Fred and Elian were totally terrified not knowing what to do until they heard raucous voices, clinking glasses, and the clack of billiard balls coming from the other room. Elian commented to Fred, "They'll soon be drunk and hungry, so let's get the servant to make a meal for them; that will take their minds off us."

The meal was prepared, and the revolutionaries were invited to the dining room to partake of a delicious and filling repast. They were all a little tipsy, but they were young men in their late teens and early twenties and so happy to have been sent to occupy such a luxurious place not to mention to enjoy the food and drink. They became friendly with Elian and Fred and stayed to enjoy several days of fun and games.

At one point when they were all very drunk, their leader took Fred aside and told him, "You know we were sent here to scope out your place and see what you were doing. We're supposed to report to our captain what we found here and when would be a good time to come to arrest you. We like you; we suggest you leave so you don't go to jail."

The following morning, another Revolutionary Guard barged in shooting his gun in the air. He saw that all his men were feeling no pain, so he went to the bar area and ordered the guards to pour every bottle of liquor down the toilets. They went through all the cupboards and poured out over a hundred bottles of liquor and wine.

"I'm taking my men away now. You've made them all drunk with your illegal drinks! We will be back to take the two of you to prison for your acts against God and the Islamic Republic." The Revolutionary Guards left the big, ultra-modern house of the Elghanians.

"Fred, what are we going to do? We'll be killed like your father! They have already taken your company and most of our money. Now, they'll take our farm and put us in prison! My babies! They're away! What will happen to them when we're dead? Oh God! Help us!" Elian was hysterical and crying.

"Elian, get in the car. We're leaving this place now."

"But my clothes, my jewelry! And what about the horses?"

"Forget about all of that if you want to live. I know some people from the factory. I'm sure I can find a place for us to hide in Tehran. I'll get in touch with the family in New York. I'll find a way for us to escape. Don't worry. I'll take care of you!"

He hoped he could keep that promise. He told the two grooms at the stable that they were leaving and to expect the revolutionaries to come and take over the farm. "Save our horses if you can," he told the two young Turkomans, "but save yourselves first."

The two young grooms, Ahmed and Reza, had been working for the Elghanians for several years. They had come to Karaj from the Turkoman Sahra looking for work at age fourteen. They were uneducated, but they had worked with their father's Turkoman race horses. Over four years, they felt they were a part of the family. They too were afraid of what was to come, though they promised to take care of the horses until the revolutionaries came to seize the property, which they most certainly would within a few days. Fred gave the boys the address of one of his friends so they would be able to find him and he could pay them their salaries, which were due.

He sped out the long drive with Elian crying uncontrollably and went to the home of one of his faithful factory workers who lived in the southern part of Tehran in a small, two-room, mud house that was very neat and clean. He put his arms around Elian and almost carried her into the front room as she continued to cry. His friend was not about to join the revolutionaries, but said that most of the young men who lived around him were in the Revolutionary Guard and it would be dangerous for them to stay with him and his family. He would try to find someone he trusted to keep them safe until they were able to get out of the country. He left them with his wife, who gave them tea and some sweets. Elian continued to cry while Fred got on his cell phone and tried to contact people who might be able to help him get them out of Iran. It was then that I received that phone call telling me that Fred and Elian wanted help getting out of Iran.

A small house in the center of Tehran was found where they could stay unnoticed by authorities. They didn't previously know the people they were housed with, but they were very kind and drove them around when they needed to go out and do errands. Fred had given his car to his factory worker to do what he wanted with it, but he warned him to keep it hidden for a few weeks until they were gone.

One evening at dusk, there was a knock at the door. Their host told them there were a couple of scruffy-looking young men looking for Fred. They were carrying several large sacks and said they were the grooms of Fred's stable who wanted their pay. They entered the house with their large saddlebags and stood shyly in the hall to await their wages. When Fred came with it, he customarily kissed them on both cheeks and learned that the guards had come to his farm and taken over. Ahmed and Reza had gone into the house, packed as much of Elian's and Fred's personal belongings they could fit into the saddlebags, and left the farm quickly with the belongings.

"Elian, Elian! Come here and see what is here!" Fred shouted to his crying wife. She came red eyed into the room and hugged the boys. Her tears became tears of joys when she realized that the boys had risked their lives to bring her so many things that were dear to her. There were photo albums, clothes, jewelry, and personal papers these two dear, young Turkomans had saved.

Fred gave the boys their money and wished them good luck getting back to the steppes. They left with big smiles as Fred had been very generous in paying them. Who knew when they would ever be paid again?

"My God! How did they find us, Elian?" Fred asked as the door closed behind them.

"Fred, they loved us and were so loyal! I can't believe it. And now we will never see them again. I hope God will be good to them and keep them from harm." She began to sob again, her shoulders shaking as she howled.

There was a type of underground in Iran not unlike the Mafia, so when a rough-looking man came to the house to take Fred and Elian to have passport photos taken, they knew an underground gang would arrange their escape. A message came that the New York branch of the family had purchased plane tickets for them on a direct flight to Paris in a week.

Several days after the photos were taken, the Iranian thug brought their false passports telling them that they were on the flight to Paris in three days. The tickets were in their false names. They were not sitting together, but they were in first class. Fred, who had grown a beard as a disguise, was to dress well and wear a hat for the flight, and Elian was to wear a chador.

"Your family has paid dearly for you to get out of this godforsaken country, so don't make any mistakes. Know your passport names and the backgrounds I have given you by heart. *Bon chance.* I wish I were going with you," were the thug's parting words.

They took a taxi to the airport and went to immigration to retrieve their passports, which had been handed in as was the law two days earlier. There was always the fear that immigration would pull their passports and thus prevent exit from the country, but miraculously, theirs were handed to them with no problem. They waited fearing they would be spotted, but when the flight was called, they boarded without a hitch. They held their breath hoping nothing would prevent the plane from taking off.

Once the Air France plane crossed the border into Turkey, the flight attendants popped the corks off champagne bottles and served the passengers a celebratory drink. They all toasted their escape.

Qasr Prison

CHAPTER 6

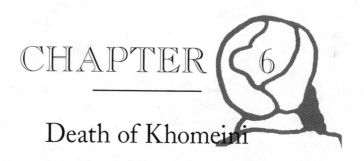

Death of Khomeini

The clerics had mobilized the Iranian masses. They exerted their influence from the remotest villages to the largest cities. Of the many opposition groups in the country that participated in the revolution, the clergy dominated Iran's political system. None of the other factions had the benefit of the traditional legitimacy of religion that would hold the population together.

The new Islamic government tapped into the clergy's power to achieve its agenda, but after the war, the regime established a symbiotic relationship that would shape both politics and the next generation of clerics. Any clerics who thought or behaved outside the framework of the regime's specific Islamic ideology were not tolerated, and many were excommunicated for heretical interpretations of Islamic theology.

The judiciary has played a vital role in preserving Iran's Islamic system as it falls under the authority of the Supreme Leader. It also implements the Islamic penal code including stoning, amputations, and flogging, and it is responsible for Iran having become the country with the largest number of executions in proportion to population in the world. During the first three decades of the Islamic Republic, crime rates, drug-related offenses, and financial crimes rose substantially. Allegations of corruption and bribery in the judiciary were rife, and though overhauls of the system were been promised, it was a slow process.

During the past four decades, the world has known little about what really has been happening in Iran with the exception of what we learn from a biased press controlled by the government. We rarely receive true information about the internal workings of Iran, which has become the most developed and modern country in the Middle East.

Iran is blamed for supporting ISIS and other jihadist organizations, which is totally untrue. The Iranian military has been and is still fighting ISIS; it has lost many brave young men to ISIS. Iran has over these past years wanted a dialogue with the West, but the West has not been interested in Iran unless it was for financial gain.

Iran had opposed and condemned the Taliban and al Qaeda for years, and after 9/11, the country privately offered to assist American efforts to overthrow the Taliban regime. Iran had influence with the Northern Alliance, the insurgency that had been battling the Taliban since the mid-nineties. Tehran used its influence to help the United States secure agreement among all elements of the Afghan opposition on a new government that took office in Kabul in December 2001. A month after that, Bush called Iran the new "axis of evil" and threatened to use military force to halt its nuclear program. Even so, Iran continued to offer cooperation on Afghanistan and volunteered to help the US raise and train a new Afghan army, but the Bush administration ignored its offer.

Over the years since the US and Iran severed relations, there has been some unofficial interaction between the two countries starting in the time of President Mohamed Khatami (1997–2005), a moderate reformer. The Nuclear Deal of 2016 has helped greatly with the relationship, and Iran is fulfilling its part of the deal in hopes of having more sanctions lifted and being able to create more dialog with the West.

But how has life been for the ordinary people of the country? Of course life continued and the population went on its way. There were arrests, imprisonments, and executions for anything from improper dress for women to the most heinous crimes one can think of, but on the whole, if you minded your own business and didn't verbally or actively oppose the regime, life was changed only by the limitations the war caused.

When the war ended, there were more executions; in one month, the administration hanged 2,500 prisoners, so the population became wary and more careful of its actions. The economy had been devastated by those dreadful years of the war, but it slowly began to grow as oil prices increased starting at the beginning of 1989 and as the National Iranian Oil Company began to produce more oil from its wells, many of which were under reconstruction and improvement.

Ayatollah Khomeini died at age eighty-six in June 1989. He had successfully destroyed all secular opposition, beaten down the Kurds, and seen his country through a monstrous war. However, he did not have a qualified successor because he had disqualified the two ayatollahs expected to replace him. The first, Ayatollah Shariatmaderi, had allegedly been in a plot against Khomeini and had been disgraced, tortured, and forced to recant. The second, Ayatollah Montazari, had also denounced Khomeini saying publicly and in writing, "Your prisons are far worse than those of the Shah and his SAVAK."

His successor was the fifty-year-old Seyyed Ali Hoseyni Khamenei, a former secretary general of the Islamic Republic Party who had been president from 1981 to 1989. Khamenei was not an ayatollah but a lesser cleric. Since the constitution stated that the Supreme Leader must be an ayatollah, the Constitutional Reform Council, against Shari'a law, declared him and his close friend Ali-Akbar Hashemi Rafsanjani ayatollahs. Rafsanjani was the elected president from 1989 to 1997.

Khomeini's death was a drama. He died in a clinic next to his home in north Tehran in the presence of his family and members of his inner circle. It was decided by officials not to announce his death until the following day; the government declared five national days of mourning followed by forty days of official morning as was the Muslim custom.

His body was prepared for burial as per his instructions and shrouded, as was the custom. On June 5, the body was taken to a vast wasteland in the hills north of Tehran designated as a place of prayer. His remains were in an air-conditioned glass case covered by a white shroud; his feet were facing Mecca, and his black turban was on his chest, an indication of his lineage from the prophet Muhammad.

Within a few hours, thousands of mourners were trying to get a last glimpse of their beloved leader. Due to the inadequate arrangements for such a crowd, eight people were killed and hundreds were injured in the crush.

It had been planned to have a funeral procession from these hills through the streets of Tehran to his burial place in Behesht-e-Zahra, the graveyard of the martyrs of the revolution and the war, but the crowd was so large that it was impossible for the procession to move. As hard as the Revolutionary Guard tried, they could not gain control even with the use of water cannons and firing into the air. The funeral was postponed.

When it did take place days later, it was chaotic. It was attended by millions of inconsolable mourners. The hearse was stopped repeatedly, and the crowd eventually took the coffin and started passing it over their heads. A helicopter finally arrived, but it was too late, and even the armed *Komiteh* guards couldn't stop the body from falling out of the coffin as the helicopter landed; they tore at the white shroud so that Khomeini's frail white leg was exposed. Shots were fired into the air to push the crowd back, but the guards were unable to retrieve the body. When it was eventually recovered, it was placed in an ambulance and taken to the helicopter for transport back to north Tehran to repeat the shrouding ritual.

The body was put in the grave, a simple vertical hole that accommodated it so that it faced Mecca. The crowd of mourners was huge; the media announced that dozens of people had been killed and over 10,000 were suffering from injuries, exhaustion, heat, and loss of consciousness.

CHAPTER 7

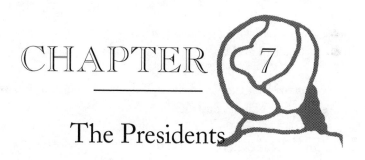

The Presidents

Akbar Hashemi Rafsanjani (1989-1997) was born to a wealthy family of pistachio farmers in Kerman Province. At age fourteen, he went to Qom to study theology as he did not see himself as a farmer. While studying, he came under the influence of Ayatollah Khomeini and became interested in politics.

When the Shah exiled Khomeini in 1963, Rafsanjani stayed in Iran to represent the Ayatollah. He continued to create opposition, which led to his imprisonment for clandestine activities against the Pahlavi regime seven times for a total of four years and five months. During the late sixties and early seventies, he traveled to twenty states in the US making speeches against the Shah and spreading revolutionary ideas to thousands of Iranian students there.

When Khomeini returned to Iran, he appointed Rafsanjani as the financial manager of the revolution and the Islamic Republic. Due to Khomeini's complete trust in him, he became one of the most powerful politicians in Iran. He was instrumental in establishing the Revolutionary Guard, and as second in command of the Joint Chiefs of Staff during the war, he persuaded Khomeini to accept UN Resolution 528 that ended the eight-year war.

He was elected president in August 1989 and served two terms until 1997. During his presidency, his policy was the economy first. He accomplished privatization of many companies that had been state owned and operated after the revolution. He was especially popular with the upper and middle classes due to his economic reforms and his successful support of human rights compared to those during Khomeini's time.

Unfortunately, his reconstruction efforts failed to reach the rural or war zones where they were most needed, which made him unpopular with veterans, farmworkers, and the working class. He was accused of corruption during his time and had confrontations with the Supreme Leader Khamenei, who gave increasing power to the Revolutionary Guard, which ordered many executions of political dissidents, drug offenders, Communists, Kurds, Baha'is, and even some Islamic clerics.

He was the first Iranian to show support for a nuclear deal as he did not believe weapons of mass destruction were a part of the Islamic culture, but he was unable to finalize a deal. He ran for a third term in 2005 but lost to Ahmadinejad. He died of a heart attack at age eighty-two in January 2017.

Mohamed Khatami (1997-2005) was elected president in 1997 with 70 percent of the vote; he served two terms until 2005. The son of a high-ranking cleric from Yazd Province, he became an ayatollah at a young age. He attained the highest level of education in Iran, studying in Esfahan and Tehran. In 1978, he was sent to Germany, where he chaired the Islamic Center in Hamburg for two years.

Before serving as president, he held many important government positions. As the first reformist president of Iran, he ran on a platform of liberalization and reform and advocated freedom of expression, tolerance, a civil society, constructive diplomatic relations with other states, and an economic policy that supported free markets and foreign investment. He believed in democracy and the inclusion of all Iranians in the political decision-making process.

Unfortunately during his presidency, unemployment remained a big problem due to the shortage of available jobs; the unemployment rate was 14 percent. Public and private investment in the energy sector, construction, and other industries increased, and the country's external debt was decreased by $5 billion, but 40 percent of the people were classified as poor during his time as president. His policies of reform led to repeated clashes, which he lost, with the hardline conservative Islamist members of the Guardian Council. By the end of his term, many of his followers had become disillusioned.

The controversial sixth president of the Islamic Republic was Mahmoud Ahmadinejad, who served two terms from 2005 through 2013. He was born to a poor family in the village of Ardan in northcentral Iran. His mother was a Sayyida, a descendant of Muhammad, and his father was a blacksmith with the surname of Sabbaghian or "thread painter," which is the lowliest job in the traditional carpet-weaving industry. To better the family's economic situation, his father moved them to the Narmak District of Tehran; to avoid discrimination, he changed the family name to Ahmadinejad, which means "race of Muhammad."

He earned a degree in engineering at Iran University in Tehran, where he became an anti-shah activist. He secretly produced and distributed a propaganda magazine called *Jiq va Dad*, "Scream and Shout," and joined the Islamic Association of Students, the group that took the hostages at the American Embassy. After the end of the war, he continued his higher education and became a professor at Iran University. In the 1990s, he held a number of government positions; he was appointed governor of Maku and Khoy in Azerbaijan and of Ardabil Province, a position he held for four years. In 2003, he was appointed mayor of Tehran during which time he imposed new cultural restrictions favored by the mullahs.

He ran for the presidency in 2005 with the support of the Guardian Council on a platform promising to address poverty and social injustices and to end corruption. He played a simple man, one of the people, and formed a strong bond with the deeply religious working class. Though the political elite ridiculed his pedestrian mannerisms, the common man identified with him. He was elected president of Iran on June 24, 2005.

His ultra-hard-liner intentions were made evident by the cabinet ministers he appointed when his term commenced in August. He was a common man and a demagogue. Never had the country had leader like him. It had had monarchs, learned clerics, aristocrats, and scholars but never such an uneducated, boorish man. He was a small, wiry, and cocky man who spoke in a very uneducated tongue that appealed to those of the lower socioeconomic group. He had no political experience and little acumen.

Under his leadership, the country went into decline. He found ways to spend the petrodollars importing goods and produce, rather than encouraging home production and farming. International relations worsened. He sped up Iran's nuclear program, which made the West believe it was aimed at making nuclear weapons. The UN and Western countries imposed sanctions, which worsened the country's economic problems.

His remarks that there was no such thing as a holocaust and that Israel needed to be wiped off the face of the earth turned Iran into a pariah state. During his time as president, he condemned the US for its proliferation of weapons of mass destruction and its climate of "intimidation and injustice." At the same time, he professed his desire to pursue Iran's nuclear technology program, which he claimed was for peaceful purposes. The UN Security Council passed resolutions to terminate Iran's nuclear enrichment programs and imposed sanctions on the country's imports and exports with the exception of those for development and humanitarian aid.

He instituted measures to control free speech, and he suppressed opposition with harassment, arrest, and imprisonment. He was unsuccessful in fulfilling his economic campaign promises, and despite the huge oil reserves, he was unable to stop the squandering of the profits. Inflation was between 30 and 40 percent during his presidency.

When the elections of 2009 were held, the people thought that they would be free of this autocrat. The polls said that he would be defeated by his rival, Mir-Hussein Mousavi, for whom there had been tens of thousands of supporters marching throughout the cities chanting their slogan, "Ya shasoon Mousavi," "Long Live Mousavi."

When the polls closed on June 12, 2009, Ahmadinejad was in the lead. Mousavi claimed that the Revolutionary Guard and Ahmadinejad were rigging the votes. The next day, Ahmadinejad's interior ministry announced that indeed he had won with 24 million votes; only 13 million had been cast for Mousavi. Mousavi, with a silver beard, had served as prime minister under Khomeini and had openly criticized his opponent; he had wide support especially from the reformist groups. His supporters became known as the Green Movement, which had incorrectly predicted his victory.

People were referring to the elections as a coup d'état staged by Ahmadinejad and the Revolutionary Guard. Green demonstrations took part all over the country demanding new elections that would never happen. There were demonstrations in the streets of millions of protesters, and hundreds of Green Movement activists were jailed, but the Supreme Leader, Ayatollah Ali Khamenei, formally endorsed Ahmadinejad as president anyway. The Green Movement was put down violently; its people began being spirited off to prison in the middle of the night to serve unknown terms. It was the largest uprising seen in Iran since the 1979 revolution.

Though inflation and unemployment did decrease during his second term, he was accused of continuing to implement cronyism and corruption, and human rights deteriorated during his time as president. He was a true hard-liner.

Hassan Rouhani's (2013-present) father was an ayatollah who owned a spice shop in the town of Sorkheh and had been politically active against the Shah. When he was twelve, he was sent to the seminary in Semnan to study and then on to Qom to continue his religious education. He attained a bachelor's degree at Tehran University (and a PhD from Glasgow University in Scotland in the 1990s).

After receiving his undergraduate degree, he traveled about Iran making speeches against the government of the Shah and his support for the exiled Khomeini and was arrested many times by SAVAK. He was finally informed by his religious comrades that it would be safer to leave the country, so he went to Europe, where he began making anti-shah speeches to Iranian student groups. When Khomeini arrived in France, he was summoned to be a part of his entourage.

He was instrumental in setting up Iran's military after the revolution and was elected to the Majlis in 1980. During his twenty years in that capacity, he held many important positions including deputy speaker of the house, head of the defense committee, and head of the foreign policy committee. He was also in charge of the supervisory council of the Islamic Republic of Iran Broadcasting immediately after the revolution.

Up until he announced his presidential candidacy in 2013, he had been the representative of the Supreme Leader at the Supreme National Security Council (SNSC), secretary general of the SNSC, national security advisor to Presidents Hashemi and Khatami, a member of the Expediency Council, a member of the board of trustees of Tehran University, and managing editor of three academic quarterlies in Persian and English. Hassan Rouhani had been a busy man!

His biggest accomplishment during his first term as president was the signing and implementation of the nuclear deal. Though his economic policies were disappointing in this term, he was reelected in May 2017 on a platform of long-term economic development, boosting the purchasing power of the people, reducing the wealth gap, improving the rights of women, more personal freedom, and improving relations with the world. At present, he has a high percent approval rating, so hopefully, he will accomplish much of what he plans for his country in the next four years.

CHAPTER  8

Iran's Nobel Prize

Shirin Ebadi was the first Muslim woman to receive the Nobel Peace Prize. She grew up in a big, two-story house on Shah Avenue in Tehran that like most old Iranian homes was built around a courtyard with a large fish pond around which grew beautiful roses that Iran is famous for. Though they lived in the city, her father had a farm in Hamadan, several hours northwest of Tehran.

While they were visiting the country home when she was about six, Mossadeq, a popular prime minister, was toppled by a coup. For the religious, the working class, the *bazari*, and many wealthy Iranians, Mossadeq was a beloved national hero and a leader fit to guide their great civilization with its 2,500-year history.

The Iranian constitution of 1906 had established a constitutional monarchy, and the country ran well under the reign of Reza Shah (1926–1941), a wise dictator who ruled with total authority and popular support. In 1941, Reza Shah was forced to abdicate in favor of his son, Mohamed Reza Pahlavi, after the British and Russians forces occupied Iran during World War II. The country seemed to be governed well by their elected representatives, and early in the new regime, Mossadeq was elected prime minister. The young Shah became nervous as his new prime minister nationalized the Iranian oil industry and began to rise in popularity.

Iranian generals, the US, and Great Britain, who backed the Shah, were incensed at the nationalization of Iran's oil. The two major powers awaited the right moment to help stage a coup d'état. Kermit Roosevelt came to Iran to reassure the skittish Shah and direct the coup. He had $1 million to spend on paying crowds of poor people in south Tehran to march and bribe newspapers to run spurious headlines. It took only four days to topple the elderly prime minister and restore the Shah to power. The Shah thanked Roosevelt: "I owe my throne to God, my people, my army, and you."

Iranian people were humiliated to watch the foreign intervention of their country as if it were an undeveloped country. The foreigners had saved their interests in the oil industry, which was a considerable income for them. In fact, they earned more than the Iranians did off the country oil's revenue. Mossadeq received the death penalty at a military trial that the merciful Shah commuted to three years in prison. He spent part of those years in a Tehran prison but was allowed to retire to his village of Ahmadabad, where he died on March 5, 1967.

In most Iranian families, sons are given special treatment; they are spoiled and permitted to do anything without admonishment. They feel they are the center of the world; they have exalted positions, and their fathers love them more than they do their daughters.

But that was not the case in the Ebadi family; Shirin never felt that her father cared for her brother, Jafar, more than he did for her. After the coup, her father, who was a longtime supporter of Mossadeq, lost his job as Deputy Minister of Agriculture and languished in lower posts never again to be given a senior position. He hid the fact of his demotion and eventually a lack of a job from the children, the norm in Iranian families as children were seldom privy to family problems.

In 1965, Shirin entered law school at Tehran University. In the Iranian system, a judge is not required to practice law first, so she decided to go into the study of judgeship; she had no idea how absorbed in politics she would become. It seemed that almost all the other law students were consumed with politics. Though she spent hours with her classmates studying criminal and domestic law, she became focused on the politics that were in the forefront. There were protests as there are still in universities today, but Shirin became overly attracted to them. These protests were followed closely by SAVAK on the campuses, the streets of most Iranian cities, and in the United States and Europe, where there were many Iranian students studying and demonstrating.

The students at the university were mostly from middle or working-class families. The women didn't wear the veil, but they also didn't date in the American sense; they gathered as mixed crowds at coffee houses or went on weekend trips together as a group. Though the women and men studied together in the library, in class, the women sat at the front while the men were at the back.

Shirin graduated in 1970 at age twenty-three and became a judge. As she was one of the top two students in her class, she spent the last two years of her studies interning with various branches of the judiciary. Once the district judge felt she had mastered the legal code, she was permitted to preside over a courtroom. She joined an institution of an unpopular government, but she did not take sides. Within five years, she was appointed president of the Tehran City Court. In those days, Iranians appealed to the courts for anything from divorce to fraud and had confidence that the legal system was fair and uncorrupt. Political opponents were prosecuted in military courts, which were kept out of the public justice system.

She made a love match with an electrical engineer, Javad Tavasolian, whom she married with the blessing of her family. She continued to work after her marriage, but the tone and the atmosphere in the streets of Tehran were changing. In 1977, the Shah's regime tried to reduce the jurisdictional power of the court by creating a Mediating Council, which would adjudicate cases outside the formal justice system. Some of the justices wrote a protest letter, which Shirin signed. The signatories of the letter were threatened with expulsion from the courts, but that didn't happen, and she continued with her job. There were demonstrations at the time, but it was not evident that they were anything more than overheated politics; it was not understood that an Islamic revolution was beginning.

The mosque had always been a place where grievances against the government could be aired behind the semi-protected walls of a holy building. Iranians didn't feel it was shocking or foreboding to hear Ayatollah Khomeini broadcasting his denunciations on radio and tapes from exile. But by the summer of 1978, the protests had grown, and she began to feel herself drawn to the side of the opposition that hailed Khomeini.

When the revolution happened, she felt that she too had won, but it took her less than a month to realize she had participated in her own demise. She was a woman, and the revolution became her defeat. Everything in Tehran changed. The first thing that happened was that the women were forced to wear the hijab, the head scarf. The government officials who had always been beautifully dressed in smart, dark suits with ties and shiny shoes started wearing plain, ill-fitting pants and collarless, wrinkled, and stained shirts. Offices that used to smell faintly of cologne started sporting a stale, musky smell.

And then it happened. She was stripped of her judgeship. She was called into a meeting in front of a committee of men, two of whom were judges she knew well; one had actually been her junior until the previous year. She was at the time seven months pregnant with her first child, and these men let her stand while they sat behind a long wooden table not thinking to ask her to sit. Without other words, one judge rudely threw a sheet of paper at her and said, "Show up at the legal office for work tomorrow." That in effect meant she was being demoted to the position of a legal clerk.

Shirin showed up for work punctually the following morning but stubbornly refused to do any work; she just sat there. She continued her strike until she became almost crazy with boredom as hours blurred into days and days blurred into weeks.

Finally, one morning, she decided it was time to do some work. Her first task was to read the morning paper *Enghelab-e Eslami*, the imaginatively named "Islamic Revolution." She was in shock when she saw the headline "Islamic Penal Code Overhauled." She could not believe what she was reading: the value of a woman's life was half that of a man, a woman's testimony in court as a witness counted only half as much as a man's, and a woman had to ask permission for a divorce. The laws turned the clock back fourteen hundred years to the days when the stoning of women for adultery and chopping off hands for thievery were considered appropriate sentences.

It was becoming apparent to educated people that the revolution was veering in a vicious direction, and violence seemed to be growing. The revolution was losing sight of its ideals of freedom and independence and was alienating Iranians with its own rampant corruption and repressiveness.

And then came the Iran-Iraq War. Khomeini was orating about his determination to spread his revolution around the region claiming that Islam had no borders and that God had commanded the war. However,

Saddam Hussein declared that it was a border dispute in which he wanted to take control of Iran's oil-rich southern province.

During the first days of the war, normal life ground to a halt. Government and most other offices closed early, and restaurants and movie houses were not open after dark because the citizens wanted to be safe in their homes when the air raids started. People listened to their portable radios constantly to not miss an alert. The stores ran out of staples such as flour, sugar, rice, and detergents. When rationing was put into effect by the government, people had to stand in line for hours at the stores to reach cashiers who would dole out their rations.

The political repression of the early revolution had not stopped. The papers were full of lists of the executed, which included most of the Shah's officials and counterrevolutionaries who had been hanged or shot by firing squad. There were macabre pictures of bodies, but people were afraid to express their anger at the fact that the revolution had deceived them. They had to support the only government they had, and even though they were at war with a brutal tyrant, the majority of the Iranians knew that Khomeini's revolution had not united them; it was the war that had done that.

As the war went on, the television showed footage of young recruits wearing bandannas with the keys to heaven around their necks boarding buses for the battlefields. The reports that came back were horrific— hundreds of thousands of Iranians were killed.

Everyone became terrified that their homes would be searched and books or publications deemed to be anti-regime would be discovered and they would be arrested. Shirin took any books with objectionable titles off the shelves and lugged them out to the garden, where she burned them not wanting to have anything that could be construed as anti-regime in her home.

Her second child, a daughter, was born in 1983. Civil servants, and Shirin was one, were allowed to retire after fifteen years, so the day after her fifteen years was up, she handed in her resignation, which was accepted readily. She felt the system was not going to change any time in the near future; it had already killed the careers of women.

After her retirement, life became a struggle because Javad's company had been closed on the grounds that it was infiltrated by Communists, which of course was not true. There were times when they had little income; inflation was high, and raising two children was expensive. They cut their spending habits to afford necessities such as powdered milk and diapers.

The world seemed to watch silently as the war continued. UN missions investigated the chemical warfare but did nothing; the US, hoping to contain a government it deemed hostile to its interests in the area, aided the Iraqis by providing satellite images of Iranian deployments and battle-planning assistance.

With the world's superpower aiding Saddam Hussein and the Islamic Republic bent on prolonging the war, Iranians started fleeing their country. Right after the revolution, many who had opposed it and those connected to the Shah's regime had left for Europe or America to start new lives. Now, some managed to obtain visas and departed by plane from Mehrabad with their dignity intact, but hundreds of thousands of others took to the desert and mountain routes paying bandits to smuggle them into Turkey and Pakistan. These smugglers made vast sums shepherding Iranians through desert passes and gorges in the dark; it was dangerous, but so was staying in Iran.

Shirin began writing legal books hoping to contribute to the legal fields, and many foreign journalists began to seek her out because she was an expert on women's rights. One evening, she was invited to meet with a reporter at the posh former Sheraton Hotel. She was totally shocked as she saw stylish men and women in the restaurant listening to piano music and devouring steaks and fancy desserts while the rest of the city's population had coupons or could not get what they needed. It seemed to her that the wealthy were experiencing the war in a far different way than ordinary people were.

In July 1988, the USS *Vincennes* fired a heat-seeking missile at an Iranian civilian airliner killing all 290 people onboard. President Reagan could not explain how the ship, equipped with the most sophisticated radar gear, could have mistaken the huge airplane for a supersonic, sleek, fighter plane. When the ship's captain received a medal for his actions, the Iranians could not believe it had been a mistake. The mullahs had to reevaluate the war; was the US finally going to take sides? American intervention would help Iraq recover lost ground and endanger the revolution.

After nearly eight years and a half a million dead, they decided to end the fighting and accept the UN cease-fire resolution. Khomeini broadcast a radio statement: "I pledged to fight to the last drop of my blood, and though this decision is akin to drinking a chalice of poison, I submit myself to the will of God."

In 1992, the judiciary passed a law permitting women to practice law, so Shirin opened her law practice in an office on the first floor of the building they owned and lived in. She specialized in commercial and trade cases but would occasionally accept a pro bono political client. Most of her cases were business oriented—getting clients' money or property back from their debtors, suing for damages, or defending them against unjust allegations. Often, her cases would never get to the courts, as clients would tell her that the prosecution had accepted bribes and their cases had been settled.

The courts were corrupt. She decided that as her family had survived on Javad's income for years, she would give up the law that earned her an income and start taking only pro bono cases that would let her show the injustice of the Islamic Republic's laws. She took cases that showed the theocracy's discrimination against women, and she became co-founder of the Association for Support of Children's Rights.

She wrote an article about a young girl who had been raped and killed by three young men. They were arrested and put in jail, but one of them confessed and somehow hanged himself. The other two were sentenced to death. However, because a woman's life was worth so little, the judge ruled that the girl's family would have to pay for the execution because she was worth less than the two men. This was very hard for the family, which was from Sanandaj in Kurdistan and very poor. They sold what they could but still did not have enough, so the girl's brother and father decided to sell their kidneys. It turned out that they were both rejected, but the doctor was shocked when he heard their reason for wanting the money. He wrote the head of the judiciary threatening to report the case to the international organization, Doctors without Borders, unless the treasury made up the difference needed for the execution.

The judiciary agreed, but then, one of the prisoners escaped prison. The court reopened the case, which had never been closed; Iranian law is ambiguous and even a closed case always remains subject to further review. This article illustrated how outrageous the laws were and how they treated women as non-people. The paper in which it was published was sold out immediately, and reprints were necessary. One member of the Majlis told reporters, "Someone stop this woman or we'll shut her up ourselves." The system was beginning to fear her work.

During the 1990s, she was arrested several times mostly for improper Islamic dress but sometimes for no apparent reason as on the day she was in Ramsar near the Caspian Sea, where she and her family were vacationing over the Now Ruz holiday. In 1999, she was arrested for her outcries against the regime's treatment of women. There seemed to be little that anyone could do for protection against a state that wished to impose a climate of fear.

On June 28, 2000, she was arrested concerning the trial of the killers of a student in the riots of that time; the police chief and some of his officers had been charged with the murder. She was representing the family of the dead student, who wanted the murderers to be sentenced. She had heard gossip that she would be arrested because of the case, so when the phone call came for her to report to the precinct, she was not surprised. She had packed a bag with her things and had her husband drive her there.

The session with the judge lasted only twenty minutes. She was ushered outside to a dimly lit parking lot where she was put in a vehicle that would take her up the mountain to the infamous Evine Prison. Her kind driver stopped at a kiosk on the way so she could quench her thirst with a soda. When she arrived at the prison, she was asked if she was there for a moral offense, to which she replied, "No! What are you talking about? My offense is political." It seemed that most late-night arrivals were prostitutes.

She was put in a cell that was covered in filth. The sink had no running water, and the toilet in the corner was rust-rimmed and dirty. With her chador as a pillow, she fell asleep only to be wakened a few hours later to a breakfast of a piece of bread, a small square of salty cheese, and some tea. She was taken to administration, where she was fingerprinted and had a numbered tag hung over her head and a mug shot taken; she was ready for her stay. Shirin was moved to two more prisons during her imprisonment and was interrogated almost every day for at least two hours by the same interrogator.

Finally after three weeks, she was awakened one morning to be told she should dress for her trial. It went well, but she was sent back to prison for ten more days. She was finally informed that she would be released on a bail amount of 20 million toman, about $25,000. Her husband took the deed to their house to the court, and she was released the next day. An ambulance took her from the prison to an intersection where the driver asked a taxi driver to transport her home. What a way to be released!

When she inquired about the case she had been imprisoned for, she was told that it had been dismissed. After all, the student had been an agitator, and though he had been killed in the dormitory by paramilitaries, the state permitted to prey on its citizens, he was dead and that was the end of it. Neither the government nor the judicial system cared for such cases.

As the new millennium unfolded, things in Iran became a little easier. The enforcers became more lenient about the hajib and dress of young women, the internet became available to all, cafés began opening around Tehran, and parks began holding outdoor concerts; art galleries opened up and held regular exhibits. The young people were fighting back with boldness, and with their numbers, it was difficult for the state to impose itself as it had in the 1980s and 1990s.

Shirin continued to fight for women's rights and representing pro bono anyone who came to her with a problem she felt she could help with, especially if it had to do with women's or children's rights.

Her eldest daughter left Iran to study in Canada in 2003, and Shirin became busier with her work. When fourteen women were elected to the Majlis, she became involved as they asked her to draft a bill that would broaden women's rights but be compatible with Islam. Once it was drafted, it became stuck in a preapproval commission, and she was asked to plead its case in front of the commission, which she did; however, the bill failed to pass.

When she was invited to attend a seminar in Paris, the Iranian Embassy tried to prevent her participation on the grounds that her beliefs were counter to the official positions of the Iranian government. It seemed that the system believed it could control what was said or thought about the country anywhere. The Iranian Embassy threatened to prevent its county's films and works of art from leaving the country for the event if she were allowed to attend, but the French organizers refused to be cowed by that, and finally, the Iranian government gave in, and she took her daughter with her to the event.

The evening before she was to return to Iran, she stayed with an old colleague from the pre-revolutionary judiciary who was at the time vice president of the International Federation of Human Rights. They had a good time reminiscing about the old days in Tehran before the revolution.

The next morning as she was leaving his house, a call came for her; someone said she had won the Nobel Peace Prize. She hung up thinking it was a prank. When she was called the second time, she was convinced that she had in fact been awarded the Nobel Peace Prize for her efforts for democracy and human rights especially for those of women and children.

She asked her friend what she should do; he suggested she stay in Paris until the announcement was official; there, he could arrange a press conference for her, which would be difficult to do in Tehran.

When she arrived at the crowded conference room he had arranged for, she was bombarded with questions from the press even before she stood behind the podium. Being a very articulate woman, she answered calmly and quickly all she could manage. An emissary from the Iranian Embassy arrived to congratulate her and give her a Quran as a present; the ambassador, who said he was too busy to attend, called her on the phone.

The incessant interviews she was asked to give began to wear her out, so she decided to return home with her daughter on an Iran Air flight. Word had gotten out about the prize, so when they boarded, the captain congratulated her and moved her and her daughter to first class. Many passengers sent congratulatory notes to her, so she stood when they were at cruising altitude and went up the aisle shaking people's hands and thanking them. The captain announced that he was naming the journey the Flight of Peace and invited them up to the flight deck. She was surprised that he was not steering and watching where he was going, so he had to tell her about autopilot!

When she arrived at Mehrabad Airport, a huge number of Iranians were waiting for her. She saw her mother's proud, smiling face; she gave her a hug and kissed her hand before she noticed the crowd. Ayatollah Khomeini's granddaughter placed a wreath of orchids around her neck. As she walked through the throng of people encircled by police, she shouted out as loud as she could, *"Allah-o-Akbar!"* One of the popular vice presidents was there and greeted her warmly. She was hoisted up on a makeshift platform, and she looked over the thousands of people in the terminal to the outside, where she figured there had to be over a hundred thousand people. Not since the return of Khomeini had there been such a massive welcome. Most of the welcomers were women, some in black chadors but the majority in colorful head scarves and veils waving gladiolas and white roses. That was a proud moment; she had realized some of her goals for women and children's rights in Iran. That, she hoped, would give the people who worked in human rights more courage to continue their work.

The Islamic Republic officials either ignored or were critical of the pro-Western institution's award and criticized her for not covering her hair during the presentation. President Khatami did not even congratulate her; belittling the honor, he said that though the scientific Nobel Prizes were important, the Peace Prize was nothing and was presented to her for purely political reasons.

In Iran, she continued to defend prominent political prisoners, journalists, students, and women as well as continuing to call for reforms in the country. She let her belief that change could happen only peacefully be known loudly throughout the country. She was not imprisoned after her Nobel Prize, but she was often threatened by the authorities telling her to stop working for human rights and calling for reform.

Her husband was arrested in Tehran and severely beaten, but she continued to criticize the government for its suppression of opposition protests and urged that new elections take place that would be monitored by the UN. That made her become even more unpopular with those in power.

In 2008, these threats intensified. Her life and those of her family were said to be in danger. She was criticized for defending the Baha'i community, and her youngest daughter was accused of converting to that faith, which was a capital offense in the Islamic Republic. In December that year, her office of the Defenders of Human Rights Center was shut down by the police. In 2009, "demonstrators" probably hired by the regime attacked her home and place of work.

The controversial elections took place while she was on a speaking tour in Spain. As the world knows today, it was a totally rigged event, and the cruel incumbent, Ahmadinejad, was again president. She was advised not to go back to Iran. Since then, she has been living in exile mostly in Great Britain.

In November, on the orders of Tehran's Revolutionary Court, her Nobel medal was confiscated by the raiding of her safety deposit box; as well, her bank accounts were frozen, and $410,000 was demanded for taxes on the $1.3 million Nobel Prize money.

While she was out of the country, Iranian agents set her husband up and videotaped a supposedly romantic physical encounter he had with a woman. He was taken to the Evine Prison, where he was flogged for having drunk alcohol, and later, he was sentenced to stoning for having committed adultery. He was forced to go on national television to admit his crimes and denounce his marriage to his wife. After that, she felt it was only fair to allow him to divorce her and hopefully escape more persecution from the administration.

To this day, Shirin Ebadi is championing her causes for women's and children's rights around the world by her lectures and writings. She truly believes,

> The Western world should be spending money funding education and an end to corruption rather than fighting with guns and bombs. The Islamic State stems from an ideology based on a "wrong interpretation of Islam." Physical force will not end ISIS because it will not end its beliefs.

"Until We Are Free", Shirin Ebadi.

CHAPTER 9

Other Women of Note

After the revolution, the way of life for women changed greatly. Gone were the days when they could arise in the morning and pick from their many colorful, Western-style skirts and dresses that they would wear for the daytime activities whether under a chador or not. Now, Khomeini had decreed that all women must wear the chador in public; those caught without the *hajib* could face public whipping or time in prison. What was the use of dressing up if no one would see you?

Since the time of Reza Shah in the 1920s, women were given universal education and increased career opportunities. The government had forbidden the wearing of the chador, and they were given the right to vote. The Family Protection Laws in 1967 gave them the right to divorce their husbands and petition for custody of their children. Before 1979, the Women's Organization of Iran, which was under the patronage of the Shah's twin sister, Ashraf, helped women gain freer education and economic independence, abortion was made legal, and labor laws were revised to eliminate sex discrimination and encourage equal pay for women. Women were encouraged to run for public office, and some were cabinet ministers, governors, and mayors; one was an ambassador. Iran's women had become westernized.

Then came the revolution. The women were persuaded to demonstrate and take part in this revolution that promised true democracy and equal rights for women. They ran with the masses and took part in the marches with hundreds of thousands to demonstrate their loyalty to their would-be Supreme Leader. They were among the frenzied mob when Ayatollah Ruhollah Khomeini disembarked from the chartered Air France plane that brought him back to his homeland after fifteen years in exile. They shouted, *"Khomeini, O Imam, Allah-o-Akhbar!"* with the crowd of millions expecting that he would be the leader who would personify their aspirations, restore their spirituality, and bring them freedom, independence, and justice. But he enforced Islamic dress on women, banned alcohol, and began to impose what was in effect the religious culture of the urban lower middle classes on everyone. The rights that women had gained under the Shah were systematically removed.

Mary Gharagozlou, who was running her Arab stud farm just outside Shiraz, was walking across her courtyard one day several weeks after the revolution when a group of shabbily dressed Revolutionary Guards came smashing through the wooden gate to her small compound surrounded by a high mud wall.

"Where is Mary Khonume?" they shouted waving their ancient rifles.

"I am here!" she answered.

"You're under arrest!"

"What have I done to be arrested?"

"You have tried to start a revolt of the tribes. Your file has been found, and you will come with us!" shouted the big, bearded, burly man who seemed to be the leader. "You will come with us now," he said as two of the men roughly grabbed her arms.

"Wait! Please wait! I need to tell my workers to make sure my horses are taken care of while I'm gone," she pleaded.

"Very well, but hurry! We need to get you to the transport depot. You will be going to the Qasr Prison in Tehran," the captain said.

Mary rushed to the stable where the grooms were resting as it was the middle of the day and hurriedly told them that she was being taken to prison and that they must see that the horses, the property of the Royal Horse Society, were taken care of while she was gone. Since the revolutionaries had taken over, who was to know if the horses would continue to be a part of the government's responsibilities? She had received no money to date and had been buying feed and necessities from her own meager savings; she just hoped that the regime would establish itself soon and the Asil Arabs she had worked so hard to produce and get recognized by the world would continue to be a part of the heritage of the country.

The Pasdaran men roughly pushed her toward an old Land Rover outside the gates and at gunpoint told her to climb in. Sitting in the back, being jostled on the uneven dirt track that led to the main road to Shiraz from her compound, she reflected on how she had arrived in this place after having the wonderful life she had had in Aghili during the winters and at her family home high in the mountains near Hamadan in the summers till just before the revolution.

Under the direction of Kambiz Atabai and thanks to the many Bakhtiar contacts and the Shah, the Royal Horse Society had agreed to take responsibility for her herd of beautiful horses when she was almost penniless. After her husband, Majid, had been killed, his family did not let her have any of his estate because she had divorced him to work with the tribes to help them modernize their agricultural methods at the time of the Shah's land reform.

The small stable Majid had bequeathed to her in his will was where she and her herd of beautiful Arab horses spent their winters, while in summer, she drove the herd north to her old home near Hamadan. In the late 1970s, she was told she must move the stud farm to a more central location near the city of Shiraz, and she would not be allowed to continue the nomadic trek she made every year with the herd.

The Persian Arab had in effect been recognized by the World Arab Horse Association; the official studbook Mary was working on needed to be completed. Kambiz felt that the horses should be in a place where tourists and other interested people could appreciate them. The move had not been to her liking, but Mary had been allowed to design her stable and home, with the help of the royal architects, in the traditional Persian style, so when the actual move took place, she was very happy with her situation.

She was a long way from Tehran and far enough from Shiraz that when the demonstrations started, she wasn't affected at all. However, as they became more frequent, she began to watch what was happening on TV, for which she usually had no time. Then when the departure of the Shah and her savior, Kambiz Atabai, occurred, she was unsure what would happen to her. Next came Khomeini and at first no government at all. Her small savings began to dwindle rapidly when funds from Tehran ceased. And then came her arrest.

She was shoved from the Land Rover to a battered, old school bus with about forty other men and women who had also been arrested for one thing or another. Everyone declared his or her innocence of the charges placed upon them to no avail. They were on their way to the Qasr Prison, a two-day trip. The bus stopped several times along the way so people could relieve themselves, and they were offered water and stale *nun-e-barbari*.

When they finally reached their destination, they were blindfolded and herded like sheep toward the prison. Mary heard some people tripping over things and the guards shouting, "What's the matter with you? Are you blind?" She was led into what she thought was a small room that smelled like vomit and urine.

"Put your hands out!" shouted the person who was pushing her, and she fell against a wall. Her hands were tied together, and she was pushed to the ground. Her blindfold was pulled off, and she saw a bearded man staring down at her. "Why did you tell the sheik that he should not join the forces of the Ayatollah?" he yelled.

"I did no such thing!"

"We have found a file that you have been telling all the tribespeople who live in your area that they should not be a part of our revolution. You have been arrested for corruption and acts against Allah and therefore you will be executed!"

"Your time will come soon," shouted another big, rough-looking man with short, black hair and a trimmed black beard who had entered the small cubicle. They left.

She saw a small slab of wood on short legs that she realized must be her bed and in the corner a bucket for her to use as her toilet. As well, there was a rusty sink that had no water. The room was cold, but luckily, there were two rough, brown blankets rolled up on the bed. She had lost track of time, but she felt it was probably late in the evening. There was no window in her cell, so she had no idea if it was night or day. She was exhausted after the long trip from her comfortable and formerly safe home, so she put one blanket under her and the other over and slept.

Mary had heard nothing but horror stories about life in Iranian prisons whether it was during the time of the Shah or now in the time of revolution, so she was surprised when her door was opened and a decent breakfast of nun, fruit, and tea was brought to her cell by a woman guard after she had awakened from a fitful sleep the next morning.

Later, the woman guard returned and told her she was being moved to the women's prison and would be put in a ward with many others. She was led through a dark, dank corridor to the barred metal door of a room about twenty-five by fifteen feet with a brown, worn carpet; it was full of women of all ages. One of the women pointed to a spot in the far corner and indicated that would be Mary's domain. Amazingly enough, the room was quite clean. The food brought to them three times a day was not terrible, and for some reason, she was not taken to interrogation every day as most of the others were.

As time went on, women left one by one usually to be shot by a firing squad though some were released on bail. Each night when she went to sleep in her corner, she wondered if it would be her last. Days, weeks, and months continued with no torture and not much interrogation, so she began to think she might be spared for some reason.

Finally, the day came when her name was called on the loudspeaker; she was told to report to the matron of her unit.

"Mary Gharagozlou, you are a very lucky woman!" said the matron when she entered the small, dingy office with rusty steel furniture. "You have obviously been cleared of your charges and without a trial. You are being released. The tribesmen you worked with over the years banded together and have demanded that you be set free. I have never heard of such a thing since the return of our Ayatollah, but I wish you luck."

Mary was ushered through the door and directed to get into a taxi, which took her to the city center. When she got back to her stud farm, she found that her horses and men were all well and that the Islamic Republic was paying for their care.

But as the war set in, the Islamic Republic lost interest and had no time for its equine heritage; government money trickled to a stop. She still owned a small piece of what had been extensive lands of her family near Hamadan, so she moved with her horses and dogs back to the Gharagozlou tribal area. She had no money to speak of, and when she was down to her last resorts, she wrote to a friend,

> Many things have happened, and my life is topsy-turvy. I am in a small property near the town of Hamadan. I have a house, a stable, my horses and a new German shepherd

puppy. All the money I have left does not amount to one hundred dollars, and we all have to eat and have heat through the winter. God is great!

One evening when she was unable to sleep, she went to the stable and mounted her favorite horse, Khabiseh. She rode to the top of a barren hill just below the Alborz Range and dismounted. Standing at the side of the mare with her arms around its neck, she searched for the new moon as it set, looking for the face of her horse to be seen in that moon. It was a tribal superstition that if you saw the face of your horse in the new moon, it would bring you luck. As she found the image in the moon, she said to her horse, for she had started talking to them at that point, "We have a place to live, but what are we going to eat? I cannot feed myself let alone you horses."

Shortly after sunrise, her caretaker came running to the top of the hill where she had been standing with Khabiseh and said, "Madam, there is a telegram from outside [meaning outside Iran] for you." She was completely flabbergasted; she didn't think even her sister, who lived in Italy, could have found her. In a panic thinking it was bad news, she told him to bring it to her directly. She opened it with shaking fingers and read, "I have six thousand dollars with me for fodder for your horses. Signed, Don Ford." He was the president of the World Arab Horse Organization (WAHO).

She eventually decided to sell the little place at Hamadan so she could move nearer to Tehran. Mary took that money and what little of her savings was left and convinced some of the supporters of the Persian Arab horse to help her build a stud farm near Kordon, a small town on the mountain slopes west of Tehran. Having been forbidden to leave the country after her release from prison, she spent her time finalizing the Persian Arab studbook, which was submitted to the WAHO and accepted; due to this accomplishment, she was allowed to go to England accompanied by a minder to present the Persian Arab to be recognized internationally.

Her traditional arched house at the foot of the mountains and stable block of dried mud construction were where she lived her final years on air and windfalls from occasional benefactors surrounded by her horses and cared for by old tribal retainers.

Mary died on September 14, 2011. Her funeral was attended by hundreds of tribespeople along with her horses standing at graveside.

Louise Firouz had joined forces with Kambiz Atabai and the Royal Horse Society for a second time in 1977. The society had formed the World

Caspian Association, which included Caspians that had been exported to Canada, the US, and New Zealand as well as the small herd that had been presented to the Prince Phillip, Duke of Edinburgh, by the Shah during the spectacular celebrations for 2,500 years of the royal dynasty of Iran in 1971.

Though there were probably still Caspians in the forests of Mazandaran, Louise's small herd was appropriated by the Royal Horse Society as it had declared that all Caspians in Iran were to become property of the society. Louise it seemed was expected to keep feeding and caring for what were now not her Caspians any longer.

During that time, she and Narcy were almost bankrupt and could hardly afford to feed the animals. Louise wrote a letter stating that the nationalization of the herd should include her facilities at Ghara Tepe Sheikh in the Turkoman Steppes as she was not able to finance the maintenance of what was claimed to be a national heritage. The Royal Horse Society was still talking about what it was going to do! It was finally decided that the herd would be moved from Ghara Tepe Sheikh, where they were, but it took months for the society to eventually move them to the racetrack at Gonbad-e-Kavous. Louise was paid for the past keep of the horses and hired on for four months with a salary to manage the herd and get it settled at the new location.

Once the four months were up, Louise returned to her farm at Ghara Tepe Sheikh to find the locals anxiously awaiting her. She first went to the summer grazing pastures in the mountains nearby to collect what was left of the Turkoman mares that had not been wanted by the Royal Horse Society. Life at her small farm would continue as it had before minus the herd of Caspians.

It was late summer of 1978, and there were rumors of demonstrations in Tabriz and other cities, but her farming and reorganizing of her stud farm kept her busy, and she paid little attention to what was happening in the country. One day, some local Turkomans visited her and warned that the situation was getting serious and she should consider leaving. She shipped a number of books and all the research on the Caspians to England. She had several dogs and her horses that would be taken care of by her loyal help who came from the village, so she left for an extended trip to visit her children in England and the US.

When she returned in the late fall, she wrote,

I found the country in a state of euphoria. It was as if occupants of a giant kindergarten had seized the reins, the teachers powerless to stop their charges from overturning and incinerating cars and busses, defacing walls, chopping down trees to block roads and everywhere dashing vigilantes speeding on motor bikes Paul Revere-like announcing the approach of authority. To the cry of *Azadi* [freedom] the emancipated crowds cheered each other on. Although there was anger evident, the prevalent mood was buoyant and it was impossible to escape the sense of convivial joy exhibited by everyone but the authorities.

She was fascinated with what was happening and was possessed by the spectacle of anarchy.

When Khomeini returned in February 1979, there was a brief period of freedom of the press and a longer period of executions and death photos of the victims prominently displayed in the papers. This appalling slaughter of those of the Shah's regime will remain an enigma forever.

Louise and Narcy were in Ghara Tepe Sheikh planting potatoes when the Shah's air force rebelled and the uneasy truce between the two governments running the country ended. They decided to get in their white Volvo station wagon and drive to Tehran to see what was happening. The city seemed in chaos with Chieftain Tanks immobilized by Molotov cocktails lying drunkenly on the sidewalks, burned-out buses and cars in the streets, and children squatting in doorways making gas bombs. Posters in the streets showed how to assemble guns, and soldiers were instructing the crowds on how to fire rifles.

Narcy and Louise got in their car the next day to go sightseeing around the city that was in revolution mode. They first went to Evine Prison, which was being stormed. The stream of traffic up the newly built Shah-an-Shahi Boulevard was getting snarled, and cars filled with gunners honked to pass tourists; they warned them to keep to the right lane to make room for the revolutionaries. The stream of vehicles carried them past Qasr Prison in time to see the break-in that freed all the Shah's prisoners!

The following evening, there was a call from one of the grooms at Nowruzabad, where the Royal Horse Society still had Caspians and other horses. He was worried about safety there as revolutionaries were trying to steal horses. Though she felt it was really none of her business, Louise called several of the local horse dealers to go out and secure the property. When she arrived there, sixteen horse dealers were proudly brandishing guns and yelling, "Here comes Khonume Firouz."

By that time, some officials from the society appeared, so Louise made a hasty retreat. Caught in a traffic jam on her way back to the house on Damghan Avenue in Tehran, she looked up to the rooftops to see men with cloth-wrapped heads firing bullets over the tops of the cars. That was too much, so she and Narcy decided to drive back to Ghara Tepe Sheikh, where hopefully life would be less dangerous.

As they were negotiating their way around Maidan Ferdowsi on their way out of town, a Pasdaran, Revolutionary Guard, jumped into the Volvo and told them they were under arrest. It was in front of a mosque into which the guard told them to march. Marching for Louise was difficult for she had broken her leg in a fall a couple of weeks before; she had a pin in her ankle, and she was still on crutches. Inside the mosque, long queues of people stood arguing with guards and mullahs. When it was their turn, after much talk and more arguing, they were finally released. Their white Volvo station wagon had been thought to be one of the Shah's government cars and thus their arrest.

When they finally arrived at the farm that evening, they smelled spring flowers and heard the comforting sounds of the neighbor's lambs. It was a relief to be back where the revolution was hardly occurring.

A few days later, news passed along the steppes that there were counterrevolutionaries in the city of Gonbad. The Turkomans of the steppes whose land had been confiscated by the Pahlavis many years previously had stayed faithful to the monarchy until the end for some inexplicable reason. They had never been revolutionaries, so that was why these people were now being called counterrevolutionaries; that was the Turkoman logic. They weren't really pro-shah, but they were in definite opposition to the revolutionary force.

An announcement came on the radio that the people of Gonbad should surrender or be obliterated by artillery and bombs. Refugees fled the town using any form of transportation they could find from Paykan cars to horse and oxen-drawn carts. They streamed over the steppes pushing cars and carts through deep, muddy ruts and camping in mud and brick villages along Alexander's Wall. Forty kilometers away in Gonbad, guns boomed and planes were circling, but no bombs fell, and the radio announced that

Gonbad had capitulated and that Kalaleh, a town just ten kilometers away, had been captured by the air force.

When they returned to Tehran after Now Ruz, they learned that Narcy's brother had been incarcerated; he ended up being imprisoned for six years. Mary Gharagozlou had been arrested and was in Qasr Prison, where she was to stay for four months. People seemed to disappear with no warning, but on the surface, life in Tehran continued mostly unchanged. People's jobs limped along, parties continued, and play reading initiated by the staff of the British Embassy provided weekly entertainment.

The horses seemed worse off than most ordinary people. When she was released from prison, Mary went to Farahabad, the former royal stables, where she along with the Shah's former grooms saved the Royal Horse Society Arabs from slaughter. Fanatics were trying to execute the Shah's horses on the grounds that they were monarchists.

The Caspians in Gonbad were not doing well. At first, they were completely neglected and then put in a barbwire enclosure to stand in mud up to their hocks. They were dying from lack of even straw and water. Louise made several trips to the stud farm to plead for her precious horses that were a part of the heritage of Iran; she argued that if they were not going to care for them, they should at least release them and let them fend for themselves on the Turkoman Steppes or at least shoot them to put them out of their misery.

The Revolutionary Guards were powerless to do anything—they were not allowed to feed them, and they were not allowed to shoot them. It was not a malicious plan; no thought at all had been given to the poor animals. Finally, the guards decided to hold an auction, and as she was not informed about it, she did not attend. If she had known, she would have bid her last rial to repossess them. The horses were sold for fifty to a hundred toman each—$6 to $12. They were mostly bought by Kazakhs, a horse-eating tribe from Central Asia. Because they were so cheap, they took them home, slit their throats, and ate them.

In September 1980, Louise had planned to go to England to meet her daughter Roshan, who was living there. She had travel documents and an airline ticket. One morning a few days before she was due to leave, she was in the house alone waiting for Narcy to return from a business trip when uniformed Revolutionary Guards showed up with a search warrant. As she was not yet dressed, she told them to wait while she dressed and made coffee. When she finally opened the door for them to enter, one of the guards handed her the English-language paper *Kayhan International* that had been on the front step. She was questioned mostly about whom she knew, to which she answered that most of her acquaintances had either left the country or had been executed. They found Narcy's large collection of hunting rifles, ammunition, and knives, and they began playing games with the knives in a light-hearted manner nicking each other and drawing blood while they waited for Narcy's return.

Narcy arrived and stared in disbelief at his welcoming committee of eighteen Pasdaran. He was taken into a separate room for his interrogation while Louise fixed a lunch of scrambled eggs for Narcy and herself. The guards were served lunch by a van that was delivering lunches to them.

About four o'clock, they were instructed to pack an extra set of underwear and any toiletries they needed for an undetermined stay. Louise opened a box of cornflakes and filled bowls with water for the four dogs that weren't invited to go along. They were blindfolded and driven to an unknown location having been told not to speak and to keep their heads down so they wouldn't be seen.

Louise's blindfold was taken off when she entered a small, gray cell. She saw two cots upon one of which was a headless body, the stump of which was covered by a Palestinian-looking scarf. In this unrealistic setting, she was brought a meal that she declined to eat having decided to eat nothing while in prison.

The following morning, she was ushered into a filthy bathroom that had cockroaches in the sink and a pile of garbage from prisoners' meals in a corner. She was interrogated daily by a faceless questioner; her only diversion was the sound of the air raids. She mentioned that she had a reservation to fly to England in a few days and was told that the airport was closed. When she questioned why, she was told Iran had just gone to war with Iraq.

Two weeks later, she was told to collect her things as she was being released. She was driven blindfolded to her house, which had been sealed. Once the seal was broken and she entered, she saw a ransacked house that would take days to clean. Luckily, the guards had fed and given the dogs water. Narcy was held another six weeks before he was released.

Iran began a life-and-death struggle during the war with Iraq. Shortages of food and fuel put a cruel strain on the populace. There were no vegetables or meat, and lines to buy bread were extremely long; it would take hours to get it. The one foodstuff that was readily obtainable was caviar. As the royal court no longer had the monopoly on it; it flooded the market, but there were few left who had developed a taste for this delicacy, and so it went unsold. Narcy, Louise, and their friends ate it for breakfast, lunch, and dinner.

The scud missiles were terrifying; buildings were here today but gone tomorrow, and Tehran began to have a vast number of parking lots as the bulldozers leveled stricken buildings. A scud missile that came through the roof of the house on Damghan Avenue was the last straw for Louise, who decided she wouldn't live in such danger any longer. Her father had died and left her a small legacy with which she bought a little fruit garden in the town of Kordon on the slopes of the Alborz about fifty-five kilometers west of Tehran. Though Narcy never did move his clothes out of the house on Damghan Avenue to the new farm, he did run the farm. His construction business had been confiscated, but that was to his relief—it had not been turning a profit and had heavy debts.

In 1989, with the help of Narcy, Louise discovered more Caspians that were being held in paddocks by the revolutionaries at Jalalabad, which had been the remount station during the time of the Shah. These small horses had been collected to go to the front to clear minefields, but the experiment hadn't worked, so when Louise and Narcy offered to buy them, the revolutionaries were happy to let them go.

This herd became known as Persicus Caspians, and in 1994, she sold this rescued herd of the miniature horses she had discovered many years before to the Iranian Ministry of Agriculture, which has continued her breeding and research programs and kept these ancient horses as part of the national heritage of the Islamic Republic.

In the spring of 1994, Louise was in Ghara Tepe Sheikh when her son Caren called to tell her that Narcy was desperately ill and in the hospital. She drove as quickly as possible to Tehran and found Narcy lying comatose; the doctors said he was in kidney failure. They said there was no hope, but he rallied for ten days before his heart finally stopped. He was buried in the graveyard of the village of Kordon, and the Turkomans held a memorial service for him on the steppes at Ghara Tepe Sheikh.

In 1999, with the help of individuals from Canada and the United States, Louise, sixty-five, started what turned out to be her final Caspian breeding program on the remote farm at Ghara Tepe Sheikh. On one of her treks that spring, she rescued two foundation Caspian stallions and eight foundation Caspian mares. With her regal ability, she experienced until her death the joy of watching newborn Caspian foals thrive under her watchful eye. This herd has been assimilated into the national herd of Caspian horses at Gonbad in the Turkoman Sahra.

Friends had mentioned to Louise that the amazing rides she had taken them on through the forests of Golan in the steppes could be extended to include paying visitors. She liked the idea and connected with a travel company that specialized in arranging horseback riding trips through exotic destinations. This business became quite successful, and the proceeds kept her and her horses in the manner in which they were accustomed for the whole year.

Over the years, she had several falls; she broke a leg one time, which necessitated surgery in Tehran. In 2006, she had a fall that damaged her shoulder, and when the doctor suggested she was foolish to be riding, she replied, "No. I was only foolish to fall off!"

Many of her friends felt she was mad to live a life in the wild, but they couldn't realize the true freedom of the Turkoman Steppes; they had no understanding of the exquisite beauty of the primeval forests of northeastern Iran. She lived there with her dogs and horses and the trees she and Narcy had planted; his memory was forever green.

She died on May 25, 2008, at age seventy-four. Louise, who had come from a patrician home in Virginia and married into one of Iran's royal families, would not have exchanged her life for another.

Nazila Fathi is an Iranian journalist who was a longtime reporter for the *New York Times* in Tehran. She grew up there during the times of the Islamic revolution. At age eleven, she could no longer choose what clothes she could wear as the new regime dictated that black, dark blue, brown, or gray were the only colors women and children could wear. She and her family lived in a large, modern, gated community of fourteen twelve-story buildings that had been among the first high-rises in Tehran not unlike the condo complexes in the US. There was a lush, green, seven-acre garden with a large swimming pool at the center where the children could swim and have fun during the hot summer months.

As the cool weather came in the autumn of 1978 and the swimming season ended, the demonstrations grew bolder, and her mother was afraid to let her and her sister out of the apartment. One afternoon, they were finally able to persuade her to take them to the big department store on Pahlavi Avenue for ice cream. It was January 16, 1979, and as they walked out past the guardhouse of the complex, they saw people in the street yelling and celebrating. Their mother tightened her grip on the girls' hands as they moved toward the ice cream parlor. When they got to the store, they saw frenzied people waving newspapers in the air with the bold headlines "*Shah Raft*,"—"The Shah Left." When they got home, their father had returned from work and was watching a newscast showing the teary-eyed Shah with his wife walking toward an airplane.

Just two weeks after the Shah left, the same newscaster announced that the revolution had triumphed. A seventy-eight-year-old cleric had just returned to Iran from exile. He was Ayatollah Khomeini. As he rode past the huge crowd of hundreds of thousands, they shouted, "Once the monster left, the angel appeared!"

Nazila's parents had never heard of Khomeini; they were shocked to see so many educated people on TV captivated by his passionate speeches against the Shah. The audience was panned by the camera and looked to be mesmerized by the Ayatollah's words.

"We are going to elevate your financial status as well as your morality," he stated in his singsong voice. "Don't think we will only build you housing. Electricity and water will be free. Public transportation will be free."

Her father was shocked. How could he give free electricity and water to a country of 30 million? He was mad to think he could run the country like a seminary.

The people began to clap, but a cleric next to Khomeini signaled them to stop. "*Allah-o-Akbar*" he shouted, and some in the crowd followed his signal. It seemed that the new leader of the country felt that clapping was much too Western and not Islamic. On TV, they saw people looking confusedly at each other, but the "*Allah-o-Akbar, Allah-o-Akbar*" began to resound.

In September 1981, almost a year after the war with Iraq began, a law was passed in the Majlis enforcing the veiling of women; they were forced to cover their hair and bodies with the hijab—loose, knee-length coats, pants, and head scarves. Women were banned from wearing makeup, perfume, or high heels. The regime upheld this rule with an iron fist; the Pasdaran roamed the streets and arrested women who were not complying. The Iranian penal code stated that the punishment for violating the new law was imprisonment, a fine, and up to seventy-four lashes.

Women and girls over age nine were banned from swimming, so the girls in the complex could only sit around the pool sweating in their hot manteaux and scarves watching the boys diving in and having all the fun.

One hot afternoon, the girls got together and decided to ignore the ban. They removed their head scarves and dove in in their heavy clothes. The joy of the occasion didn't last long as the parents, fearing the Pasdaran might come into the garden, forced them out.

Nazila had been attending the American school, a co-educational, Western-type academy where students could wear T-shirts and blue jeans. Then, the schools were segregated with male teachers only in the boys' schools and women teachers in girls' schools.

When Nazila graduated from high school, she was accepted at Azad University in Tehran to study English translation; she went to a French tutor to study that language as well. Her tutor had connections with Western reporters who all needed translators, and so as her languages became fluent, she became one of their regular translators.

It had been difficult for foreign reporters to gain entrance to Iran until the devastating earthquake of 1990 that killed 35,000. Most of the reporters who came to Iran at that time, however, were more interested in the way of life in the country than they were in the earthquake. Nazila was by then very interested in journalism and had the luck to be assigned to the *New York Times* reporter Judith Miller. After an interview Judith had with Ali Akhbar Mohtashamipor, a hard-line cleric and fierce opponent of President Rafsanjani, she was bitten by the journalism bug. A few days following that interview, she received a call from the Intelligence Ministry asking her to go down to answer some questions.

She of course was extremely nervous about the interview, and she couldn't figure out how they had discovered her phone number. She had always been careful to ask the reporters she worked with not to mention her name in their reports. By that time, she had worked with many foreign journalists, who called her their fixer. Besides translating for them, she made appointments and fed them news stories.

One of her friends who was working with a BBC reporter had been pulled out of an interview, held for several hours, and threatened with being charged as a spy. *But what can the ministry want from me?* She wondered. She went to see her father in his office to tell him where she was going, and he told her not to worry as she had done nothing other than translate. He didn't think they wanted her to stop doing her job; if that had been the case, they would have threatened her over the phone.

When she got to Ershad, the office of the Intelligence Ministry, wearing her most conservative clothing, she parked her car in front of a small convenience store knowing that if she didn't return, the shopkeeper would call the police as he would want to keep an open space in front of his store. She walked along the street of affluent, old houses to the ministry. When she entered, the guard inspected her purse and led her to a small, windowless room that looked like an interrogation room. After several minutes, a small, rotund man with a mustache and no beard entered and sat behind the desk opposite her. He informed her that they had been monitoring her for several months and knew that she was working with foreign correspondents. That was not a problem, but they wanted her to fill in some forms for their records.

It took quite some time to complete the questionnaire as it was extremely detailed and wanted names of family and friends as well as other personal information. She knew that her family had never done anything that could be a threat to the regime though they disliked it, so she had no problem putting down their names. Of her friends, she mixed first and surnames feeling that if she were questioned, she could say she had made a mistake. Once finished, she left with no adieu and immediately called her father to say all was well.

Two weeks after her interview, she was summoned to a second one, this time at the Office for Alien Residence. A deep-voiced man had called her, so she recognized him by his voice when she was ushered into a room with two men awaiting her arrival. She was asked to sit. Tea and pastries were on the table. The meeting was mostly congenial except when the second small, shabbily dressed interviewer suggested that an article Judith Miller had written about censorship was totally untrue. She had helped Judith with that article about the censorship of Iranian movies and couldn't believe this little man had no idea that many Iranian movies that portrayed disillusioned Iranians and had won awards at foreign festivals had been banned for viewing at home. She was afraid that might prevent her from continuing her work with the foreign media and she would have to go back to her teaching job, which paid very little.

The deep-voiced man complimented her on her command of English and said that they thought she was an intelligent woman they could trust. They would like her to continue to work with the foreign media, who were sometimes spies in disguise, and inform on them if she suspected any of them were indeed spies. She finished her tea and pastries and left after telling them because Iran was her homeland, of course she would do as they requested.

She continued acting as a translator and guide for foreign journalists taking them to sights that were on the list of most important to see. The mausoleum of Ayatollah Khomeini was always first on the list. He was lying in a sarcophagus in a golden cage on the edge of the national cemetery, Beheshteh Zahra, just outside south Tehran. The second stop would always be the martyrs' cemetery close by, where tens of thousands of men killed in the war lay under identical gray stones.

She met Babak Pasha in 1991 shortly after he had returned to Iran from spending eleven years in San Diego, where he had lived to escape the war. He had come home to help his father in his business. Their first date was a picnic on the top of a hill with a spectacular view of the twinkling lights from the city below them. They had barely spread out their blanket and taken the wicker basket from the car when a big Basij SUV pulled up and three members got out shouting at them. How dare they be together in a public place when they were obviously not married? Nazila was about to explain that they were in a *sigheh* marriage, an arrangement between a man and woman where for a certain sum of money, they could have a conjugal relationship that could be terminated at any time—days, hours, or minutes. That was legal in Iran, whereas to be seen together in public, a woman and man had to have been married!

Babak, having lived in a free country, didn't understand that he should lie; he apologized saying they were on a date. That was it. They were taken away to a detention center, where their parents picked them up. They had to leave the deeds to their properties as bond to ensure they would appear in court a few days later. At the trial, her father stated that they were engaged to be married, which saved them from detention and sixty lashes.

For five more years, they snuck around and lied about their relationship, but finally, being the strong woman she was, Nazila proposed to Babak, and they were married in a traditional Persian ceremony. In defiance of the regime, she refused to wear a head scarf on her wedding day.

She was called into Ershad one day in 2000, and at the end of her interview, she was issued a letter that authorized her to work as a reporter. She had finally made it. She became a journalist for the *New York Times* but also wrote for magazines such as *Time* and the French *Agence France-Presse*. She began her career as a journalist in earnest and was constantly on the move with her work.

The press in particular was hit hard after the Green Movement demonstrations in 2009. Journalists were banned from working with the foreign press. Nazila ignored the ban and continued to go out into the streets to report what she was seeing. One day about ten days into the protests, she received a call from a friendly Basij commander warning her that government forces had given her picture to snipers; she was not to go out into the streets.

Her next warning was when she began to see men with full beards and shabby clothes watching her apartment building. Then one afternoon when Babak was taking the children out in their car, she saw from her window that he was stopped by riders on motorbikes who demanded that he open the windows to see if she was in the car.

That evening, they decided to leave their homeland. They quickly packed a few things, imagining they would soon return, and drove to the airport expecting to be stopped. She had luckily bought airline tickets for their summer visit to Canada, so with those in hand, they arrived at the airport and gave their passports to the officer at the wicket. She endured the longest wait in her life as their documents were scrutinized and was relieved when they were amazingly returned to her. A few hours later, they were on the flight out of Iran to Canada. She has never returned to her native land.

Louise Firouz

Louise Firouz with Caspian horse

CHAPTER  10

The Business World

During the war with Iraq, Iran limped along somehow continuing with business as usual in everyday life. The wells pumped oil, the refineries produced their products, export and import businesses flailed but were able to operate, cars were built, aluminum and steel were produced in a limited capacity, and other industries struggled to survive; the country was fighting for its life.

Once things settled down after the end of the war, the regime slowly started to pay attention to its infrastructure. Iran was a country of great resources and highly capable and intelligent people; it was time to make up the financial losses that had been incurred over the past eight years. A series of five-year plans were put into effect to grow the country's economy. By the end of the fifth Five-Year Socioeconomic Development Plan, the country had become a modern nation as far as business and industry were concerned.

After the revolution, the United States placed economic sanctions on Iran and expanded them in 1995 to include any companies dealing with the Iranian government. In 2006, the UN Security Council imposed sanctions after Iran refused to suspend its uranium-enrichment program. These sanctions targeted investments in oil, gas, and petrochemicals, exports of refined petroleum products, and business dealings with the Iranian Revolutionary Guard, which encompassed banking, insurance, shipping, and web-hosting services for all commercial endeavors. These sanctions were crippling to a country that was still recovering from a revolution and a war, but even so, the country slowly developed into a nation with the many successful and prosperous industries it has today.

The oil and gas industry is the most active in the country. Iran has the fourth-largest reserves of oil and the second-largest reserves of natural gas in the world. Though the sanctions have been eased, it has been slow trying to revive oil and natural gas production. Since the government has made changes to investment terms that encourage outside funds, there are foreign oil companies looking to invest in the Islamic Republic. This financial influx will greatly help recover and modernize this major industry. There are plans for pipelines and reviving liquid natural gas to entice foreign entities as well.

In the 1990s, the country tried to attract foreign companies to develop its crude oil reserves because it lacked the technical and financial resources to do so itself. The deal was that the foreign companies would develop the field and would be paid back in the crude oil produced. Ultimately, the fields would be returned to the control of the National Iranian Oil Company. These arrangements did not satisfy foreign investors, and threats of renewed sanctions led most of the Western companies to leave.

Now that the nuclear deal of 2015 is in effect for all the signed countries with the exception of the US, which was pulled out by Trump, and the lifting of sanctions in January of 2016 took place, there is renewed interest in Iranian oil due to the fact that the new Iranian Petroleum Contract allows foreign companies to participate in exploration, development, and production. European, Chinese and Japanese companies are already showing interest in oil production and the new refineries that are planned.

Iran is OPEC's second-largest producer of oil and the world's fifth-largest globally. Its oil sector is one of the oldest in the world. Production started in 1908, and as a result, Iran has one of the most mature oil sectors in the word. It has already produced about 75 percent of its reserves, but it has made some new, important discoveries in the past decade.

Its gas production has increased an average of 10 percent a year for the past two decades, but it has depleted only 5 percent of its reserves. Unfortunately, its ability to produce has lagged behind its domestic needs due to increased demand because of economic and population growth. It must continue to develop its reserves at a rapid rate to keep up with demand. The infrastructure also needs to be developed rapidly because gas production is in the south but the bulk of the demand is in the north. There is an impressive pipeline network to transport gas, but the growing demand dictates a need to expand these pipelines domestically and to Turkey, Oman, and the United Arab Emirates where the gas is sold.

The lifting of some international sanctions is beginning to revive investment in the oil and gas sector, and that will help economic growth. It will also boost Iran's plastics industry as it is a derivative of the petrochemical industry. At the 2017 Plastics Exhibition in Tehran, five hundred local and four hundred foreign plastics companies conferred about the highly versatile material that can be shaped into any form. From the time of the Elghanian's Plasco, the first plastics company in Iran, to today, Iranians have been big consumers of plastic products. Iran makes and exports millions of dollars' worth of toys, dishes, and other items and produces polymeric water pipes. Fifty billion dollars' worth of that pipe was exported a year even before the sanctions were lifted.

The aluminum and steel industries are flourishing in today's markets. The Iralco (Iranian Aluminum Company) plants in Arak and the south are expanding with the help of Chinese investment. Iran is producing aluminum, and alumina, from which the metal is produced, is being refined in the country. The National Iranian Steel Industries has many plants around the country, and many private industries produce steel and steel products. There is a great demand for steel domestically, and Iran exports much steel; by the end of the Iranian year 1392 (March 2018), 8 million tons of steel were exported.

The Chinese see Iran's competitive advantage in production factors such as iron-ore resources, cheap and skilled labor, and abundant natural gas; thus, they are investing heavily in this industry. Iran's mining industry is underdeveloped, and yet it is one of the most important mineral producers in the world ranking among the top-fifteen mineral-rich countries. Mineral production contributes only 0.6 percent of the country's GDP, but 30 percent of investments made by Iranians are in the mining field. The list of minerals hidden in the country's mountains and deserts is long, but some of the most important are coal, metallic minerals, sand, gravel, chemical minerals, and salt. Iran is the eighth-largest producer of iron ore in the world, it makes the over 17 million tons of steel that allows Iran to be self-sufficient in its steel production.

Bauxite from which alumina is extracted to make aluminum is mined in the north of Iran in Azerbaijan and Khorasan Provinces. Most of the alumina, which in the seventies was imported from Australia, is refined at home now. As Iran is the largest producer and supplier of aluminum in the Middle East producing over 1 million tons each year, it still must import some of its alumina. A government-to-government agreement to buy and refine bauxite and import alumina to Iran has recently been signed with Guinea.

The Saar Cheshmeh mines in Kerman Province contain the world's second-largest lode of copper ore, and Iran exports over a billion dollars' worth of copper each year. The National Iranian Copper Industries Company is the largest non-oil exporter in Iran.

Iran has an estimated total of coal reserves of 50 billion tons. It produces almost 2 million tons per annum and uses about the same amount, but plans are to produce up to 5 million tons a year in the future. Coke, zinc, lead, uranium, and gold are also mined in large quantities not to mention many semiprecious and precious stones.

The list of successful industries in Iran today is endless, but here are some facts compiled over the last few years.

- Iran is producing 59-seat aircraft, and with the help of Russia and the Ukraine, there are plans to build 90- to 120-seat planes in the near future. Military-attack airplanes such as the F-313 fighter are also being manufactured there.
- Iran is self-sufficient in designing and operating dams and power plants and has won many bids to build such structures abroad.
- It is one of only six countries in the world that manufacture gas and steam-powered turbines.
- Iran is the world's eighth-largest producer of cement and in the Middle East second only to Turkey.
- Textile mills that produce huge amounts of cotton fabric cannot keep up with the local demand, and so overseas companies smuggle in illegal textiles and apparel at a rate that is decimating the manufacturers and costing Iranian jobs.
- The government owns 90 percent of all mines and related large industries and is seeking foreign investment to develop that sector.

- The automotive industry is the second most active industry in the country, and Iran is the eighteenth-largest automaker in the world.
- Iran now manufactures many types of arms and equipment including its tanks, armored personnel carriers, guided missiles, submarines, and other military vessels. It exports military equipment and weapons to over fifty-seven countries.
- Iran's beautiful terrain and lovely ancient historical sites put it among the top-ten most touristic countries.
- The Tehran Stock Exchange, which first opened in 1967, has a market capitalization of over $100 billion and is a founding member of the Federation of Euro-Asian Stock Exchanges. It has been one of the world's best-performing stock exchanges since 2002. Its advantage is the thirty-seven industries directly involved in it. Automotive, telecommunications, agricultural, petrochemical, mining, steel, banking, insurance, and other industries trade shares at the stock market, which makes it unique in the Middle East; it has more than 300 listed companies.
- Another advantage is that most of the state-owned firms are being privatized and people are allowed to buy shares of the newly privatized companies. The market has jumped more than 25 percent since sanctions were lifted in January 2016. The surge in the market has been driven mostly by domestic investors.
- The country has the largest educated population in the Middle East and the largest market, so it follows that it will be the regional economic leader in days to come. Iran is the last, large untapped emerging market in the world. The economy has many investment opportunities and is forecast by Goldman Sachs to reach the highest economic growth from now until 2025.
- Unfortunately the Trump administration is trying to destroy a country that could possibly become a major economic world power. Only time will tell what happens.

Iranian made F-313 Fighter

CHAPTER 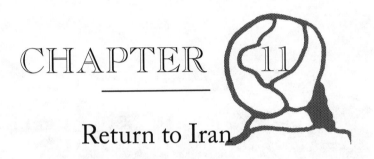 11

Return to Iran

When I was writing this book, I began to realize I would need to go to Iran to see firsthand how life was now in the country I had so loved and been so saddened by the events of the past forty years. I searched the internet and saw it was indeed possible to visit Iran. There were many travel agencies that advertised tours of the country.

I learned that the only way to visit Iran was to take a planned tour, guided by an official government guide. The tours all looked very interesting and something that would really suit someone who had never been to the country before. They started with a few days in Tehran seeing the many sights there including the Golestan Palace, which is one of the oldest historic monuments in Tehran having been built on the site of the historic citadel of the Safavid by the Qajars with its amazing Hall of Mirrors. As well, the crown jewels in the vaults of the National Bank, the Saadabad and Niavaran Palaces, which had been the official homes of the Pahlavis, and the many wonderful museums in the city were included. Then there would be a whirlwind tour of such places as Esfahan, Shiraz, Mashhad, Tabriz, and many other beautiful and historic locations.

That wouldn't suit me at all because I had visited most of the places on the itineraries. Not that I wouldn't want to see some of them again, but I also wanted to see what was happening in the horse world, which had been mine while I was living there. I wanted to go to the horse shows, the races, and the polo matches and see if I could encounter old friends. I called and emailed at least ten agencies to learn that the only way to visit Iran was on one of these tours and that it was impossible to go anywhere without a preplanned itinerary and with a guide—no exceptions. Private tours were not normally available to British, Canadian, or US citizens.

Next, I contacted an Iranian horse magazine, *Iran Horsey*, which is a part of the Sepanj Group, a Middle Eastern conglomerate. I happened across this information when searching LinkedIn, so I sent them a message. Almost immediately, I received a reply telling me that they had heard of me, would help me plan a trip to Iran, and supply me with a personal guide.

We emailed back and forth a few times, and then they sent me some pictures of me taken while I was in Iran that they had found in the archives of the Iranian Equestrian Federation. When I checked the website of the Equestrian Federation, I found that my book *All the Shah's Men* was listed.

Of course, everyone I talked to about my trip kept warning me that it would unsafe for me to go back to Iran due to my association with the Shah and his Imperial Stables. But I had been in contact with people who had gone there, and they all had said it was extremely safe, the horse world was flourishing, and many of my imperial riders and friends were anxiously awaiting my arrival.

I had hoped to take the trip in September 2016, but my visa did not come through in time. When it finally did, it was for December, and I didn't want to be away from my family over Christmas, and it can be very cold at that time of year in Tehran. Of course in the end, it didn't really matter because the Iranian government decided to cancel all visas of Americans due to the election of Donald Trump and his travel ban.

Once the holidays were over, I started emailing my contacts in Iran but to no avail; no one responded. I went to the internet and called agencies in the US, Canada, and Great Britain. No, there weren't any tours to Iran because no visas were being granted.

I finally found the telephone number of an Iranian travel company in Tehran and called them—Bingo! They emailed me the forms to fill out for my visa and informed me on April 16 that I should make my air reservations to arrive on May 20. They had sent me an itinerary that looked perfect, so with excitement, I made my plans. But the next morning, Mehdi, the owner of the agency, contacted me to say that Iran had declared an election for May 19 and all visas were again canceled. Another letdown.

In Iran, anyone over age eighteen can register as a presidential candidate, but the Election Monitoring Agency managed by the Guardian Council—an unelected panel appointed by the supreme leader—approves only a handful of those who register. That year, 1,636 individuals put in their names, including 137 women, but on April 20, it was announced that only six candidates were approved—Moustafa Hashenitaba, former head of Physical Education and Heavy Industry; Ebrahin Raizi, former head of General Inspection and Attorney General from 2014 to 2016; Hassan Rouhani, president since 2013 and former speaker of Majlis; Moustafa Mir-Salim, former Minister of Culture and supervisor of Presidential Administration; Eshaq Jahangiri, first vice president and former Minister of Industries and Mines and Metals and governor of Esfahan Province; and Mohammad Bagher Ghalibaf, mayor of Tehran.

Of these candidates, the two front-runners seemed to be Rouhani, the incumbent who was a moderate and reformist, and Raizi, a conservative hard-liner. Under Rouhani's administration, the deal that limited Iran's nuclear program in exchange for sanctions relief was signed in 2015.

Campaigning in Tehran was fierce with billboards everywhere and activists from both sides flocking to the streets. At first, it was announced that no live debates would be broadcast on TV—only prerecorded debates would be aired—but after the candidates and public criticized that decision, live debates were allowed. The reformists and the conservatives used Telegram instant messaging, the most widely used messaging application in Iran. It is reported that 45 million in a country of 80 million use it as a platform to express their political views, so it played an important role in the election.

As Election Day approached, Eshaq Jahangiri declared that he would curtail his campaign in support of Rouhani, and then Mayor Ghalibaf and Mostafa Mir-Salim threw in the towel in favor of hard-liner Raizi. According to the polls, Rouhani would not be the shoo-in it was thought he would be. I, of course, was hoping Rouhani would be elected for a second term. He was the reformist who had managed to get sanctions lifted and was pledging to persuade the US to lift more sanctions as well as to improve relations with the Western world and improve the Iranian economy.

I rejoiced when on May 20 I heard Rouhani had won by a landslide; he had defeated the hard-liner from the Combatant Clergy Association with his Moderate and Development Party—57 percent to 38 percent. He had won a clear mandate to push through domestic reforms and pursue talks with the West. As president, he commands the country's vast bureaucracy and can shape foreign and domestic policy, but all state matters must eventually be approved by the Supreme Leader, Ayatollah Ali Khamenei, and the Guardian Council.

About 70 percent of Iran's population of 80 million cast ballots in the elections; as many voted in 2016 in the election for members of the Majlis (congress or parliament) as well as the powerful body of the Assembly of Experts, which is the committee that chooses the Islamic Republic's Supreme Leader. Interestingly enough, Rouhani and former president Rafsanjani, both reformists and moderates, were elected to the Assembly of Experts, which will be electing a new leader upon the death of Khamenei, who is seventy-six.

The elections over, I contacted my travel agent in Iran, and he was ecstatic about the results. We could move forward again to get my visa and make plans for a September trip.

After much correspondence including sending a PDF of my book *All the Shah's Men* to the ministry via email and talking and texting with WhatsApp, I was finally emailed an official-looking document with my picture on it and the visa number I would need to take to the Iranian Interest Section of the Pakistani Embassy in Washington to get my official visa. How exciting! I had finally been approved. I called the office to make an appointment and was told that was not necessary. I just needed to get to the office before 11:00 a.m. to receive my document the same day.

My friend Suzie Ruane, who had lived in Iran with her Iranian husband while I was there, came along for the ride the Wednesday I went for my documentation. She was to sit in the car while I went to the office because I was sure parking in Washington would be impossible.

We got to the city and to where I needed to be by 11:00 a.m., but the address I had been given on the phone was not correct—there was no Iranian office there. I decided we should go to the Pakistani Embassy, which we found after three U turns and twenty minutes. I went to the entrance and read a sign: Embassy Personnel and Visitors Only. I pressed the intercom button and learned that the Iranian Interest Section was on 33rd Street NW.

Another ten minutes brought us to a construction site at the new address. I called the Pakistani Embassy, and after about five minutes of recorded messages, I finally spoke to a human who told me I had the wrong address; she gave me yet another one.

Ten minutes later, we were in front of a beautiful office building with a huge Mexican flag over the door. As the building number was correct, I pulled over and parked in a miraculously empty space right in front of the building. I left Suzie in the car and ran up the steps and through a huge, plate-glass door to a breathtakingly beautiful lobby of beige and brown marble. On the right was a door to the Indian Embassy, and straight ahead was the massive entrance to the Mexican Consulate, but where was the Iranian office? I spotted a small, frosted-glass door in the left corner with a small Iranian flag and smaller letters reading Iranian Interest Section of Pakistan. I sighed in relief. I had finally reached my destination, and it was just noon. I cautiously opened the door and walked through a metal detector; I reached a desk, and a small Iranian man stared at me with a shocked expression.

"Do you have a scarf?" he asked me. It had totally slipped my mind that I would need the hijab in the Iranian office; after all, I was in the US.

"No." I answered.

"Then you may not come in!"

"*Behbashid, Aga. Nemitunam. Mota'assefam.*" I apologized in Farsi.

His lips quivered in a smirk; he reached into a drawer, pulled out a scarf, and handed to me. "Do you know how to put it on?"

Of course I did, but a pleasant Iranian woman came up to me and said, "Let me help you." Once my scarf was on, the little man told me I had to fill out applications for a visa. I waved my email at him telling him I had already filled out the applications electronically, but he insisted I needed to do it again. I had to remember my answers to the tricky questions I had put on my original application. When I had completed the form, he gave me a number; not glancing at my papers, he sent me upstairs.

I was number 103. When I reached the upstairs waiting room full of Iranians awaiting renewed passports, visas and other documents, the number board was at 94. To pass the time, I decided to read the instructions on my application, which I had neglected to read before filling it out. The price for a Canadian to obtain a visa was $40 cash only, and I had only $10. I phoned Suzie in the car and asked her if she could lend me $40. I left the room and ran down to the car.

When I got back to the waiting room, my number was on the board, so I went up to the counter to be told by another little Iranian man that I needed to have a picture taken with the scarf on my head. He ushered me into the next room, where a photographer was taking the picture of a beautiful Persian woman with a wine-colored scarf. She needed the picture to be retaken six times before she was satisfied. With me, he took one picture, and I was satisfied with what looked like me, a *babushka*.

I went back to my Iranian interviewer, who looked over my application, passport, visa confirmation from Iran, and picture; he seemed quite satisfied. "Everything seems in order. Do you want your visa tomorrow?"

"No. Actually, I would like to have it today. They told me on the phone that I could get it the same day. You see, I live in Richmond, and it's a long drive."

"Well, I guess I can do that. You can pick it up before three this afternoon."

"Thank you so much!" I said effusively.

"That will be a hundred and fifty dollars."

"One hundred and fifty? Do you take credit cards?" I asked rhetorically.

"No, no. Just cash."

"I'll have to go to the bank. Can I bring the money back when I come for the visa?"

"Yes of course. Be sure to be here by three though."

After the bank, we had a delightful lunch while parked illegally in front of a restaurant just around the corner from the visa office. When I went upstairs again, the office was jammed with people waiting for their documents. During my wait, I chatted amicably with several Iranians all of whom were interested in why I wanted to go to Iran. One woman had come to Washington from Vancouver, Canada, to renew her passport. A man wearing a yarmulke asked me for some change stating, "I can't believe this embassy doesn't take credit cards! This is ridiculous! We are in America!"

When my little friend signaled me to come up to retrieve my documents, he said, "I can't seem to find your papers." *Oh, no!* I thought. *Now what?*

"Did you pay me?"

"No. Do you remember I said I had to go to the bank?"

"Oh yes. Let me look again," he said as he went back into the other room.

He came back out to the desk all smiles. "Here it is. How much did I say it would be? A hundred and twenty-five dollars?"

"Yes, I think so," I said happily. My $40 visa would cost me only $125. I handed him the cash, and he handed me the passport with a beautiful gold and silver visa in it that had the picture of the babushka.

At the time, I had no idea how hard it had been to get a visa to visit Iran. Apparently, I had been turned down three times since March, when I had sent the PDF of my book. In August shortly before I was given permission, I was turned down again, but luckily, Mehdi pulled some strings, and the department told him it was just a glitch in the computer software that had caused the problem. I was the first ex-employee of the Shah who had been granted a visitor's visa to the country.

I had envisioned Khomeini Airport as a glitzy, new, and modern airport from the tourist information I had looked at on the internet. That it was not. We disembarked down the front stairs of the plane, which parked on the tarmac near the terminal. Walking through the dingy, dark tunnel toward the immigration lines, I had a moment of despair thinking that this trip might have been a mistake. The low acoustic ceilings, which dated the building, were cracked and yellowed with age though I knew the building was only about ten years old. The new Tehran airport had originally been planned under the Shah's regime and construction was started in 1979, but it was not completed until after the revolution in 2004 with the final cost being $350 million. There were operational problems and construction difficulties because the runways were built over old *qanats*, underground waterways, which was a safety concern; the official opening did not take place until October 2007.

It took me over forty minutes to clear security and customs; my suitcase hadn't made it, and my driver and guide were not waiting for me. There I was in this dumpy terminal wondering what to do next. Luckily, a lovely Iranian woman I had met on the plane waited while I called my contact, Mehdi, who told me that my escorts would be there momentarily. We went to the airport information booth to wait for them.

I had been asked by many people before I left for Iran if I thought I would know anyone when I got there, and my answer was always, "I'm not sure. Most of the people I knew are either dead or have left the country, but maybe some of the men I trained at the Imperial Stables are still living. I've been told that I have friends waiting to see me, but I really don't know."

Golestan Palace, Tehran

CHAPTER 12

The Horse World

Sajad Bamdad, my driver, held his hand out to me as introduction, which surprised me because I had understood that men and women did not touch each other in public, but obviously, that was a misconception. He was very tall—over six feet—with strong, broad shoulders, a kind, brown-eyed face, and a shock of white at the front of his almost-black hair. He looked to be in his early thirties, and he spoke beautiful English he had learned in Australia, where he had lived until he was eighteen while his father was studying in university on an exchange program sponsored by the Iranian government post-revolution.

Accompanying him was an attractive, dark-haired woman with a rather severe expression. She wore blue jeans, a black, loose-fitting top that came almost to her knees, and a black head scarf completely covering her hair. She did not shake my hand but introduced herself as Leilah Mohasab. She had just flown down from Mashhad, where she usually guided people who were making a pilgrimage to the shrine of Imam Reza or were interested in the religious and archeological sites. I learned she was a specially selected guide, one of twenty, from the Department of Tourism who accompanied visitors to Iran who it was believed might be of interest to the security of the country. Being an ex-employee of the Shah, I was obviously of interest.

We walked to the parking area, which was jammed with cars as it was the beginning of a holiday weekend, and Iranians love to travel when they get four days off. Sajad drove his white Peugeot sedan to pick Leilah and me up minus my suitcase, and in we climbed. I was expecting the traffic to be dreadful as I had read and seen pictures of Tehran's impossible traffic, and I remembered how bad it had been forty years earlier when I lived there. But cars were moving swiftly along the highway as we passed the golden shrine of Imam Khomeini on our way into the city. Though it was under renovation with huge scaffolds around two of the four eighty-seven-(his age when he died)-foot golden minarets or towers, it was an impressive landmark. The great golden dome was adorned with seventy-two golden tulips symbolizing the martyrs who had fought and died with Imam Hossein, the third imam of Shi'a Islam in 680 BC at Karbala, Iraq.

As we drove toward the north of Tehran, where my hotel was, I searched the horizon for Mount Damavand, the beautiful stratovolcano that is the highest peak in Iran and the Middle East and the highest volcano in Asia. As it is only sixty-six kilometers, about forty-one miles northeast of Tehran, it had been visible from the balcony of my house. Why could I not see it? "Where is Damavand?" I asked Sajad.

"Damavand? I don't think I've ever seen it from here. Actually, I haven't seen it at all in the past few years. You know, we have terrible smog here now. It probably wasn't this bad when you were here last. Maybe you'll be able to see her when we drive back from Gorgon toward the end of your trip."

"I hope so. I loved looking at that mountain. You know, it is said to have mystical and magical powers, and its name means the mountain from which smoke and ash rises. I do want to see it," I mentioned forgetting that he was the guide, not me.

The Esteghlal Hotel looked familiar as we drove into the circular drive. Once in the lobby, I thought I recognized the place, and then it struck me that it was the Sheraton before the revolution. I had been there many times. My room looked out to the foothills of the Alborz Mountains, where there were tall apartment buildings and offices that had not been there the last time I'd been in the hotel. We used to ride horses in those hills, and my brother had a small *bagh*, a garden, there where he kept his Turkoman horses. Now, it was all part of the huge city of 12 million.

Tehran's population had been only about 3 million when I was living there. The total population of Iran in 1976 had been 30 million; now it was 80 million.

The following morning, Sajad picked Leilah, who was ever by my side, and me up to see the Golestan Palace. This palace complex dates back five centuries and has been modified during the Safavid, Zand, Qajar, and Pahlavi Dynasties. The earliest structures are from the Zand Dynasty (1750–1794). Karim Khan Zand made Tehran his capital; in 1760, he had the old citadel renovated, and it became his administrative and living quarters.

When the Qajar Dynasty came to power, they also selected the Kakheh Golestan to be their palace. During the Pahlavi era (1925–1979), the Golestan was used for formal royal receptions. Both Reza Shah and Mohamed Reza Pahlavi were crowned there. There are many beautiful halls, but the most amazing is the Hall of Mirrors, which has its walls and ceilings covered with mirrors; in the past, it was used for receptions. The Peacock Throne and the Kianid Crown had been kept in this spectacular room until they were moved to the Museum of the Crown Jewels, which is in the main branch of the National Bank, shortly after the revolution.

"The horse federation is having a show this afternoon at seven at Dashte Behesht. Do you know the place?" Sajad asked me as we headed to a restaurant for lunch.

"When I was here, some of my friends had their clubs there," I told him; by clubs, I meant riding stables. "I used to drive out there at least a couple of times a week. I would drive along the Karaj Highway going about a hundred and forty kilometers an hour. It would take me only about a half an hour to get there."

"It takes more than that now. The traffic between Tehran and Karaj is terrible. I think we should leave about six."

Luckily, my bag arrived at the hotel before we were due to leave as we were going to spend a couple of nights as the guests of someone I had never heard of, out in the country. We left northern Tehran about six and headed toward the Karaj Road. It was bumper-to-bumper traffic going at a stop-and-go snail's pace. I couldn't believe the scenery. What had been mostly desert and mountains was high-rise after high-rise, and once outside the city limits, there were factories hugging each other on both sides of the road.

After about half an hour, I heard Leilah coughing in the back seat and then heard her asking Sajad to stop the car. He cautiously pulled over onto the shoulder. Leilah jumped out and retched onto the dry, brown ground. She was car sick. "I'm so sorry," she said trying to regain her composure. "I'm not used to sitting in the back seat in such terrible traffic, and Tehran's smog is really getting to me."

"Not to worry," I told her. "I'll sit in the back. It won't bother me at all." So we changed positions.

It took almost two more hours to get to Karaj, and on the way, Leilah kept receiving calls on her cell from someone who seemed concerned we hadn't arrived. Iranians are notoriously late, so I couldn't see what the concern could be.

When we finally got off onto what used to be a narrow, two-lane road through the desert to Dashte Behesht, I saw that it was four lanes and the desert had turned into one long strip of houses and shops. There were cars and trucks starting, stopping, and making U turns, which made the going very slow. Sajad stopped once to get Leilah some Tums for her nausea and came back with a power drink.

After many wrong turns and having been talked in on the cell phone, we arrived at a huge, black, iron gate in a tall mud wall. When Sajad pressed the intercom button, a little, old, gray-haired man came out to open the gate. We drove into a beautiful Persian garden with fountains, paddocks, stables, and a large house at the end of the drive.

Our host, Ali Hojabr, came out to greet us, and after introductions, I saw that Ezat Vodjdani, one of my *djelodars*, riders, from the Imperial Stables, was standing beside him smiling at me. We hugged each other with joy; I had trained Ezat to become the first Iranian show-jumping champion in 1973. He had been a talented young man of about twenty-five when I first knew him. He was hard working and had a great love of horses; he became an excellent student who listened well and got results. I couldn't believe he was there. It had been forty-one years since I had last been in Iran, so we had both aged, but he was still the handsome man I remembered.

Ali and Ezat, who is his trainer, showed me around the stables, riding rings, two indoor arenas, and the fancy clubhouse with a restaurant and bar. I was impressed with the facility but more so with the sixty or so beautiful European Warmblood horses he had in the stalls. It is a modern and well-appointed equine center that could compare with the best of any European or American counterpart.

Once our tour was finished, I was led into a lovely garden area filled with people. It seemed there was party going on. I entered the garden and realized the reception was in my honor; many of my old students were there to greet me. There was applause, and everyone was shouting "Welcome back, Khonume Rose! *Khoshomadid*!" I was almost in tears; I was so touched and relieved to see so many of my friends. The horse world was making me feel at home again.

The evening went on till the wee hours with the typical fruits, sweets, and tea to start and then a delicious Persian meal with all sorts of rice, *khoresh* (stews) and salads. After the meal, everyone sat around a carpeted *takhte*—a wide bench about a foot and a half above the ground. All who had known me stood on it one by one telling stories of when I had been in Iran. Many were very amusing while others were serious and touching.

Then it was my turn to reply to all these tributes. My Farsi was very halting as it was only my second day in the country, but I did my best with the help of a couple of translators. At one point, I became quite choked up, but I was able to finish with a funny story about my first day at the Imperial Stables in 1972 when I had been run away with by one of the newly imported and very expensive German horses.

Of the twenty or so *djelodars* with whom I worked at Farahabad, nine of them were still living in Iran and were at the party. There were tales of those who had left us. Colonel Neshati had been killed in a car accident, Reza Hadavand had died of an overdose, Maleki had had a heart attack, and Khanlahani and several others had died of old age. The saddest one was Mahmad Sarbazi, who was in his late teens when the revolution occurred. When the Revolutionary Guard took over the Shah's stables right after the revolution and renamed it Shahidabad, the Martyrs' Place, they arrived to introduce themselves. They lined all the *djelodars* up against a wall and explained how things were to be run from then on. At the end of the lecture, one guard shot Mahmad in the forehead and said, "This is what happens if you do not follow our orders."

On Friday, which is like our Sunday, there was an International FEI-sanctioned show-jumping event. I was invited to sit in the VIP section and was greeted by many old friends from the horse world. The event was well run, and the horses and riders were of really good quality. Any of them could have competed in Europe or America successfully. Of course most of the horses were expensive European imports, but the riders had obviously had good instruction either abroad or from European trainers who were invited to come to Iran as guest trainers.

Many of the horses had also been trained by my boys, who were among the leading trainers in the country then. When I was the chairman of show jumping in the seventies; there were eight clubs in the Tehran area; now there were fifty-five. The sport has grown immensely over the past forty years, which makes me especially proud of the work I did and of the young men I trained.

When the last class of the day, which was a 1.50 m to 1.60 m Grand Prix (international height) with thirty-eight horses competing was finished, I was asked to go into the ring for the presentations. I was presented a beautiful, hand-painted Esfahani vase, and it was announced that it was in gratitude for my being the first trainer of the Iranian show-jumping team and founder of the sport there. I was then asked to make the presentations to the winners. I felt much honored to do so, but I was surprised that each rider seemed really thrilled that it was me presenting the checks and ribbons.

After the awards ceremony, the riders, trainers, officials, and I stood around talking and telling stories about the days of the past, so Persian. When we dispersed, the winner of the class came up to me and asked, "May I please walk with you, Khonume Rose?"

"Absolutely! I would be delighted. You and your horse preformed beautifully today. It was a pleasure to watch you," I commented.

"I just want to tell you, Khonume, that I am honored to meet you. When I was young, I lived near Louise Firouz, and she helped me learn to ride. I would go to her stable every day to help out and ride. She had good things to say about you. You know you are really a legend in the horse world here. It is said that without you, we would not have this wonderful sport we have now. I just want to say again that I am truly honored to have met you, and I hope we will see each other again soon."

I was flabbergasted and shocked that I was held in such esteem after forty years. "Thank you, Majid. I really appreciate what you have told me, but for me, the legacy is that the riders I trained as imperial servants have now become such good trainers themselves and are successful in their own jobs and businesses."

As we parted, I reflected on the fact that what I had done all those years ago in this Middle Eastern country had had an impact I could never have imagined.

I spent the following week being saturated in equine activities. We visited all the clubs my boys either owned or worked at and saw the many horses most of which had been imported from Europe. The Azmon Club, next to the east side of the famous Azadi Stadium where the Asian Games have been held 1974 and had been built by the Shah, was founded by Reza Aladadi, a wealthy Iranian businessman who has a great love of horses. He has imported hundreds of horses from Europe over the past twenty years.

He brings planeloads of Warmblood and purebred foreign Arabian horses several times a year, and he has his own quarantine station for seventy horses where the animals are kept for their period of quarantine imposed by the Department of Agriculture. His club, which he has since sold, has over 400 stalls occupied by horses belonging to wealthy Tehranis. The club has two indoor arenas and nine outdoor rings as well as a beautiful, big grand prix ring with excellent European footing. Davoud Bahrami one of my imperial boys, who was junior champion of Iran every year I was there, is one of the trainers at this huge complex. He asked me to help him school one of his horses, so there I was again in the middle of a ménage in Iran.

The Bam Club, where Ali Rezai, another of my boys, (Iranian champion of 1975) is the manager, is another spectacular modern facility. The 400 stalls are filled. The grand prix ring is 300 meters long; there are nine other outdoor rings and two indoor arenas. There is a very active riding school where new horse enthusiasts learn to ride. There is a well-equipped veterinary clinic and six guest houses for visiting riders and trainers. They hold several horse shows a year in the main ring, which has a large, comfortable covered stand, VIP boxes, and restaurants. This horse complex would hold its own anywhere in the world.

Of course, the most thrilling stable for me to visit was Farahabad, where I had been the trainer and manager. Right after the revolution, the Pasdaran or Revolutionary Guard had taken over the running of the Shah's stable. Khomeini had ordered that none of the historic buildings or palaces should be damaged after the revolution. Farahabad had been the Imperial Stables not only during the Pahlavi reign but also during the almost hundred and fifty years of the Qajar rule, so it was a historical site. Even though they changed the name to Shahidabad, the Martyrs' Place, everyone in the horse world still calls it by its old name. During my time and for centuries before, it had been a part of the *shikargar sultaniteh*, the royal hunting grounds. It was in the southwestern corner of a vast piece of desert and mountainous land that was fifty miles square and was owned by the royal family in power. There was a beautiful old hunting lodge by the back gate, which I used to enter when I arrived for work every day, that had been built by Fath-Ali-Shah at the end of the eighteenth century.

As we drove south down one of the main north/south Tehran roads, I said, "There it is! Do you see the high wall on the top of that hill on the left? That's it!"

Sajad was not familiar with the horse world and the countryside because he was usually the driver/guide for businessmen from China, Europe, or Japan looking to invest in or start joint ventures with Iranian companies, and they spent their time in Tehran and other industrial cities. We had been lost more times than not looking for my horse clubs, so he was relieved when I recognized our destination. Of course the roads had changed a lot, but I was able to direct him past the gates of the old Imperial Guard, now a Revolutionary Guard military installation, and into the front entrance of Farahabad.

What had been the Shah's domain was now a boarding or livery stable where about 200 horses were kept by various owners. Aside from the fact that the place was not as well kept up as it always had been, it was the same. It was like going home. My "boys" were all there waiting for my arrival, and they all clapped and hugged me as I got out of the car. Nosrat Vodjdani was the current manager and main trainer; he had never left the employ of Farahabad through the subsequent owners who had followed the Pasdaran. We toured around looking at horses and the buildings including my old office, which has been turned into a cantina.

"Khonume Rose, do you want to see the museum?" Nosrat asked me.

"Yes, yes!" all the boys answered for me.

"Is it the same museum we had when I was here?" I queried.

"Yes the same," Ali Rezai answered. "Some of the things are gone, but there are some new ones too."

A young woman wearing a colorful head scarf came over from the office with the key to unlock the door. The museum had always been kept locked those years ago, so it seemed things had not changed. When we entered the building, I saw the same white walls and arched ceilings I remembered. The stuffed head of one of the Shah's favorite horses was hanging on the wall where it had always been, and the small leather elephant encrusted with brass and semiprecious stones that had been given to the Shah by the Indian ambassador was still on display; it had been a favorite of mine. Some things had changed, but I was delighted when Ali showed me the pictures of me jumping and receiving trophies; I had been well remembered.

Lunch was served in the new, very modern restaurant the club members used. It overlooked the green fields, which Kambiz had so painstakingly managed with irrigation, seed, and fertilizer, but they were now brown and overgrazed. Out the huge glass windows, I saw the majestic old Qajar hunting lodge and tall, scalloped mud walls reminiscent of the days of the shahs. Many stories of the forty years gone by were told that afternoon. The most memorable and disturbing was told by Davoud Bahrami.

"Shortly after you left, Khonume, Kambiz was taking Crown Prince Reza up to the mountains to try to shoot a mouflon [Persian red sheep]. He was just learning how to shoot, and it was to be his first hunt. It was a *Jomeh* [Friday], and I was off school. I didn't usually go out with the hunting party, but Kambiz saw me riding a young horse as they were leaving the stable area and called me to join them. I told him that the mare I was riding wasn't very well trained, but he insisted I go with the hunting party anyway.

"When we viewed the first herd of sheep, he and the Crown Prince along with a couple other *djelordars* got off their horses to get a good spot to shoot. My little mare had not been behaving very well, and as Kambiz was directing Reza where to shoot, she reared up and started to whinny. That spooked the sheep, and they ran off, so the prince didn't get a shot.

"We found two more herds, but each time, my horse misbehaved and the game ran off. As the sun started to fall, we found more sheep. Kambiz turned to me and shook his fist at me as a warning because he really wanted the prince to be able get a shot. He said, 'If you let that mare scream again, I will shoot you,' and he pointed his gun at me. I was really scared, and I could tell Kambiz was really angry.

"I stayed back as he kept his gun trained on me while he showed Reza where to position himself. It was a very tense moment, and no one said a word until the Crown Prince broke the silence. 'Kambiz, put your gun down! I don't care if I shoot a mouflon or not. Davoud is my friend. I don't want to shoot him.' So Kambiz put his gun down and looked me in the eye. 'I don't know what I was thinking, Davoud. I'm sorry,' he said. But that is how he was. He would do anything for their majesties, even kill someone."

And that was indeed how it was in those days. The generals, courtiers, and servants held their royal family in such esteem that they would do almost anything for them to stay in their favor.

We spent time visiting clubs specializing in Iranian-bred horses found around the capital. The Turkoman, Akhal-Teke, Darashouri, Fars, Asil Arabs, and Caspian horses are all well represented, and their bloodlines have been kept pure in a country so proud of its equine heritage.

I was lucky enough to visit the small farm of my deceased friend, the defender of the Persian Arab horses, Mary Gharagozlou. The couple to whom she left her place seemed happy to welcome an old friend and were proud to show me a young foal of Mary's bloodlines. I was invited to the house for tea and had a nostalgic feeling to be seeing so many of Mary's lovely things again.

It was beautiful on the day we drove up into the mountains near Kordon, where Louise and Narcy Firouz's place, which they had built just before the revolution, is situated. The trees laden with fruit and the flowers in glorious bloom would have made their hearts sing. The brick barns with their arches had several horses Louise had bred before her death nine years previously. Her son, Karen, has several Caspian horses, the small, ancient horses his mother discovered, in his adjoining garden, which was equally well kept with fruit and blooms abounding and horses grazing in the paddocks. Visiting Louise and Narcy's lovely *bagh* brought to my mind the many wonderful times we had spent together years earlier. Though they are gone, their legacy remains.

When I arrived at a polo match one afternoon, it was announced over the PA, "The first trainer of the Iranian show-jumping team is with us this afternoon. After forty years, we are happy to welcome her back." There was applause, and I stood. I was surprised at this announcement but was pleased I had been remembered by the horse people of Iran. I had always been a polo aficionado and had seen many games played at the dusty old sand field at the Khargooshdareh grounds those years ago. I was amazed at how much the sport had changed. The players played well on a beautiful, green grass pitch that had been built at the south end of Farahabad. The game was fast, and the players and horses could definitely have been successful if they were playing in Canada, Great Britain, or the US. The sport had advanced as well as show jumping had.

On our way to the races in Gonbad-e-Turkoman (Gonbad-e-Kavous, pre-revolution), we stopped at the home of the racing secretary, who welcomed us and invited us in to his home for tea. He seemed to know about me and took me into his office to see pictures on his computer of the best horses of the day and explain their bloodlines. He also gave me some good tips on which horses would be the winners in the afternoon's races. Under Islamic Shari'a law, gambling is generally seen as illegal, but thanks to certain religious rulings, race goers are permitted to put money on the horses as long as they're only "predicting" through official channels. It was the day of the Iranian Championships, the final day of racing in the north. He told me there were two really good horses that had been battling each other throughout the racing year, and he was not sure which would win the championships, so he told me to bet them both.

My brother Clarke, who had been a successful horse trainer in Canada in the seventies, had come over to Iran at the invitation of my friends Ali Reza and Mahmadi Soudovar for the two months prior to the Iranian Championships in 1974 and 1975 to train their horse Shahnazar in hopes of winning the coveted Aryamehr Championship Cup. As well as winning many other races with their horses, he was successful in winning the championship with Shahnazar both years.

"Do you remember the horse Shahnazar who was champion in 1974 and 1975?" I asked.

"Shahnazar? Of course! He won the championship in 1353 and 1354 in the Persian calendar. He was a great race horse and became an excellent sire. His blood is still in many of our good horses today. He was trained by a foreigner the Soudovars brought here, to be sure they won."

"Yes I know. He is my brother," I commented.

"I knew him well! He was a great trainer, and he really knew his horses. Is he still with us?"

"Yes. He's still riding and training horses in America."

"You must give him my best when you go back home," he said.

The parking lot at the racetrack in Gonbad-e-Turkoman was full of cars when we arrived, and we had a long walk to get to the stands and paddock. We followed crowds of men all talking about which horse they thought would win this or that race as we approached the gates. We went to the paddock, which was enclosed with a chain-link fence that hadn't been there before, and we looked at the horses with their tasseled neck pieces and colorful bridles. They all looked healthy with enough flesh and shiny coats. After checking out my tips for the race, we walked over to the stands, which had not changed in the forty-one years I had been away; it was still a three-tiered building of dingy-gray concrete with rickety, green iron steps leading to the second and third levels. I carefully climbed the stairs through throngs of men up to the third level to my VIP front-row seat. I sat, and the man next to me nudged me and pointed to the number 6 horse in the field of twelve. "My horse!" he said in accented English.

"*Bon chance! Enshalah aval mishe!*" I wished him luck and hoped he'd be the winner.

It took about twenty minutes to get the horses to the starting gate; when they finally got there, one horse broke out and ran around the track twice with men on foot chasing it and finally scaring the poor thing so that it jumped over the fence and fell.

When the bell finally sounded, the eleven remaining horses flew out. Jockeys juggled for position bumping and pushing at each other while a pickup truck full of stewards raced alongside in the infield watching for infractions and the ambulance followed behind kicking up more dust. As the horses headed for the finish line, they were spread out; I noticed that two were without riders. The winner was three lengths in front, and number 6 was nowhere. My neighbor pounded his fist on the rail and got up to leave in disgust.

"*Behbashid, Agha,*" I gave him my condolences.

In pre-revolutionary Iran, horse racing was an elite sport. The Shah was a very keen horseman and was aiming to expand racing. Under Islamic law, betting is *haram*, illegal, but the Iranian Racing Commission was able to receive permission from the Ayatollah and his Assembly of Experts to have betting at official race meets. Nowadays, people from all walks of life attend the races in Gonbad in the north and at the Nowruzabad track just outside Tehran. The betting windows, which have computer screens showing odds and results, are usually manned by women with head scarves taking the predictions and handing out the winnings. Tickets can be bought for as little as 10,000 rials, about 25¢, with no upper limit, though large bets are rare at the windows. Though people are reluctant to place big bets at the tote window, there is always a long line of small-money bettors. The big bets are usually made unofficially with the winnings being exchanged hand to hand.

The day continued with the rest of the races being quite entertaining; I saw rider less horses running up the stretch, ambulances picking up the fallen around the track, and the mostly male betters grumbling when the favorites were not winning. Horse racing in Iran had not changed much in forty years.

I had visited the many horse farms and clubs in the Tehran area most of which were show-jumping stables and full of imported European Warmblood horses. The next stop was Esfahan to the south. We drove out into the desert to the farms where the Persian Arab and Darashouri horses were bred and used for endurance, hunting, and pleasure riding. The farms were smaller, and the stables were of the more traditional, old Persian style—mud and bricks with high-domed ceilings. The horses were either tethered or allowed to roam free in the desert and mountains. Each owner had fewer horses, but the majority were well kept, and the breeders took great pride in the fact they were keeping the pure Persian horse breeds from becoming extinct or mixed with horses of unknown pedigree.

When we drove into the irrigated apple orchard of Agha Sirturk (Esfahan is known for apples), I was amazed at the lushness of the grass in the orchard and the pastures alike. In nine years, he had turned about fifty hectares—just over 120 acres—of desert into a beautiful setting for his home and horses. His five stallions were tethered to tall posts around the edge of a paddock filled with clover and fescue. The mares out in a huge field were also tethered, but the foals, all of which were several months old, were allowed to roam free to take advantage of the green grass and their mothers' milk. There were no stables, because he drove the herd south to Khuzestan for the cold winter months. These horses were direct decedents of the Darashouri horses made famous by Zia Khan, his grandfather, during the late nineteenth century. Sirturk is a true lover of the horse and proud of the pure lineage of his herd.

Reuniting with my old friends and students from the 1970s and meeting so many new friends in the horse world were highlights of my trip. I had not dreamed that the horse world in Iran could have developed as much as I found it to be after forty-plus years. Show jumping there is the equivalent of the sport anywhere in the world, and polo, which had been founded in Persia hundreds of years ago, is excellent. Racing is entertaining and a place for the Turkoman, Persian Arab, and *dokhun* (Turkoman/thoroughbred cross) horses to compete. Hundreds of imported foreign Arab horses are displayed and judged at many Arab beauty shows, and Persian breeds are protected and are flourishing. A few breeders are starting to breed European Warmbloods as well, so in Iran, the horse world is as extensive and as complete as anywhere in the world.

Tea with the racing secretary (in white) Hoor
Mansuri and Sajad Bamdad (L)

Asil Arb foal with dam from Mary Gharagozlou line

Author with her Imperial "boys"

Clarke Whitaker on Turkoman race horse

Darashouri stallion from Louise Firouz line

Ezat Vodjdani Champion on Shahbrang

Authors office at Farahabad

Turkoman racing in Gonbad

Village school children

Polo match

CHAPTER 13

Dor Dor Bazi

As we were driving through the posh Niavaran area of Tehran early one evening, I noticed many fancy and expensive cars driving slowly up Darband Street—Porsche Panameras and Cayennes, convertible BMWs, Mercedes-Benzes of all types, Audis, Lexuses, and some cars I didn't recognize. Most had a good-looking young man at the wheel and one or two other male passengers. They seemed to be driving up the street and making U turns at the top to come back down again. They were moving slowly, and the traffic seemed to be getting more and more jammed up. Every now and then, a car would stop in the middle of the street and bring traffic to a complete stop.

"What's going on with this terrible traffic?" I asked Sajad.

"Oh it's just the time of day for *dor dor bazi*," he explained.

"What's *dor dor bazi*?"

"That's the way young guys meet attractive girls."

"I don't get it. How do they meet girls if they're driving?"

"Well, they look for attractive girls driving the other way, then they stop their cars and exchange telephone numbers. Then the guys go someplace where they park their cars and decide which girls they want to call to hook up with. Or sometimes, the girls take the number and call the guys they think look cool. You see, the girls are checking out the fancy cars and what the guys look like, and they'll agree to meet the guys who look promising and have fancy cars at one of the nearby cafés. Then who knows what will happen?"

"What about the girls? Do they have fancy cars too?" I asked.

"Some do, but it really doesn't matter what car they have as long as it's nice and clean and polished; the girl just has to be good looking."

"Well, that shouldn't be hard. Most young Iranian girls are attractive with beautiful complexions, lovely, dark eyes, and dark-brown hair," I said. "But I thought young people couldn't just hook up like that here."

"Who's to stop them?" he asked.

"I thought you had morality police who checked dress code and made sure couples weren't seen together in public and other things like that."

"That was years ago. There are no rules or police like that now. The young people are as promiscuous here as they are in America I'm sure. Maybe they're worse here. You might be shocked. Do you think my girlfriend and I are chaste? No way. We Iranians don't marry at young ages. Most of us live with our parents till we're in our thirties. We don't pay rent, and we have plenty of opportunities to go out to cafés and parties and have sex if desired. We want to be sure before we marry, and we want to have enough money to have a good life together, so we wait. Even so, the divorce rate is high in this country."

Leilah, the hard-liner, was probably squirming in the back seat. "Well, I want you to know that eighty-five percent of marriages are not arranged in this country, but the divorce rate in that group is almost ninety percent! In arranged marriages, which are about fifteen percent, the divorce rate is only about two percent. Anyway, I've never heard of *dor dor bazi*. I'm sure they don't have it in Mashhad, where I live."

"Oh I'm sure they do," Sajad said. "Maybe if you tried it, you would find yourself a husband, Leilah. You're always complaining that you haven't found the right guy yet."

"I don't have a fancy enough car. I have a twenty-year-old Honda Accord."

In Gorgon, which is north in Mazandaran Province near the Caspian Sea, the foliage is a lush green on the northern side of the Alborz Mountains. As we were flying across the mountains to get there, I saw a distinct line where the south side of the mountains stopped and the north began—desert south and green forests north. I was looking forward to this part of the trip because I had been in the north of the country many times in the past and had always had an enjoyable time.

Hoor Mansuri became my second guide while I was in the north. He was one of Iran's leading environmentalists and had been chosen to guide me in an area of the country that was completely new to Sajad and Leilah. He would teach all three of us about the wonders of the northeastern Iranian countryside.

The first morning as we got in the car to drive to the small village of Shahpour, high up in the Alborz, Hoor began singing a Persian love song to make sure we were all in the mood for a drive to this romantic village that had been a stopping place for Shah Abbas in the sixteenth century. As we drove south up the mountain, the lush green trees and grass abruptly turned into barren mountain terrain as we neared the top.

Halfway up the mountain, we stopped to talk to some nomads who were beekeepers. There were hives alongside the road, and their tent was pitched on the side of the hill overlooking the valley where their sheep were grazing. Two sheepdogs lazily glanced down at the contented sheep below. The men were happy to see us, especially as I was a foreigner, and answer questions about their bees, sheep, and their nomadic travels.

They invited us into their tent, which had a beautiful Turkoman carpet on the floor. We reluctantly acquiesced using the custom of *taarof*, a meeting together, to seem polite. We chatted while they served us delicious Iranian tea and *nun-e-barbari* (bread), the most delicious I had in Iran. They had bought it that same morning from a nearby bread shop where it had been baked in the traditional way, in a stone oven. The fresh honey from the queen bee, which is the most treasured, was offered to us, so we spread it liberally on the bread.

After a delightful half hour or so eating bread and honey and chatting amiably, they were at first reluctant to take the rials we offered them, which was another example of taarof. It is polite to refuse an offer of food or some other thing by someone who will continue to press the offer until you reluctantly but gratefully accept.

The remaining drive to the village was steep and winding with startling views of oases, valleys, and steep gorges while the road became more and more narrow. We entered Shahpour; its streets were one lane with barely room for our car. We passed a man and a donkey with loaded saddlebags, a shepherd herding his sheep up a lane, and a tractor chugging along on its way to a field to plow. There was no *dor dor bazi* in this town.

Gonbad-e-Turkoman is the main town in the Turkoman Sarah area of Golestan Province near the Caspian Sea. Since I had last been there, it has grown immensely, but it still has a small-town atmosphere. It is famous for its horse racing, which I described earlier. The inhabitants are mostly descended from the nomadic Turkoman tribe and speak a western Turkoman language as their first tongue. There are also Korisani Turks, Baluch, and other Iranic peoples residing in the area.

The tall, proud tower on a hill in the center of the city is Gonbad-e-Kaboos, Tower of Kaboos. This tower was once a part of a fortress of Ibn Washmgir, King of Ziyarid, who ruled over that area from 927 to 1090. This mystical structure is totally featureless with the exception of an inscription of the king's name and year of his death. It is fifty-five meters high set on a fifteen-meter mound with a brick foundation of seventeen meters in depth, so the total height is seventy-two meters, making it the world's tallest brick tower. The entrance leads to a cylindrical chamber built in the shape of a pencil with a ten-pointed star at the top; this is totally empty all the way up to the roof. The tower became the king's tomb after he was killed by his son as was predicted to him by the stars.

I visited the tower at dusk one afternoon; each step I took while inside reverberated in a strange, eerie way. When I went outside, I stood about twenty meters from its entrance and began talking; my voice came back to me after bouncing off the inner walls and ceiling in a way that made me think an invisible person was standing next to me.

As we drove along the main street of the town to have dinner, the traffic was becoming heavy. Cars were starting and stopping, and the narrow street was congested.

"It looks like they're doing *dor dor bazi* in Gonbad," Sajad commented.

"I don't see any fancy cars though," I said.

"In the smaller cities and towns, it really doesn't matter. You just need any kind of car to do it."

"I guess I'd better come to Gonbad then with my twenty-year-old car," Leilah said with a laugh.

Esfahan, called by the Persians of old, Nisf-e-Jahan, meaning that after seeing it, one had seen half the world, is about 2,500 years old. It is one of the most beautiful cities in the world with its monuments, tiled mosques, and palaces. It was the capital city during the time of the Seljuk Dynasty in the eleventh century. In those days, the city center was a square bordered on the north by the great mosque of Esfahan, which is still one of the chief architectural glories of the city.

After the fall of the Seljuks, the city declined, but Shah Abbas I (1587–1629), who later unified Persia, made it his capital in 1598 and rebuilt it into one of the largest and most beautiful cities of the seventeenth century anywhere in the world. It continued to be the capital until the Qajars chose Tehran as their capital in 1722. It is renowned for its many great historical buildings and monuments and its life-giving river, Zayadeh-Rood. The city has been an oasis settlement noted for its fertile lands and prosperity for centuries.

The evening I went to visit the bridges over this more than 200-meter-wide river, it was dry. "What happened to the water?" I asked Sajad when we were at the Khaju Bridge.

"You may know we have a dreadful water shortage in this country. Since the revolution, we have built many dams. In an arid country as we have, dams are essential so water can be stored to assure the reliability of supply for our domestic, industrial, and agricultural requirements. We also need them for flood control and hydroelectric power. The Chadegan Dam was built upriver in 1972 as a hydroelectric power project and to stabilize water flow and generate electricity. The dam has helped prevent seasonal flooding and gives us the electricity and water we need, but the water is held in the reservoir and not allowed to flow in the river until the rainy season begins in the fall. During Now Ruz, the water flow is increased for the holiday and is stopped in the dry season. We're in the dry season, but in a few weeks, they will let the water flow and the river will have water."

Eleven bridges crossed the Zayadeh-Rood in Esfahan, but the two most famous and beautiful are the Alaverdi Khan Bridge and the Khaju Bridge. The former was built during Safavid times under Shah Abbas I to connect the north side of the river with the south side, where he had constructed huge gardens and palaces. He had many Christian Armenians brought to live there to grow commerce in the city; these people were allowed to retain their Christian faith.

The bridge is 298 meters long, built over the widest part of the river, and it has thirty-three pier arches, thus giving it the popular name of *Si-o-Seh Pol*. Alaverdi Khan, an Armenian, was the most powerful general of Shah Abbas I's time. He funded the bridge and hired a Russian architect to build it between 1599 and 1602. It has footpaths and a wide cobblestone road for pedestrian and carriage crossing. It has served as a dam as well as a bridge and an important place where people can meet to socialize.

The Khaju Bridge, three miles to the west, has been described as the finest example of Persian architecture at the height of the Safavid culture. It was built by Shah Abbas II around 1650 on the foundations of an older bridge. Its twenty-four arches extend 133 meters with a 12-meter-wide road and pedestrian walks. Serving as a dam as well, it links the Khaju quarter on the north bank of the river with the Zoroastrian quarter on the south. It served as a place for public meetings and today is still a meeting place for young and old.

Shah Abbas built himself a pavilion on it in the middle, where he could sit and admire the views and the beauty of the bridge that was once covered with paintings and tile work. The bridge regulates the water; when sluice gates under the archways are closed, the water level behind the bridge is raised to facilitate irrigation of the many gardens along the river upstream.

On the upper level of the bridge, the central lane was for horses and carts and the vaulted paths on either side were for pedestrians. Octagonal pavilions in the center on both sides provide vantage points for remarkable views. The lower level can be accessed by pedestrians and is a popular shady place for relaxing.

The rich, cultural heritage of this city makes it attractive for tourists. It is famous for its handicrafts of silver and copper work, woodwork, brass work, and pottery. The arts of tile making and carpet weaving, which had died out, have been revived in recent years.

The people of Esfahan are a very socially oriented and enjoy walking or driving around of an evening for entertainment, so it wasn't surprising that we saw many fancy cars roaming the streets participating in the national Iranian youths' pastime of *dor dor bazi*.

The bazaar, as in most Middle Eastern countries, is the center of commerce. Each of its many sections specializes in a particular item for sale. For instance, there are sections for fruits and vegetables, meat, spices, copper, silver, gold, plastics, fabric, and dry goods, artifacts, and other commodities. A lot of walking is involved, but it is interesting to traverse the usually enclosed alleyways where you can find just about anything you want.

I had received a *tala* by my maid Azizeh for my birthday one year when I was living in Iran. It was a gold chain with six coins dangling from a thin gold bar. I was very touched that she and her family had bought me such an expensive and meaningful gift. Each small coin on the chain represented one of the central bodies of Shi'ism. Azizeh told me I must wear this necklace at all times and I would be protected. I wore it most days while in Iran and continued to wear it when we had left and settled in America. Then one day, a gold coin fell off. When I realized that, I looked but was unable to find it. I put my precious necklace in the drawer of a Persian chest I had brought back with me; it stayed there for forty-one years. When I returned to Iran, I brought the necklace with me in hopes that I could find a replacement coin of Imam Fatimeh.

When I told Leilah about my necklace, she said the best place to find a Fatimeh charm would be the gold bazaar in Esfahan, so the first morning we were there, we headed for the bazaar. Up to that point, I had not been able to change more than $100 at any of the money changers or banks. I decided to try the hotel that morning and was told they had only enough rials for $50. "Maybe you will be able to change some money in the bazaar too." Leilah suggested.

In the bazaar, I went to the first booth that had a lot of handicrafts and items for tourists; I asked the merchant if he could change some American dollars for me.

"How many do you want to change?"

"Could you change a few hundred for me?" I tentatively asked.

"Of course, no problem. How many hundred do you want?" I was surprised because the money changers and banks seemed so stingy with their exchanges. When we decided on the amount, he took my few hundred dollars and came back with a wad of rials. He gave me 39,000 rials for each American dollar, where the hotel had given me only 34,000 per dollar. I was a millionaire! My purse was busting at the seams.

We walked along the crowded alleys of the bazaar passing the copper, silver, clothing, and many other sections until we came to the area where there was nothing but gold to be seen in the small shop windows. It took some time and many questions to find the kind, little, gray-haired, balding goldsmith who said he would try to help me find a replacement coin for my tala. He buzzed around talking to his neighbors in their shops and finally told me, "I don't think we will find another coin like the others. This is a very old and delicate piece you know. They don't make them anymore. I haven't seen one of these for many years. I think if I just move one of the coins on the side to the middle, then you will have five coins hanging evenly. It will look perfect."

"But what about Imam Fatimeh? I won't have her with me."

"Well, maybe we can find a Fatimeh charm and you can put it on a separate chain and wear it with the old one. Then you will still have all six of the coins."

His repair shop was on the second story of the gold bazaar; we watched while he worked on the delicate piece of gold. It took only a short time for him to remove the coin from the right side and put it where Fatimeh had been in the middle.

"There," he said as he polished a small, rough edge from the bar. "Now it looks better." He showed me the small amount of gold he had taken from the slim bar and told me he was going to pay me for the gold.

"*Naher, Agha.*" I declined the money. "What do I owe you for the work?"

"*Nada, Khonume.*" He didn't want me to pay. We bantered back and forth in the Persian way of using *taarof* until it was decided that I would not pay him, he would not pay me for the small piece of gold, and we would go together to find a Fatimeh charm and a gold chain for me. It took some time, some walking, and some talking to finally find a Fatimeh piece and an appropriate chain. I was very happy with my purchase and especially that the seller was only too happy to accept US dollars.

When we were in the north, Hoor took us to the small village where he lived in a garden with his parents and his seventeen-year-old daughter. The town was very small, but it had a bazaar of course, and a main street with many small shops. As we drove down the narrow streets, we passed a shop with a green neon sign that read Computer Repair in English. "That's my shop," Hoor said smiling as we drove by slowly. It looked neat, and though it was small, it seemed full of people.

"It looks busy, Hoor," I commented. "Who works there when you are off guiding people like me?"

"I have a couple of computer science students who go to the university in Abbas Abad who take care of things for me."

"Is there a university near here? It seems we are a long way from any major city."

"Iran today has universities everywhere. We are only about forty minutes from Abbas Abad, you know."

"But how do the kids get to school living so far away?" I asked.

"There is great public transportation in this country, and almost everyone can afford a car. That's one of the reasons for the bad traffic and pollution. Anyone in Iran can get a college education if he or she wants to now. We are a very well-educated nation. There are really almost too many universities; practically every city has at least one."

"I had no idea! When I was here, the Shah was expanding higher education, but there weren't that many colleges, and many students were sent abroad for university education."

"We have a large network of private, public, and state-affiliated universities. Non-medical schools are under the supervision of the Ministry of Science and Technology while medicals schools are under the arm of the Ministry of Health. Here, we have free education and physical training for everyone," he explained.

"That's fantastic! What about your daughter? Is she going to university yet?"

"Yes. She's in her first year at Azad University in Abbas Abad."

We drove on, and he pointed to a large, two-story stone house. "That's my house," he said proudly. "I just finished the final touches last week. It has taken me two years to build it. I have an apartment for ecological tourists who come here during the winter months, so it will provide me with some income too. My parents live in the guest house by the gate."

"Where do these tourists come from?" I asked.

"Each year as the cold season arrives, the wetlands, where we were today, turn into a haven for migratory birds. The Mazandaran and Gilan Provinces, here in the north, are destinations for many breeds of birds including swans, pelicans, all types of gulls and seabirds, tern, and quail that come from Siberia and Central Europe. The Department of Tourism has been arranging bird-watching tours in the fall and winter to help boost tourism in the colder months when we don't get many travelers. It's becoming quite a successful endeavor, and I expect to have my guest rooms full most of the winter.

"We show interested people the rural lifestyle, culture, and customs and give tours of villages and natural landscapes. A lot of them are interested in watching net fishing and shopping for fresh fish on the beaches, so a number of eco-lodges such as mine have been built.

"Iran's considerable wetlands are all important globally as they are used by migratory birds from India, Eastern Europe, and Africa. Due to the appropriate range of temperature and all the soaring peaks of the Alborz and Zagros in the north and west of the country and the lesser ranges in the east, center, and south, each different climate zone suits the existence of various plants, mammals, birds, reptiles, and aquatic organisms. In Iran, we have mammals weighing just two grams, lighter than a coin, and a species of whale that weighs a hundred and thirty tons.

"Unfortunately, humankind has slaughtered many species and destroyed habitats over the years, but even so, the variety of fauna and flora in Iran is greater than what is found in all Europe. Iran hosted the first convention on wetlands of international importance at Ramsar, on the Caspian Sea, in 1971. The outcome of this convention was that the Department of the Environment in Iran and the UN Development Program/Global Environmental Facility developed a project to demonstrate how to conserve wetlands. After the revolution, in 2005, the government commenced again to protect and save the wetlands with the Conservation of Iranian Wetlands Project, which focused on the development and application of the ecosystem approach at the contrasting wetlands.

"A cross-sectorial and participative approach demonstrated how to rehabilitate and conserve wetlands while continuing to achieve ecological and socioeconomic goals. This approach has been utilized successfully in many regions around the world. In July 2017, in an effort to counteract the combined effects of climate change, water crises, and human activities that had turned the once-thriving wetlands into sources of dust and sand storms, the Majlis passed a law to protect, restore, and manage the country's wetlands. The Wetlands Protection Law will protect and fund projects aimed at achieving the goals of the law."

We drove through the black metal gate to Hoor's house, and I saw a large garden with all sorts of fruit trees and flowers his mother was watering. I was impressed that this young man in his early thirties had the money to build such a lovely house and garden. He was very enterprising; he was an ecologist and guide who also had a shop and a bed and breakfast. He had a charming mother and father, and his lovely daughter made us tea and served fruit and sweets.

I asked his daughter about school and if she had a boyfriend. She smiled sheepishly to the latter and explained that she did not.

"Well, you will have to go do a little *dor dor bazi* and find one," I chided.

"No daughter of mine will be doing *dor dor bazi* while I'm around," Hoor declared.

Alaverdi Bridge, Esfahan

Gonbad-e-Kaboos

Author with Leilah Mohasab

Shah Mosque, Esfahan

Town of Shahpour

Enjoying tea with nomads

Friends in Shahpour

Iranian countryside

CHAPTER  14

Places of Interest

Though this book is not a tourists' guide, I want to demonstrate that Iran is a gold mine of tourist attractions. To see all the worthwhile sights would take a lifetime, so I will discuss just a few of my favorite places I haven't mentioned so far.

Persia's history is long and complicated but certainly worth a cursory look for the traveler planning to visit. The Achaemenids ruled 550–330 BC during which time they tried but failed to conquer Greece. In 330 BC, Alexander the Great conquered the Persian Empire, which was dominated by the Greek Seleucid Empire until 140 BC. Then the Parthians and the Sasanians ruled with Zoroastrianism being the dominant religion.

The Arabs invaded the area, ended the Sasanian Dynasty, and brought Islamic rule in AD 636. Until 1501, when Shah Ismail became the first Safavid ruler and Shi'a Islam was declared the state religion, there were a series of dynasties including Seljuk Turk, Mongol, Turkic, and other Iranian tribes. The last Safavid ruler was deposed in 1736 by Nadir Shah, who was deposed by Karim Khan of the Zand Dynasty.

In 1794, Mohammad Khan Qajar killed the last of the Zands to restore stability to the country until power was seized by Military Commander

Reza Khan in 1921. Parliament voted to have him crowned king in 1925, and the Pahlavi Dynasty reigned until the revolution of 1979 deposed Shah Mohammad Reza, his son.

Thakht-e-Jamshid, Persepolis, is one of the world's most magnificent ancient sights. It is about sixty kilometers northeast of the beautiful, old city of Shiraz, which is known as the city of love and poetry. The sight includes a 125,000-square-meter terrace artificially constructed by cutting out the side of Rahmet Mountain; three sides are surrounded by high retaining walls while the third side rests on the mountain itself. It is thought that the Achaemenid King Cyrus the Great selected the site, but his son Darius I actually started its construction in about 515 BC. It was the elegant residence and ceremonial capital of Persia. To the ancient Persians, it was known as Parsa, which is also the word for Persia, but it was believed that the mythological figure Jamshid built all the monuments, and thus it was called *Takht-e-Jamshid*, Throne of Jamshid.

Alexander the Great invaded Parsa in 330 BC and had the palaces burned as an act of revenge for the Persians' burning of the Acropolis. It takes about a full day to see this eerie place, but I would suggest staying until the evening to experience the beautiful sound-and-light show. I also recommend visiting the tomb of the poets Hafez and Saadi, the lovely old Qavam House, and the many magnificent Persian gardens.

The city of Yazd, about 270 kilometers southeast of Esfahan, was named for the Sassanid ruler Yazdegerd I and is an important center of Persian architecture. The city's heritage of being a center of Zoroastrianism with its Tower of Silence on the outskirts and its *ateshkhaneh*, which holds a fire that has been kept alight continuously since AD 470, makes it a fascinating place to visit.

To deal with the extremely hot summers, most of the old buildings were built with wind towers thus giving it the nick name of City of Wind Towers. It also has one of the largest networks of qanats, underground waterways, in the world; its qanat makers are said to be the most skilled in the country. As well, there are prime examples of *yakhchals*, which were used to store ice from the glaciers in the nearby mountains.

The Jame Mosque, built in the twelfth century, is an example of the finest Persian mosaics and architecture. Because of its remote desert location and difficulty of access, it remained largely immune to battles and the ravages of war; the beautiful, old adobe buildings are intact. This noble city has a family-centered culture and is said to have a very low rate of divorce. Today, the majority of the people are Muslim though there is still a sizable population of Zoroastrians and some Jews including Moshe Katsav, the former president of Israel.

Just south of Yazd in the desert is the Zoroastrian sanctuary and destination for pilgrims called Pir-e-Namaki. It is believed that Naz Banoo, the daughter of King Yazdegerd, ran to the base of the cliff of Mount Naraki to escape the Arabs who were invading the area. When she got to the wall of the mountain, she prayed to her God to save her. A cave-like opening appeared in the rock in front of her, so she entered. Once she was safely in the cave, the opening closed and a spring began flowing out of the mountain. To this day, the spring still flows and fragrant flowers bloom around it in the springtime. This mystical Zoroastrian pilgrimage site is well worth the visit.

Five other Zoroastrian shrines near Yadz were also used as holy places long before the birth of Islam. The yearly pilgrimage or *hadj* to these shrines is an occasion of gathering of members of different villages, an important religious time of the year, an undertaking of spiritual significance, and an opportunity for feasting, music, and dancing.

The most holy city in Iran is Mashhad, near the Afghan border, which originally was the little town of Sanabad, where trade caravans would stop at the caravanserai on the way to Turkmenistan. In AD 818, the eighth Shi'ite imam, Ali Bin Moussa Al Reza, the great grandson of Imam Ali, who was the cousin and son-in-law of Muhammad, was poisoned by the *calif*, the religious and civil ruler of the time. As Imam Reza was buried in Mashhad, Shi'as and Sunnis began visiting his grave on pilgrimage.

By the end of the ninth century, a dome was built on the grave, and many buildings and bazaars sprang up around it. The *haram*, shrine complex, was ransacked and rebuilt a number of times during the next thousand years. This shrine has become the third most holy site for Shi'ite Muslims after Holy Kaaba in Saudi Arabia and Karbala in Iraq. Today, this ever-growing *haram* commemorating Imam Reza's martyrdom is a magical city within a city with dazzling clusters of domes and minarets in blue and pure gold behind fountain-cooled courtyards and magnificent arched arcades. It is one of the marvels of the Islamic world and worth visiting at different times of the day to see its changing moods. Even though non-Muslims are allowed in most of the *haram's* outer courtyards, they are not given access to the holy shrine and Gohar Shad Mosque.

I was lucky enough to visit the mosque and holy shrine itself when I went to Mashhad with Crown Prince Reza in the seventies. It was awe inspiring to see the amazing gold lattice *zarih*, or cage, under which the imam's tomb was displayed in the room decorated with mirrors and tiles. Witnessing the many tearful pilgrims kneeling and kissing the *zarih* on the floor of which coins, paper money, and jewelry had been tossed was a moving experience.

In this city, some women stay covered at all times while others dress and act like Westerners, but even so, it is evident that public opinion matters a great deal to them. In the beginning of the revolution, there were gruesome public hangings there, but the people protested against them, so they were slowly curtailed. Today, mass killers and child molesters are sometimes put to death in this way, but because of the disapproval, there are few spectators.

At the heart of Iranian Shi'a, a religion of mourning and loss, there is always the hope for better things to come even though its adherents still feel a bleak loss over the defeat and murder of the three great Imams, Ali, Hossein, and Reza, which took place over 1,300 years ago. Shi'as await the return of the "hidden" twelfth imam who disappeared in AD 878 and may reappear at any time with Jesus at his side to restore peace and goodness to the world. When one sees the devotion of the pilgrims at Imam Reza's tomb, it is hard to come away without a feeling of respect for this faith. Iran's unique brand of Islam seems a sweet, sad mystery and is quite unlike the hard, aggressive faith found in the Arab states.

Nader Shah, the founder of the Afshar Dynasty, ruled from 1736 to 1747. He was an enigmatic figure in Iranian history. As head of a group of bandits, he raised a large army to help Shah Tahmasp, the Safavid king, regain the throne his father had lost three years before; he then deposed Tahmasp in favor of his infant son, who soon died; Nader had himself proclaimed shah.

Although he restored national independence and protected Iran's territorial integrity at a dark moment in history, his obsessive suspicions and jealousies plunged Iran into political turmoil. He was a Sunni by birth and upbringing, but he was a great benefactor of the Shi'a shrine of Imam Reza. He was often called the Napoleon of Iran as this bandit leader created an empire that stretched from northern India to the Caucasus Mountains. His syphilitic rages and crazed decisions contributed to his assassination in 1747 after only eleven years as shah. His tomb and museum are in a beautiful garden in the heart of Mashad less than a mile from Imam Reza's haram and are definitely worth a visit.

The city of Kashan remains a largely undeveloped tourist attraction. It is in Isfahan Province along the Qom-Kerman Road, which is on the edge of Iran's central desert. It dates to the Elamite period, and the Sialk Ziggurat, a rectangular tower sometimes surmounted by a temple, still standing in the western suburbs after 7,000 years, reveals that this region was one of the primary centers of civilization in prehistoric times. This ziggurat, where the remains of people who lived there can be seen, is the oldest in the world. At present, there is still excavation and restoration being done on this amazing site.

Kashan was the leisure vacation spot for the Safavid shahs and where Shah Abbas I had the beautiful Bagh-e-Fin, Fin Garden, with its pools and orchards built in the style of the classical Persian vision of paradise. Unfortunately, the massive earthquake of 1778 destroyed most of the lovely Safavid buildings and gardens in the area as well it killed over 8,000 people. The buildings in the Bagh-e-Fin were destroyed, but fortunately, the pools and waterways remained intact.

During the Qajar Dynasty, the town was rebuilt; numerous large houses from the eighteenth and nineteenth centuries illustrate the finest examples of Qajar architecture. The town is divided into two parts, the mountainous and the desert. Part of its charm is the contrast between the parched immensities of the desert and the greenery of its well-tended oasis. The west side is near two of the highest peaks of the Karkas chain, Mount Gargash and Mount Ardehaal. The former is the site of Iran's national observatory, which has the largest astronomical telescope in the country.

It is fun to get pleasantly lost walking the beautiful lanes while going to visit the Agha Bozorg Mosque and the many beautiful houses of Kashani residential architecture, which are open to the public. There are also many beautiful rose gardens to see as well as the traditional methods for rose-water production for which Kashan is famous. Today, the city is also famous for its carpets and silk as well housing most of Iran's mechanized carpet-weaving factories.

Just a few miles north of Kashan is the small town of Noushabad. The city was named because one of the Sassanian kings when passing through stopped to drink water from a well, and he found it extremely cold and tasty. He ordered a city to be built around the well and named it

Anoushabad, which means cold and tasty water. The name was eventually shortened to Noushabad.

About fifteen years ago, a citizen of the town was digging a well near his kitchen when the earth fell away and he discovered a tunnel that went deep into the ground. He notified the town fathers, and they began to excavate and discovered a city under the town. Archeologists dated it to the Sasanian Dynasty, about 1,500 years ago. It was used to shelter inhabitants against invasions and attacks particularly from the Arabs.

The city consists of a labyrinth of corridors, rooms, and wells. Entrances to the city were from population concentration points such as water reservoirs, markets, and individual houses. It is an amazing feeling to walk bent over in the many spaces and rooms of about six feet in height that are connected by angled corridors in this temporary settlement. There were toilets, supply rooms, gathering rooms, and guarding places. Light was provided by fat-burning lamps, and there was natural air conditioning and water provided by ancient engineering wonders. This masterpiece of ancient architecture is definitely worth a visit.

Among the oldest cities in Iran is Hamadan, which is green and mountainous and in the foothills of the Alvand Mountains in the Midwest of the country. It is at an altitude of 1,850 meters above sea level, and it dominates the wide, fertile plain of the upper Qareh Su River. It is believed to have been occupied by the Assyrians in 1100 BC, and it was the capital of the Medes around 700 BC. It is mentioned in the Bible (Ezra 6:1–3), and there is a tradition of Jewish association with it. The putative tomb of Esther there is in reality that of Queen Shushandukt, wife of the Sasanian King Yazdegerd I and mother of Bahram V, the great hunter. She, a Jew, helped establish a Jewish community in the city. Her tomb and that of Mordecai, Esther's uncle, are both places of pilgrimage surrounded by beautiful, lush green gardens. This city of tall cypress trees, lovely roses, and green grasses was badly damaged during the Iran-Iraq war of 1980–88, but it is developing into a modern city with a pleasant, cool climate in summer though the winters are long and harsh. It has winding, tree-lined roads and boulevards and is a great place to pick up ancient artifacts and handmade carpets.

Tehran itself, Iran's colossal, ugly, and yet charming capital, has a myriad of sights that are of interest to foreigners and Iranians alike. This is a cosmopolitan city with great museums, parks, restaurants, and warm, friendly people. Visitors could spend weeks in the city and not see everything if they could handle the dreadful smog for that long. I spent ten days there, and every evening back at the hotel, I would blow my nose free of black soot and grime. Driving around the city during the non-rush hours was a breeze. The traffic on the well-constructed and designed roads moved along quickly and smoothly though there was no speeding or running red lights allowed. Cameras pan the roads everywhere—not only in the cities and at stoplights but also on the fast-moving highways many of which are eight lanes. The small villages too were equipped with these overhanging cameras most of which would blink with a small white light that showed they were in operation.

"If you are caught making any infraction by the cameras, it is recorded by computer, and once a month, they send out tickets. There is no way to dispute the fines, so you just have to send in your money. If you don't send it in in a timely manner, the fine is doubled and extra points are taken off your license. Lots of people lose their licenses by not paying the fines," Sajad explained to me as he pointed out a camera.

One day as we were leaving the city on our way to one of the horse clubs, we were flagged down by a pair of traffic policemen standing at the side of a roundabout. Sajad pulled over and got out to see what the problem was. He returned in five minutes and said, "They saw me with my cell phone in my hand, which is illegal. I explained that I had an important visitor in the car and was using my GPS. They were pretty good about it and just gave me a warning. They were just young guys serving their military time. As you may know, we have conscription in Iran, and a lot of the young soldiers serve their time as traffic police. Maybe you noticed they didn't have guns or anything. Most of the police here are unarmed, so we don't have the police violence you have in the US."

Traffic during rush hour was a different matter. One afternoon, we were driving back to the hotel during the height of it. We had been invited to a very posh restaurant for dinner where I was being honored as Iran's first international trainer. Leilah and I had wanted to go to the hotel to change before the party, but as we drove into Tehran, we saw that the usually four-lane road to the north had turned into seven lanes all of which were blocked. We were creeping along at a snail's pace.

"I hate to tell you this, girls, but I think we need to go directly to the restaurant. You won't have time to go to your hotel to change. With this traffic, we'll make it to the restaurant on time, but if you go to the hotel, you will be at least an hour late," Sajad told us. So off we went to the most chic and expensive restaurant in Niavaran in the clothes we had been wearing all day.

I had been to Saadabad Palace when I was working for the Shah, so I was excited to learn that the beautiful, unique and very large garden in the almost two-hundred-acre complex along with the historical buildings have become one of the most important tourist attractions in Tehran. The Darband River extends from the north to the south of the garden, and the diverse vegetation includes natural forests with different species of needle-leaf and wide-leaf trees. The decorative plants around the palaces add beauty to the complex.

Since the revolution, the many palaces of the Qajars and Pahlavis are open to visitors. During the Qajar Dynasty (1794–1925), Saadabad was the royal families' summer palace. After the coup of 1921, it was expanded and became the summer residence of the Pahlavis. There are about seventeen buildings most of which are palaces on the grounds that have been turned into the Saadabad Cultural and Historical Complex. Each museum building has a theme. Everything from the furnishings of the palaces and the Fine Arts Museum to the Royal Cars and Royal Weapons Museum has been carefully documented and renovated for the many tourists from Iran and abroad to see.

Niavaran Palace, where the family of Mohammad Reza Pahlavi lived during most of the year, has also been turned into an interesting tourist attraction. There, you will see the bronze statue of the boots of Reza Shah; his body and head were desecrated shortly after the revolution before Khomeini had decreed that monuments should not be destroyed.

Though Tehran has the unenviable reputation as a smog-filled, traffic-clogged, and featureless sprawl of concrete bursting at the seams with 12 million residents, you can find an endless number of nice, cozy places in and around the city. Tehran has 800 well-kept parks the most famous of which is the Jamshideh Park built in the Qajar times and named after Prince Jamshid Davallou. During the Pahlavi era, it was renamed for the Empress and became Farah Park. After the revolution, its name reverted to Jamshideh Park. A beautiful stone garden with a waterfall and pond are central to its design. Many paths follow the narrow channels that bring water from the pond to the lower areas of the park creating smaller water features. In the 144-acre park are numerous restaurants, traditional *chai khoneh*, which are tea houses, picnic areas, and hiking trails from the lower areas of the park all the way to the top of the mountain. It is a great place to meet locals, but non-holidays are best as it is not crowded then.

When I had arrived in Tehran in January 1972, the first thing that caught my eye after leaving Mehrabad Airport was the huge Shahayad Tower. Its 8,000 blocks of cut marble from Esfahan glistened a sparkling white in the spotlights surrounding it on that dark evening. The Shah commissioned it to mark the 2,500th year of the foundation of the Imperial State of Iran and the first Persian Empire by Cyrus the Great.

Hossein Amanat, a young architect, was the winner of the competition to design the monument that had already been named Shahayad Aryamehr, King's Memorial, which would be the new gateway to Tehran. His design ideas were based on classical and postclassical Iranian architecture and popular influences on the arts of the 1960s. At the time, Iran's art industry was undergoing a renaissance due to the increasing wealth. The monument was supposedly funded by a group of about 500 industrialists and cost $6 million to build. The Council of Celebrations for the 2,500th anniversary, which was headed by Court Minister Asadollah Alam, planned Shahayad; after the revolution it was named, *Azadi*, Freedom, and it is still an amazingly beautiful archway to the city, with a museum of Ancient Persian artifacts, documents, and art beneath the tower.

As we drove to the north of Tehran the afternoon I arrived in September 2017, I saw a big, three-tiered bridge that crossed the Modarres Highway in the Abbas Abad area that took me to my hotel. Sajad said the bridge was called the *Pol-e-Tabiat*, Nature Bridge. This bridge was designed by a young woman architect, a genius, Leila Araghian. She had a vision: "A bridge is not just a structure to connect one point to another; it is also a place to stay on and enjoy." The bridge soars 270 meters across the highway connecting two parks. From the west on Ab-o-Atash (Water and Fire) Park, the bridge, making it feel still a part of the park, opens with a 60-meter-wide entrance with flower gardens. It crosses east to Teleghani Park, where there are many places for sports activities such as tennis, handball, extreme biking, and rollerblading. The evening I went to spend time on this three-tiered bridge, I was mesmerized for quite some time watching the bikers and rollerbladers practicing on the large and diverse course used for national competitions at the junction of the park and the access to the bridge across from the planetarium. Multiple paths lead to it from each of the parks, and all the levels are connected to each other by stairs and ramps that provide multiple paths throughout the bridge to get to another level.

On one level are many cafés and restaurants ranging from fast food to fine dining, another level is for walking, running, and biking, and the third is for viewing the highway below or the Alborz Mountains, which tower beyond the skyline of the city. Sajad, Leilah, and I had a delicious trout dinner with a salad of cucumber, tomato, and onions in a tart lemon and oil dressing and of course honey-sweet baklava for dessert. It was a beautiful, warm, dry evening, and as we ate, the local cats of which there are thousands in Tehran sat quietly by in the open-air restaurant waiting for us to finish. The waiter told us not to feed the cats the remainder of our fish by the table but to take it over to the garden wall, which we did, and they seemed quite grateful.

The best time to visit the Tabiat Bridge is shortly before sunset to experience both day and night views and have plenty of time to wander and enjoy the scenery before settling in for the evening meal.

After the revolution, the construction of the Milad Tower commenced in 1997. It took eleven years to complete what is considered the sixth-tallest free-standing telecommunication tower in the world. Bagher Ghalibaf, the mayor of Tehran who ran for president in 2017, and the city council officially opened this 435-meter needle in February 2009. It consists of five main parts—the foundation, lobby, structure shaft, head, and antenna mast. The underground floors are used as data centers. The ground floor is the visitors' reception area with a well-appointed modern lounge where artwork by the famous Iranian artist Farshid Mesqali is exhibited. There are banks and ATM machines, and an introductory film is shown there.

The first three of the six lobby floors consist of eleven food courts, a cafeteria, and a commercial products exhibition hall. Six speedy elevators are in the main core or shaft of the building. The head of the tower is built around the concrete shaft and has twelve stories and an area of 12,000 square meters.

On the different levels of the head, you will find open and enclosed observation decks, a revolving restaurant that holds 400 diners, a special VIP restaurant for a hundred, a cafeteria, art galleries, and the radio/television antenna of the Islamic Republic of Iran Broadcasting. The tower was designed like a wind tunnel for airflows as fast as 140 km/hr and can withstand gusts up to 220 km/hr. This also makes the building virtually earthquake proof, which is a must in a city that expects one every hundred or so years.

You can see the Milad tower soaring into the sky from almost everywhere in the city. The best time to visit is at dusk, but it is open every day from 9:00 a.m. to 11:00 p.m. It is exhilarating but a bit frightening to walk out on the observation deck on a cool evening. You can see lights coming from every angle from homes, cars, other tall buildings, highways, and shops. This is Tehran at its finest, a capital to be reckoned with.

The restaurants offered tasty food; everything was hot and well presented. The service was excellent as it is in most places in Iran; the people are so welcoming to their visitors. This is a must-see on your tour.

The last day I was in Tehran before my return to North America, I was entertained at the office of the Surfiran team, who were the ones who had finally obtained my visa and set up the itinerary I wanted. Mehdi Eshraghi, the owner, introduced me to the attractive girls who had done most of the work and reiterated what a difficult time they had had trying to get me a visa due to the sensitivities associated with visa arrangements for those with connections to the Shah.

"I hope you have enjoyed the past three weeks in Iran," he commented. "There is one place I want to take you this afternoon that I think you will be surprised to see. Have you been to the American Embassy?"

"I was there a few times when I lived here, but I have not been by it this time. I hear it is all boarded up and not accessible."

"It was until just a few months ago. One side of the complex has been used for the education and training of the young Basij when they first join, so it was off limits to anyone who was not a military or government official, but they have now opened what were the embassy offices to tourists. The cadets are the tour guides. I went there last week for the first time and thought it would be interesting for you to visit, so after lunch, we'll go there. I think it is open from about two in the afternoon till four."

We walked from the office to a small, well-appointed restaurant with orchids on the tables, mirrors on the walls, and excellent Iranian fare. Near 2:00 p.m., we strode a few blocks to the American Embassy. The walls of this once-deserted embassy where ninety American embassy employees were held hostage were painted with bright murals right after the revolution; they are old and flaking after forty years, and no one pays much attention to them now. Liberty with a face of a cadaver, a blue wall with a handgun painted as an American flag, and the portrait of Khomeini with a background of the Iranian flag gave a foreboding appearance to the tall walls with iron spikes and barbwire on top.

We arrived just after 2:00 p.m., but the gate was not open. We waited for about fifteen minutes and still no one appeared. Gradually, a few other tourists appeared, but as the gates were still closed, people sat on the high curb entertaining themselves with their cell phones. I was thinking this was going to be a bust when Mehdi said that he was going over to the side door to see what was going on. He returned and said a guard told him it would be open in about five minutes. Five minutes went by and then another five, so Mehdi went to speak to the guard again. He came back with the news that the key for the front gate had been misplaced; they were hoping to find it soon.

After a few more minutes, a nice-looking, bearded young man with a swarthy complexion came to the gate to tell us that the extra key had been located and was being brought over from the administrative office; we would be admitted in just a couple of minutes. As the couple of minutes dragged on, I asked Mehdi about the large, black plaque with gold Persian writing and an etched picture of Khomeini next to the front gate.

"Khomeini had that put up right after the revolution when the hostages had been taken. It is just a lot of insulting words about America. Nobody pays any attention to it now as it seems so ridiculous."

"Why don't they take it down?"

"It's part of history now, and we never destroy historical monuments you know."

Finally, another young bearded man with glasses came with the key to let us in. It was interesting to see the embassy offices that we were told looked just as they did the day the hostages were taken. I could believe it because the place was so dusty. It looked like it hadn't been cleaned in thirty-eight years. We were told that their American prisoners had been well treated; each had a single bedroom with a bathroom *en suite* and that a special French chef had been flown in to prepare their meals. Ha! We were shown the Glass Room where all sorts of spying had supposedly taken place; it was a glass-walled room within a room so nothing could be heard from outside its walls.

Three mannequins sitting at the small conference table in the room looked like spies; one looked like Robert Kennedy! The other rooms on display had old teletypes and other antiquated machines used for communication in those days. Waste baskets were filled with old papers and tickertapes supposedly not ever moved from where they were at the time of the takeover.

At the end of the tour, we were ushered into a small theater with a bronze statue of students climbing the embassy wall; we watched a fifteen-minute video full of ridiculous Iranian anti-American propaganda. If you want a bit of a chuckle, the American Embassy is a sight to see.

Rooftops in Kashan

Persepolis

Mosque at Imam Reza's Shrine in Mashhad

Persepolis with tent city in background

CHAPTER 15

Iran Today

While I was in Iran, I noted a great number of interesting facts that perhaps people in other parts of the world don't know. I want to divulge some of these things to let others know more about this fascinating and growing country. The press reports on television and social media as well as in the printed news tell us what is supposedly happening in Iran today, but most of that information is convoluted and false. The West seems to want to hear the news in derogatory terms.

Iran entered the twenty-first century as a major regional power in the Persian Gulf and the Middle East. With close to 80 million people, it is the largest country in the region. It plays a key role in the Organization of Petroleum Exporting Countries, is the world's third-largest producer of oil, and has the globe's second-largest proven reserves of gas and oil. It will remain important as long as the hydrocarbon age lasts.

Since ages past, Iranians have had a deep-seated love of the written word as well as a long history of arts and sciences. Great poets and authors since the tenth century are still read and appreciated today; the works of Ferdowsi, Sa'adi, Hafiz, Attar, Nezami, Rumi, and Omar Khayyam are classics still enjoyed in all parts of the world. In this country where literary censorship is an official government policy, it is surprising that the biggest bookstore in the world was opened in the summer of 2016. Previously, according to the Guinness Book of World Records, that title was held by a Barnes & Noble bookstore in New York, which covered 156,250 square feet and twelve miles of bookshelves.

The head of Tehran's Arts and Cultural Organization announced in July 2016 the opening of *Bagh-e-Ketab*, the Book Garden, which is a roughly 65,000-square-meter (700,000 square feet) center with movie theaters, science halls, classrooms, and over 400,000 books for children alone. The mayor of Tehran said, "The opening of the Book Garden is a big cultural event in the country, so that our children can make good use of this academic opportunity." The center is a beautiful, modern learning complex that includes sixteen permanent book exhibition areas divided into literary genres, galleries, and lounges, and it will become home to creative artists who will keep the Iranian heritage of the arts alive. It is a part of the Sacred Defense Garden that is accessible from the Tabiat Bridge and next to the National Library and Archives of Iran.

Though the country is considered one of the top-ten most censored countries in the world, many improvements have been made in the cultural sphere since pragmatist President Rouhani was first elected in 2013. Bans on many books and films have been lifted, and the young in particular are being encouraged to read more. Iranians' lack of interest in printed books can be blamed on censorship as it takes months for a new book to be passed by the Ministry of Cultural and Islamic Guidance. After a book has gone through the intricate process and interpretation of Islamic Law, words and phrases as well as whole chapters are often removed.

Online book publishers bring out writers' works as eBooks that would otherwise have no chance of passing censorship, and illegal books can be downloaded through the internet. As well, Fidibo, a digital company, produces eBooks that have publishing permission from the government. Though there are only about 1,500 bookstores in a country of so many millions, it is hoped that this high-profile Book Garden will bring Iranians back to the written word. I was overwhelmed when I visited this amazing center; it had a vibrant atmosphere and was filled with enthusiastic book lovers.

Alcoholic beverages are officially forbidden in Iran today, but their consumption is widely practiced in private homes and clubs. Armenians, Jews, and Zoroastrians still produce wine, and local moonshine is found in the rural towns and villages. The most popular beverage is vodka distilled from grain, grapes, or raisins. Alcohol is found at most celebrations and weddings as long as they are private. My guide watched me like a hawk when we were at any parties or private homes, and though I was surreptitiously offered a drink of alcohol a few times, I was afraid to accept it not wanting to suffer the ire of Leilah.

There are no bars as such in the country, but every street corner has a café or *chai khoneh* where young people sit and socialize playing backgammon or chess or using the internet, which is available everywhere in the country. When Sajad, Leilah, and I went to these cafés, the atmosphere was always congenial, and we were included in conversations. As I was obviously a foreigner, I often became the center of attention with people wanting to know where I was from and why I was in Iran. I always explained that I was Canadian but lived in the United States. All were interested in both countries, and many claimed to have relatives living in one or the other country, so I was asked if I knew this place or that. The majority of those I talked to loved Americans and especially American music and films, but they all stressed their dislike of President Trump. They felt he was a very dangerous man and were incensed at his saying that Iran was not complying with the nuclear agreement. Of course it is! The sanctions are very hard on the country making it difficult to get foreign investment, which is desperately needed for its continuing growth.

As we drove south of Esfahan into the desert on our way to visit some of the horse farms in that area, we passed a huge military installation with wire fences and tall walls that went on for miles. Several entrances and guard towers were at intervals along the perimeter. I saw guards with machine-guns standing on the small balcony at the top of the towers.

"What is that place?" I asked. Leilah said not a word.

"That is the Nuclear Technology and Research Center. It's the largest in the country, and about three thousand scientists work there. It was built by the French in 1975 when the Shah was still here to provide training for the personnel to operate the Bushehr reactor, which is on the Persian Gulf. Since the revolution, it has been expanded and now encompasses around 4.5 million square meters," Sajad said.

"Sajad, we're not really supposed to be discussing anything about the military or politics with Gail you know!" Leilah said sharply.

"Don't be ridiculous, Leilah!" he said. "The Chinese signed a nuclear cooperation agreement in the early nineties, I think, and there are reactors, but no nuclear weapons technology is being created here or anywhere in Iran. Our county is strictly complying with the nuclear agreement signed in 2015. Despite what the American president is saying, we're following the rules, and the inspections have proven it."

"Is this the only such facility in Iran then?"

"No," said Leilah. "Now that we have brought up the subject, let's get it straight. Iran has no intention of producing or using nuclear weapons. Our Supreme Leader Ali Khamenei declared a *fatwa* [a ruling on a point of Islamic law given by a recognized authority] against the acquisition, development, and use of nuclear weapons in the mid-1990s though it wasn't made official until the meeting of the International Atomic Energy Agency in Vienna in 2005. Our country has a great aversion to nuclear weapons especially since the war with Iraq when chemical attacks were used against us that killed 20,000 people and injured 100,000 more. We never even sought revenge for those atrocities.

"This fatwa is consistent with Islamic tradition, which states that the stockpiling and use of nuclear weapons is forbidden. Yes, there are many other nuclear facilities in Iran, but they produce electricity, are research facilities, or have another reason for their existence. Arak produces heavy water and radioisotopes for medical and agricultural purposes. Karaj has the Center for Agricultural Research and Nuclear Medicine. Anorak near Yadz has a nuclear waste storage site. The Bushehr Nuclear Power Plant, which was destroyed in the war, has been rebuilt with the help of Russia and now is operated solely by our people. So you see, we use our nuclear knowledge for reasons other than bombs."

As I have stated before, Persian girls and young women are very beautiful. Why then do you see so many of them walking the streets proudly wearing bandages across their faces? Because about one in every fifty has plastic surgery on her nose because she wants to change her prominent Iranian nose to look like what they think are beautiful, straight, Western noses seen in European and American films. Iran is the country with the most nose jobs per capita in the world; it is a status symbol, and women and some men can be seen displaying their bandages long after they are healed. This desire for the perfect nose is most probably prompted by the authority's attempts to make women look like bats and crows in *hijabs*.

If invited to a private party in an Iranian home, dress in your finest. The women are very stylish with their attire, which can be purchased from the many chic women's clothing shops in malls or along the sidewalks of the wealthy residential areas of most cities.

The women walking along the streets of cities such as Tehran and Isfahan look as stylish as do Parisian women in Paris. Somehow, with a belt here, an adjustment there, and a selection of color, they manage to make their *manteaux* or jackets look stylish and chic. They laugh and chatter as they walk together along the streets shopping or looking for fashionable cafés where they sip milkshakes, designer coffees, or tea for hours. Most probably, they have made arrangements to meet their boyfriends away from the intrusive eyes of their families.

You will often see these same young women frolicking in parks and playing games having taken off their head scarves, which is of course illegal, but no one seems to notice anymore. In days gone by, the dress-code police would have been there to fine or arrest them, but today, things have become very lax in that regard. Most of the young women wear their head scarves half on anyway so all can see their beautiful, well-styled, and often blond hair. With the tolerant reform administration in power now, I wouldn't be surprised if women were granted the right to discard the head covering altogether.

Of course you see many women wearing the chador, which covers the head and entire body to the ground, with only the nose and eyes visible to see, but they are from the more religious group of Muslims who still do exist all over the country especially in rural towns and the less-affluent parts of the big cities. In the mosques and shrines, it is of course only a matter of respect that women cover their crowning glory. When I was in the Jameh Mosque in Isfahan, my scarf, which I had been having trouble with all day, slipped off my head unbeknown to me.

"Your head scarf! Your head scarf!" Leilah said sharply touching my shoulder. "It has fallen. You must keep it on your head in respect for Allah and this place of worship."

Embarrassedly, I pulled it up rumpling my already messy hair even more. The one thing about wearing the head covering that I enjoyed while I was in Iran was that each morning, I didn't have to fuss with my always difficult hair as it would be seen by no one all day. I say, let's wear head scarves in America!

Iran is not a medieval theocracy where females are hidden away and forced to do as they are told. Men and women sit together in mixed groups at lunch or dinner tables conversing as equals. Young couples are seen holding hands as they walk down the streets or through the parks. Though movies are still strictly censored by the Department of the Interior, Iranians of all ages enjoy the cinema, and there is usually a long line to get in the theaters. In the past few years, censorship has become less stringent; even many European and American movies are shown on the silver screen. From the back of the theater, you can see couples with their arms around each other necking in the style of the sixties, a night out that could have been prompted by *dor dor bazi*.

Life for the young Iranian girls is not very different from what it is for girls in the West. Most are well educated, and when they have finished with higher education, they take jobs, which are readily available. Even after marrying and having children, most middle-class women continue to earn incomes to help with the ever-rising cost of living. The $795 monthly rent on a three-bedroom house may sound very cheap, but when the actual income of a family is factored in, it becomes equivalent to what we find in many cities in the US. The actual cost of living per month in Tehran is about $457, $1,638 for a family of four, which is 61 percent lower than that in the United States.

There is plenty of extramarital and illicit sex now with some sanctioned by Islamic law, which allows *sigheh*, temporary marriages. Prostitutes are seen patrolling the streets at night; the enforced morals have failed to prevent that ancient profession. It is said that the holy city of Qom has more women of ill repute than does any other city in the country. Many young girls of the wealthy class who have had premarital sex have "revirginization" operations before they have their extravagant social weddings to handsome, well-to-do grooms who may or may not have been chosen by their families.

Iran and its people have been interested in the cinema since the inception of the silent movies. After the Islamic revolution, the industry slowed down especially during the ruinous eight-year war. Slowly, the industry is making a comeback, and this year under moderate President Rouhani's second term, the film *Nafas*, "Breath," which is about a young girl whose fantasy world helps her escape the hard realities of growing up in the country in the aftermath of the revolution, was directed by a woman, Nages Abyar. It had been selected for an Oscar for the foreign-film division, but it was not nominated. If it had been, she and her husband would probably not have been able to get visas to attend the ceremony due to President Trump's travel ban. The forty-seven-year old director and writer remains confident in the power of art to bridge cultural and political divides. "Cinema, culture, and art do not recognize any border, but in fact bring humanity closer together," she told the press.

Three Iranian films—*No Date, No Signature, Beyond the Clouds*, and *Yeva*—were presented at the Palm Springs Film Festival the winter of 2018 as well as an animated film, *Release from Heaven*, that was presented at the International Peace and Film Festival in Orlando. The Iranian movie industry is on the move.

Iranian society has always had a special place for sports. In ancient Persia, physical strength and courage were needed to defend family and homeland. The Zoroastrians prayed first for the beauty of heaven and second for physical strength and mental power. In the sacred books of the ancient religions, champions and sportsmen were held in higher esteem than were saints and men of God. The young men were all trained in such sports as horsemanship, polo, dart throwing, wrestling, boxing, archery, and fencing. Today, these sports are still an important part of the life of girls and boys, but on the whole, Iranians are not as physically fit now as they once were, and 30 percent of young Iranians never play any sport. The first city in Western Asia to host the Asian games was Tehran in 1974, which still continues to host and participate in international sporting events.

There is a long history of wrestling in Iran, and it is still popular today, which makes it not surprising that Iran won five medals for wrestling in the 2016 Olympic Games in Rio de Janeiro. A team of fifty-four men and nine women athletes competed in the games though men's volleyball was their only team sport.

In 2017, a federal judge temporarily suspended Trump's ban on nationals of Muslim countries including Iran from entering the United States; Iranian officials responded by allowing the previously banned US wrestling team to compete in the World Wrestling Match in Kermanshah. Since the curtailment of diplomatic relations between the two countries, the 2017 wrestling team became the first official American sports team to visit Iran since the revolution. The team was greeted at the airport with red roses and smiling and cheering local fans. Iranians and Americans had a moment of sports diplomacy amid crumbling relations between the leaders of both countries.

Soccer is the most popular sport in Iran and has been for many years even before the revolution. The national team won the Asian championships three times in the sixties and seventies, and it made its World Cup debut in

1978. The revolution and the Iran-Iraq war left few resources to devote to sports, and the new regime regarded sports as a rival to mosque attendance. However, since the 1990s, there has been a revival in sports due to the enormous public support for sports, especially for soccer, that could not be suppressed.

In 1998, when the Iranian football team qualified for the World Cup, it was the first time since the revolution that people realized they could appear in huge numbers. The whole country cheered the team's victory, and massive numbers of people paraded and cheered in the streets all over the country.

Iran attained gold medals at the Asian Games in 1990, 1998, and 2002. With the launch of Iran's Premier Football League, the sport has made great advancements. Many Iranian players have been drafted into the European leagues, and Iranian clubs are hiring European players and coaches. Iran's largest stadium is the Azadi Stadium, the third-largest football venue in the world with a seating capacity of 100,000. This is the home stadium of the two most popular teams, Persepolis and Esteghal, and where national matches take place. Iran's national Team Melli represents the country in international competitions and is governed by the Iran Football Federation. Since 2014, this team has been the highest-ranked team in Asia, and according to FIFA's November 2017 World Rankings, it was thirty-second in the world. They have already qualified for the 2018 World Cup, and their Spanish manager plans to see the team through until that time. Unfortunately they did not make it into the final rounds.

If you're interested in snow skiing, visit Iran to experience the best skiing in the world. There are many mountains in the country from north to south and east to west with the Alborz and the Zagros ranges being the highest. An abundance of snowfall begins in early November and lingers until May in the mountains, a long skiing season. The snow, which is a beautiful powder in consistency, almost always falls at night, so the sun usually shines on the skiers. I don't remember a day when it was cold and blustery with no sunshine when I was skiing, and I went often every winter I lived there. It was and still is a popular sport. It would just take a phone call from a friend to tempt me to take a day off from the stables in winter.

Skiing began in Iran when the Austrian and German railway engineers came to build Reza Shah's railway; they saw that the winter months had plenty of snowfall and the mountains were conducive to skiing and building slopes. The Germans brought their own skis and spent winters touring the country on them. As well, Iranian students who were studying in Europe learned to ski, so they brought the sport home with them. Abdollah Basir, who studied abroad to become a medical doctor, became an avid skier and learned how to make skis. When he arrived back home, he instructed carpenters in the art of the production, and thus skis became available to all. The first ski trails were in the Telo hills known as Lashkarak, which became the prime destination for ski clubs, which had been formed, and American soldiers who were stationed there. Soon, more resorts were being built, and Iranians became passionate skiers.

Today, there are thirteen good ski resorts in Iran, but there are three main ones. Dizin is the biggest and has the longest pistes. The highest is 3,600 meters, 11,800 feet, has a drop of 510 meters, 1,660 feet, and is 2,960 meters, almost two miles in length. The well-kept modern hotel is at an altitude of 2,500 meters, 8,000 feet. A three-day, two-night stay including ski passes and meals costs about $245.

Shemshak ski resort was created in the late 1950s near an old coal-mining town that had become a leisure spot for the wealthy offering them a place to learn and practice the new, trendy European sport. Though it hasn't expanded since its opening, its proximity to Dizin and Darbansar makes it the ski capital of Iran. It is known for its steep and technical slopes, black mogul pistes at the top, and numerous off-piste trails.

The newest and most modern resort is Darbansar, which was bought by private investors recently and is developing fast. New lifts, snowmakers, and groomers have been purchased for the 2018 winter season. From the top, you can see, and access on skis if you, want Dizin's last gondola lift station. Night skiing is offered, and the potential for free skiing is huge. At present, off-piste skiing is not officially allowed, but if you want to try, it's possible to negotiate with the ski patrol to get authorization, or you can just do it. Remember, Iranian rules are different for almost everything.

Author in front of American Embassy

Author in front of Embassy wall

Dizin ski resort

Tehran's Milad Tower

Sajad Bamdad with his beer

Tabiat Bridge

Surf Iran Team

CONCLUSION

With the events and protests that were reported to have occurred in Iran late December and early January 2018, the conclusion I had come to after having visited this past fall had fallen apart. I had planned to report that Iran had once again become an affluent country whose citizens have the good life they expected and that even though the Supreme Leader, Ayatollah Khamenei, and his Committee of Experts did have the right to veto any legislation passed by the acting government, they rarely acted or interfered with the workings of the country.

Suddenly, the newscasts were all about the demonstrations in Tehran and a number of other major cities by people protesting economic hardships. Rising living costs, high prices, inflation, and unemployment seemed to be the reasons for the peaceful marches. Amateur videos on social media showed antigovernment crowds marching in the streets of several cities including Tehran. One video showed protesters shouting "Death to Khamenei!" It must be remembered that in Farsi, "Death to ..." really just means "Damn the ..." whatever it is. Taxi drivers will say "Death to traffic!" meaning, "Damn the traffic!" "Death to America," which was literally translated to English forty-odd years ago, really meant "Damn America," so the people are really just damning the Ayatollah for the fact that things aren't as rosy economically as they would want.

In some cases, the numbers of participants in these demonstrations were reported to be less than a hundred, and in some areas, they were said to have been in the thousands. Though not on a massive scale, it was the largest display of unrest since the Green Movement in 2009 after Ahmadinejad's reelection. Those uprisings were initially led by the upper middle class, university students at their core, and Tehran the center.

These recent demonstrations supposedly included a broader swath of the population. Nearly all society was represented including the middle class, the underprivileged, women, and young people. Protests shifted from economic woes to rejection of the whole regime at one point.

According to some sources, after the first couple of days, the protests began to wane and rallies supporting the government occurred across the country. Most of the videos of demonstrations we've seen in the West have been shared on social media, so who knows if they actually happened?

I have been in contact with several of my Iranian friends who have sent me messages on WhatsApp or called, and they all say it is not true. To quote one friend, "There is no problem here. It's interesting that all my friends from overseas keep asking about the situation, which was a small, peaceful demonstration, and has now been made into a big problem by the press. Don't listen to that rubbish. I didn't see anything myself. Our problem here is that because of all this bad publicity, people are scared and most of the tours are being canceled." Another good friend wrote, "Fortunately, nothing really bad has happened till now. It was just a partial demonstration against economic inflation. The media always exaggerates everything against Iran."

With the reports of the demonstrations, Reza Pahlavi, the son of the last Shah, called for a replacement of clerical rule with a secular electoral democracy that would improve human rights, modernize the state-run economy, and prove to be more palatable to the West. Interestingly the age of the monarchy and the Pahlavis have retained their mystique in Iran even though the majority of the 80 million people now weren't alive to have experienced it. Young Iranians are increasingly looking to the past when the Shah's secular and pro-Western rule produced a rapid modernization program financed by oil revenues. It is said in retrospect that it was the good life. Parents and grandparents are being asked, "Why did you get rid of that system and put in this archaic, religiously rooted one?" Despite this optimism of Reza to have a type of democracy in his homeland, it must be considered that the power of the current administration will be hard to overthrow even though for countless Iranians the revolution is unfinished business.

In Iran today, most people are living the good life. Business seems to be booming with many foreign companies wanting to invest in or have joint ventures with Iran. China, India, and Japan are strongly committed to their Iranian investments in the oil and manufacturing world, and many

European companies are knocking on the door to get their foot in now as it is believed that Iran is the most stable of the Middle Eastern countries in which to invest.

There is very little visible military presence in the country as a whole. It is rare to see soldiers with guns in the streets except in front of actual military installations and some of the tourist attractions such as the crown jewels that are of great value or are security risks. I was in Mehrabad and Khomeini airports several times and never saw a soldier or a policeman with a gun. Everywhere else in the world where I have traveled recently, I see soldiers with automatic rifles and police with side arms all over the terminals. The police you see in the streets or directing traffic do not carry weapons. In the earlier days of the republic, the brutality of the military and police was well known, but in the past few years, things have changed dramatically, and as has been reported, there is little police brutality in the country at the present.

The time of the glowering ayatollahs, book-burning mobs, and fatwas of death has been slowly disappearing as the people who are the most pro-Western in the world tend to live their lives day to day. For most families, things are the same; the rich are still rich and the poor are still poor. Life under the monarchy and the Islamic Republic is almost the same; instead of one bunch of criminals running the country, there is another, but the opposition, some of whom are living in America and Europe, have little to offer. Many people today think the regime of the Shah was not so bad compared to what they now have. They forget there was corruption, secret police savagery, and wild incompetence, which actually still exists today, and they yearn for the monarchy to come back or to live in America.

Thirty-nine years after the revolution, in general, life has become almost the same as it was during the reign of the Pahlavis.

The problem that is now to be faced by the Iranian people is how much damage will be done to them by the administration of President Trump, who seems to have a real hate for the country, the people and the administration.

EPILOGUE

During the time of Shah Mohamed Reza Pahlavi, the majority of Iran's population was made up of the middle class, but now, post-revolution, most people would be considered to be in a lower socioeconomic bracket.

The revolution of 1979 has provided plenty of food for thought for Iranians. It was inspired in no small way, in my opinion. by their dissatisfaction with themselves, not just their rulers. It was inspired by tradition, not religion. Now that the people have an Islamic government, few people want anything to do with the religion, which the government has destroyed with its early revolutionary actions. The young, who are the largest percentage of the population (60 percent under age thirty), have no feeling for religion and sadly don't even understand the words of the call to prayer one hears all over the country three times a day. They can be heard saying, "Shut that guy up!" when the loud, usually recorded, voice is heard in the streets. Many people who never went near a mosque to pray marched in the demonstrations calling for Khomeini and an Islamic Republic. They wanted to show their disgust with the Shah and the way Iranians were being forced further into the quagmire of corruption and dishonesty. They wanted a cleanup, and they saw this as the first real hope of getting it, but they were not marching for religion itself and they did not get what they expected.

Just as we in the West have based our secular societies on Christian values, the Iranians and Arabs will base theirs on Islamic values. Those of us who sympathize with Iranians in the confusion they have found themselves during the Shah's reign, and in their present situation, will look forward to the day when they will enjoy the kind of society in which they will find their true liberty.

Tehran in February 2018

INDEX

Carter, President Jimmy, xx, 103–4, 182, 188–89
Chafik, Ahmad, 20
Chehelsotoun, 44
Contadoro Island, 190
Cyrus the Great, xiii, 112, 152, 325, 332

D

Dabscheck, Ron, 71, 213
Darius the Great, xiii, 41
Davallou, Prince Jamshid, 331
Diba, Farideh, 30
Diba, Kamran, 2, 33, 38
Diba, Madam (mother of Empress), 14, 30, 79
Djahanbani, General Nader, 10, 57, 62, 116, 132, 188, 217, 219, 231

E

Ebadi, Shirin, 120, 247–55, 258
Echo of Tehran, 152
Elghanian, Elian, 58, 214, 231, 233–36
Elghanian, Fred, ix, 214, 231, 233–36
Elghanian, Habib, 110, 171, 232
Emami, Leila, 51
Emami, Sharif, 112
Eqbal, Manuchehr, 184
Esfahan, 43–45, 195, 242, 284, 286, 304, 313–16, 321, 325, 332, 340
Eshraghi, Mehdi, 334

F

Farahabad, xviii, 5, 10, 27, 29, 87, 158, 203, 268, 296, 298–99, 301, 308
Fardoust, Hossain, 159
Farman (newspaper), 154
Fathi, Nazila, 271
Fawzia, Princess of Egypt (Shah's first wife), 3, 9
Firouz, Iran Ala, 77
Firouz, Louise, 69–70, 77, 84, 128–30, 265–71, 301
Firouz, Narcy, 26, 77, 128, 130, 265–71, 301
Friouz, Safieh, 77
Frost, David, 152

G

Ganji, Manuchehr, 55
George, James, 46
Ghaffari, Farrokh, 38, 40
Ghalibaf, Bagher, 286, 333
Gharagozlou, Mary, 121–25, 130, 260–64, 268, 301
Ghavam, Mirza Ali Muhammad, 19
Ghisletta, Luigi, 159
Ghotbi, Reza, 33, 38
Gonbad-e-Turkoman, 301–2, 313
Gotbzadeh, Sadeq, 190

H

Hadavand, Reza, 296
Hashenitaba, Moustafa, 286
Helms, Richard, 103
hijab, 210, 250, 272, 288, 341
Hojabr, Ali, 295

Hoveyda, Amir Abbas, 15, 23, 26, 48, 51–56, 176, 181–82, 204
Hughes, Ted, 41

I

Iralco (Iranian Aluminium Company), 92, 162–63, 165–66, 169–70, 280

J

Jahangiri, Eshaq, 286
jihad, 203

K

Kadjar, Roqnehdin, 163
Kaminski, Luba, 219
Karbala, 293, 326
Kayhan International, 153, 159, 269
Khalkhali, Sadeq (blood judge), 204, 216
Khalvati, Kay, 125–28
Khalvati, Sohrab, 125–27, 172
Khamenei, Ayatollah Ali Hoseyni, 207, 244, 287
Khatami, Mohamed, 59, 217, 238, 242
Khatami, Mohammad Ali (head of Iranian air), 111
Khomeini, Ayatollah Ruholah, xx–xxi, 131, 183, 221, 232, 239, 241, 249, 256, 272, 275
Khosrodad, General Manuchehr, 40, 59, 63–66, 188, 204, 215–16
King Hussein of Jordan, 156

M

Macken, Eddie, 57–59
Mansour, Hossain, 53
Massoudi, Farhad, 46
Menuhin, Yehudi, 41
Mesbahzadeh, Mostafa, 153–54
Mesqali, Farshid, 333
Miller, Judith, 273–74
Mir-Salim, Moustafa, 286
Mohasab, Leilah, 292, 321
Mohtashamipor, Ali Akhbar, 273
Mossadeq, Prime Minister Mohammad, 8, 103, 154, 247–48

N

Nahavandi, Hushang, 55
Najaf, 196–97, 221
Naqsh-e-Rostam, 40, 42
Nasser al-Sabah, Shaikh, 101
Nassiri, General Nematollah (head of SAVAK), 106, 126–27, 172, 174, 183–84, 204, 216
Nawsh-e-Jehan, 44
Nemazi, Mohammad, 77

O

O'Donnell, Jim, 156–58
Oveissi, General Gholam Ali, 122–23

P

Pahlavi, Abdul Reza, 25–27, 75
Pahlavi, Ashraf, 8, 18–24, 27–28, 33, 54, 94, 106, 123, 136–38, 176, 215, 259, 364

Sullivan, William (Bill), 103–4

T

Tavasolian, Javad, 249
Taylor, Kenneth, 102–3
Tehran Journal, 153
Teleghani, Ayatollah, 232

U

Underwood, James, ix, 45, 152, 160

V

Vodjdani, Ezat, 295
Vodjdani, Nosrat, 299
von Lilianfeld, Georg, 102

W

Wright, Sir Denis, 101

X

Xenakis (Greek producer), 41–42
Xerxes, xiii

Z

Zahedi, Ardeshir, 9, 21, 31
Zolghadr, Ali, 106
Zolghadr, Soraya (Zorik), 106

BIBLIOGRAPHY

Abrahamian, Evand   A History of Modern Iran

Alam, Asadollah   The Shah and I

Azadi, Sousan   Out of Iran

Azadi, Susan w/Angela Ferante   Out of Iran

Baker, Patricia & Hillay Smith   Iran

Christ, David   The Twilight War

Cooper, Andrew Scott   The Oil Kings

Cooper, Andrew Scott   The Fall From Heaven

Delforoush, Ali   The Iran Chronicles

Duguid, Naomi   Persia

Ebadi, Shirin   Until We are Free

Ebadi, Shirin   The Golden Cage

Ebadi, Shirin   Iran Awakening

Elliot, Jason   Mirrors of the Unseen

Fathi, Nazila   The Lonely War

Firouz, Louisew/Brenda Dalton   Riding Through the Revolution

Hooman, Majid   The Ayatollah Begs to Differ

Hopkirk, Peter   The Great Game

Hoveyda, Feridoun   Fall of the Shah

Hughs, Stephan E.   The Rise of the Islamic Republic of Iran

Huyser, General Robert E.   Mission to Tehran

Iranian.com
Iranrights.org
Kapuscinski, Ryszard   Shah of Shahs
Kinser, Stephen   All the Shah's Men
Kursmn, Charles   The Unthinkable Revolution in
                                Iran
Kurzman, Charles   The Unthinkable Revolution in
                                Iran
Milani, Abbas   The Shah
Milani, Abbas   Policics and Cuture in
                                Contemporary Iran
Moin, Baqer   Khomeini, Life of the Ayatollh
Nafisi, Azar   Reading Lolita in Tehran
Nemat, Marina   Prisoner of Tehran
Pahlavi, Ashraf   Faces in a Mirror
Pahlavi, Farah   An Enduring Love
Pahlavi, Mohamed Reza Arymehr   The White Revolution
Pahlavi, Mohamed Reza Arymehr   A Mission for My Country
Pahlavi, Reza   Winds of Change
Raji, Parviz C.   In Search of the Peacock Throne
Reeves, Minou   Behind the Peacock Throne
Saikal, Amin   Rise and Fall of the Shah
Sami, Ali   Parsagrad
Secor, Laura   Children of Paradise
Smith, Anthony   Blind White Fish in Persia
Sofer, Dalia   The Septembers of Shiraz
Stevens, Roger   The Land of the Great Sofy
Sykes, Ella c.   Through Persia on a Side-Saddle
Wickipedia.org
Wright, Robin (editor)   The Iran Primer

Printed in the United States
By Bookmasters